Still Jewish

Still Jewish

A History of Women and
Intermarriage in America

Keren R. McGinity

NEW YORK UNIVERSITY PRESS

New York and London

NEW YORK UNIVERSITY PRESS
New York and London
www.nyupress.org

Library of Congress Cataloging-in-Publication Data

McGinity, Keren R.
Still Jewish : A history of women and intermarriage in America /
Keren R. McGinity.
p.   cm.
Includes bibliographical references and index.
ISBN-13: 978–0–8147–5730–7 (pb : alk. paper)
ISBN-10: 0–8147–5730–8 (pb : alk. paper)
1. Intermarriage—United States. 2. Jewish women. 3. Jews—United
States—Identity. 4. Jews—Cultural assimilation.   I. Title.
HQ1031.M394 2009
306.84'30882960973—dc22   2008039062

New York University Press books are printed on acid-free paper,
and their binding materials are chosen for strength and durability.
We strive to use environmentally responsible suppliers and materials
to the greatest extent possible in publishing our books.

Manufactured in the United States of America

c 10 9 8 7 6 5 4 3 2 1

Dedicated with love to my mother, who gave me life, and to Shira for making it meaningful.

From every human being there rises a light that reaches straight to heaven. And when two souls that are destined to be together find each other, their streams of light flow together and a single brighter light gives forth from their united being.

—Baal Shem Tov

Women's significance in groups considered marginal must not be allowed to obscure their centrality in maintaining what scholars traditionally have called the "mainstream." Women's history is American religious history.

—Ann Braude

We only grow when we are introduced to other faiths. Diversity is part of God's plan. The problem is when we try to turn others into a copy of ourselves. We should view them instead as opportunities for growth.

—Abraham Joshua Heschel

Jewish feminism began as women felt left out of Jewish life; it is continuing as women determine they have something to contribute. In the future, we shall see how Judaism itself is transformed by their participation.

—Susannah Heschel

Contents

Preface

One of my earliest childhood memories is of going to my cousin's house and sensing that something was different, that is, not Jewish. I knew I was Jewish; my parents were both born and bred in the Bronx, and we celebrated Jewish holidays. I knew my paternal aunt was also Jewish. But something about her husband, my uncle, and their children felt alien to me. It was as if we spoke different languages. And what in the world was that Christmas tree doing in their living room? The collection of impressions from that day, when my brain was too young to grasp the notion of interfaith marriage, was the seed for this book.

My intellectual curiosity about an issue that perplexes many couples and alarms the organized Jewish community deepened and broadened over my lifetime, as did my intimate knowledge of the topic. After more than twenty-two years, my parents' marriage culminated in a bitter divorce when I was ten. Both remarried non-Jews soon after, and both remain married to their spouses thirty years later. If nothing more, their life courses taught me that endogamous marriages are not the panacea for marital bliss, and exogamous marriages are not doomed to fail. I became a *bat mitzvah*, went to Israel, attended Jewish summer camps, and sought out High Holiday services while traveling in Europe. Experience with intermarriage in my family was a significant influence on my scholarly interests and dating choices. I wrote my first research paper on intermarriage as a sophomore in college, during which time I continued dating my Gentile boyfriend from high school, and a second one during a summer graduate course in religion. I could not, however, anticipate how my life would evolve outside the classroom.

Although I made concerted efforts to meet an eligible Jewish bachelor, my commitment to marry a coreligionist was weak. At age twenty-four, I became engaged to a man of Irish Catholic background. The verbal prenuptial negotiation included my acceptance of his surname and his agreement to raise our future children as Jews. A fair deal, I thought, for my betrothed wanted to perpetuate his family name, and I wanted to contribute to the decimated Jewish population. The only heated argument we had prior to our 1992 marriage was about World War II. I was named for my maternal great-grandmother who perished in the Holocaust, and I was deeply troubled by what I felt was his superficial understanding of the horrific genocide of millions. That discussion, and his deceptive behavior preceding our wedding day that had nothing to do with religious differences, should have deterred me from this particular intermarriage. But love is a powerful emotion, perhaps the most compelling one.

A professional garden of historical scholarship bloomed from what had started as a seed of personal curiosity. During the course of my nearly fourteen-year intermarriage, I was constantly defining myself in contrast to my non-Jewish spouse. Rather than simply locating myself in the negative, someone who does not do this or that, I strove to decide how to live a Jewish life that felt good. In the process I wrestled with the question, what does being Jewish mean to me? And how am I Jewish? Pregnant for the first time, I sought and helped create a welcoming Jewish community. The birth of our daughter generated more questions. No longer was I simply a Jewish woman married to a Gentile; now I was a Jewish mother of a Jewish child with a non-Jewish father. How and to what extent would I impart Jewish heritage and religion to my daughter? Was this responsibility mine alone, or would my spouse share it with me? The actions that came about in direct response to these questions, for example, choosing a Hebrew first name, observing Shabbat weekly, and agreeing that Shira would receive a formal Jewish education, encouraged me to reevaluate the role of Judaism in my life. In the process I became "more Jewish." Was I alone, an anomaly, or did other intermarried women experience something similar? Did my inheritance of the incomplete gains of feminism play a role and, if so, how?

This book is an attempt to answer my own questions in an effort to elucidate the meaning of intermarriage. Trained as a historian who studies change and constancy over time, I structured my investigation to span a century. This lengthy time period would explain, I hoped, whether my experience was unique or shared by my intermarried predecessors and contemporaries. Moreover, by looking at my life and those of other women within their respective historical contexts, I hoped to better understand the various influences on women's personal lives and the outcomes of the choices they made.

This book benefited enormously from my own intermarriage in that I knew what to look for in the archives and which questions to ask, and, because I was an "insider," the women who participated expressed comfort in talking openly with me. I could relate to their experiences, empathize with the hardships they faced, and exult in their personal triumphs. Moreover, I was acutely sensitive to the potential for bias, and therefore vigilant about ensuring that the words and experiences of others shaped the narrative. The knowledge produced as a result of my effort was a by-product of my social location as an intermarried Jewish woman, my analysis of the sources, and my interactions with the respondents. The relationship between interviewer and subjects was reciprocal; my personal experiences informed my analysis, and my analysis contributed to the decisions I made about my own life.

The personal answer to the riddle of how I could intermarry yet still claim the Jewish identifier and raise a Jewish child has a three-part explanation: religious observance, community, and education. In order to teach my child about Judaism, I learned to practice it daily by living according to Jewish time, creating rituals for everything from *brit bat* (covenant of a daughter) to bedtime. To enable her to feel proud of her Judaic heritage, we became increasingly active participants in the Boston Jewish community by bringing food for Family Table, taking classes at the local Jewish Community Center, and attending board meetings at our temple. But perhaps my most important decision was to enroll her in a Jewish school, where Jewishness is in the air the children breathe. During her preschool years she learned more about Jewish traditions and Hebrew than I ever could have imagined. Her comment to me one day illustrates this well: "Ema, I think I'm a little more Jewish than you." Whereas I grew up fully aware that I was a Jew in a Christian country and with the ghost of anti-semitism lingering over my shoulder, courtesy of a brick thrown through my living room window during childhood, Shira is free to develop a fresh perspective. "America is a great Jewish place to be," she commented at age four. There is plenty of time for her to learn about demography.

Sadly my marriage did not withstand the challenges of dual careers and divergent views on parenting within intermarriage. During the final stages of editing this book, my spouse and I formally separated and divorced. Although I searched my respondents' experiences for signs that differences of religion caused marital disharmony, it was my own union that exemplified this concept more than any I encountered during my research. The women's lives I studied suggested that issues relating to economics, politics, and infidelity were more often the cause of strife than anything having to do with one spouse being Jewish and the other not. In my own case, however, that I consistently refused to bring our preschooler to church or allow her to receive presents from Santa Claus caused irrevocable damage. Although my spouse remained a lapsed Catholic, his resentment over what he considered to be my "inflexibility" about these particular issues escalated over the years, eventually becoming intolerable. I, on the other hand, was profoundly disappointed that he would not live up to the bargain we had struck. I was prepared to raise our Jewish daughter single-handedly. To do so, however, with someone who vacillated from being a *ger tzedek* (righteous Gentile) to begrudging my efforts to cultivate her love of Judaism was, in the end, unhealthy for everyone. We are each responsible for our choices and their repercussions. I chose Jewish continuity over an unsatisfactory marriage founded on an imbalance of love, commitment, and emotional nourishment.

The reader has a right to know about the person who writes history for public consumption, especially given the controversial nature of the topic at hand. Although I share my personal history in the interest of intellectual honesty, this book is not about me or about my life. Nor should the reader misconstrue my own story as a verdict against intermarriage. I am neither for nor against it, rather a knowledgeable witness to it. I hope, however, that anyone interested in intermarriage and gender will take note that mine is a success story in terms of the future of the Jewish people. Would things have turned out differently had I married a coreligionist the first time around? Perhaps yes, perhaps no. It is not religion that binds or breaks a marriage but the individuals who practice it. The same is true for whether a child of intermarriage will be raised to identify as a Jew and continue to do so after she becomes an adult and establishes a home of her own. Parents can only provide the tools . . . and pray.

Acknowledgments

My deepest gratitude is to the forty-six women who generously, and in three cases posthumously, shared their personal intermarriage stories that made this book possible. Their trust and experiences motivated me to persevere with the utmost resolve. Intermarried Jewish women, *yasher koach* (may you have strength)!

Numerous members of the Brown University community participated in this endeavor. Mari Jo Buhle was an exemplary adviser: her standards exactingly high, her feedback swift, and her support unwavering. She is a model of intellectual engagement and efficiency to which I will always aspire. Howard Chudacoff taught me to remember the "forest." Lynn Davidman showed me the ropes of contemporary ethnography. Ken Sacks and Jim McClain appointed me to teach courses related to my research. Diligent librarians located materials near and far. The Computing and Information Services folks saw me through many technical difficulties.

My project received financial support from Brown University, the Memorial Foundation for Jewish Culture, Wellesley College, the National Women's Studies Association Jewish Women's Caucus, and the Hadassah-Brandeis Institute.

Eric Zinner, Emily Park, Ciara McLaughlin, and Despina Papazoglou Gimbel at New York University Press expertly guided this book from proposal to production. Paul Spickard and several anonymous reviewers supplied knowledgeable critiques that significantly improved the manuscript. Sherry Israel and Mae Shafter Rockland Tupa read the page proofs with keen eyes.

I was lucky to have multiple mentors whose passion for scholarship combined with their devotion to their children provided much inspiration and encouragement by example. Thank you Joyce Antler, Hasia Diner, Deborah Dash Moore, Pamela Nadell, Riv-Ellen Prell, and Judith Tick. Deborah was an invaluable resource from when I crafted my research proposal in the summer of 2000 to the present. Joyce, too, deserves special appreciation for always making time to discuss a work in progress and for countless pearls of wisdom.

When I began my research I was told by those in the know to contact Egon Mayer, *z"l* (of blessed memory). I hesitated, thinking I should first make some headway, only to answer my phone one day and hear him say: "Hi, I hear you're working on intermarriage. How can I help you?" His pioneering approach to studying intermarriage at the micro level of personal experiences, mixing qualitative and quantitative studies, impressed me profoundly. I regret that this book was not finished in time to share it with him.

Jonathan Sarna's continuous interest in my progress accompanied me to the finish line, as did his prolific scholarship on American Jewish history.

Clergywomen and men of many faiths and denominations pointed me in fruitful directions and shared insights, namely, Jack Ahern, Binyamin Biber, Robert Bulloch, Samuel Chiel, Nicholas Ciccone, Walter Cuenin, David Danner, Steven Dworken, Irwin Fishbein, Ron Friedman, J. Robert Giggi, Zachary Heller, Gordon Hugenberger, Miriam Jerris, William Joy, Jan Kaufman, Judith Kummer, Kathryn Michael, Joseph McGlone, Jack Porter, Allan Press, Benjamin Samuels, Sanford Seltzer, Dennis Sheehan, Charles Simon, Barbara Symons, Robert "Skip" Windsor, and Elaine Zecher.

I also thank the following dedicated professionals: Julie Albanese and John Hurley, Unitarian Universalist Association; Steven Bayme and David Singer, American Jewish Committee; Paula Brody, Union of American Hebrew Congregations Northeast Council; Ed Case, InterfaithFamily.com; Rhea Chapman and Dorothy Estes, Christian Science Headquarters; Kari Colella, Felitia Forger, Robert Johnson-Lally, Maria Medina, and Melissa Wodzinski, Catholic Archdiocese in Boston; Jennifer Davis, Hebrew Rehabilitation Center for Aged; Lena Dmitrieva, Wilstein Institute; Fiona Epstein, Beth Waldorf, and Marc Sokoll, Leventhal-Sidman Jewish Community Center; Lisa Gallatin, Workmen's Circle; Paul Golin and Gail Quets, Jewish Outreach Institute; Leonie Gordon, Harvard Institute for Learning; Dru Greenwood, Union for Reform Judaism; Josh Klein, Sarit Meir, Ben Phillips, and Jim Schwartz, National Jewish Data Bank; Judith Krell, Combined Jewish Philanthropies, Boston; Clara Marton, Jewish Community Housing for the Elderly; Charlotte Millman, Brookline Senior Center; Catherine MacDonald and Jay Rock, Presbyterian Church USA; Paula Panchuck, Lasell Village; Elana Kling Perkins and Diane Richler, Jewish Family & Children's Service; Sandra Sudak, Episcopal Diocese of Massachusetts; and Stanley Wayne, Ethical Society of Boston.

I thank the skilled archivists, reference librarians, and administrators at the following institutions: American Jewish Historical Society, Center for Jewish History, Congregational Library in Boston, Cornell University, Episcopal Divinity School, Hadassah, Historical Society of the Town of Greenwich, Jacob Rader Marcus Center of the American Jewish Archives, Judaica Reference and the National Center for Jewish Film at Brandeis University, Methodist Library of Theology at Boston University, National Marriage Project at Rutgers University, Newton Public Library, Schlesinger Library, Temple Israel Library, Titus Foundation, and Yale University.

A brief mention cannot do justice to the help I received from Richard Alba, Robert Allison, Arthur Antin, Tzvi Black, Paul Buhle, Joshua Comenetz, Lila Corwin, Arnold Dashefsky, Sergio Della Pergola, Anita Diamant, Sarah Dutton, Edward English, Kirsten Fermaglich, Leslie Fishbein, Sylvia Barack Fishman, Gerald M. Friedman, Edith Gelles, Calvin Goldscheider, Bethamie Horowitz, Matthew Frye Jacobson, Jacqueline Jones, Josephine Kanarek, Debra Kaufman, Helene Kenvin, Ariela Keysar, Adrian Koesters, Susan Koppelman, Amy Kronish, Laura Levitt, Maud Mandel, Allan Mazur, Judy McCarthy, Jim O'Toole, Joel Perlmann, Kristen Petersen, Bruce Phillips, Shulamit Reinharz, Anne Rose, Anne Ross, Judith Rosenbaum, Evelyn Salz, Jeff Scheckner, Philip Silverman, Ellen Smith, Miriam Sokoloff, Werner Sollors, Stanley Tamarkin, Aviva Taubenfeld, Shelly Tenenbaum, Miriam Tick, Elaine Trudeau, Lana Wilder, Hasdai Westbrook, and Ruth Wisse.

Various audiences asked thought-provoking questions, affirmed my exercise in reflexivity, and confirmed the validity of my findings for women living in other parts of the United States. They include the staff of the Jewish Women's Archive, participants in the American Association for Jewish Research Seminar on History and Memory held at Vassar College, the Jewish Feminist Research Group at the Jewish Theological Seminary, the Association for Jewish Studies, the Boston Seminar in Immigration and Urban History at the Massachusetts Historical Society, the Scholars' Conference on American Jewish History, the Boston College Conference on the History of Religion, the Knoxville Jewish Alliance Women's Network, the Klutznick-Harris Symposium at Creighton University, and the New Women's Voices in Jewish Studies series at Hebrew College. Brown University students, particularly those enrolled in my course, Interfaith, Interethnic, Interracial America, and select Stonehill College students voluntarily personified the terms "half-Jew" and "cashew."

As the publication date neared, the amazing staff of the Jean & Samuel Frankel Center for Judaic Studies at the University of Michigan and the Ann Arbor community warmly welcomed my family into their midst.

New and old friends—Sharon Albert, Alejandro Botta, Julie and David Chivo, Sandy Falk, Jill Gibson, Janna Giesta, Julie Goodman, Michelle Hall, Shiho Imai, Ellen Jawitz, Dan Judson, Jeff Korn, Rob Leikind, Vince Martinelli, David Miller, Carmen Padilla, Josh Sens, Orna Teitelbaum, Joshua Wachs, Barbara Walter, and Caragh Whalen-Feinblatt—were my social lifeblood. Temple Beth Avodah and Rabbi Keith Stern provided a spiritual home. The extraordinary faculties and administrators at the Solomon Schechter Day School of Greater Boston, the Rose and Jacob Grossman Camp, and the Gan Yeladim Early Learning Center nurtured and educated my child so that I could focus on writing with peace of mind and a satisfied heart.

My parents fortified me: my mother stocked my freezer with edible love, Myron found my transcription machine on eBay, and I got the skinny on publishing from my father. Members of the Adams, Goodman, McGinity, Murray, Rockland, Stanley, Tenenbaum, and Thomas families consistently expressed confidence in my ultimate success. My daughter, Shira, came with me, in utero, to many of the interviews and much of the archival research. Her presence in my life improved my ability both to compartmentalize and optimize time for this project, while keeping its significance in healthy perspective. Shira's question at age two and a half, "Work hard today, Mommy?" and her incessant demand "Play with me!" captured my blessed fragmentation. At press time Shira is a gifted first grader. I hope someday she will read this book and know that, while yesterday is history, hers is the future to decide.

To all the above, I am eternally grateful.

Introduction

I was born Jewish and I'll die Jewish. I will always just be plain Jewish.

—Intermarried Jewish Woman (2001)

Hannah Noble met her husband in medical school. He moved in with her on their second date, and they named their future children. Though he was Methodist, Hannah, raised as a secular Jew, knew she wanted to marry him and did not think that their different backgrounds would generate problems: "I didn't really think about having a Jewish life back then." However, they discussed religion during their engagement; her betrothed refused to raise his children as atheists and Hannah refused to raise them as anything but Jews. As a result, what had been a non-issue when they first met and later wed in 1992 became a new way of life: "I'm much more Jewish, *now* . . . than I was then. . . . My parents think I'm a religious fanatic now because I say the prayers on Friday night."[1] Hannah's comment about her parents illustrates a common phenomenon in the recent history of Jewish women, namely, that daughters become more observant than their parents. The couple joined the Jewish Community Center, researched which temple to join, and began having Shabbat dinners with friends. Hannah's story is not unique.

This book is the first history of American Jewish women who intermarried during the twentieth century.[2] The history of intermarriage has largely been the history of men, written by men about men. This trend is not to say that women did not intermarry—for most certainly they did—but the vast majority of work has neglected to consider gender. The few studies that mentioned women did so only cursorily. They pointed out that fewer Jewish women intermarried compared to Jewish men, and that the gender gap decreased late in the century. In this book I seek to answer three main questions: What did intermarriage mean to and for women who were Jewish at the time they married Gentile men?[3] In what ways did Jewish women shed or retain their ethnic and religious heritage despite marrying "out"? And how was intermarriage portrayed by the mass media and religious activists? This endeavor strives to understand how women's lives changed over time according to their exogamous marriage choices and whether they further integrated into non-Jewish society or contributed to Jewish continuity by self-identifying as Jews and raising Jewish children.

In this book I discern how assimilation or transformation has occurred among Jewish women by "entering" their homes to assess the influence of intermarriage on their lives. By looking at the intersection of intermarriage and gender across the twentieth century, I describe the lives of Jewish women who intermarried by taking into account historical factors. To date, Jewish-Gentile intermarriage has been a topic studied largely by sociologists, whose scholarship brought the topic of intermarriage out of the family closet and into public discourse. My analysis uses this body of work as evidence while integrating the variable of change over approximately one hundred years to contextualize the historical significance of several dozen intermarried Jewish women.

Although the issue of intermarriage has intrigued scholars and concerned the Jewish community nearly since permanent Jewish settlers arrived on America's shores in 1654, sociologists became fascinated by the topic only in the twentieth century.[4] Melting pot observers generated a plethora of social science research about intermarriage as a barometer of assimilation. Prior to 1930, the only large-scale study of American intermarriage was by Julius Drachsler in New York City, covering the years from 1908 to 1912. Drachsler wrote, "The subtle interplay in mixed marriages of different types of mind and culture has thus far almost completely eluded the observation of the scientific student.[5] Scholars devoted unprecedented attention to marriages between different groups of people beginning in the 1930s, following the great "wave" of immigration from Eastern and Southern Europe, and interest continued during the 1940s and 1950s. Intermarriage studies focused on rates and factors leading to marriage between groups, characteristics of both intermarriage and those who intermarried, and marital adjustments and outcomes. Many of the studies incorporated rhetoric concerned with biological and cultural mixing between groups, illustrating the social preoccupation with assimilation and amalgamation.[6] Some scholars in the 1940s and 1950s advanced a "triple melting pot" hypothesis that intermarriage occurred across ethnic lines more often than across religious ones.[7] Intermarriage as an index of the assimilative process had reached a level of national interest.

Although much has been written about inter-religious marriage during the past quarter-century, previous scholarship has insufficiently accounted for the passage of time and the role of gender. The vast majority of scholarly books on intermarriage are sociological. For example, Egon Mayer's classic *Love and Tradition: Marriage Between Jews and Christians* (Schocken, 1985) and Sylvia Barack Fishman's recently published *Double or Nothing: Jewish Families and Mixed Marriage* (Brandeis, 2004) do not account for change over time. The meager historical literature that does exist does not use gender as a primary category of analysis. Anne Rose's *Beloved Strangers: Interfaith Families in Nineteenth Century America* (Harvard, 2001) has some useful insights about women and religion, in general. However, until now, no studies have delved deeply into Jewish women's intermarriage in twentieth-century America. Although the historian Paul Spickard's *Mixed Blood: Intermarriage and Ethnic Identity in Twentieth-Century America* (Wisconsin, 1989) discusses Jews in one part of a work admirably devoted to multiple groups, it treats gender as immutable. Hence *Still Jewish* aims to contribute significantly to a topic that has heretofore received sparse attention from historians of women and Jewish studies.

Two major debates are currently being waged by scholars of Judaic studies and activists in Jewish organizations. One is academic, and the other regards policy decisions and programming; both are political and inform each other. The academic debate is between assimilationists and transformationists; the former believe that intermarriage will eventually eliminate the Jewish people,[8] and the latter see intermarriage as an aspect of ongoing change. For them, unlike assimilationists, change means transformation, not necessarily crisis. Calvin Goldscheider, a transformationist, contends that high levels of intermarriage are not equivalent to assimilation, as many intermarried Jews take part in communal life, or else were marginal to it in the first place, and therefore these marriages cannot be a cause of weakening.[9] The two groups differ over several key issues, including their definition of Jewish continuity, the import of modernity, and their assessments of American life in terms of its receptivity to ethnic and religious subcultures. The debate within Jewish institutions is how to handle intermarriage as an issue of Jewish survival, which I discuss in the conclusion of this book. One camp promotes outreach to intermarried Jews and their Gentile spouses, conversion if possible, as well as Jewish learning for Jews who are uneducated about their heritage.[10] The other camp encourages "in-reach," otherwise known as prevention.

Although this book primarily focuses on the meaning and representation of intermarriage, I use the assimilation versus transformation debate as a framework for understanding the significance of a history of intermarriage and its ramifications for Jewish continuity. By "assimilation," I intend the definition proposed by the scholars Richard Alba and Victor Nee: "the decline of an ethnic distinction and its corollary cultural and social differences."[11] I use the word "amalgamation" to mean the blending of two or more parts to create something new, and "acculturation" to signify integration without ethnic disappearance. This book is concerned with describing the experiential and cultural issues generated by intermarriage. This research effort contributes to the debate by suggesting a new paradigm that expands the discussion of continuity as it relates to religion and ethnicity by including gender.[12] The changing relationship between women and men influenced intermarried Jewish women's identities. Intermarriage, like all marriage, is a relationship of power, and gender is a primary way of signifying this relationship.[13] Therefore gender must be fully taken into account to accommodate this fluidity of identity so that the stories of intermarried Jewish women are no longer marginal. I specifically examine how gender politics in intermarried women's lives impacted their experiences and what this history can tell us about ethnic survival and whether intermarriage was "good or bad for the Jews," to quote the sociologist Shelly Tenenbaum.[14]

Continuity

Next to the fate of the State of Israel, continuity is the number 1 concern in the organized American Jewish community, and has been for at least the past two decades. The rising rates of intermarriage over the twentieth century in America seem to illustrate, on the surface, that total assimilation draws nearer with every passing decade: increasingly fewer Jews are marrying fellow Jews, resulting in fewer Jewish offspring. Prior to 1940, the rate of marriages between Jews and non-Jews was estimated to be between 2 percent and 3.2 percent, doubling to approximately 6 percent between 1941 and 1960.[15] According to the latest national sociological research, the percentage of born Jews who remained Jewish before marrying

"Whose Faith for the Kids? Mixed Marriages, Holidays, and Hard Choices," *Newsweek*, 15 December 1997, cover.

non-Jews increased roughly as follows: from less than 13 percent before 1970 to 28 percent between 1970 and 1979; from 38 percent between 1980 and 1984 to 43 percent between 1985 and 1995; and reaching an all-time high of 47 percent between 1996 and 2001.[16] The numbers alone suggest that concern about the future of American Jewry is highly warranted.

The grave alarm over intermarriage is based on the assumption promulgated by religious and academic authorities alike that once American Jews intermarry, they becomes fully assimilated into the majority Christian population, religion, and culture. The common belief, throughout the twentieth century, was that Jews who intermarried were "lost" to the Jewish community. The Anglo-Jewish newspaper *The Hebrew Standard*, for example, warned in 1905 "against matrimonial alliances with those outside the faith, because *"the Jew must remain a Jew."*[17] The sociologist Milton Gordon contended in his 1964 book, *Assimilation in American Life*, that intermarriage spelled "identificational assimilation." Gordon's theory was that intermarriage leads to ethnic dissolution. He postulated that once minorities enter the social milieu of the majority, intermarriage will occur and the minority group develops a sense of peoplehood based on the majority society.[18] The assumption by some Jewish advocates was that those who intermarried had essentially forsaken their Jewishness; their Jewish identity was no longer important to them and would never be so. Illustrating this perception was the 1997 statement by Alan Dershowitz, a distinguished law professor and Jewish activist, in his book, *The Vanishing American Jew*: "A decision by a young Jewish man or woman to marry a non-Jew is generally a reflection of a well-established reality that their Jewishness is not all that central to their identity."[19] The possibility that being Jewish remained a vibrant identification to someone who intermarried, or that it might become such in due course, was persistently beyond the comprehension of those who wrote about the issue.

Jewish identity is dynamic, constantly interacting with and being influenced by environmental factors, such as partner and lifestyle. Self-identifying as Jewish for the women in my study meant integrating the ethno-religious identities they inherited at birth and their intermarried lives within their respective historical contexts. Being Jewish for the women in my study meant maintaining allegiance to the Jewish people and, for those who intermarried in the later decades, making Jewish choices regarding observance and education despite having married outside the tribe. Although intermarriage affected women's identities, diluting them earlier in the century and accentuating them toward the end, being Jewish was a persistent part of women's ideological makeup. It influenced their self-perceptions, their view of their immediate social circles and the world at large, and their notion of how others saw them. Moreover, Jewish identity within intermarried women's sense of self was an intricate mixture of religion, ethnicity, and race. Whereas religion could be accepted or rejected, ethnicity and race were malleable but permanent.

The inherent tension between the selection of a Gentile husband and the maintenance of a Jewish self evolved over the twentieth century, as American women gained more political rights and personal power within their most intimate relationships. While democratic culture enabled Jewish women to blend into the mainstream, and some did when they intermarried, it also increasingly encouraged them to assert their Jewishness. In the words of the literary scholar Ruth R. Wisse: "American Jews find themselves in the tough position of having to bless America precisely for what endangers them, and of proving the depth of America's hospitality by refusing to be absorbed into its folds."[20]

The paradox of pluralism in America enabled the Jewish women discussed in this book to intermarry while forcing them to determine for themselves the ways that they wished to integrate into the American population and retain their ethnic and religious heritage despite marrying "out." America, with its religious freedom, ethnic diversity, and marital opportunities, offered Jewish women the chance to choose their own spouses and how they would self-identify. In the process, the meaning of religious identity became increasingly personal and individualistic, as it did for many moderately affiliated American Jews.[21] Because they were married to non-Jews, however, women who identified as Jewish needed to go beyond their most immediate personal circles to find Jewish fellowship, for example, at their synagogue, through their children's Jewish education, and through Jewish cultural activities. Intermarried Jewish women increasingly expressed and enacted their Jewish identities through explicitly public means. Lest she be utterly alone, the "sovereign self" of the modern intermarried Jewish woman, the principal authority for contemporary American Jews described by Steven Cohen and Arnold Eisen in *The Jew Within,* reached out to organizations and institutions to connect her private Jewish self with the larger Jewish community.[22]

The assumption that an intermarried person ceases to identify as a Jew is exacerbated by the assumption that a Jew who marries a non-Jew does not raise Jewish children. Although this project focuses on Jewish women rather than their offspring, the more crucial issue for people interested in Jewish continuity regarding intermarriage is not how the individuals involved identified but how their children were raised and what that would mean for the future of the Jewish people. The recent statistic that roughly only a third of the children with intermarried parents are raised as Jews, combined with the low fertility rates of Jewish women that are below replacement levels, make the *halakhic* position—that is, the one that accords with Jewish law—against intermarriage all the more pragmatic.[23] If approximately half the American Jews intermarry and less than half raise Jewish children, the Jewish future would indeed seem to be in jeopardy. American Jews who care about continuity, many of whom now have adult children, want an answer to the question: "Will my grandchildren be Jewish?" I would respond to this question with another question: "Do you have an intermarried daughter or son?" If it is a daughter who intermarried in the late twentieth or early twenty-first century, the likelihood is strong that she will raise children to identify as Jews.

The historical stakes for my study of intermarriage are high: using gender, it will reconceptualize how intermarriage is understood to affect Jewish continuity according to the histories of forty-six women who intermarried between 1901 and 2000. The evidence illustrates that women who intermarried later in the century were more likely to raise their children with strong ties to Judaism than women who intermarried earlier in the century. In the chapters that follow I discuss the particular historical circumstances that influenced women's own identities and choices on behalf of their children. Here I summarize how the women raised their children with respect to the issue of continuity. Of the three women who intermarried in the first decade of the century, two had children and both raised them without any discernable Jewish identity. Seven of the Jewish women I interviewed who intermarried between 1938 and 1960 raised their children as Unitarians, five as Jews, one as Catholic, and one was childless. Ten women who intermarried between 1963 and 1979 raised children who identified as Jewish, the children of two identified neither as Jewish nor Gentile, and the children of two others identified reportedly as "both." Finally, of the fifteen Jewish women who intermarried between 1980 and 2000, twelve were raising children to identify as Jewish, two were childless, and one was pregnant at the time of the interview. Although drawing generalizations using a sample of only forty-six women would be imprudent, the steady increase in the ratio of women who raised children to identify as Jews is unmistakable.

Recent scholarship suggests that Jewish women who marry non-Jews raise Jewish children at higher rates than do intermarried Jewish men. Prior to the new millennium, the minimal attention to the gender of the Jewish parent suggested the disinclination, perhaps inadvertent, on the part of scholars of intermarriage to truly confront the role of gender in the construction of families in general, and in intermarried families in particular. It should be emphasized, however, that how children were raised to identify is no guarantee of how they will identify when they reach adulthood. Nevertheless, the presence of Jewish mothers married to Gentile men in intermarried households is a stronger predictor of Jewish identification than are non-Jewish mothers married to Jewish men. Although the study of the children of intermarriage is still young, a 2002 report by the Higher Education Research Institute at the University of California, Los Angeles, found that college freshmen tended to affiliate with the religion of their mothers. Of students with a Jewish mother and a Gentile father, 38 percent identified as Jewish compared to 15 percent of students with non-Jewish mothers and Jewish fathers.[24] In a 2005 study of a nonrepresentative sample of ninety young adult children of inter-married couples, 77 percent of respondents with Jewish mothers reported that their Jewish parent encouraged them to "identify with the Jewish religion" compared to 45 percent of respondents with Jewish fathers.[25] According to Fishman, "households with Jewish mothers are more connected to Jewishness and less connected to Christianity in every measurable aspect of Jewish life than households with Jewish fathers."[26] Quantitative data strengthen what qualitative research patterns suggest: an analysis of the 2000-2001 National Jewish Population Survey (NJPS), thought to be representative, found that of the roughly one-third of the children of all currently intermarried Jews being raised Jewish, 47 percent were children of intermarried women and 28 percent were children of inter-married men.[27] These findings from contemporary sociological research reinforce my historical research about the roles of intermarried Jewish women and American religious life.

Jewish History and Matrilineal Descent

A twentieth-century history of women and intermarriage in America has as its background an ancient Jewish story resulting in a monumental conflict of interests. Whereas Americans believe in "life, liberty, and the pursuit of happiness," Jewish law warns Jews not to intermarry, and sages told those men who did to purge Gentile wives from the Judean tribe. The classic biblical prohibition of Jewish-Gentile intermarriage is Deuteronomy 7:3-4: "You shall not intermarry with them: do not give your daughters to their sons or take their daughters for your sons. For they will turn your children away from me to worship other gods, and the Lord's anger will blaze forth against you and He will promptly wipe you out."[28] After the ban against marriage with members of the seven larger non-Israelite nations, Jews were warned against marriage with people of *all* lands and nations, urged by Nehemiah only to marry fellow Jews. In the fifth century BCE, Ezra took the decree further, aiming to expel "foreign" wives and their children from the Jewish community.[29] This ancient writer expanded the notion of holiness and extended the requirement of genealogical purity, formerly required only of Israelite priests, to lay Israelites. According to Ezra and Nehemiah, the distinction between Israelites and Gentiles was genealogical, not moral or ritualistic; hence intermarriage and conversion became impossible because the holy seed of the Israelite could not be joined with the profane seed of the Gentile.[30] Jewish marriage was between two Jews, period.

The intense religious objections to intermarriage held by today's traditional *halakhic* Jews (those who follow Jewish law) reinvigorate Ezra and Nehemiah's ancient discourse regarding tribal boundaries, as well as the discourses of subsequent Talmudic rabbis who devised the principle of matrilineal descent. Previously the issue of genealogical purity was not gendered; although descent was formerly inherited from the father, and, correspondingly, the children of an Israelite man and a non-Israelite woman were considered to be Israelites, the idea of the people of Israel as a holy seed excluded Gentile females and males such that only children of two Israelite parents could be Israelites.[31] In the words of one scholar, the idea for the matrilineal principle first appears in the Mishnah "like a bolt out of the blue," and may date from the end of the mid-second century CE or the late fourth century. According to two textual segments, the offspring of a Gentile mother and a Jewish father follows the mother; similarly, the offspring of a Jewish mother and a Gentile father follows the mother. Whereas the law penalized the Jewish man by making his child born of a Gentile woman also Gentile, the law penalized the Jewish woman by making her child conceived from a Gentile man a *mamzer* (illegitimate) but a Jew nonetheless. The basis for the bastardization of the child is that there is no potential for a valid marriage in these circumstances. Although there was dissent between some rabbis who considered the child of a Jewish father and a Gentile mother Jewish, and rabbis who considered the child of a Jewish mother and a Gentile father Gentile, the matrilineal descent principle became nearly universally accepted within rabbinic circles and, I argue, outside them as well.[32] (I discuss the adoption of the patrilineal descent principle in the 1980s by the Reform Movement in chapter 4.)

In an important historic twist, the matrilineal descent principle contributed to making the experiences of Jewish women who married exogamously less noteworthy and therefore less visible from the earliest centuries to the twentieth century. Previously the author of the Book of Jubilees, who reworked biblical text, did not know the matrilineal principle and condemned the intermarriage of Israelite women more vociferously than those of Israelite men in his paraphrase of Genesis 34:

And if there is any man who wishes in Israel to give his daughter or his sister to any man who is of the seed of the Gentiles he shall surely die, and they shall stone him with stones; for he hath wrought shame in Israel; and they shall burn the woman with fire, because she has dishonoured the name of the house of her father and she shall be rooted out of Israel.[33]

What, then, can be surmised about Israelite women who had unions with Gentile men? The biblical figure Dinah, daughter of Leah and Jacob and great granddaughter of Sarah and Abraham, defied the reported word of God when she had sexual relations with and married Shechem, a Gentile Egyptian prince. Although some scholars interpret the story of Dinah as a rape, it seems equally plausible that she intermarried and that the charge of rape was subsequently issued to explain the unthinkable: a Jewish woman marrying a non-Jewish man.[34] That Dinah "went out" of the Jewish tribe and that Shechem did whatever was necessary to keep her as his wife, including being circumcised, suggest that intermarriage was the real issue. Moreover, her brothers' slaughter of her husband and all the males in his kingdom was apparently an attempt to physically eliminate any other potential Gentile mates for Jewish women (Genesis 34:1-27).[35] Thus, although the injunction against intermarriage applied to Jewish men as well as Jewish women, the union of a Jewish female with a non-Jewish male was by far the more grievous offense.[36]

Patriarchy supersedes the matrilineal descent principle both before and after its invention. Whereas the Jewish woman who joined her body and life with a Gentile man "shall burn" and "be rooted out of Israel" (Book of Jubilees 30:7-8), the Israelite warrior could take captive a non-Jewish woman he desired. He could bring her home, change her appearance by cutting her hair and discarding her clothes, allow her a month to grieve for her parents, and "after that you may come to her and possess her, and she shall be your wife" (Deuteronomy 21:10-14).[37] In contrast to the silence surrounding Dinah, numerous biblical accounts describe Jewish heroes and kings who intermarried. Such pairings included Judah with a Canaanite woman, Joseph with an Egyptian, Moses with a Midianite and an Ethiopian, David with a Philistine, and Solomon with "women of every description."[38] Subsequent rabbinic *midrash* (the interpretation of Jewish texts) generally argued that Gentile women who married Jewish patriarchs were not actually foreign, as the women were either of Israelite origin or had converted to Judaism prior to their marriages.[39]

Gender explains why, paradoxically, more Jewish men intermarried than women despite the matrilineal descent principle. The negative portrayal of intermarriage was in highly gendered terms, with dire consequences for individual women if they disobeyed, but more significant consequences for Jews as a group if men did. There was considerably more concern about Jewish men becoming idolatrous, because it was a patriarchal society in which everything of importance was men's domain. Regarding this imbalance, the scholar Shaye D. Cohen argued, "if Israelite men are incited by their foreign wives to abandon the worship of the true God, the result would be catastrophic; if Israelite women are turned astray by their foreign husbands, who would notice? . . . Hence the legal and narrative texts pay little attention to marriages between Israelite women and foreign men. Like the women themselves, they were easily overlooked."[40] Perhaps this hints at one of the reasons why Jewish women who intermarried later in history and maintained ties to their Jewish heritage were overlooked: they were less conspicuous than men to begin with and were assumed to disappear into their husbands' houses.[41]

Why Jewish Women?

Difficulty tracing intermarried Jewish women, combined with cultural assumptions about gender roles, contributed to scholarly analyses that underrepresented women. Social scientists merely reported, without much commentary, that, between 1930 and 1960, Jewish women intermarried less often than Jewish men did. As Milton Barron wrote, "Everywhere Jewish men were found to have intermarried more than Jewish women."[42] A multitude of research studies documented the sex-ratio differential.[43] For example, a study conducted by students at Hebrew Union College in Cincinnati in 1944 surveyed twenty-one cities in seven mid-western states and remarked that the most striking result was that, of the 152 intermarried Jewish individuals, 133 (nearly 88 percent) were men and only 19 were women.[44] But surveys can be misleading, at least when it comes to the meanings behind the intermarriage sex ratio. Although more Jewish men than women may very well have intermarried, the lack of critical analysis to date regarding this gender differential undermines a deeper understanding of intermarriage history.

More Jewish women may have intermarried than historians will ever know, because studies conducted between 1930 and 1960 that used "Jewish" surnames to locate interfaith couples potentially missed Jewish women who married non-Jews, changed their names, and became "invisible" to researchers. Jewish men who married outside the fold may also have been inadvertently excluded. Although scholars exercised great care in their attempts to include only actual intermarriages, others probably went undetected because numerous intermarried Jews dropped their original Jewish names and adopted non-Jewish names, sometimes even prior to marriage.[45] It is likely that more women assumed their husbands' names than men assumed non-Jewish names upon marriage, though only a study of Jewish men who intermarried could confirm this idea. For example, all the women I interviewed who intermarried between 1938 and 1960 took their husband's name when they wed. As the sociologist Erich Rosenthal wrote in the *American Jewish Yearbook 1963*, "the data on intermarried Jewish women do not lend themselves to consistent analysis."[46] In the case where a non–name-based methodology was employed, intermarried Jewish men still far outnumbered women. The states of Indiana and Iowa asked the religious affiliation of the individuals who purchased marriage licenses. Based on this information, a study including the years 1953 to 1959 found that 75 percent of the mixed marriages of Jews in Iowa involved a Jewish male, and only 25 percent involved a female.[47] The question was, why? Answers, though not plentiful, suggest that Jewish women who intermarried were exceptions.

The perception of intermarriage as a "men-only" course of action obscured the actual history of intermarried Jewish women. Students of intermarriage intertwined speculation about why Jewish women presumably intermarried less frequently than Jewish men with gender stereotypes reinforced by double standards.[48] Social scientists in 1934 surmised that Jewish men had more opportunity to meet Gentile women in business, and that religion exerted more influence on Jewesses (a term used for Jewish women in the early twentieth century) than on Jewish men. These scientists' observation that "many Jewish businessmen marry their Gentile stenographers" overlooked the fact that Jewish stenographers could also marry Gentile businessmen. They specifically cited the difficulty in ascertaining how Jewish women became acquainted with Gentile men.[49] Tacit approval of Jewish males' sexual relations with non-Jewish females, allowing greater access to Gentile women, is illustrated by a Yiddish saying for Jewish boys: "In the Torah it is written, that you may lie with a Gentile girl, but if the girl does not let you 'have' her, may she be afflicted with Cholera!"[50] The saying is a cultural manipulation of the aforementioned biblical text (Deuteronomy 21:10-14) that, although not discussing any ailment, dealt with the treatment of sexually desirable non-Jewish women who are captured in war that includes marriage, intercourse, and conversion to Judaism.[51] As late as 1968, the psychologist Louis A. Berman contended that men, "whose sex role designates a greater degree of independence and aggressiveness," were more likely to violate the social taboo of intermarriage, whereas the Jewish daughter "would seem more vulnerable to threats of ostracism."[52]

Whereas Jewish men could engage in sexual relations with Gentile women that might lead to marriage, it was more difficult for Jewish women to cross the religious line, because, in addition to their friends being carefully screened for Gentiles, they were expected to remain chaste until marriage. There is also a Yiddish aphorism to this effect—"No Chuppe, No Shtuppe" ("No Wedding [Canopy], No Sex")—reflecting the expectation that Jewish girls will avoid premarital sexual relations.[53] The prospect of being marginalized probably made some women think twice about marrying a non-Jew. The writer Toby Shafter observed the following in a 1949 *Commentary* article about her Maine community:

> The announcement that a young man is about to marry or has already secretly married a *shiksa* hardly creates a sensation by now. The few Jewish girls who have married Gentile men have, on the other hand, been subject to vehement criticism, coffee-hour gossip, and unending speculation. In all cases except one, they have not remained in town.[54]

Keren Hadass's 1941 booklet, *A Marriage Guide for Jewish Women: Especially Prepared for the American Jewish Woman,* concerned endogamy only.[55] How many Jewish women intermarried despite social pressure against doing so is undeterminable. One thing is certain, however: Jewish women who intermarried defied the cultural expectation that they would "save" themselves for Jewish men, some of whom made other plans.

Although it became clear in the 1960s and 1970s that Jewish women were, in fact, intermarrying, Jewish women's intermarriage stories went untold. In 1970, for example, the *American Jewish Year Book* reported that analysis of a survey by the National Opinion Research Council (NORC) suggested that the gender differential between Jewish women and men was not as great as earlier intermarriage studies suggested. Acknowledging that more Jewish women might have intermarried than suspected, one scholar explained: "The narrowing gap between male and female intermarriage rates may have resulted from the inclusion of that portion of the Jewish population most frequently underrepresented in intermarriage studies—the Jewish girl who marries out and is lost to the Jewish community."[56] The increased awareness of Jewish women marrying non-Jews extended from Jewish communities in the Diaspora to Israel, causing the Israeli Minister of Religious Affairs to publicly lament, in May 1971, about the number of Jewish females who married Muslim men.[57]

Still, the actual experiences of those Jewish women who crossed the religious line remained concealed by the contention that they were reluctant to intermarry before second-wave feminism.[58] Moreover, the oft-cited 1970-72 National Jewish Population Study finding that the Jewish husband-Gentile wife marriage was "about twice as prevalent" as the Jewish wife-Gentile husband combination curtailed extensive inquiry or commentary about Jewish daughters who married "out," perpetuating in the process the assumption that intermarriage was largely the domain of Jewish men rather than women.[59] This assumption was overturned in the last decade of the twentieth century, but the imprint of its long history lingers. Only through interrogating the relationship between gender and intermarriage does it become possible to effectively illustrate that Jewish women, those in my study and I suspect many others, may not have been so reluctant to intermarry after all and that most remained Jewish after they wed. They may have indeed intermarried in fewer numbers than their Jewish brothers for most of the century, but this assumption should not be used to explain why Jewish women were ignored.

Methodology and Chapter Overviews

I define "intermarriage" as follows: the legal union between a born Jew and a born non-Jew who has not converted at the time of marriage. I use the anthropological terms "exogamous" (marriage outside one's own group) and "endogamous" (marriage within), interchangeably with "intermarriage" and "in-marriage," respectively. I include a Jewish woman whose spouse converted sometime after their wedding day. For example, a Jewish woman who married a non-Jew in 1970 and whose husband converted to Judaism in 1980 would no longer be considered "intermarried" by the present standards of Jewish organizations or by most people (although some rabbis would disagree). I include her, however, because she originally wed a Gentile and her spouse's conversion to Judaism is part of change over time. This trend is not in any way to discriminate against women who are Jews by choice or to stigmatize conversionary couples as still intermarried, but rather to accurately trace the changing meaning of intermarriage to Jewish women and in public discourse. Although same-sex couples and long-term heterosexual partnerships are often also interfaith, this study focuses on male-female relationships defined by conventional marriage under current law. I also do not include marriages between born Jews of different backgrounds (for example, Conservative-secular, American-Israeli, or German-Russian marriages), despite that sometimes these unions are considered to be "intermarriages" by the individuals involved and by some scholars, in both different and strikingly similar ways.[60]

This is a multigenerational history, beginning with women who immigrated to the United States in the early twentieth century, using two methodological techniques.[61] The first involves collecting women's self-reports to describe the experience and meaning of intermarriage. "Jewish women" is loosely defined as those who were raised Jewish and either did or did not later identify as Jews. In cases where women have parents of different religions, I rely on women to identify themselves as Jews at the time of marriage (rather than using matrilineal or patrilineal descent as a determinant). I augment interviews with letters, memoirs, biographies, and novels about women. I consider how contextual factors such as immigration trends, world wars, the Depression, antisemitism, and the Civil Rights and Feminist movements influenced intermarriage.[62] The second technique is to integrate throughout my study an analysis of how interfaith relationships and intermarriage were portrayed in the mass media, advice manuals, and religious community-generated literature to situate women's self-representations within larger discursive contexts.

The meaning of intermarriage and gender is best understood through individual experiences within their respective contexts. To obtain these life stories, I conducted in-depth personal interviews with women who intermarried.[63] This methodology produced the oral history narratives that enabled me to interpret what intermarriage meant to and for Jewish women within their particular social milieus and how this changed over time. This approach embraces the "personal" as an epistemological tool and uses individual experiences to uncover and chronicle the meaning of intermarriage. It employs contemporary ethnography which assumes that, in one noted scholar's words, "all knowledge in the field is produced through the interactions between a researcher, who is a socially situated self with particular life experiences, and her respondents, who bring to the dialogue their own embedded assumptions and meanings."[64] The interviewees' own intermarriage histories constitute the content of this scholarship. By asking women "How are you Jewish?"—and not "How Jewish are you?" —this book considers the "invention of ethnicity," to borrow the title from a work by another scholar, Werner Sollors. This book looks at intermarriage as a historical process during which women defined and re-defined their own ethnicity, that is, the ways in which they belonged to an ethnic group, as well as how others perceived them as belonging.[65] I recognize the fluidity of ethnicity and that it involves personal choice by describing and analyzing a woman's ethnic identity as her subjective orientation toward her religious origins.[66]

In addition to archival research about three women who are deceased, I conducted forty-three interviews in fourteen towns and cities in the Boston area with women of mostly Ashkenazi descent and assorted generations whose intermarriages occurred in seven twentieth-century decades. This sample does not strive to be random or representative. Rather, it selectively sheds light on the complex histories of some Jewish women who intermarried and whose voices have yet to be heard. This sample size is large enough to illustrate some common experiences among women who intermarried and the meanings these experiences generated at various points across time. The interviews were conducted in the Boston area for convenience; a multi-regional study, though enviable, was beyond my resources as the sole researcher. Unless otherwise noted, the phrase "intermarried Jewish women" in my text refers specifically to the women in my sample. Italicized words situated within direct quotations indicate the women's own verbal emphases. Pseudonyms are used to preserve the women's anonymity. As a historian, I longed to include women's actual names. However, anonymous participation strengthened my research by enabling many women to share intimate details and emotions un-self-consciously, information they would otherwise have omitted for fear of their friends and families someday reading this book and identifying them. I do use the real surnames of the semi-famous immigrant women discussed in chapter 1, as their personal papers are accessible to researchers, and also the actual name of the published novelist discussed in chapter 2.

Three minor limitations should be pointed out regarding the makeup of my sample. None of the women I interviewed married Muslim men; none married men who were devoutly religious; nor did any of the women formally convert to Christianity. Certainly such intermarried women exist, but that none of these particular women chose to participate in my study suggests two important points. First, there were probably fewer such women than women who married non-religious Christian men. Second, and more significant, that most women in my sample who married non-Jews during the twentieth century continued to identify as Jewish illustrates the unique "tenacity of Jewishness" in American society.[67] It also suggests that, when studied historically, intermarriage, at least involving Jewish women, may not be "bad for the Jews" in the long run. My sample is self-selected and all women volunteered their time, that is, no incentives or compensation was offered. More important is that this was not a skewed group of women who felt proudly Jewish and therefore participated. Rather, the women illustrate the ways in which being Jewish and intermarrying was experienced differently depending on the time period.

In chapter 1, I discuss the intermarried lives of three well-known immigrant Jewish women: Mary Antin Grabau, Rose Pastor Stokes, and Anna Strunsky Walling. Their experiences shed new light on the inner workings of intermarriages early in the twentieth century that disputes the conventional idea that religious differences were the primary cause of marital failure. The lives of lesser-known women who intermarried between 1930 and 1960 are analyzed in chapter 2, where I argue that diminished religiosity, assimilation, and wider social contacts increased the possibility of intermarriage and that antisemitism was sometimes a contributing impetus. Chapter 3 illustrates how the liberalism, ecumenism, and feminism of the 1960s and 1970s simultaneously created more room for Jewish women to intermarry and, for an increasing number of women, to proactively define themselves as Jews. In chapter 4, which covers the years from 1980 through 2004, I show how multiculturalism, combined with rampant changes in religious affiliation and individualism in American society, meant that, although Jewish women married Gentile men who were often not religious, their encounters with the "other," paradoxically, inspired many women to reconnect with their Jewish heritage and communities. The Jewish women in my sample who intermarried toward the end of the twentieth century initiated what I call a Jewish-feminist modus vivendi by creating meaningful ethnic self-identities that were non-halakhic (counter to Jewish law) yet authentic, and by charting the religious courses for their families.[68] In the conclusion I summarize my findings and discuss the polarized Jewish community's response to intermarriage, which is known as the "outreach/in-reach debate." Suggested avenues for further inquiry may be found in the afterword, followed by an appendix that includes seven tables containing relevant statistical information for the reader's reference. It is my hope that this book will convince anyone interested in pursuing research on intermarriage of the absolute necessity of analyzing gender.

1

Immigrant Jewesses
Who Married "Out"

My grandchildren, for all I know, may have a graver task than I have set them. Perhaps they may have to testify that the faith of Israel is a heritage that no heir in the direct line has the power to alienate from his successors. Even I, with my limited perspective, think it doubtful if the conversion of the Jew to any alien belief or disbelief is ever thoroughly accomplished. What positive affirmation of the persistence of Judaism in the blood my descendants may have to make, I may not be present to hear.

—Mary Antin, *The Promised Land*, 1912

Immigrant Jewish women who intermarried in the early decades of the twentieth century were highly independent thinkers who refused religious conformity as a way of life. The Jewish women I consider here immigrated to this country between 1886 and 1894, and subsequently married Gentiles. Their Eastern European places of origin were similar, as were their Orthodox beginnings, and as activists they shared some political views and experiences. The lives of Mary Antin Grabau, Rose Pastor Stokes, and Anna Strunsky Walling illustrate freedom of choice and expression in the New World. These immigrant women who intermarried did not cease to self-identify as Jewish or to exemplify Jewish values as was presumed to be the case for those who married "out." They contributed to a new subculture of modern American life that permitted intermarriage at a time when it was uncommon, without entirely forgetting their heritage. As Progressives during a period of bountiful public activism, they worked on behalf of the tired, the poor, and "the huddled masses yearning to breathe free."[1] In some cases they formed new religious identities.

All their experiences expanded what it meant to be a "Jewish woman" by illustrating the growing elasticity of religious identity in modern American culture. Each romance in its own way suggests something about the mechanics of intermarriage between Jewish women and Gentile men that defies conventional ideas about the influence of intermarriage on identity.

Antin, Pastor, and Strunsky are well-known historical figures because of their political activism and literary works. However, the personal details of life within their homes and marriages, and how their families responded to their marital choices, have received little attention to date. These three women are the focus here, because they became celebrities of sorts as a result of their ambitions, their professional accomplishments, and their marriages to prominent non-Jewish men. These women demonstrate that despite the lack of social acceptance that inhibited large-scale intermarriage—between less than 2 percent and 3.2 percent of Jews married non-Jews prior to 1930—for some Jewish women (and men) intermarriage was a way to join the dominant culture.[2] The American rate of Jewish intermarriage was significantly lower than in Germany where, by 1930, twenty out of one hundred Jewish marriages were interfaith.[3] These women's stories also shed light on the meaning of intermarriage by dismantling prior assumptions about the reasons for the failures of some mixed marriages.

Antin, Pastor, and Strunsky helped make intermarriage a topic suitable for public discussion. In the years following their marriages, other immigrants began voicing their personal concerns in the print media. Most immigrants had a humble outlet for their angst: the *Jewish Daily Forward,* a Yiddish newspaper in America started in 1897. It attracted many immigrant readers, became their confidant and adviser, and, by the early 1930s, had a circulation of a quarter-million. In 1906 Abraham Cahan, the *Forward*'s editor, began printing letters from readers and the paper's responses in a column titled "A Bintel Brief" (A Bundle of Letters).[4] The topics ranged considerably, including woes of unemployment, poverty, starvation, illness, husbands who deserted their families, protests about boss's actions, complaints against family members, and issues related to intermarriage. Those who intermarried wrote some of the letters, as did their relatives. The topic of intermarriage was an issue of interest, whether or not the *Forward*'s staff members fabricated any of the letters for their readers. "What is the matter with the Jewish girls and boys of the East Side?" asked the *American Jewish Chronicle* in a 1916 article titled "Intermarriage on the East Side." In a thinly veiled reference to the Pastor-

Stokes and Strunsky-Walling couples, the author alleged that the inter-marriages that occurred some years earlier between certain social workers of a non-Jewish social center were the greatest impetus to intermarriage on the East Side.[5] Although articles in the Jewish press may have exaggerated the influence of their marriages on people's behavior, the articles illustrate that these immigrant Jewish women put intermarriage on the kitchen table.[6]

Yet other writers maintained that, although Jewish women and men might entertain the idea temporarily, they were unlikely to intermarry in large numbers. In a March 1925 interview with *Der Tog (The Day)* the advice columnist Beatrice Fairfax disclosed her readers' perspectives. Commenting on the tensions between mothers and daughters, she wrote: "Way down deep the girls have a very strong traditional sense, and would not marry out of the fold at any price. Comparatively few of them do. They tell me so in their letters." Fairfax also contended that Jewish boys' involvement with non-Jewish girls should not be misconstrued to imply impending intermarriage. She argued, "What right has any Christian girl to think that a Jewish fellow takes her out for any other reason than to have some fun? And these boys write to me about these presumptuous *Schickses* who are annoying them because they misunderstood their intentions."[7] In her estimation, then, neither Jewish women nor Jewish men had any serious intentions of committing the unthinkable act of intermarriage. "Some fun," as Fairfax described it, likely referred to the idea that Jewish men may have been willing to "experiment" and "learn" on Christian women but not to marry them. Jewish women, of course, did not have the converse implicit privilege with Christian men.[8]

In addition to being mentioned in the Jewish press, Pastor and Strunsky inspired quasi-autobiographical literature concerning intermarriage. A direct reference to Mrs. Walling and Mrs. Stokes suggests that their marriages fostered the creation of the 1926 book *I Am a Woman—and a Jew.*[9] This work was hailed by the *New York Times* for its "utter frankness" and sincerity, for shedding original light on the cleavage between Jew and Gentile.[10] The *Hebrew Standard* reported that the book revealed with sincerity how a woman, "by marrying a Gentile, became a stranger among her people" and that it should be viewed as a "composite autobiography."[11] Similar to Antin, the protagonist's aspirations reflected not so much a rejection of Judaism as an embrace of the ideology of modern womanhood that included delaying marriage so as to better preserve independence and individual fulfillment.[12] This intermarriage story about a woman's struggle for a career and her belief that Jewishness was inescapably racial suggests how an immigrant Jewish woman who intermarried in the early twentieth century navigated the complications of being a Jew by birth and marrying a non-Jew. Her individuality was sacrificed at the marriage altar, but her Jewish inheritance clung to her without fail.

The high visibility of the Antin-Grabau, Pastor-Stokes, and Strunsky-Walling unions heightened awareness in the organized Jewish community that some Jewish women were leaving the fold. Initially, published letters regarding a Jewish man's marriage, or prospective marriage, with a Gentile woman belied the existence of Jewish woman-Gentile man alliances. The author Harry Golden reinforced this idea in his commentary by pointing out that, "much has been written and said about the terrible scene that takes place in a Jewish home when a son marries a *shikse*—the parents sit *shiva* in mourning for the boy."[13] I did not find any letter regarding a Jewish woman who intermarried in the twentieth century prior to the three women I discuss in this chapter, each of whom married between 1901 and 1906. Beginning in 1905, however, letters and references to intermarriage in ethnic press articles, some of which allude to these women, indicate that concern about Jewish women marrying out increased as time went on.

Immigrant Jewish women who intermarried had similar ideals about married life as immigrant women who married coreligionists. The historian Susan Glenn, in her book *Daughters of the Shtetl: Life and Labor in the Immigrant Generation*, contended that Jewish working women's involvement in two overlapping contexts, urban mass culture and political activism in the garment industry, eased constraints on female behavior. Their involvement in these contexts fostered women's optimism about relationships with the opposite sex based more on a partnership model, not necessarily equal but certainly more collaborative than Orthodox Jewish cultural patterns. Paradoxically, girls entered the workforce and became involved in union activities, thus expanding the traditional female sphere. Once they married, however, they settled back into domestic life. As Glenn wrote, "One image emphasized women's ability to fight side by side with men to help earn a living and to struggle for workers' rights. The other stressed the respectability and romantic promise that women sought in the role of modern wife-companion." Moreover, "[for those involved in labor unions] gender equality was never as important as working-class equality." If women gained some modicum of social equality it was the result of their radical activities rather than agitation specifically about women's needs.[14]

This Jewish version of New Womanhood, which combined socializing with the opposite sex and political activism, prompted those who inter-married, as well as those who in-married, to seek companionate marriages but not necessarily equality with their husbands. And if they did strive for gender equality in theory, it was unattainable in practice. American family social values opposed women's full emancipation as individuals by maintaining a hierarchy of domesticity that viewed women as having a special nature as wives and mothers. By the early twentieth century the new justification for suffrage was that women had a special contribution to make to society because they were different from men, and not as a way of securing political expression for women's self-interests. Moreover, women were classified as physically weaker than men. In 1908, for example, the Supreme Court ruled in *Muller v. Oregon* that protective labor legislation for women was constitutional; restricting women's factory employment to ten-hour days in an effort to preserve women's health was, in the justices' unanimous opinion, "an object of public interest." By 1917 nearly all states limited women's hours of employment.[15] Politics and voting became extensions of the home; the responsibility for its upkeep and the care of children were women's and not shared equally with their male companions.[16]

Like their immigrant sisters, Jewish women who married non-Jews chose their mates rather than accept arranged marriages, evidence of the growing individualism in modern America. The New World presented many new opportunities for immigrant Jewish women, among them the ability to earn their own living and, with it, the potential to select their own spouse. Certainly some immigrants still utilized the *shadkhen* (marriage broker) to help them secure an appropriate marriage partner, but they were increasingly in the minority. The rising "price of husbands" also made the old dowry arrangement an unaffordable luxury for some immigrant families.[17] Although parental approval remained a factor, young Jewish women, shortly after they began to earn an income, married and began raising families.[18] While earning potential replaced the role of the matchmaker and the dowry, a middle-class ideal of respectability pervaded immigrant and American culture alike. Women were expected to stop working for wages after marriage. In the words of the historian Elizabeth Ewen: "Both middle-class American culture and immigrant men in particular, considered it demeaning for women to work outside the home after marriage. It was assumed that husbands who allowed this were incapable of supporting their families on their own."[19]

Antin, Pastor, and Strunsky succeeded in attaining contemporary marriage standards of a less-than-equal partnership, notwithstanding criticism for intermarrying and their in-laws' mixed-emotional responses. Marriage in America was defined by specific characteristics. As the historian Nancy Cott wrote in *Public Vows: A History of Marriage and the Nation,* "Political and legal authorities endorsed and aimed to perpetuate nationally a *particular* marriage model: lifelong, faithful monogamy, formed by the mutual consent of a man and a woman, bearing the impress of the Christian religion and the English common law in its expectations for the husband to be the family head and economic provider, his wife the dependent partner."[20] The male breadwinner ethic was clearly evident in Jewish women's intermarriages, often causing strife between spouses. By selecting husbands sufficiently well off so as not to require their wives' incomes, immigrant Jewish women fulfilled the American marital promise. Moreover, women who transcended their class by marrying men of considerable wealth put romantic hope "into the heart of every unwedded working-girl," according to a 1906 article titled "Poor Girls Who Marry Millions."[21] However, by surrendering their independence and accepting marriage as the natural route to fulfilling the roles of wife and mother, women's individuality was suppressed by the needs of their new family.[22]

Getting married provided a way of buying into the American family ideal. As the American studies scholar Riv-Ellen Prell wrote in *Fighting to Become Americans,* "To create a new household and family was part of becoming attractive Americans with an outlook focused on pleasure and consumption." In other words: "marriage was the route to Americanization."[23] Marriage as a purely social and economic arrangement had already begun to break down in the Old World, where young people began requesting their parents' approval after falling in love. Western ideas about love and marriage infiltrated the *shtetlekh* (small Russian and Polish towns) and were reinforced among Jewish immigrant women in America; love, freely chosen, took precedence in the modern age over *yichus* (prestige) brought to one's family.[24] Americans were committed to marriage founded on serendipitous love that neither obeyed rational discipline nor answered family considerations or monetary concerns.[25] As the immigrant character in one of Anzia Yezierska's stories exclaimed: "America is a lover's land."[26] And as Prell eloquently stated: "Romance and Americanization were baked together into a single wedding cake."[27] If an immigrant woman married for love rather than religion, as did all three of the women examined in this chapter, she exemplified an American ideal and therefore the zenith of acculturation.

Although immigrant Jewish women who intermarried bought into the American family ideal, their lives also reflected contemporary criticism of marriage and the "new morality" that became a mass phenomenon in the 1920s.[28] The feminist Charlotte Perkins Gilman (1860-1935) identified women's economic dependence on men in marriage as the core problem for women, because it hindered their personal and intellectual growth. She argued that only economic independence through work outside the home would grant women true equality with men. Although Gilman's ideas were largely ignored at the time in favor of a focus on suffrage, Antin, Pastor, and Strunsky all experienced firsthand the consequences of economic disparity in their marriages.[29] Modern views on love and marriage, most notably espoused by the anarchist Emma Goldman (1869-1940), also apparently had some impact on the women's perceptions of their right to "free love" and intellectual equality with men, albeit within the confines of legal marriage.[30] Antin, Pastor, and Strunsky qualify as American moderns, as the historian Christine Stansell wrote in her book by that title: "those willing to repudiate the cumbersome past and experiment with form, not just in painting and literature, the touchstones of European modernism, but also in politics and love, friendship and sexual passion."[31]

Religious differences, contrary to the claims of the clergy and ethnic press authors, did not cause marital disharmony for immigrant Jewish women.[32] Political dissension and financial disagreements instigated the eventual erosion of all three marriages discussed here. However, because all three women came from working-class, immigrant families and their husbands were native-born, upper-class Protestants, cultural differences such as psychology, habits, and sensibilities may have influenced how they disagreed with each other. Whether, as the *Hebrew Standard* contended, the intermarriages of Antin, Pastor, and Strunsky actually influenced other immigrant Jewish women to consider marrying non-Jewish men is difficult to ascertain without direct testimony to this effect.[33] What is apparent is that these particular intermarriages that occurred during the first decade of the twentieth century sparked an outpouring of interest, coverage in the ethnic press, and commentary by Jewish religious figures and organizations that lasted well into the third decade. Understanding their intermarriage stories tells us as much about American history as it does about the history of Jewish women.

Photograph of Mary
Antin with American
flag and schoolchildren.
Courtesy of Anne Ross
and Rose Richards.

Mary Antin (1881–1949)

Mary Antin, author of the classic immigrant autobiography *The Promised Land,* illustrates the ways in which intermarriage contributed to religious experimentation without causing her to cease being Jewish, as she defined it. Her beginnings were similar to those of many Jewish immigrant women. Born in the small Russian town of Polotzk within the Pale of Settlement, Antin immigrated to Boston aboard the steamship *Polynesia* on May 8, 1894.[34] It was there that her intermarriage took place, along with a quest for a new spiritual understanding of life's meaning. Antin met Amadeus W. Grabau, a German-American Lutheran geologist and paleontologist doing graduate work at Harvard, through the Natural History Club at Hale House. She and Grabau married on October 5, 1901, in Boston (Antin was twenty, and Grabau thirty-one).[35] The minister of the South Congregational Church, Edward W. Hale, performed the ceremony in his home.[36]

The response to the Antin-Grabau marriage was mixed, and some controversy surrounds how Antin's family reacted. Despite the social taboo against intermarriage that would have made a negative response understandable, one relative contends that Antin's family never publicly criticized her selection nor that of her sister, Ida, who also married a non-Jew.[37] Perhaps Antin's mother actually accepted her daughters' choices, because she herself had been party to an arranged marriage. In nineteenth-century Russia some affluent Jewish women married Christian suitors, ran away from home, or converted to thwart arranged marriages that they considered undesirable.[38] A woman without means and who did not have a choice might wish that her daughter would have more of one. However, Antin's youngest sister Clara, who was two years of age when Antin married, described their mother as shedding tears of anguish when her eldest daughter married "out." Clara's memory, recorded in 1972, may well have been influenced by factors other than their mother's feelings about intermarriage in 1901.[39] That Grabau was an academic may also have earned him points with Antin's parents. If Antin's family did not object, her friends and benefactors certainly did. In a letter to the English author Israel Zangwill announcing her marriage, Antin wrote:

> I . . . hope that none of my old friends will think that I can spare them now. I want them all as much as ever, particularly since I have lost many to whom my marriage was displeasing on religious grounds. They might find these reasons unfounded if they could realize that I have not changed my faith.[40]

Long before Antin intermarried, she questioned her Orthodox Judaism. Although her queries started at a very young age and before she left Russia, they accelerated once she began the process of Americanization. Her parents did not deter the loosening of Jewish tradition. In fact, Antin's father had asked her mother to leave her wig, a symbol of Jewish Orthodoxy, in Russia. And although they lit candles on the Sabbath, her parents kept their store open until Sunday, the Christian day of rest.[41] When Antin began her American education, her pursuit of learning replaced her traditional observance. As the historian Jonathan Sarna described, "school became her surrogate house of worship."[42] Antin reveled in American ideals of freedom of choice. To her, the prospect of American citizens choosing their own religion, choosing whether or not to believe in God, was the ultimate freedom. "In Russia," she declared, "I had practiced a prescribed religion, with little faith in what I professed, and a restless questioning of the universe. When I came to America I lightly dropped the religious forms that I had mocked before, and contented myself with a few novel phrases employed by my father in his attempt to explain the riddle of existence."[43]

Antin had already begun to explore nature's explanation for being and the process of evolution by the time she married a Lutheran man. The Natural History Club in Boston added new perspectives to her religious repertoire. According to the historian Sam Bass Warner, "for her, the outings and lectures of natural history began a lifelong endeavor to unite her Judaic inheritance with the modern romantic tradition of Emerson and Thoreau."[44] And in Antin's words: "By asking questions, by listening when my wise friends talked, by reading, by pondering and dreaming, I slowly gathered together the kaleidoscopic bits of the stupendous panorama which is painted in the literature of Darwinism."[45] This process was emboldened by Antin's friendship with Josephine Lazarus, sister of the poet Emma. Lazarus believed in transcendentalism and insisted that, "in God's boundless universe all truth, all spirit, are one, alike for the Jew and the Christian who live in the spirit and the truth."[46] This kind of thinking might have appealed to Antin, as it offered a justification for aspects of her own life, including her marriage to a non-Jew.

A woman who intermarried could express ambivalence about Judaism by experimenting with other religions, yet also maintain her Jewish identity, as Antin did.[47] Evidently the Antin-Grabau couple celebrated Christmas, perhaps in a secular rather than religious manner. Antin wrote of her illness to her brother- and sister-in-law in December 1905, pointing out that, "it's all I can do by way of celebrating the holiday, to send a few short letters to the few dearest friends, and look on while Amadeus trims the Christmas tree. I hope to be more lively next Christmas."[48] Although some endogamous Jewish families have also celebrated Christmas, such as the family of the late U.S. Supreme Court Justice Louis D. Brandeis for whom Brandeis University is named, it was specifically Antin's intermarriage that introduced this practice into her life.[49] Although never formally converting to another religion, clearly Antin came to accept aspects of other religions as at least defensible, if not downright appealing. Writing in 1914, Antin showed definite signs of accepting some Christian precepts. "I know that 2,000 years after righteousness was urged on us we still have to be coaxed to behave ourselves," she wrote, alluding to the teachings of Jesus. "Christianity, as I understand it, is the Mosaic law expressed in another form."[50] It is also apparent that the First World War figured in her thinking about the meaning of religion and brotherhood at home and abroad.

Antin's Jewish identity was manifest, for example, in the specifically Jewish celebrations held in her home many years after she intermarried. In his autobiography, Rabbi Abraham Cronbach, a friend, described the joyous Chanukah party he attended at Mary Antin's house in 1916, where, at her request, he officiated at the Jewish ritual of dedication. By this time the Antin-Grabau marriage had become quite strained, which explains why Grabau was absent for the celebration. The evening was a gala affair: many of Antin's relatives and other guests were present, including a skilled pianist; Chanukah candles were lit, followed by the singing of the traditional Chanukah hymn "Rock of Ages"; and a lavish dinner was served.[51] Thus, as both Rabbi Cronbach and Antin's daughter have testified, Antin observed the major Jewish holidays in her home after her marriage while also exploring "many forms of religion and religious philosophy." Antin spent parts of her final years as a disciple of two different spiritual leaders: Meher Baba and Rudolf Steiner.[52] Her nephew contends that she "fully accepted being Jewish without accepting the dogma of the religious tenet."[53]

Antin's diminished religiosity in terms of traditional Judaism was common within the larger historical context. Although immigrants who became less Orthodox did not necessarily align themselves with another branch, critics used the lessening of observance as an opportunity to attack Reform Judaism. In a 1923 article, "Steps from Synagogue to Church," the unidentified author lambasted Reform Judaism as eventually becoming merely a variant of Christianity. The marriage of the Jewish granddaughter of a famous financier family of Reform Jews to a Gentile in a church was cited to illustrate this point. "Were the young lady quite irreligious, and had she determined to marry a non-Jew, without any religious ceremonies, the matter would bear a different complection [sic]: it would represent another problem."[54] Hence the blame for intermarriage and apostasy were to be laid at the feet of Reform Judaism. Reform Judaism, however, remained steadfast in its opposition to intermarriage as contrary to Jewish faith (discussed below), dispelling notions that Reform Judaism was complacent about Jews marrying non-Jews.

Although Antin's intermarriage may have added fuel to her religious meandering, the seed for this lifestyle was planted *before* she met her husband and continued to grow long *after* they eventually parted. The historical evidence suggests that, rather than keeping or discarding one identity or another, she continued to identify as Jewish *and* in non-Jewish ways. In a 1925 letter, Antin described how she self-identified: "I am not a Christian—not in any technical sense of adherence to orthodox Christian dogma; not in any popular sense. One friend defines me as 'a Christian *and* a Jew,' making a distinction from the popular rather distasteful conception of a 'Hebrew Christian.' I don't care what I am called, but I want to be sure I don't mislead anyone."[55] This statement illustrates a coalescence of religious identities that defies simple categorization.

Rather than prevent identification with the Jewish people, Antin's marriage and interests outside Judaism contributed to her belief in helping others regardless of differences of faith. In a powerful article written during World War II, Antin rationalized the support she gave to a Catholic priest building a chapel that surprised two Jewish men who also sought a contribution to start a Hebrew School. "It was known, of course, that I was married to a Gentile—a Protestant. Still it was assumed there were limits to my apostasy."[56] She had begun to read the New Testament: "I was not yet aware of the supreme role of Jesus of Nazareth in mediating the Hebrew tradition to the modern world. That was to come later; but already I was a queer enough fish from the orthodox Jewish standpoint."[57]

Yet from early in her marriage to long after she and her husband separated, Antin identified as a Jew and with other Jews, particularly during times of active antisemitism in the world. In a letter dated 1905, when violent pogroms occurred in the Pale, Antin wrote: "Yes, truly my heart is in Russia these dark days. . . . At last accounts, my near relatives had all survived the murders . . . The blood that then cried for rescue may now be crying for vengeance. And so it does, for my brothers and sisters were the victims in any case."[58] The words "brothers and sisters" in this instance refer not to her siblings, all of whom were safe in America, but to her coreligionists in Europe. Thirty-six years later, her connection to the Jewish people remained strong.

> For decades I lived cut off from Jewish life and thought, heart-free and mind-free to weave other bonds. There was nothing intentional or self-conscious in this divorcement. It was simply that my path in life ran far from the currents of Jewish experience. Today I find myself pulled by old forgotten ties, through the violent projection of an immensely magnified Jewish problem. It is one thing to go your separate way, leaving friends and comrades behind in peace and prosperity; it is another thing to fail to remember them when the world is casting them out. I can no more return to the Jewish fold than I can return to my mother's womb; neither can I in decency continue to enjoy my accidental personal immunity from the penalties of being a Jew in a time of virulent anti-Semitism. The

least I can do, in my need to share the sufferings of my people, is declare that I am as one of them.

And finally, "In all those places where race lines are drawn, I shall claim the Jewish badge; but in my Father's house of many mansions I shall continue a free spirit."[59]

Antin's eventual embrace of a racial Jewish identity epitomized what the historian Eric J. Goldstein referred to as a new "realism" in regard to Jewish racial identity; Antin initially sought to integrate through intermarriage, only to learn that she would always be a Jew.[60]

Antin's use of the word "race" is fitting given the complex history of Jewishness in America. Religion was but one element that identified the Jewish people as distinctive. During the second half of the nineteenth century, there emerged a "visible, physical—biological—Jewishness in common American understanding"; Jews did not make, in the words of the historian Matthew Frye Jacobson, "the final transformation toward Caucasian whiteness" until after World War II.[61] Amid the controversy about whiteness scholarship, Jacobson's work has been criticized by scholars who contend that the category of whiteness is ill defined, that race as a social construction is an idea accepted long ago by most academics,[62] and that the lack of focus on how African and Afro-Caribbean immigrants became black confirms blackness as "identification, authoritative, and external," whereas whiteness is merely identity.[63] In the earliest years of the twentieth century, many Jews sought to affirm "their place as unqualified whites," according to Goldstein, "demonstrating a clear social distinction between themselves and America's principal outsiders, African Americans."[64]

The insistence on being distinct from African Americans came to coexist with Jewish racial distinctiveness during the 1920s and 1930s. Construing Jewish racial distinctiveness in a positive light, for example, by highlighting Jewish contributions to the arts and Jews' success in sports, also helped fuel arguments defending a preference for endogamous marriage. In 1922 Julian Morgenstern, the president of Hebrew Union College, the Reform rabbinate, opined: "We may continue to be Jews by race as well as by religion and steadfastly oppose intermarriage."[65] Thus, by the time Antin used the word "race" in her 1941 article, "House of the One Father," there was a certain acceptance of the "racial" characteristic of Jewishness among American Jews, some of whom did not see religion as an explanation for their secular Jewish communal involvement.[66]

Along with her spiritual investigations and Jewish identification, Antin believed that America held certain promises for women, including higher education. Her autobiography asserted: "A long girlhood, a free choice in marriage, and a brimful womanhood are the precious rights of an American womanhood."[67] This contrasted with the traditional gendered view of Jewish women and marriage described in Antin's story, "Malinke's Atonement," where she wrote: "What are daughters worth? They're only good to sit in the house, a burden on their parents' neck, until they're married off."[68] In the Old World women lived in a gender-defined world, where learning and religion were reserved for men, and women were given the realm of domesticity to organize and master.[69] "It was not much to be a girl, you see."[70] She was saddened by what she considered to be her elder sister Frieda's premature marriage at the age of seventeen. Frieda's youthful union was common for immigrant women.[71]

Antin's views on marriage and women's potential to live multifaceted lives reflected the heightened individualism of many women who courted, delayed, and in some cases abstained from marriage between the late 1870s and about 1910. The age at marriage among the first generation of college women, for example, was higher than the general population and 11 percent never married, which was the highest proportion in American history. In 1900 the median age at first marriage was 21.9 for women (25.9 for men). That some women delayed getting married may not indicate a negative attitude toward marriage so much as a sign that women viewed marriage as a choice rather than their destiny.[72] The opportunity for women to pursue higher education had increased significantly beginning in the post–Civil War decades with the founding of four women's colleges that became national institutions (Vassar in 1865, Wellesley and Smith in 1875, and Bryn Mawr in 1884); after the 1870s coeducational institutions attracted the majority of female enrollments. Between 1870 and 1900 the number of women enrolled in institutions of higher learning multiplied eightfold, from eleven thousand to eighty-five thousand.[73]

Though Antin was an atypical immigrant Jewish woman because she had the opportunity for formal learning, she, like the majority of American women, did not have a liberal arts education. Immigrant daughters were often pulled out of school so that they could work and supplement the family's income once they reached the legal age of fourteen; in Antin's case, her sister Frieda labored to help keep Antin in the Boston public schools.[74] Although the female proportion of the total college population rose, from 21.0 percent in 1870 to 39.6 percent in 1910 and 47.3 percent in 1920, the percentage of college women remained small among females eighteen to twenty-one years of age: 0.7 percent in 1870, 2.8 percent in 1900, and 7.6 percent in 1920.[75] Moreover, the vast majority of college women were native born and only 23.8 percent of all female students at sixty-three colleges had immigrant parents in 1911.[76] However much she pitied her sister's fate, Antin did not attain what she had destined for herself after she was married. Having once set her goal of attending Radcliffe, Antin relinquished this idea when she married and moved to New York with her husband, where he assumed a professorship at Columbia University. She studied at Columbia's Teachers College and at Barnard College but did not complete a degree.[77] Antin never achieved the level of higher education that she had dreamed of throughout her Americanization, perhaps the result of illness combined with the reality of married life.[78]

Marriage constrained women's individualism; immigrant Jewish women, like all women, had difficulty balancing marriage with the effort to reach their full intellectual potential through education and careers. Although Antin benefited from the expanded sphere of domesticity in the early twentieth century that included promoting the public good, she was also responsible for managing home life, including all aspects of entertaining household guests. Meals were served in the building where Antin and Grabau lived after they wed, which was located in the apartment wing of Columbia's new Whittier Hall dormitory at West 121st Street and Amsterdam.[79] Although this convenience likely spared Antin from having to cook, she dutifully fulfilled the part of a faculty wife—even referring to herself as "Frau Professorin" —and once they moved to their own home in suburban Brooklyn she faced more domestic chores.[80] In a December 1905 letter to a friend, Antin wrote: "I cannot invite you for dinner that day, because I do not know how many Christmas guests my husband will bring me. My housekeeping is on a very small scale, of course."[81] She clearly assumed the responsibilities that hosting guests entailed.

Although Antin maintained the use of her maiden name in her published work, she also identified socially as Mary Antin Grabau, illustrating the tension in being a married professional woman. Antin's 1913-1918 national lecture circuit about the importance of immigration and the ability of immigrants to become good citizens, issues she emphasized in her book, *They Who Knock at Our Gates* (1914), expanded her work far outside the home.[82] She was fortunate eventually to have domestic help from cousins who served as maids and from her sister, Frieda, who became Antin's housekeeper in Scarsdale, New York, after her own marriage ended.[83]

However, responsibility for their home remained predominantly Antin's, and it was she who placed their young daughter in boarding school rather than in the care of the girl's father while she lectured around the country.[84] In the long run, she was left to raise her child single-handedly when Grabau left the country altogether.

Conflicting nationalistic loyalties and wage competition, not religious differences, caused the eventual marital dissolution. Her marriage deteriorated over time, accelerated by World War I. Grabau was of German ancestry, and Antin was fiercely patriotic about America. Therefore, Grabau's refusal to believe that Germany was in the wrong and Antin's support of the Allies created significant friction between them. In later years their daughter, Josephine, described her perception of Antin's and Grabau's differences by saying, vividly, "he was waving the German flag out of one window and she was waving the American one out the other."[85] Disparity in their earning capacities suggests a different rationale for discordance. Antin received fees when she lectured on the national circuit as well as royalties from her writing, increasing her earnings markedly. Grabau's salary at Columbia did not appear to increase from his initial salary in 1901 of $2,500 per annum, even after he was promoted to full professor in 1905, and remained the same as late as 1917.[86] According to his biographer, Susan Koppelman, "there is reason to believe that this disparity in financial success discomfited Professor Grabau,"[87] perhaps because of the male breadwinner ethic. In addition, Antin became a celebrity while her husband became an outcast in his own department, which undoubtedly disturbed the original dynamic of their romance in which Grabau had been the notable professor and Antin the novice learner.[88] After *The Promised Land* was published, a friend described Antin as "the most talked-of writer—if not the most talked-of woman—in America."[89] Thus, much like other bohemian love stories such as that of Louise Bryant and John Reed, professional rivalry was often the cause of conflict.[90]

Most significant for the purpose of this book is that a difference of religion was not a significant factor in their eventual separation. Arthur Antin, Mary Antin's nephew, believes it played no part and rather that Grabau's pro-German feelings influenced the outcome of their relationship and contributed to his leaving the country.[91] In 1920 Grabau took a post as director of research for the China Geological Survey in Peking where he remained until his death in 1946. Despite their mutual inclination toward divorce, their daughter "made such a fuss about it that they did not" obtain one.[92] Evidence suggests that Grabau sought a divorce and

Antin refused; on what ground is unclear. Perhaps her resistance partly stemmed from marriage as a tenacious cultural norm; although, by the end of the 1920s, more than one in every six marriages ended in court. College-educated women in the 1920s also exhibited a strong preference for marriage over career.[93] In a letter to her younger sister, Rosemary, dated 31 January 1946, Antin wrote: "No, I am no longer agitated about A. There is nothing I can do, so I let go of the whole matter. The letters have stopped coming. I did send A. the lawyer's letter to show him officially that I could not execute this divorce."[94] Both Antin and Grabau suffered from declining health at various times.[95] No evidence suggests, however, that either of their conditions contributed to the marital failure. Antin died in 1949 at the age of sixty-eight.[96] She was buried at the Mount Pleasant Cemetery in Hawthorne, New York. Although there are Jewish sections in the cemetery, Section 6, where she was buried, is nonsectarian. Given Antin's spiritual journey, her final destination is not surprising. However, visitors to her grave will find small pebbles atop the tombstone, which indicate that Antin's Jewish relatives and friends did not forget her.

Rose Pastor (1879-1933)

Rose Pastor intermarried a few years after Antin, and the resulting personal notoriety catapulted the public fascination with intermarriage from the stage to the pulpit, the ethnic press, the bookstore and the film screen.[97] Although issues other than organized religion dominated her life, Pastor did not relinquish her identity as a Jewish woman. Born Rose Harriet Wieslander in Augustova, Poland, she immigrated to the United States in 1890 and later took her stepfather's last name of Pastor.[98] In 1901 she began to write letters and then eventually regular columns for the *Jewish Daily News (Yiddishes Tageblatt)*, a Yiddish newspaper. Pastor was among other "Jewish New Women," Yiddishists and Zionists, garment workers, political zealots, and neighborhood journalists, who, through socialism and anarchism, embraced modern ideas about gender roles, calling for education for girls and release from the expectation of reproduction and serving the family.[99] In 1903 Pastor moved from Cleveland to New York and joined the newspaper staff.

Pastor wrote about intermarriage in her advice column "Just Between Ourselves, Girls" under the pseudonym "Zelda."[100] An eighteen-year-old reader named "B.C." disclosed that she was in love with a Christian man two years her senior who wanted to marry her. Her father objected on the grounds that a Jew should marry a Jew. The advice seeker wrote, "I think it very nice that a Jewess should marry a Christian. Don't you? . . . What would you advise me to do? Marry my Christian lover or listen to my father?" Zelda responded unambiguously that the girl should not marry him and her father was right. He "wants to save you from misery and shame; from social excommunication and from moral death; you *know* all this in the depth of your heart, in spite of what you are trying to fool yourself into believing."[101] Zelda admonished that should the girl make the ill-fated step, she would not be able to look her friends in the face, her father would curse her, and her mother's weeping would cause near blindness. These were strong words coming from someone who two years later married a Christian. Perhaps Pastor was trying to convince *herself* not to become romantically involved with a Gentile, one, in particular, whose acquaintance she made before issuing the advice against intermarriage.[102]

Pastor met James Graham Phelps Stokes, the son of one of America's wealthiest Episcopalian families and a graduate of Yale's Sheffield Scientific School and the medical college at Columbia, when she was assigned to interview him for an article. Stokes worked at the University Settlement, founded in 1887, whose male college graduate residents lived among the poor and aimed to set good civic examples.[103] The interview was congenial and the article ran in the *Jewish Daily News* on 19 July 1903. Stokes made clear that his Christianity was a private matter, and that settlement work should be nonsectarian to improve social and industrial conditions while avoiding class-consciousness.[104] His words resonated with Pastor who had to drop out of school at age ten to make shoe bows, and their romance began.[105] The Pastor-Stokes relationship illustrates on a personal level what Harvard students termed "vital contact" in the 1910s. Elite men (and women) could revivify themselves through contact with the working poor, whom they mentored about good citizenship and civic organization, making cross-class encounters mutually beneficial.[106] The American Settlement as a fertile meeting ground for interfaith romance echoes an earlier period when wealthy Jewish women met their Gentile-noblemen husbands participating in Berlin salons in the late-eighteenth and nineteenth centuries.[107]

Perhaps aware that common politics played a more prominent role than religion in determining who was best suited for her daughter, Pastor's mother did not articulate concern when Pastor and Stokes told her they planned to marry: "she showed neither surprise nor excitement, but looked glad, and said quietly, 'Well children, there's a lot of work to be done. I hope you will be very happy—and useful.'"[108] Pastor's mother's response was also probably influenced by her own experience of not being allowed to wed a Gentile man. Pastor wrote in her autobiography, "so bound by tradition was my mother, she would not marry her Polish lover—out of faith and against her father's will."[109] Her mother had encouraged Pastor's trip with Stokes to Canada and perhaps welcomed the prospect of her impoverished daughter marrying a very wealthy man, regardless of his religious heritage. Pastor wrote, "He had 'seen' me home from the Settlement on many occasions and my mother liked him;" she considered him kind, thoughtful and polite.[110]

While Pastor's family was supportive, the response from Stokes's relatives was mixed. Stokes described his fiancée to his parents as follows: "Despite her Jewish origin she is as Christlike a Christian as I ever knew— I don't know where to find another Christian who is truer to the teachings of her Master." His parents, who were on an extended tour of Europe and Africa, responded warmly in a cable to his letter that detailed his engagement: "We most sincerely congratulate you and wish you all joy and happiness. Give our love to Rose."[111] Not all his extended family was equally supportive. Two of his aunts took him to Mexico, possibly to divert his attention from, in Pastor's words, the "Israelitish maiden."[112] Stokes's Uncle William Earl Dodge, an antisemitic xenophobe, complained to a federal assistant attorney general when Pastor's socialism became too much for him. Writing in March 1918, Dodge described Pastor as: "a woman who was born under a cloud with a grievance and she is dangerous."[113] Evidently both her Jewish background and her politics dismayed some of his relatives at the outset of their relationship and for many years later.

Their engagement evoked comments and headlines. Stokes's brother, acting as the family's spokesperson and perhaps hoping to avoid scandal, made their acceptance of Pastor public with the statement, "Miss Pastor is an ideal woman, loving, true, tender hearted, gentle and intellectual. She is a noble woman and has done noble work. The family is very much pleased with the match. It is an ideal one in all respects."[114] Despite the family's official position, rumors flew in the press. The front page of the *New York Times* carried the headline "J. G. Phelps Stokes to Wed Young Jewess" on 6 April 1905. This article reported that Stokes sought to rectify two misunderstandings. The first pertained to his family opposing their union. He said, "That is entirely false. There is nothing but the utmost cordiality and delight. The second error is that there is a difference of religious belief between Miss Pastor and myself. She is a Jewess as the Apostles were Jews—a

Christian by faith."[115] Stokes sought to persuade people that his wife-to-be was different from other Jews who maintained their distinctive lifestyles and customs, and that theirs would not even be an "intermarriage."

Pastor perceived her match with Stokes as intermarriage, even if he did not. While Stokes reassured his mother that Pastor was "a very devout Christian . . . I have never met a nobler or truer Christian," Pastor told friends that she was going to "make history" by marrying the millionaire Stokes: "Riches and poverty, Jew and Christian will be united. Here is an indication of a new era."[116] When confronted with an inquiry about her earlier advice column, Pastor told the reporter, "I advised a Jewish girl . . . against marrying a Christian, but that was not as some say because I am opposed to inter-marriage. It was simply because it was obvious that the girl did not love the man . . . and I was always opposed to loveless marriage."[117] This rings of rationalization, but Pastor was hard-pressed to explain her own action given her earlier advice.

Stokes's family shared Pastor's view that the marriage would join dissimilar individuals. Although his mother responded unequivocally to Stokes directly, she expressed surprise if not reservation to his brother. "Is it not astonishing," Helen Louisa Stokes asked, "that a *Phelps Stokes* would choose for his wife a poor girl of Russian Jewish parentage, ancestry unknown[?]" Anson Jr. reassured his mother that Pastor had a sense of humor, good complexion, and sensible dress, that her "spiritual talent" was of a "very high order" and that although she had "a Jewish look about the forehead and mouth," her nose did not.[118] Although Stokes's mother and brother noted Pastor's ethnic, religious, and socioeconomic difference, they concluded that at least, by their standards, she was not "too Jewish" looking. Clearly the Stokes family construed Pastor's Jewishness in racialized terms.

The Pastor-Stokes wedding defied the gendered rule in effect through the first quarter of the century that allotted control of the occasion to the bride and her family, adopting instead a more companionate approach that involved both the bride and the groom.[119] Pastor and Stokes were married at St. Luke's Church on 18 July 1905, her twenty-sixth birthday, and the reception was at the Brick House, the Stokes's country home in Noroton, Connecticut. Similar to Antin's marriage, non-Jewish clergy performed the ceremony. Two hundred or so people attended. One of Pastor's journalist friends declined to attend because he opposed inter-marriage.[120] The couple insisted that the word "obey" be omitted from the ceremony. Pastor did not explain why, but she claimed the initiative for

Photograph of Rose Pastor and James Graham Phelps Stokes on Rose's twenty-sixth birthday and their wedding day, 18 July 1905. From Arthur Zipser and Pearl Zipser, *Fire and Grace: The Life of Rose Pastor Stokes* (Athens: University of Georgia Press, 1989).

this deletion in her autobiography. She contended to have been little interested in the wedding preparations and assured her husband-to-be that nothing was of much import; everything was fine. But, "on the inspiration of the moment I add, 'but I want the word 'obey' eliminated from the service.'"[121] Though indiscernible in the photograph of the couple, Pastor supposedly wore a cross at her wedding.[122] The *New York Times*, however, described the bride's attire in significant detail and that a pearl necklace was the only jewelry she wore.[123]

There was a generational split in the Jewish community's opinion of their union. Some of the young people living on the East Side who knew Pastor celebrated what they perceived to be a wonderful romance, the best they had witnessed.[124] There are many explanations for why the younger set was more accepting than the older of the Pastor-Stokes relationship. For one thing, it illustrated the way in which New York bohemians opened social boundaries, defying WASP and Jewish prohibitions, and antisemitism in the process.[125] Another rationale involves prioritizing class mobility over Judaism. Whereas "proper" Jewish womanhood included marriage and motherhood, intermarriage could be pardonable if it meant an elevation of the Jewish woman's socioeconomic status. Hypergamy, marrying "up" economically, superseded endogamy in importance. This rationale reflected the German-Jewish female reformers' emulation of their Protestant peers while striving to uplift Eastern European Jewish girls' stations in life.[126]

The older generation recalled Pastor's advice column, objected to her hypocritical behavior, and expressed disapproval when the engagement was announced. Two days after the wedding, an editorial assumed that the marriage entailed the renouncement by the bride of her inherited faith and expressed concern that the couple's work would bring a Christianizing influence to Jewish children.[127] A year and a half later, members of the Jewish establishment continued to voice disapproval. Rabbi H. Pereira Mendes objected to Pastor's appearance before the Sisterhood at a temple, citing that if intermarriage were encouraged Judaism would be merged into Christianity. Furthermore, he argued, Pastor should not be "promoted or brought forward, or honored in the slightest way in connection with Jewish work, by us who call ourselves Jews or Jewesses."[128] Pastor's speech was likely about working conditions and socialism, given as a member of her class to coreligionists, more than as an intended voice of the Jewish people. However, the rabbi's effort to distance Jews from the intermarried Pastor suggests that her still-Jewish voice caused consternation.

Early-twentieth-century intermarriages such as Antin's and Pastor's stimulated attention to intermarriage by religious bodies as well as individual religious authorities. The Central Conference of American Rabbis (CCAR) had its own ideas about intermarriage. The CCAR was founded in 1889 and was considered the organized rabbinate of Reform Judaism. Its interest was whether intermarriage was acceptable (it was not) and, given both the biblical injunction against it and the potential effects on the perpetuity and strength of the Jewish people, whether rabbis should officiate at such ceremonies. The very first year that intermarriage was addressed was at the 1907 conference, shortly after the marriages of Antin, Pastor, and Strunsky. The group recommended presenting a paper at the next conference, appointing a committee to consider "the disparity between some of the Mosaic and Rabbinical marriage laws on the one hand, and the theories, laws, and practices prevalent in our country," and to prepare a report to guide the Reform rabbinate.[129]

The paper, delivered in 1908 by Rabbi Mendel Silber of St. Louis, reported that, as a result of Christians becoming more open to marriage with Jews, intermarriage had become a "burning question." He refuted claims that, since Gentiles were not regarded as idolaters, the biblical prohibition against intermarriage did not apply to marriage with them. Mendel stated that "the spirit of the Bible is utterly opposed to the measure" and that "the religion of Israel must be protected from influences which make for disintegration."[130] The overarching message was that intermarriage was wrong, and hence rabbis should not perform such ceremonies. He even disapproved of intermarriages in which the non-Jew converted, judging these unions as still weak in terms of perpetuating the integrity of Judaism.

The CCAR gave intermarriage the most attention in 1909 at its annual conference. Rabbis presented several papers and passed a resolution that read:

> Your committee, after mature deliberation, recommends the following expression of the sentiment of the Conference: The Central Conference of American Rabbis declares that mixed marriages are contrary to the tradition of the Jewish religion and should therefore be discouraged by the American Rabbinate.

For the time being, this resolution settled the issue and the Conference did not debate the topic again, aside from two essays written by one individual in 1919, until 1935.[131] It is no surprise that the Conservative and Orthodox branches of Judaism also opposed intermarriage, considering the more liberal rabbinate's position.

In 1910 clubs and hotels were more popular wedding sites than synagogues, lamented the CCAR. The invitations, catering, attire, photography, and flowers became increasingly significant as weddings became parties, while the religious nature of the occasion diminished.[132] So-called Americanization involving intermarriage affected an immigrant woman's religious practices, how she raised children, and sometimes how she self-identified. The same, however, could also be said of immigrant women who married coreligionists but who became less religiously observant in an effort to seem less of a "greenhorn" and more American. The wedding itself was representative of the ways in which immigrant marriages became increasingly commercial and less ceremonial. Synagogues, customarily, had not been used for weddings in order to preserve their sacred spaces; that the organized rabbinate wanted them to be used for weddings indicates concern over the direction of weddings in general, not just of those who intermarried. The commercialization of American weddings illustrated the intensifying relationship between escalating consumerism and romance that began during courtship. Automobiles, movies, and dance halls appeared before the First World War, and by the early 1920s they became settings where couples courted leading up to their weddings in non-sacred locations.[133]

Some rabbis used their pulpits to advocate against intermarriage. Rabbi Ferdinand M. Isserman made several such pleas. In a sermon delivered at Rodeph Shalom Synagogue in Philadelphia on 11 April 1925, Rabbi Isserman used contemporary as well as biblical literature to illustrate several points about why to avoid intermarriage. His first objection was that intermarriage rarely resulted in happiness, as the two souls could not understand each other: "Where one member of the family is Jewish and the other Christian, the home cannot be harmonious." Even when conversion occurred, the difficulty of fully embracing a new faith made achieving harmony rare. Isserman's second objection was that intermarriage weakened Judaism and that increased exogamy would destroy it. He argued that the ideal of raising children without any religious affiliation, to be nonsectarian humanitarians, was a fallacy. Isserman wrote, "Jewish children who in Christian countries are brought up to respect all religions and love none will end up by assuming the color of their environment and becoming Christian." He advocated guarding against intermarriage because it was an "assault on the Jewish home" where Judaism was perpetuated. Finally, Isserman rejected the notion that opposition to intermarriage was a bigoted or narrow-minded response, declaring, instead, that it was "based on our belief that when the bars against intermarriage are removed, the death-knell of Judaism will be sounded."[134]

Regarding religious observances, one can only speculate about whether Pastor and Stokes discussed how they would keep and run their married household. While they were engaged, Pastor and Stokes traveled to Cleveland and attended a traditional Passover Seder at a friend's house.[135] According to her biographers, Arthur and Pearl Zipser, the couple did not practice any "doctrinal religion,"[136] which implies that they observed neither Protestant nor Jewish religious laws. This generalization, however, neglects to consider what threads of either their Christian or Jewish origins may have manifested in the Stokes's marriage and practices. Though little evidence exists as to the exact manner in which the couple celebrated holidays, there are some hints. For example, Stokes told Pastor, in a letter he wrote late one fall some years after their wedding, that he ordered "something beautiful for the hall and trimmed the window box plants."[137] By the sound of it, their house was being decorated for the coming Christmas season, since a tree or wreath is often located in a front hall and plants are "trimmed" with holiday ornamentation. References to a "batch of cheery Christmas mail from Rose" suggest season's greetings, though a deeper meaning is allusive.[138] Without children to educate, we cannot know what religious tradition, if any, Pastor would have imparted from her Jewish background.

How couples negotiated married life illustrated the tenacious idea accepted by most middle-class Americans that women handled the daily responsibilities of life within the domestic sphere, religious or otherwise. *Ladies' Home Journal* reported, in 1905, that "home provided man a retreat from and a reason for his work; home *was* a woman's work."[139] The industrial revolution of the nineteenth century transformed the work done in the home in the 1900s from production to maintenance and management.[140] By 1910 labor-saving devices and store-bought products increased women's mobility outside the home but also caused tension between modern "conveniences" and the fact that wives were still responsible for purchasing and using them.[141] Thus, although Pastor lobbied on behalf of working-class women in the factories, housework was her domain; it was she who "systemized her housekeeping," chose paper napkins over cloth to reduce laundry, and used many uncooked foods to minimize her time in the kitchen.[142] Moreover, Pastor took Stokes's last name. During the incubation period of their pre-marriage relationship, Pastor had told Stokes, "you will be coming to my world, not I to yours . . . We will have a flat somewhere on the East Side, and live and work among the people."[143] Although this was true initially—the couple rented an apartment on the Lower East Side with six rooms and a bath—they soon moved into a new house on Caritas Island off Wallacks Point in Stamford, Connecticut (a wedding gift from Stokes's parents). In both locations they had hired household help, suggesting that Pastor became accustomed to Stokes's way of life rather than the other way around. As Cott wrote in *Public Vows*, "Turning men and women into husbands and wives, marriage has designated the ways both sexes act in the world and the reciprocal relation between them."[144]

Similarly, although Pastor's and Stokes's politics seemed more alike than not at the outset of their relationship—both were committed to social betterment—it was Pastor who ultimately carried the emotional burden for their social work. For women active in the labor movement, such as Pastor, sharing political views with one's spouse superseded other concerns.[145] After she wed Pastor joined the Socialist Party and, using her childhood Yiddish, told a crowd at a rally that her husband's decision to join with her was "the happiest and grandest day of my life."[146] Pastor's socialism energized her, and she became an inspiring public speaker. On 5 December 1909 she enthusiastically addressed more than 7,000 people to help the Women's Trade Union League generate community support for striking garment industry workers during the "Uprising of 20,000" that began in November and lasted until February 1910.[147]

Over time, however, their different modus operandi became apparent. Pastor noted this in her diary in 1913: "He [Stokes] is very dependent on my presence and dreads the thought of my going in to the strike without him, yet feels that he is not specially fitted for that *kind* of work in the movement."[148] In her autobiography she described how Stokes sought to avoid the crowds that pressed forward to shake their hands, whereas she reveled in it.

> It was not until many years afterward that I realized why this was so with him. Then it was borne in on me that he loved the people *in theory only;* that there was no personal warmth in him for them. Often I thought I detected a look of contempt for some member or members of my class. He could not have dealt me a personal blow that would have hurt more. At times he would let fall a word . . . and I would chill with an undefined apprehension.[149]

When it became clear that their commitment to helping the disenfranchised differed, their marriage, which had been based on common interests and love, faltered, becoming instead a relationship of economic dependence. Pastor probably received an allowance from Stokes while married, as her income from speaker honorariums and occasional articles was meager.[150]

Distinct politics and gender inequity, not issues of religion, shattered the companionate ideal and eroded the marriage in the long run. World War I increased the dissolution of common political ground. In a 1914 letter, Pastor described her horror about the war: "That stupendous slaughter house—the other side of the Atlantic—has had a most crushing effect upon me."[151] Pastor and Stokes resigned from the Socialist Party in

1917—they both supported the war and the party opposed it—but only Pastor, after changing her mind about the war, eventually sought to return to it.[152] A. H. Fromenson, her former editor at the *Yiddishes Tageblatt (Jewish Daily News)*, beckoned to her to join the Poale-Zion, the socialist group sympathetic to Marxism and Communism: "This is your place, my friend, and you are sufficiently Jewish—nationally Jewish—to take your place in its ranks. You know, of course, that Mary Antin is with us. But there is room for you. Come in."[153] She moved to the Left while Stokes moved to the Right. Pastor's outspoken politics made her the target of a government indictment, and in 1918 she was convicted of attempting to cause insubordination, obstructing recruitment, and making false statements to impede the success of U.S. forces and to aid its enemies. The U.S. Circuit Court of Appeals ordered a new trial, however, and in 1921 the government dropped the case.[154] In 1922 Pastor was prosecuted again for her involvement in the formation of the Communist Party.[155] By this point the Stokes couple had become politically distant, she more radical and he significantly less. Like other Jewish Communists who had adopted Anglicized names leading up to the Depression, Pastor's class background and political beliefs motivated her actions, not her Jewishness.[156]

Their divergent paths may not have been unusual for socialist couples; socialist women met with resistance when they tried to raise women's issues along with the class issues, according to the historian Susan Ware, and socialist men "often had very traditional ideas about women's place in the home."[157] Although women may have accepted more of the domestic work, Pastor expected her ideas to at least merit equal attention as those of her husband. She was a member of the Heterodoxy Club, a quasi-secret group of radical women who met for lunch, usually in Greenwich Village, and were committed to women's self-realization within their private lives.[158] Diary entries shed additional light on the eventual demise of the Pastor-Stokes marriage. In one, Pastor described Stokes's displeasure at her interjection in a conversation he was having with someone else. She surmised, "—now, and often before, my interest in the subject doesn't seem to count." Pastor chose to let this incident slide.[159] A year later Stokes's conduct left a more permanent mark. After an exhausting speaking tour, Pastor stayed in bed late one morning attempting to recover from bronchitis and a fever. She wrote, "Today marked a deep change in me—mentally, spiritually—in my attitude toward G. He *accused me of loafing*. . . . 'Loafing!' I didn't reply. What's the good? But it put the iron in my soul, and this time I feel it's there to stay. The terrible loneliness of one's soul

in such moments!"[160] Pastor's use of the word "iron" in this instance is a
metaphor for the discrepancy between the ideal of a marriage between
equals and the reality of the power dynamics between women and men.
These experiences, together with their divergent politics, added to the
breaking point that resulted in their divorce in 1925.

Pastor's marriage helped make her famous, because it was an interfaith union between a poor immigrant Jewish woman and a wealthy non-
Jewish, American-born man. Maintaining class loyalty, Pastor stated that,
other than her marriage, "there is nothing remarkable to tell of my life. I
was but one of an overwhelming number of working women when I came
to this country and went into a cigar factory."[161] Although the religious differences in the marriage preoccupied members of the Jewish community,
it was the rags-married-to-riches story that captivated the general American reading public. *Cosmopolitan* magazine noted that it was rare for "a
Russian cigarette maker to capture an American millionaire philanthropist," but, that Pastor did so, illustrated "sufficient progress in the union
of wealth and ease with poverty and toil."[162] That Pastor's political activism
increased after she married suggests that her personal gains heightened
her awareness of others less fortunate.

Feminism and political radicalism proved more important than religion in influencing Pastor's choice of a mate, but her identity as a Jewish woman was likewise subsumed under her beliefs and efforts on behalf
of the working class. Just as education became Antin's form of worship,
advocating a better way of life for the underprivileged became Pastor's.
"God didn't make the poor, and no God will unmake poverty," she wrote,
"Only—we!"[163] Although she would not be considered a practicing Jew
by any means, her autobiography demonstrated a strong connection to
Yiddishkeit:

> What has the Jewish worker in common with the Jewish exploiter? . . .
> I embrace you, brother! Let us together make a home for ourselves in
> Zion, yes? Or here in America, you, the Jewish exploiter, I, your Jewish
> sweatshop slave! For are we not both united in Jewry?[164]

As the historian Alice Kessler-Harris pointed out, the most prominent
Jewish women who continued to be active politically after they married were those who intermarried.[165] Perhaps their continued involvement served as an outlet for their modified self-identification as Jewish
women. That Pastor did not have the social protection of marriage within

the Jewish immigrant community may have strengthened the class unity that powered her radicalism.[166] Moreover, marrying into great wealth may have accentuated her identification with the working class long after she left the cigar factory.

In Pastor's case, at least, she lived and was remembered as a Jew, even if she may not have observed as one. Through an early friendship with Miriam Shomer, a frequent contributor to the *Jewish Daily News* whose father was a popular Yiddish novelist, Pastor met the intelligentsia of the Lower East Side.[167] Her legacy was kept alive within the immigrant Jewish community long after she died on June 20, 1933.[168] Rose Pastor Stokes was the prototype for the heroine of a Yiddish novel, *Reizel of the East Side*, serialized in the *Morning Freiheit* from January to March 1942.[169]

Anna Strunsky (1877-1964)

Anna Strunsky married William English Walling on June 28, 1906, and, like Pastor and Antin, eventually split with her Protestant husband. Like Antin's and Pastor's marriages, differences in politics and fiscal perspectives—not religion—provoked the deterioration of Strunsky's marriage. Harder to identify is whether ethnic differences influenced their political and economic disagreements with each other. Although Strunsky identified as something other than Jewish in the years following her marriage, she did not renounce her Jewish heritage. Strunsky was born within the Pale of Settlement in Bibinots, Russia, moved through Germany to England, and then immigrated to New York in the fall of 1886, settling on the Lower East Side.[170] Similar to Antin, Strunsky strove to fulfill her intellectual potential by attending Leland Stanford Junior University, ending her studies just short of graduation. Whether she was suspended from Stanford for moral reasons, for receiving a male visitor in her room instead of in the parlor, or because the time she devoted to her political activities caused academic problems remains unclear. She also studied at the University of California, Berkeley, but did not earn a degree from there either.[171]

Strunsky met her future husband through a mutual friend, the famed author Jack London with whom she had a prior relationship and co-authored a book in 1903, *The Kempton-Wace Letters*.[172] Walling and Strunsky first noticed each other at a Thanksgiving picnic at which they talked long into the night. Five years later, in 1905, Walling wrote to Strunsky when he spotted a pamphlet she had written as the chairman of the Friends of Russian Freedom calling for help and democratic reforms for the Russian people. Strunsky joined Walling in St. Petersburg in September 1906, and their love blossomed in a volatile environment. Their romance was ignited when, together, they witnessed the shooting of a young student when he refused to stand and sing "God Save the Czar!"[173]

The news to both sets of parents regarding Strunsky and Walling's committed relationship, and their parents' reactions, were communicated long distance through multiple letters and cables. Strunsky wrote to her father that the shooting of the student "perhaps was the occasion which forced our love to our eyes and lips," inspiring "a new faith" and that they were "born again."[174] Strunsky's mother responded in Yiddish, "I thank God for taking you so far across a great distance to bring you happiness."[175] Her mother's acceptance may have been influenced by the fact that she herself had refused to consummate an arranged marriage, escaping from it at the age of sixteen.[176] Her father's long letter expressed his utmost joy at her newfound love, with a small reference to Walling's finances. Her father already considered Walling to be his son and asked that she convey this to him, kiss him, and tell him that her father had "enough confidence in him to trust you over to him."[177] As if relinquishing a prized possession, Elias Strunsky handed his daughter over to Walling notwithstanding that Walling was a Gentile. "He got the greatest fortune" was a double entendre. Perhaps he thought financial security would be his precious daughter's future.

Not all parents were so laissez-faire as the parents of Strunsky, Pastor, and perhaps Antin were about the prospect of their Jewish daughters marrying non-Jews. Two letters published in the *Forward* in 1926 expressed concern about the marriage prospects of Jewish women. In one, a family with four daughters living in the country was in a quandary, because "here, it's impossible to marry off a girl, because there are no Jews, only Gentiles." Evidently marriage with a non-Jew was inconceivable. The parents wanted to send the girls to a big city and avoid an impractical move themselves. The editor's reply: "We can only tell them that many Jewish families that are in the same position leave the small towns for the sake of their children. Others, on the other hand, remain where they are."[178] In a second letter, a mother confided that she once thought there was no difference between Jews and Christians, and that parents should not interfere if their child desired to wed a Christian. But now that her daughter had fallen in love with a Christian, she felt differently and tried to convince her daughter to end the relationship. The mother admitted: "True, it could happen that she could marry a Jewish man and after the wedding not be able to stand him. But with a Jew it's still different." The editor's response reinforced the mother's opinion, stating that her daughter should understand that "the match is not a good one."[179] These letters clearly illustrate that some parents had difficulty justifying their sentiments that even a bad Jew was preferable to a good non-Jew, a feeling Strunsky's father did not share.

The exchange with Walling's parents was more complicated, involving multiple communications. Walling reassured them that he had known Strunsky for several years, that she was considered a genius of a writer and speaker, and that everyone loved her including all his friends. He concluded his description: "She is young (26) and very healthy and strong. Of course she is a Jewess and her name is Anna Strunsky (but I hope to improve that—at least in private life—but we haven't spoken much of such things)." Apparently he sensed that her name, at least, would cause some concern. His father's initial response came by cable: "Surprised and anxious haste always dangerous your happiness ours." Walling cabled a response that nothing would be done in haste. Subsequent letters imply that his parents had reservations about his impulsiveness, and not necessarily about Strunsky, but he continued to assure them of her character and noble work. His parents' warning about "haste," which was the only concern they put in print, may have camouflaged other objections.[180] Walling also pointed out that Strunsky was not a "maid in waiting" and would not be a professional wife, but, in any case, he was accustomed to hiring others to do the menial tasks in life. He told his parents that their ambivalence made it "absolutely necessary" that he and Strunsky marry before returning to the U.S., and he invited them to attend the marriage ceremony in Europe. Otherwise, he wrote, "I think you should send us the same freehearted blessing her parents have."[181] The grounds for the Wallings' hesitation in offering congratulations are not entirely clear, but his father's ill health at the time probably played some role, and they did not travel to Russia. Letters from Walling and Strunsky allude to her foreign birth and assure that her father considered himself a full American and that she was American by upbringing, thus hinting that Walling's parents' position may have been xenophobic, a throwback to the nativism of the 1890s.[182] A letter from Strunsky to her father-in-law mentioned the "shock that unfortunate cablegram was," suggesting that it was more the abrupt timing of their announcement than the news itself.[183]

Employing the traditional wedding etiquette of deference to the bride and her family, Walling's mother considerately suggested that they return to San Francisco and marry in a manner that would please Strunsky's parents.[184] However, according to the couple, intermarriage was best if it occurred on neutral, European ground. Strunsky's response to her future mother-in-law, included here at length as it captures the predicaments of intermarriage, spelled out the complex reasons why she and Walling chose to marry far away and in a civil ceremony:

> My parents would of course love to have us married at home, but they are not opposed to our marrying abroad. They understand that a religious marriage is impossible. Neither English nor I belong to any creed and a religious ceremony would be farcical to us, at best, something less than sincere and beautiful. A greater reason still is that according to the law of Moses, I cannot marry English at all, and there is no rabbi in the world who could listen to our troth without committing sacrilege! From the standpoint of the faith in which I was born I must be stoned to death for what I am about to do. My parents are very liberal yet I have heard them say they would rather see me dead than marry a Gentile. I should not record this at all for their attitude towards English is perfect. They believe in him so absolutely and have so perfect a picture of his nature, his strong, pure feeling, his idealism, that they count me blessed among the daughters of Zion, and they give me to him freely. It is transformation of their whole conception of nationalism, and I count it a miracle that our love should have brought it about. Their love for me helped, too, but if they had not felt deeply that English and I were tied by indissoluble laws of the spirit that we were one though every religion in the world cried otherwise, they would have withheld their consent.
>
> You see, therefore, how it is we cannot marry at home. The Jewish religion would unite us only if English became a Jew, and another form of religious marriage is equally impossible for me. It would mean conversion on my part to have even a Unitarian minister officiate, and it would literally kill my mother.
>
> So we look upon our being in Europe as the kindest possible arrangement of Fate. It is a fortunate escape for us.[185]

In this same letter she also told Walling's mother that her attitude was not "too soft or servile" and that this suited him fine. She contended that their love was the "strong good love of equals." To her credit, Rosalind Walling wrote back to both children, sympathizing with Strunsky's parents, admiring their devotion to their religion, and admitting that previously she did not know "it was not allowed to use the Jewish rites in marriage with a Gentile." She commented, "I have seen that there is more opposition in Jewish families than in Christians to mixed marriages but I didn't know the laws were so severe."[186] The many letters Strunsky wrote to her in-laws, whom she addressed as "Dearest Mother and Father," indicate that her relationship with them grew strong with time.

Strunsky's intermarriage illustrated the modern American ideal of romantic love and the New Woman's belief that she could enter marriage willfully and on better terms.[187] Similar to the Pastor-Stokes match, the Strunsky-Walling engagement prompted headlines about a talented authoress and a rich Yankee, both Socialists, becoming betrothed in Russia. The inter-class match also exemplified the affirmation of voluntary love of American moderns in whose lives and writings, as Stansell wrote, "questions of sexuality and sex roles merged with those of class equality."[188] In a news clipping, Strunsky reportedly "defended passionately the ideal of marriage based on romantic ideal."[189] After she wed she wrote to her family that, "our love is as free as the soul. We hold each other and will hold each other forever, by no force in the world except the force of love."[190] Strunsky epitomized the Jewish immigrant woman's ascendancy to Americanism through her commitment to marry a man of her choice whom she loved. "'Marriage is a relation and not a state,' and one makes that relation according to ones talent or genius for love," she wrote [sic].[191] Her words also echoed, at least in part, those of Emma Goldman, for whom love was "the strongest and deepest element in all life; . . . love, the freest, the most powerful moulder of human destiny; how can such an all-compelling force be synonymous with that poor State-and-Church begotten weed, marriage?"[192] Strunsky and Goldman had earlier exchanged ideas on women's rights and the relations between the sexes, when the two met and became friends in San Francisco.[193]

While Strunsky explained to her mother-in-law that she had no intention of converting to another religion, her words also betray a woman who distanced herself from the faith she inherited at birth. In a 1 July 1906 letter to her family, addressed "Dearest people," Strunsky described the civil ceremony that took place on June 28 and commented afterward that "we consider it of no more importance than getting a passport."[194] The marriage ceremony, something sacred in Jewish tradition, held no import for her.[195] Perhaps she was ahead of her time; Strunsky illustrated an observation made by Judge Ben B. Lindsey in his book *The Companionate Marriage,* when he wrote in 1929 that, whereas in the past "the *ceremony* actually made the marriage 'until death do us part,' in modern marriage the ceremony is regarded merely as *evidence* of the marriage" (emphasis in original).[196] In response to a letter from her father-in-law that may have expressed concern about how the two would meld their different backgrounds, Strunsky wrote, "Neither English nor I have an axe to grind, no small panacea to propose; we have no dogma that we are aware of. I think, therefore, we shall not miss our mark."[197] Her married life, however, involved more Christian tradition later on than she might have imagined.

Although there is little historical evidence detailing Strunsky and Walling's domestic life, a few pieces are revealing. They eventually left Russia and, after visiting family in Chicago and San Francisco, settled in New York. In 1916 the couple bought a house in Greenwich, Connecticut.[198] On 21 December 1918 Strunsky wrote a letter to her mother-in-law describing the glee she felt about their Christmas tree: "The greatest news is that I bought a beautiful, large Christmas tree for the children, had it set up in the parlor, and last night I trimmed it, so that we can have it for Hayden's birthday tomorrow. It is lighted by electricity, and it is the loveliest tree I have ever seen!" She described the children's delight when they came downstairs in the morning and spotted the tree. Her concluding sentence is most revealing: "Dearest, I have never before had a Christmas tree, but I hope to trim a Christmas tree every remaining year of my life—it is such a delight-giving experience."[199] This indicates that for the first twelve years of marriage, during which she bore several children, Strunsky and Walling did not have a Christmas tree. The change over time illustrates a further deterioration of her allegiance to her heritage and an acceptance of her husband's. Some Jews who did not intermarry had Christmas trees, either in an effort to Americanize or so as not to deprive their Jewish children of what their Gentile friends enjoyed. However, Christmas and Easter holiday cards sent by their young daughter, Georgia, imply that Strunsky and Walling raised their children to observe at least two Christian holidays.[200]

Like Antin's, Strunsky's religious identity changed by adding aspects from other traditions, which does not mean that she entirely ceased to be Jewish or to associate with Jewish intelligentsia. Found among Strunsky's personal papers is a wide assortment of Christian religious literature, as well as ten publications by the Society of Friends. A membership card for The Wider Quaker Fellowship bearing the name "Mrs. W. English Walling" is among her saved items. Yet Strunsky also chose to keep the advertisement booklet from a Jewish funeral home containing the laws for mourners and dates for Jewish holidays in the years 1960 to 1965. Perhaps Strunsky used this information to properly commemorate the death of

Photograph of Anna Strunsky when she was declining to socially use her husband's last name. From James Boylan, *Revolutionary Lives: Anna Strunsky and William English Walling* (Amherst: University of Massachusetts Press, 1998).

a lifelong Jewish friend or close relative, someone who died a few years before she did, or simply to remain cognizant of the Jewish calendar. Throughout her life, Strunsky maintained relationships with other Jews, for example, her friendship with Dr. Katia Maryson who lived on the Lower East Side.[201]

Like Pastor, Strunsky was disillusioned to learn that her companion did not respect her as an equal, and she, too, experienced extreme loneliness. The summer they wed, Strunsky wrote in her diary about Walling's tone of voice when speaking to her about a minor matter: "Authority only means disrespect and irritation against perceived weakness in another's personality. It was not loving—it is not to be found in the spirit of a comrade."[202] As early as the autumn following their marriage, Strunsky made an entry detailing the bitter loneliness she felt: "I am lonely. I feel very much outside of his life. . . . Why must I live in loneliness and doubt? . . . How lonely and isolated I feel!"[203] The intermittent loneliness Strunsky documented when Walling seemed absorbed only in his work or distant from her made Strunsky more aware of her own need to work, which was hindered by the demands of motherhood placed unequally on her shoulders.

Economic disparity soon became a contentious issue when she wanted to assist her relatives and he did not. In the September after they wed she wrote in her diary, "Well, I tell myself, I must work, I must earn—when I earn I shall do what I can. I have no right to what is not my own . . . I begin to feel estranged from him, distanced by a brutal fact, that he has and I have not, that there is a barrier. . . . If I cannot earn my bread and he can than I feel inferior to him."[204] Strunsky's financial dependence illustrated the importance of paid labor for the married woman, advocated by Gilman in 1898, and the feeling of subordination associated with a lack of earning power. Although Strunsky championed social equality among spouses, she also upheld the ideal of the male provider and criticized Walling for falling short, which resembled the "neglect to provide" complaints prevalent in divorce cases between 1880 and 1920.[205] Several years before their actual divorce, Strunsky wrote to her mother-in-law: "So to my mind whatever difficulty exists arises mainly from the fact that English, who is a genius, was not a bread winner and was never intended to be one."[206] She spoke and wrote of economic equality, but Strunsky's own life did not exemplify this ideal.

An alternative to patriarchy was domesticity, which assigned a companionate role to women without absolute male dominance but still constrained the lives of wives and mothers while affording men greater flexibility.[207] When newly married, Strunsky remarked that she, too, "had a 'Cause' as men have."[208] But an entry ten years later illustrates that Walling operated as he pleased, while Strunsky cared for the home and the children. In 1916 Walling made a cutting remark questioning anyone getting any "service" out of Strunsky. She remonstrated, "What about my serving the babies day and night!" though there was much more she could have added about serving others. He left himself open so that he could decide whether to travel to Boston whenever he wished, telling her he never tied himself up if he could avoid it. "That's splendid," she told him with sarcasm. "I always tie myself up. I love freedom, but I have so many duties always."[209] Strunsky outlined her views on marriage in a five-page undated essay. She advocated a "Revolution in the home, and the function of woman as home-keeper, home-drudge, or house-manager. That eats away our intellectual life, our poetry, our comradeship. The home must be kept

by both men and women." Within her own home, Strunsky had an un-
equal share of the upkeep. Her domestic responsibilities made their marriage more gender traditional than she had envisioned when she wrote:
"but maternity and work must not be confused with domesticity." [210] True
equality between spouses was not attained.

The social pressure on women to take and use their husband's name
was also acute despite more than fifty years' resistance to this custom.[211]
Initially Strunsky intended to continue using her maiden name professionally after she married, as did Mary Antin. However, she eventually
caved to convention on this point. The summer they married, Strunsky
wrote to her brother about having to sign a paper concerning Walling's
property, commenting, "I signed Anna Strunsky Walling, my legal name—
but all of my other letters and writings I sign Anna Strunsky." Strunsky's
thumbing her nose at convention caught the attention of the press. A
December 1906 *Chicago Daily News* headline read: "Scorns the Name of
Wife/Mrs. Walling Wants to Be Known as Anna Strunsky, Though Married." She explained her position well. "This taking of a husband's name
by a woman when she marries is one of the symbols of the merging of her
individuality into his. It is a convention against which I protest."[212] Less
than two years after they wed, Walling got his wish to "improve" her last
name. Strunsky's continued use of her maiden named must have caused
her in-laws some consternation. She assuaged in 1908: "Father, dear heart,
I shall never grieve you again by using my maiden name, for I want my
daughter's name for whatever I write and do."[213] Strunsky's decision to
modify the use of her name illustrates a way that marriage and maternity
influenced gender in the early 1900s. Like others who espoused free love,
including the aforementioned Louise Bryant and John Reed, who joked
that news of their marriage should be kept quiet so as not to disappoint
like-minded friends, Strunsky did not at first wear a wedding ring.[214] In
what her biographer, James Boylan, calls another "symbolic retreat from
the notion of equality in marriage," Strunsky first purchased a wedding
ring nearly three years after she and Walling wed to avoid misunderstand-
ing about them among people unfamiliar with their status.[215]

The great expectations for marital happiness were ultimately disappointed when Strunsky and Walling went in different political directions,
as did Antin and Grabau, Pastor and Stokes.[216] Whereas she supported
peace efforts during World War I, he associated the American peace
movement with German subversion and strongly disapproved of her involvement. In addition to political disagreements and issues of gender

inequality, financial concerns added considerable stress to their crumbling marriage. There is no historical evidence indicating that their different religious backgrounds played a role in their 1932 divorce.

Although the three intermarriages I have discussed failed for political and economic reasons, the Jewish press insisted that differences of religion, race, and temperament were responsible. Whereas rabbis opposed intermarriage primarily on religious grounds, the *Hebrew Standard*, which touted itself as "America's leading Jewish family paper," warned Jewish girls in 1905 not to follow in Pastor's footsteps, arguing that intermarriages usually ended unhappily. Although Pastor and Stokes were not mentioned by name, the "certain Jewish writer downtown" and the "prominent Christian worker in the University Settlement" clearly served as the negative example. The paper criticized the notoriety Pastor received as "nauseating" and likely to attract girls who wanted to see their names in print. Implied here is what Riv-Ellen Prell has identified as the Ghetto Girl stereotype, a Jewish woman who withheld wages from her family, who dreamed of wealth and success. Contained within the stereotype is the fear that Jewish women would abandon the community because it did not have the Prince Charmings to fulfill their alleged fantasies.[217] "We do not believe in inter-marriage," the paper stressed. In most instances, the article went on, the Jewish partner in the relationship became lost to Judaism and the children were raised as Christians. The exception was the Jewish partner who remained a Jew and convinced the Christian to become one.[218] A subsequent column noted an East Side rumor that settlements proselytized and, whether true or not, that this had resulted in the Pastor-Stokes "episode." The publication besieged parents to prevent the intermarriages of their offspring: "The matter is not a religious question alone, but a question of race. Tastes, ideas, sentiments, etc., differ essentially, and it is impossible that good can come of it."[219] Jewishness, the publication seemed to suggest, was in the blood.

As mentioned above, prior to the Second World War, many Americans viewed Jews as a distinct race rather than a religious group.[220] An August 1924 article debating whether Judaism was a religion or a race concurred with the implications of both the advice giver and the man in search of a wife that intermarriage was not prevalent. The author described the biblical injunction against intermarriage and pointed out that it did not apply in cases where the Gentile who intermarried converted to Judaism. He wrote: "Partly because we have never been active in proslytising [*sic*], partly because there is little temptation to anyone to become a Jew—except in individual love-cases—we have never been faced with the problem of mass conversions and mass intermarriage from within."[221] The three women's intermarriages discussed here were "individual love cases" without conversion.

Exceptional Women

The lives of the intermarried immigrant Jewish women discussed in this chapter were similar in the ways and extent to which each woman navigated her life after marriage almost entirely outside the Jewish *religious* fold, this was not necessarily the case for *all* Jewish women who intermarried during the early decades of the twentieth century, immigrant or otherwise. Some women sought acceptance within the Jewish community. When Nellie Gutenberg married Clarence Dowd, they both signed a pledge orchestrated by Rabbi Leo M. Franklin of Congregation Beth El in Detroit, which read: "We the undersigned hereby solemnly promise that should children be born of our union we will to the best of our ability rear them in the Jewish faith."[222] The intent and wording of the pledge seems to emulate the requirements of the Roman Catholic Church, discussed in the next chapter. Presumably this rabbi stipulated that he would officiate at their marriage ceremony only if they swore to raise the children as Jews, suggesting that matrilineal descent was not considered sufficient in this case. Finding a rabbi who would officiate with or without a pledge must have been quite difficult.

Moreover, intermarriage could accentuate rather than diminish women's Jewish identities, exemplifying the contradictory nature of marital assimilation. In an anonymous 1929 article, "My Jewish Wife," the Gentile author described himself as Nordic in origin and nature, and compelled to write of his marital experience. His wife immigrated from Russia and "has never been able to escape the fact that she is a Jewess" and was "deeply race conscious." They married in haste after a three-week courtship and had been married five years when he wrote: "My wife, suddenly inducted into the Nordic world, has been made all the more deeply conscious of her race." He considered her insistence that he tell people she was Jewish unnecessary to avoid inadvertent discrimination and embarrassment.[223] Clearly, like Antin, Pastor, and Strunsky, the woman in this case did not relinquish her Jewish identity. The husband's observations about his Jewish wife also illustrate a period of heightened racial consciousness when intensified antisemitism made Jews eager to defend the reputation of their "race" and simultaneously fearful of attack.[224]

There were, of course, other immigrant Jewish women who intermarried between 1900 and 1929, but only those whose life stories were preserved for other reasons provide details. The histories of Mary Antin Grabau, Rose Pastor Stokes, and Anna Strunsky Walling are exceptional because of their nuptial choices and their impact on public discourse. They also became generators of cultural representations of interfaith marriage in the press, on Broadway, and in Hollywood.[225] Electing to marry non-Jewish men had consequences for their identities as Jewish women by increasing their exposure to Christian practices and thinking. Antin and Strunsky investigated other religions and, more likely than not, transformed their identities as Jewish women to include other ways of thinking that were not Jewish. Although they each maintained contacts with their Jewish families and friends, these three women did not stay within the immigrant Jewish fold but rather crossed over to their husbands' and the larger nonsectarian social circles. However, none of these women ever explicitly renounced her Jewish identity. In fact, Antin and Pastor claimed "the Jewish badge." Cultural assumptions can wield as much weight as legal interpretations. Although, by Jewish law, intermarriage did not dispel Jewishness, scholars and community leaders asserted that those who intermarried ceased to be Jews. But the experiences of women who actually intermarried offer a more variegated interpretation of the meaning of intermarriage and Jewishness. One could indeed intermarry and remain a Jew, provided the definition of "Jew" was enlarged.

Great care must be taken in evaluating the ways in which the women migrated away from their immigrant backgrounds or retained their ethno-religious affiliations. Although intermarriage contributed to their different lifestyles, it was not the sole culprit for the decline in Orthodoxy, secularization, or religious experimentation. When Antin, Pastor, and Strunsky elected to marry men of their own choosing, and for reasons other than purely economic ones, or to bring prestige to one's family, they did so along with their immigrant sisters who married Jewish men. The modern conception of romantic love rather than arranged marriages pervaded American immigrant culture. These three women followed the majority of Americans conforming to the marital model of free choice.[226] For some immigrant Jewish women, marriage represented freedom, and along with this freedom came secularization. Becoming Americans, particularly for immigrant Jewish women who intermarried, could supersede attachments to tradition.

Antin, Pastor, and Strunsky resembled other modern women of the 1920s who expected to have both marriage and a career, and *perhaps* have children. For example, of the seventeen women whom editors of *The Nation* invited to write articles in 1926 and 1927 in order "to discover the origin of their modern point of view toward men, marriage, children, and jobs," twelve had married but only five had children. That less than half the married women had children reflected the unpopularity of motherhood among career women early in the twentieth century.[227] Their intermarriages were strikingly different from their mothers' arranged marriages, and, except for Strunsky, they had significantly fewer (or no) children compared to the average Jewish immigrant family, which had five in the first decade of the century.[228] A further distinction is that they all married at older ages than most immigrant women did; Pastor and Strunsky even married later than women in the general population.

The tradition of patriarchy that often made immigrant daughters subordinate by constraining their independence, schooling, and sexual freedom may not seem to describe these women's lives.[229] Yet, although each woman strove to achieve some degree of equality in her marriage, all shouldered the traditional female responsibilities of running a household and, in Antin's and Strunsky's cases, of raising children. Their taking their husbands' names also reflected the prevailing gender custom. A partnership of equals was sought but not achieved, at least within the confines of their marriages. However, the reasons behind the dissolution of these unions, revolving as they did around divergent politics during World War I and continuing after that, illustrate the ways in which these immigrant Jewish women carved out independent lives for themselves. Strunsky's insistence that she, too, had "a Cause" conveys this effort as well.

Antin, Pastor, and Strunsky exemplified modern women who often faced the difficulties of combining heterosexual love and work. Unlike the nineteenth-century suffragist or feminist, these women insisted on their claims to self-fulfillment in life both outside their homes and within them.[230] Although the First World War played a significant role in the women's lives, neither the Great Depression nor the ratification of the Nineteenth Amendment granting women suffrage seemed to have directly influenced their marital lives. Indeed, Antin, Pastor, and Strunsky may have resembled their non-Jewish American sisters who considered the fight for equality between the sexes to have been won with the attainment of the right to vote.[231] Their inabilities to maintain successful marriages were measured in individual terms as personal failures rather than as consequences of the structural problems that continued to dis-advantage women in American society.[232] An essay by Strunsky suggests, however, that she learned during her marriage that only systemic change could truly make women and men equals in marriage: "Needless to say this revolution in the home cannot be affected [*sic*] before the whole structure of our present society changes. The future belongs to the worker and the woman—and that should mean all mankind."[233] Class equality re-mained as difficult to attain as gender equality.

Although their actions seem to indicate otherwise, they did not claim to be feminists; Antin defiantly told President Theodore Roosevelt: "The truth is that I am very cool about the suffrage—by no means against it, but not warmly interested in securing it. I simply haven't got religion on the subject, and you cannot count on me until I have."[234] Yet Antin also rejected the contemporary women's fashions of tight-waisted skirts and puffed blouses, and hired a seamstress to make what she considered more practical clothes.[235] Even someone who had been involved in the birth control movement could self-identify other than as a feminist. Pastor, who, as an organizer for the Communist Party in 1922, had disputed any suggestion of gender solidarity by insisting that there was no "separate woman's problem," wrote shortly before her death, "I have never been a feminist as such."[236] Nevertheless, the constitutional amendment that un-dermined the former marriage-citizen relationship may have influenced the political perspectives of Antin, Pastor, and Strunsky by giving them the confidence that their sense of nationalism could stand independently from their husband's, as did their votes. The evidence indicates conclu-sively that religious differences were not responsible for their marital dis-unions. Intermarriage did not bring about unhappiness and divorce; po-litical variance from their husbands and gendered economics did. More-over, the frequency of divorce among New York's bohemian crowd, which was higher than the national average, indicates women's disenchantment with the kind of heterosexual equality that did not extend into the home, and also with the older pattern of men's privileges and women's subordi-nation to domestic demands.[237]

The controversies generated by marriages such as the Antin-Grabau, Pastor-Stokes, and Strunsky-Walling couples contributed to widespread concern and fascination about intermarriage in the following decades, spawning articles, letters, plays, novels, films, and sounds of alarm from the pulpit. Overall, the ethnic press portrayed intermarriage negatively, observing that mixed marriages were unhappy marriages and that they threatened the very survival of the Jewish people. While their offspring independently sought romantic love alliances, immigrant parents worried about their children's marriage prospects. Intermarriage was deplored by the organized rabbinate, which tried to discourage rabbis from officiating at mixed marriages and individuals from straying from the Jewish community. Being Jewish was construed in racial, religious, and gendered terms by both those who intermarried and observers.

The U.S. government held its own position regarding the institution of marriage. The Cable Act, or the Married Women's Independent Nationality Act of 1922, undercut a woman's citizenship relative to a man's. An American woman would lose her citizenship if she married a foreigner and lived in his country for two years, or if she married a man then considered "ineligible for citizenship," an Asian, a polygamist, or an anarchist. An American man did not suffer the same consequences.[238] Congress soon passed legislation restricting immigration, essentially ending the largest wave of newcomers to America's shores. Restrictions began with the Quota Act in 1921, continued with the Immigration Law of 1924, and ended in 1929 when the national origins clause actually came into effect.[239] With the gates all but closed, my analysis shifts from famous immigrant women to their "daughters" and "granddaughters." Did the lesser-known second- and third-generation women experience intermarriage differently? In the following chapters I discuss whether intermarriage and gender were lived and represented in similar or distinct ways in the post–Depression and World War II years, and in what ways the Jewish community's response would evolve over time.

2

Intermarriage in an Age
of Domesticity

To be a Jew in the twentieth century
Is to be offered a gift. If you refuse,
Wishing to be invisible, you choose
Death of the spirit, the stone insanity.
Accepting, take full life. Full agonies:
Your evening deep in labyrinthine blood
Of those who resist, fail, and resist; and God
Reduced to a hostage among hostages.

—Muriel Rukeyser, 1944

The lives of ordinary Jewish women who intermarried between 1930 and 1960 have heretofore been invisible. Jews assumed that Jewish women who married non-Jews all but disappeared by rejecting their religion and ethnic group, and by severing their connections with the Jewish community.[1] In other words, Jewish women who intermarried were considered no longer Jewish. However, a qualitative analysis of the meaning and published representation of intermarriage and gender suggests something different. Like their more famous, early-immigrant predecessors who intermarried, described in chapter 1, ordinary Jewish women selected their Gentile husbands in the 1930s, 1940s, and 1950s. Yet their histories illustrate the meaning of intermarriage for women whose lives did not warrant publicity and went unrecorded until now, rather than for the relatively few who married into prominent families. In contrast to the political activists already discussed, these women married during a Depression-era resurgence of public opinion that reinforced traditional gender roles and, with a temporary interlude "for the duration" of World War

II, encouraged American wives to embrace domesticity and leave world affairs to men.[2]

Marrying "out" became more conceivable to some Jewish women as the twentieth century progressed, though not more acceptable within Jewish circles. The increasing visibility and, to some degree, acceptability of intermarriage in American society between 1930 and 1960 made it more plausible to defy the cultural imperative of religious endogamy. Marriage between Jews and Gentiles was relatively uncommon in the United States, as it was in the first three decades of the century. In Nazi Germany, by comparison, because of Jewish emigration, by 1939 approximately 25 percent of all existing marriages involving Jews were with non-Jews.[3] However, the number of cross-faith marriages was growing in America. The Jewish intermarriage rate was 3 percent between 1931 and 1940. It increased to 6.7 percent between 1941 and 1950, and fluctuated between 6.4 and 5.9 percent between 1951 and 1960.[4] The American culture of intermarriage changed markedly between 1930 and 1960. As marriages between Catholics and Protestants became more widespread, it eased the way for Jewish women to marry "out." In 1931 a minister advised in his sermon: "It is best . . . for Americans to marry Americans, and Presbyterians Presbyterians, and Christians Christians, and Jews Jews."[5] By the late 1950s such rhetoric was outmoded in the mainstream press and intermarriage was commonly discussed. For example, in 1957, a *New York Times* author stated: "For some years it has seemed to many Americans narrow-minded, intolerant, almost un-American to raise objections to marriage on the basis of 'creed.'"[6] A new abundance of social science studies and lay and advice literature contributed to making intermarriage seem more common in American society at large, albeit still undesirable to organized religion and many parents. Jewish communities remained vigilantly opposed to interfaith unions despite the pervasive talk of intermarriage. Thus, although Jewish women who married non-Jews did so in an American society that slowly became somewhat more tolerant of intermarriage, most Jews continued to consider their actions as malevolent. American Jews, however, comprised a disproportionate number of the whites who married blacks in the late 1940s. Despite that interracial marriage remained uncommon, even outlawed, in many states, Jews who were involved in alternative politics including the Communist and Socialist Parties were more likely to meet prospective black spouses. Moreover, uncertainty about their own racial status as "white" may have made some Jews more inclined to consider crossing the color line.[7]

American Jewry's decreasing traditionalism, combined with Jewish women's academic and labor pursuits, enabled intermarriage. The diminished public observance of religion, and assimilation, meaning the loss of distinctive ethnic characteristics, both created more leeway for marriage-bound Jewish women. Women who were more "American" and less "Jewish" in a traditional sense could more easily blend into non-Jewish environments. Further, the economic and social climate during World War II was particularly liberating for single women who gained more autonomy and independence.[8] Jewish women's college living experiences and social opportunities outside the home fostered encounters with Gentile men. Greater integration into non-Jewish circles through higher education, professionalized employment, and suburban living facilitated some Jewish women's departure from marriage within the faith.[9]

While diminished religiosity, assimilation and social contacts made intermarriage more possible, experiences with antisemitism sometimes provided the motivation. Name-calling, physical abuse, social exclusion, and employment discrimination made some Jewish women more inclined to abandon the insecurity of being Jewish and single in America. Their fear of rejection and their discomfiture with a historically anti-Jewish environment lessened some Jewish women's loyalty to their religious group and encouraged them to seek alliance with a Gentile spouse. Antisemitism prompted some Jewish women to intermarry, which in turn affected how they identified and raised their children. Antisemitism did not, however, lessen Jewish opposition to intermarriage; it may even have exacerbated the notion that someone who crossed religious lines married the "enemy." Traditionally, and through the 1950s, the exogamous Jew was dead in the eyes of the Jewish community, with few notable exceptions.[10] This was certainly the practice among Orthodox Jews, though the Reform and Conservative branches of Judaism also practiced excommunication to some degree. Thus Jewish women who intermarried often faced strong responses from their families of origin.

The emerging patterns from even a small group of oral histories enable me to identify and address themes that suggest what intermarriage meant to and for Jewish women. For this book, I conducted a total of forty-three oral history interviews in thirteen Boston area communities with women who intermarried during the twentieth century. Although this sample does not necessarily represent all intermarried Jewish women, it does shed light on the complex histories of some Jewish women living in a specific geographic area who married non-Jews. In this chapter I interweave testimonies from women who intermarried between 1938 and 1960 with more conventional sources, such as periodical literature, to discuss two principal themes: how parents reacted to their daughters' intermarriages and how Jewish women formed their identities. Because variations occur according to time and place, it is not possible to generalize about intermarriage with universal validity.[11] However, I can ascertain the ways in which some intermarried women shed or retained their ethnic and religious heritage and describe familial attitudes toward marrying non-Jews.

Jewish women who intermarried came from various backgrounds, married men with diverse religious attachments, and had a wide array of experiences. Fourteen of the forty-three women I interviewed appear in this chapter, including two immigrant refugees, and eight second-generation and four third-generation Americans. All but one of the women were of Ashkenazi descent, and their denominational affiliations at birth included Reform, Conservative, and Orthodox Judaism. Their husbands' religious affiliations included Congregational, Presbyterian, Methodist, Unitarian, Italian Catholic, and Irish Catholic, representing an increase in diverse backgrounds from the pre-1930 period. A difference in socioeconomic class was a contentious issue for four women; two of them married Catholics and the other two married Protestants. Most women had less higher education than their husbands. Only one woman experienced conflict owing to regional differences; her husband was a Southerner and she felt that his relatives were against her "as much for being a Yankee as for being Jewish."[12] Moreover, because the women came from locations throughout the United States and married in different cities, this book makes no attempt to evaluate different regions of the country. Some had a Justice of the Peace officiate at their marriage ceremonies; others managed to find a rabbi, a priest, or a minister willing to perform the rites. At the time of the interviews, five of the women I discuss here were married to their non-Jewish spouses, five were divorced, and four were widowed.

The period from 1930 to 1960 was a transitional one in the history of Jewish women's intermarriage. Before 1930 intermarriage was not a conspicuous threat to American Jewish culture because it occurred infrequently; the available histories of immigrant women who did intermarry indicate that these were indeed exceptional cases. Beginning in the 1960s, however, marriage demographics changed markedly, prompting communal activists and scholars to clamor for more research on intermarriage. The national Jewish intermarriage rate nearly tripled, from 5.9 percent between 1956 and 1960 to 17.4 percent between 1961 and 1965; the first conference on intermarriage was held by the Theodor Herzl Institute in New York; and articles appeared with titles such as *Look* magazine's 1964 "The Vanishing American Jew."[13] This chapter focuses on what happened in the intervening years to make intermarriage a front-burner issue in the Jewish community and a more viable marital choice for Jewish women. In the following pages I argue that all Jewish women who intermarried did not reject their heritage, cease identifying as Jews, or completely disappear from Jewish life. Although antisemitism encouraged assimilation for some women who had thin connections to Judaism, their histories show the various ways that their Jewishness coexisted with their intermarriages. Moreover, whether or not women chose to assume new religious identities and "melt" into the mainstream, they could not escape the Jewish label. I also argue that, although intermarriage became more commonplace among Christians and in the public eye, Jewish parents tenaciously objected to their daughters leaving the Jewish fold. By looking at the intersection of intermarriage and gender across time, Jewish women's experiences and self-defined identities will uncover the personal meaning of intermarriage.

Leaving the Fold

The majority of Jewish women coming of age in the mid-twentieth century did so in religiously unobservant families and in culturally ambiguous homes. After the immigration gates all but closed in the 1920s, survival and economic success rather than Jewish education or observance preoccupied many Jewish parents in the 1930s.[14] Their children and grandchildren, the second and third generation, were Americans whose ties to Judaism were sometimes loosely defined. The separation of Jewishness as an ethnicity and Judaism as a religion enabled Jewish parents to perceive of themselves and their offspring as "Jewish" without necessarily affiliating with a synagogue or maintaining *Halakhah* (Jewish law) in their homes.[15] Parental lack of religiosity, the desire to be 100 percent American, and efforts to "get ahead" left little room for women to value their Jewish heritage. Jewish cultural objects, such as portraits of rabbis, *yahrzeit* (memorial) plaques, and Sabbath candlesticks, were replaced with copies of Great Masters' paintings or relegated to the bookshelf. According to the historian Jenna Weissman Joselit, "most Jewish homes in the interwar years were essentially devoid of explicitly Jewish markers, especially when compared with earlier tenements."[16] Harriet Mansfield's experience illustrates the toll assimilation took on some Jewish women's sense of Jewishness. Born in 1921, she migrated from the East Side to the West Side of Manhattan as her father, a self-made businessman, achieved financial success. She attended secular private schools and was cared for by a Scottish Presbyterian nanny. Harriet stated frankly: "I had no emotional feeling towards my Judaism, nothing came out of my family and Sunday School didn't inspire me in the slightest."[17] Harriet intermarried in 1942 with very little sense of her Jewish heritage. Once Eastern European Jews had proven they could be Americans, the question became whether their descendants would remain Jews.[18]

The decreasing role of religious observance in the lives of a growing number of Jews and the increasing popularity of secularism enabled women to marry outside the Jewish group without totally relinquishing their Jewish identification. Diminished attendance at religious services was a visible sign of the decline in observance, as was the declining consumption of kosher meat, which fell by 30 percent in the decade after World War I.[19] Less frequent public prayer and slackened adherence to Jewish dietary law meant a reduction in customary rituals governing Jewish life, including marriage. In the interwar period, a sense of belonging based on Jewish peoplehood, promoted by Conservatives, Reconstructionists, and the American Jewish Congress, rather than religion kept secularizing Jews in the community.[20] Mavis Rue, who was born in 1922 and grew up in Brooklyn, New York, remembered her parents speaking strictly "perfect English" at home rather than Yiddish, their *mamaloshen,* or mother tongue.[21] Though historians disagree about the exact trajectory of the Yiddish language, by 1940 few native-born Jews spoke Yiddish or actively maintained it once they left home; without a specifically Jewish language, ethnic Jewishness had questionable staying power.[22] American Jewry had become, according to historian Henry Feingold, "a voluntary association."[23] The case of Margaret Doherty exemplifies how the unbraiding of the religious and ethnic components of Judaism enabled some women to conceptualize tradition apart from faith. Doherty was born in Brooklyn, New York, in 1929. When she married in 1950, she promised to raise her children as Catholics, a prenuptial requirement of the Roman Catholic Church for a dispensation to be granted.[24] She insisted, however, that she be allowed to teach them their Jewish heritage, "not so much the religion itself," she said, "but the *traditions*"[25] which included celebrating Jewish holidays such as Chanukah and Passover in a secular fashion. Freedom of choice fostered some Jewish women's departure from tradition.

Jewish women's ties to their parents' hearth and home weakened between 1930 and 1960, creating opportunities to meet more individuals outside their immediate circles. The rise of mass consumer culture in the 1920s, and its proliferation thereafter, facilitated the efforts of second-generation women to achieve emotional autonomy from their parents. As the historian Lizabeth Cohen argues, rather than an outright rejection of ethnic identity, young people incorporated mass culture into their lives, by going to the dance hall, for example, from within their respective ethnic peer groups.[26] Once outside the watchful eyes of their immigrant forebears, however, the chances of Jewish daughters and granddaughters meeting Gentiles multiplied. Hetty Miller was born in Boston in 1933 and, after attending Dorchester High School, undertook secretarial training. The way she met her husband illustrates the casual potential of meeting Gentile men. "A friend and I happened to be in Boston and we met some guys . . . and I bumped into him somewhere else the second night . . . and I knew at that point I was going to marry him."[27] Multiple interviewees described knowing they had met their mates the first or second time they saw them. Some of these impulsive matches lasted, and, not surprisingly, others did not.

Although the majority of Jews in New York, Boston, and other cities rarely socialized with Gentiles in the 1930s, and were therefore not tempted to date non-Jews,[28] some Jewish women found wider social circles. The war years 1939 to 1945 increased the scope further. As the historian Hasia Diner wrote, "Jews of both genders . . . in the military and on the home front . . . went places, did things, and met people they would never had encountered during peacetime."[29] Social mixing was not limited to those in uniform or those in the war industries but extended to people not directly involved in the war effort. Carolyn Jasper was born in Jamaica Plain, Massachusetts, in 1924 and spent her childhood in Watertown. She described socializing in the early 1940s: "We all had boyfriends who were in the service and they would come home on leave and we went out on double dates and we all just had a very good time together when we did . . . it was quite a mixed group and everybody was very accepting of everybody else."[30] Her experience reflects Jewish women's increased social independence from parental authority and the rising interfaith peer culture that included unsupervised dating.[31] Peer socialization enabled Jewish women to fraternize with women and men of similar ages and stages of life but with different religious backgrounds, generating avenues for romance with non-Jewish men.

The increased pursuit of secular education among women in the 1930s and 1940s made it more likely for them to meet Gentile men in the classroom, as well as face cultural contradictions about female roles. A high school diploma was the minimum expectation of Jewish youth by the 1930s, and three-quarters of the girls in New York City studied bookkeeping and shorthand diction.[32] Secular learning acquired in college was considered the path to a career for Jewish women and men alike.[33] By 1934 at least 52.1 percent of all female students in New York City's colleges were Jewish women, many of whom attended teacher-training schools.[34] Alice Lawrence, who was born in 1938, grew up in Brookline, Massachusetts, and married in 1960, met her husband in one of her Pembroke College classes at Brown University.[35] A fellow Pembroke graduate wrote in *Brown Alumni Magazine*, "I was from a Jewish ghetto in New York City, and on my first day in Providence, I met more Christian men that I had known in my entire life!"[36] In a study of coeducational college seniors in 1942 and 1943, the sociologist Mirra Komarovsky found that women had to navigate between the prevailing feminine ideal of the homemaker and the "career girl," whose fundamental personality traits were "diametrically opposed." Komarovsky concluded that women who achieved the middle ground, who were intelligent but not brilliant, "able to stand on her own feet and to earn a living but not so good as to compete with men," were most content and able to manage "modern role anxiety."[37]

While public attitudes about women's traditional domestic responsibilities remained constant and their employment was viewed as temporary, women's greater participation in the wage labor force brought them into contact with non-Jewish men in the workplace.[38] Second-generation Jewish women, along with Jewish men, moved into white-collar jobs in the 1920s and 1930s.[39] Although popular belief was that available jobs should go to men during the Great Depression, which made women often unwelcome in the work force, Jewish daughters shared the burden with sons to find employment and provide income to help sustain their families.[40] World War II, while ending the Depression, also created a critical labor shortage, which Jewish women helped to fill.[41] Between 1940 and 1945 the female labor population increased by 50 percent, and, by 1950, 29 percent of women were in the work force.[42]

As teachers, secretaries, and other professionals pursuing "women's work," employment that was redefined as an extension of domesticity during the economic mobilization for World War II and later reconstructed during the Cold War, Jewish women often had non-Jewish colleagues.[43]

Eleven of the fourteen women discussed in this chapter attended some college and, job segregation by sex notwithstanding,[44] several of them met their husbands at their workplaces. Marilyn Rinalto, born in 1927, was a high school teacher when she met her husband, a fellow teacher and the department head.[45] Tamar Reynold, born in 1908, became a legal secretary; she married her boss in 1958, after working for him for many years.[46] Yvonne Evans was born in 1926 and remembered fondly: "It was an office romance! I worked for Raytheon, which was a large engineering company, and it was just *full* of young, unmarried men. It was wonderful!"[47] Sometimes working with Gentiles lessened reservations about marrying the "other." Georgia Summer, European-born in 1924, did not hesitate to date the man whom she eventually married in 1949 because, as she said, "basically we had been working together . . . we had adjacent benches in this lab where we each were working."[48] In addition to enabling them to meet more men of diverse backgrounds, earning an income and becoming financially independent from their parents may have emboldened some women regarding their choice of a mate. Barbara Adams, born in Boston in 1919, had worked and saved war bonds for a long while when she married her husband on her lunch hour in 1956.[49] The postwar years brought more opportunities for "adjacent benches," which some Jewish women readily took.

The goal of matrimony, which many Americans aimed to achieve at increasingly young ages, fueled some Jewish women to seek eligible mates regardless of religious background. Until World War II, women and men married at the age and rate characteristic of the nineteenth century. The 1940s ended this stability, when the marriage rate rose and the median age at marriage fell; more than half of all women were married by the age of twenty-one in the late 1940s. By 1950 the average marriage age for women was twenty, and many women married between the ages of fifteen and nineteen.[50] Jewish women who intermarried at least fulfilled the social expectation that they would marry, albeit not coreligionists. One woman summed up the matrimonial assignment: "We used to say that marriage is a trap you're better in than out of . . . in the days when I was raising four children around the clock, I would've liked other options."[51] Another reflected, "I only got married because I thought it was the thing to do."[52] Their comments indicate that they felt social pressure to marry. Particularly after World War II, the diminished supply of single men made many women of various faiths rush to the altar, fearful that otherwise they would miss their chance at matrimony.[53]

The marriage ideal, together with the apotheosis of motherhood that resulted in the Baby Boom, seemed to offer individual security that took precedence over Jewish group solidarity during the Cold War. Headlines about atomic secrets, Communist espionage, the House Un-American Activities Committee, and loyalty oaths fueled insecurity and prompted Americans to cultivate their own protection by creating a family. The historian Rosalind Rosenberg wrote, "To those who had grown up in the poverty of the Depression only to confront the trauma of World War II, the importance of security, both in monetary and emotional terms, took on an almost religious significance."[54]

Civic nationalism, a model of citizenship and national identity, encouraged Jews and other European ethnic groups to declare their loyal allegiance to the American nation.[55] Despite the proximity of many women's marriage dates to the Holocaust, none of my interviewees expressed concern about intermarrying in light of the decimation of the Jewish people. Yvonne Evans noted that, when she dated, young single people did not talk much about the fate of the Jews: "the war was over and people were coming home and what went on in Europe was past. [People were] getting married."[56] Her reflection alludes to the historical debate about the significance of the Holocaust in the American Jewish memory and illustrates a distinction between personal choice and intra-communal initiatives. According to the historian Arthur Hertzberg, the minority status of all Jews encouraged "group amnesia," a preference to look away from the death camps so as not to stand aside from the rest of America.[57] Hertzberg's analysis exemplifies the view that, from 1945 until the first half of the 1960s, discussion about the destruction of European Jewry was extremely limited.[58] Recent scholarship suggests, however, that American Jews were haunted by the persecution of their coreligionists and did not experience memory impairment. Citing numerous examples of Holocaust imagery used to describe contemporary events, Diner wrote, "While in the 1950s and 1960s American Jews did not place the events of World War II at the top of their public and communal agenda, they did make room for it in communal discourse and political strategy."[59]

Residential proximity mixed with attitude, education, and employment, generated opportunity for cross-religious romance. Moving from Jewish neighborhoods to the more religiously heterogeneous suburbs enabled Jewish women still living with their parents to befriend larger numbers of non-Jews than in earlier decades. Between 1945 and 1960 the social and economic profile of American Jews more closely resembled the wider American population with a larger percentage living in the solidly middle-class suburbs and professionally employed.[60] Approximately one out of every three Jews left the big cities for the suburbs between 1945 and 1965. Some clustered together in suburbia, and others ventured to the suburbs with few coreligionists.[61] In either case the proximity to Gentiles was greater than it had been before 1945. However, according to one observer writing for the *Forward* about the self-segregation in the New York City neighborhoods of the 1920s: "four-fifths of all the Jews . . . practically have no contact with Gentiles."[62] The historian Elaine Tyler May described the move to suburbia as follows:

> Second generation European immigrants moved out of their ethnic neighborhoods in the cities, leaving their kinship networks, along with their outsider status, behind. . . . Jews and Catholics joined Anglo-Saxon Protestants in these all-white communities, even if they could not join their country clubs or social gatherings.[63]

Although most Jews, Catholics, and Protestants continued to marry their coreligionists, the residential proximity between groups increased the likelihood of a Jewish woman meeting, falling in love with, and marrying a non-Jew.[64] In *Jewish Identity on the Suburban Frontier,* Marshall Sklare observed that twice as many respondents in 1957-58 spent more time socializing with friends than with family compared to their parents' generation, reflecting the pervasive peer culture of American youth. He hypothesized, "The shift to a group which is self-selected rather than inherited may portend the end of in-group solidarity." The 7 percent who reported that non-Jews constituted an equal number or a majority of their close friends suggest that there was room for enduring interfaith relationships to develop in suburbia.[65] Carolyn Jasper's story exemplifies how living and socializing among non-Jews could lead to intermarriage. She originally met her husband through his mother, her Girl Scout troop leader.[66] Carolyn's experience also supports the assertion of the historian Ellen K. Rothman that the more young people participated in commercial amusements, school, and other activities outside the family circle, the more they selected marriage partners beyond their parents' influence.[67]

Ripple Effects

Jewish-Gentile liaisons caught the attention of the Reform rabbinate, which devoted unprecedented attention to the issue of intermarriage in the 1930s and 1940s, signaling increased concern. The Central Conference of American Rabbis published papers on Jewish-Gentile marriage in the 1937 and 1947 annual journals, ending twenty-eight years of relative silence since its 1909 resolution condemning intermarriage. The conference discussed whether to tell rabbis not to officiate or simply to discourage intermarriage while leaving the decision whether to participate up to the individual clergymen. The official stance of the CCAR suggests an openness to dialogue with interfaith couples among some Reform rabbis. In a paper published in 1937, Louis Mann suggested that, rather than refuse to participate, rabbis should do everything possible to discourage the intermarriage and, failing that, to welcome the couple. Mann concluded by reaffirming the 1909 resolution to discourage intermarriage but not, as a whole, advocate nonparticipation.[68] When the issue was raised again a decade later in 1947, the CCAR once again reaffirmed the 1909 resolution, which read: "The Central Conference of American Rabbis declares that mixed marriages are contrary to the tradition of the Jewish religion and should therefore be discouraged by the American Rabbinate."[69] Numerous Reform rabbis contributed to the discussion, indicating the extent to which intermarriage had become a heated topic within the Reform rabbinate by the late 1940s.[70] Intermarriage was not a topic of public discourse for the Conservative and Orthodox rabbinates during the years from 1930 to 1960. The Rabbinical Assembly, the Conservative organization founded in 1901, did not address the issue of intermarriage at its annual convention until 1964.[71] Members of the Assembly could not officiate or even attend mixed marriages.[72] The position of the Orthodox organization formally founded in 1941, the Rabbinical Council of America, was that *Halakhah* required that a marriage be between a Jewish male and a Jewish female, and published no further commentary.[73]

Although Jewish leaders decried intermarriage in the 1930s and 1940s, concern about interfaith marriage in the mass media was primarily focused on unions between Catholics and Protestants. This would change by the 1950s, when an author asked his readers: "Would you approve of your child's marrying a Protestant? A Catholic? A Jew?"[74] A Conservative rabbi was quoted in 1931 as saying, "Intermarriage is . . . a blow to Jewry and Judaism."[75] The founder of the Reconstructionist movement

Mordecai M. Kaplan warned in his 1934 book, *Judaism as Civilization*: "Jews must be prepared to reckon frankly and intelligently with intermarriage as a growing tendency which, if left uncontrolled, is bound to prove Judaism's undoing."[76] However, the proportion of marriages between Jews still greatly outnumbered those between Jews and Gentiles in the 1930s and early 1940s, and sociological findings regarding religious endogamy curbed Jewish communal concern. For the time being, at least, intermarriage was considered an aberration, a personal and family crisis, but not a threat to Jewish continuity. World War II would change this perspective.[77]

The Roman Catholic and Protestant leaders, on the other hand, quarreled over doctrinal differences concerning intermarriage from 1930 through the 1950s, as concern about its pervasiveness grew. In March 1932 the Federal Council of Churches of Christ in America, representing the majority of Protestant denominations, protested the Vatican's decree to tighten the Catholic Church's rule that children of intermarriage be raised as Catholics.[78] In response, Catholics beseeched Christian brethren to join pens and tongues to prevent or lessen the "evils possible in these mixed unions."[79] Summarizing the dire outlook of the times, one observer contended in June 1941: "It seems to be true that of all mixed marriages, the one most likely to lead to incompatibility is that of the mating of a Catholic and a Protestant."[80]

Without a large influx of European immigrants as possible coreligious marriage partners, the mid-century ushered in more vocalized apprehension than ever before about rising interfaith marriage, Christian-Christian and Christian-Jewish, particularly from religious advocates. In January 1949 intermarriage research sponsored by the Church Federation of Greater Chicago entailing a house-to-house religious census in a large and anonymous city made it clear that intermarriage between Christians permeated American society by illustrating that more than one-third of intermarriages were between Lutherans and Roman Catholics.[81] In the researcher's words: "It is abundantly clear that interfaith marriages have unfortunate results for organized religion."[82] The divorce rate for Catholic-Protestant marriages was reportedly nearly triple that of non-mixed marriages.[83] Concern about Jewish-Gentile intermarriage resurfaced in the mass media. "Intermarriage is a serious threat to the survival of the Jewish people and consequently to the survival of Judaism," wrote a Jewish activist in December 1949.[84] Alarm regarding Jews leaving the fold was exacerbated by the Pope's Christmas message inviting non-Catholics into the Catholic Church.[85] A 1958 book authored by a rabbi about intermarriage

"Mixed Blessings" cartoon of Catholic-Protestant family divided between houses of worship. From *U.S. Catholic* 55, no. 3 (March 1990): 34. Don Pract, artist. Courtesy of Anita Jackson-Hall.

cried out to the Jewish community to "save the Jewish home from the destructive fire of mixed marriage."[86]

Increasing intermarriage rates among Protestants and Catholics provoked rising anxiety within and outside organized religion. "Sociologists have joined churchmen in recent years in their concern with mixed marriages," two scholars wrote in 1956. The number and proportion of Lutherans who married non-Lutherans grew from 46 percent for the years 1936-40 to 58 percent in 1946-50, according to one study. That almost three-fifths of non-Lutherans married members of other Protestant churches did not lessen the concern of the United Lutheran Church.[87] While noting that rates varied significantly from one region of the country to another, the priest and sociologist John L. Thomas contended, in 1951, that the intermarriage rate of Catholics averaged 30 percent of all marriages sanctioned by Catholic nuptials, and was steadily increasing.[88] Presbyterian authorities warned their flocks not to marry Catholics.[89] Interfaith marriages should not occur, advocated an Episcopal vicar.[90] In June 1951 the Southern Baptist Convention joined with Roman Catholics in alerting the public to the "dangers to harmonious home life in mixed marriages."[91] Clergy loudly lamented that more than one-third of all Catholics married non-Catholics.[92] "Catholics Assail Mixed Marriages" read the headline for an article about the twenty-fourth National Catholic Family Life Convention held in Boston in March 1956.[93] Religious leaders reportedly spoke "with one voice" against intermarriage, outlining reasons why interfaith marriages were unusually hazardous and urging that they be avoided.[94]

The assault on intermarriage reflected the uneasy relationship between religion and culture in America following World War II. The general society highly valued religion after 1945 and America's confrontation with the Soviet Union and atheistic communism. For example, the words "under God" were added to the Pledge of Allegiance in 1954, and, beginning in 1955, "In God We Trust" was printed on all American currency.[95] Although a postwar religious "revival" included the reorganization and strengthening of the nation's Christian churches, the eventual downward statistical profile of the various denominations' memberships illustrated that, by the 1960s, Christians were becoming less "religious" and more secular.[96] Outwardly, American Judaism appeared to flourish, with the number of synagogue congregations and memberships peaking after 1945.[97] Paradoxically, however, paying dues did not translate into greater religiosity; social and cultural activities seemed more popular than worship. The conflation of Judaism and Jewish identity meant, as the historian Edward Shapiro pointed out, that "American Jews seemed to have opted for a Judaism of affiliation without ritual observance or synagogue attendance."[98] The historian Jonathan Sarna argued that, in the 1950s, "affiliation, suburban institution-building, and a new interest in theology had cheered the hearts of rabbis." However, a true multifaceted revival in American Judaism that included greater emphasis on ritual and spirituality would not flourish until the 1970s.[99] Hence, although the prevailing national ideology revered religion during the postwar years, Americans of different faiths actually became less devout by 1960.

Religious advocates warned against intermarriage because, as the strict definitional borders between the three major religions in the United States blurred, increasing intermarriage rates diminished religious and denominational distinctiveness. If Protestantism, Catholicism, and Judaism belonged to the same American religious puzzle, interfaith marriages threatened to make the puzzle pieces indistinguishable. The sociologist Will Herberg theologized in 1955 that religious identification and affiliation demonstrated Americans' social necessity of "belonging" that was not exclusively based in faith. Religious identification was indicative of Americans "locating themselves socially" in a way that was "quite compatible

with the prevalence and even growth of secularism." Protestantism, Catholicism, and Judaism could be described as three branches of "American
religion," he contended: "three diverse representations of the same 'spiritual values' American democracy is presumed to stand for."[100] Intermarriage thus shook the foundation of religious separatism. Moreover, the
idea that Judaism was an equally valid expression of American religion as
Protestantism and Catholicism helped raise the status of Judaism, and, in
the process, helped diversify the marital options of Jewish women.[101]

Once Judaism reached equal standing with other "American religions"
and intermarriage between faiths became a popular topic in the 1950s, it
was more conceivable to Jewish women that they, too, could marry "out"
as many other Americans had done. However, as discussed in the introduction, because of social and cultural influences, they could not do
so at a rate comparable to that of Jewish men. Popular literary authors
pondered the question of whether people of different religious backgrounds should intermarry and what the personal consequences might
be. Parents frequently sought expert advice regarding their children's interfaith romantic liaisons. Authors commented in 1956 that intermarriage
had become "an everyday occurrence." They also believed that interfaith
marriages were far more precarious than interracial ones, because social
acceptance lulled the former into a false sense of security. The popular
consensus was that, although intermarriage was difficult to sustain, it was
still possible.[102] The late 1950s literature indicated a turn toward slightly
more positive thinking; while intermarrieds faced many challenges, love,
understanding, tolerance, compromise, and mutual respect could enable
successful marriages. One author wrote in 1959 that in the face of many
risks and difficulties, "some couples today *are* managing."[103] Regardless of
whether intermarriage was seen as negative or encouraging, the public
discourse about Americans who married across religious lines shattered
the cultural impression that a Jewish woman's only choice was to marry a
coreligionist. The depiction of intermarriage in popular culture changed
dramatically between 1930 and 1960. Whereas earlier representations illustrated interfaith relationships between members of two low-status ethnic groups, Jews and Catholics, literature and film in the 1930s, 1940s, and
1950s focused on Jews marrying higher-status Gentiles. Although stories
of lower-class Jewish-Catholic marriages did not disappear, changes in the
religious and ethnic composition of many portrayals of fictional couples
suggested that Jews could marry into the upper social echelons of Protestant America.[104]

Along with growing attention in the mass media, intermarriage advice increased in the literature, from scant references in the 1930s to abundant attention two decades later, demonstrating that intermarriage in American society, by the 1950s, had not only become more common but had also become a preoccupation. Initially advice givers of all stripes (clergy, social scientists, and intermarrieds) discussed religious differences between people as impenetrable barriers that should not be bridged. Rebecca E. Mack, illustrating the ongoing Jewish opposition to intermarriage, warned Jewish youth not to make the same "mistake" that she had. In her thirty-nine-page pamphlet, she argued vociferously that intermarriage was "an everlasting life destroyer" and that antisemitism was what a Jewish wife could expect from a Gentile husband.[105] Similarly Rabbi Jacob J. Weinstein encouraged Jewish parents in 1941 to help daughters "achieve simple, unpretentious standards" so as to avoid intermarriage.[106] He believed that Jewish men were driven to marry Gentiles because Jewish women expected the same standard of comfort as their mothers, reflecting a negative stereotype of Jewish women as excessively materialistic.[107]

Other literature focused on how to handle rather than prevent intermarriage. For example, the June 1941 issue of *Ladies' Home Journal* advised intermarrying couples to make several decisions at the time of engagement. These included the wedding location, who would officiate, and the religious training of the children.[108] The author apparently assumed that the wedding would be a religious ceremony and that children would be reared with a religious orientation. Another columnist suggested that the interfaith couple should decide "just how the active believer in one faith is going to look on the casual follower of the other faith and vice versa," and to choose a single faith for children to follow.[109] This advice illustrates the belief that religion was often more important to one spouse than to the other in an intermarriage.

Intermarriage presumably affected so many people by the 1950s that advice came in new forms of significant depth and with complex Jewish connections, suggesting to Jewish women that ancestry was not destiny. Moreover, in the postwar years, brotherly love and the idea that one God heard everyone's prayers shifted advice in a more ecumenical direction.[110] In 1954 the Public Affairs Committee, a nonprofit educational organization, announced in the *New York Times* the publication of a twenty-eight-page advice manual titled "If I Marry Outside My Religion."[111] The publication was authored by Algernon D. Black, a leader of the Ethical Culture Societies in America, and offered balanced counsel on the issues confronting those who took the interfaith leap, though he personally did not. Felix Adler, the immigrant son of a German rabbi who likewise married endogamously, had founded the Ethical Culture Movement in 1876 and was subsequently marginalized by the New York City Jewish community. He remained the movement's moral and spiritual leader until his death in 1933. A professor of Hebrew and Oriental Literature at Cornell University, Adler delivered one ill-received address to his father's Reform congregation titled "The Judaism of the Future," which proposed ridding the religion of what he considered superstitious traditions in order to better focus on ethics.[112] The Jewish publication *The Day* referenced Ethical Culture in 1924 as "founded by well-meaning Jews who were out of touch with the true nature of the Jewish problem."[113] Although on the periphery of organized religions, the Ethical Culture movement grew to include Societies in twenty cities across America, including the Ethical Society of Boston established in 1955, which still exists today.[114]

Jewish women who were interested in intermarriage could readily find cogent advice by the end of the 1950s. One book, for example, pinpointed the problem in all marriages, intermarriages and otherwise, as the lack of significance of formal religion in the couple's life. Though by no means advocating intermarriage, the author saw it as an opportunity to foreground religion by choosing a singular Church representing both individuals' convictions; in his words: "then there will be no mixed marriage. And that is the end of the problem."[115] Others suggested that compromise was the best method to mitigate cultural differences.[116] These ideas of uniting people in one house of prayer and of compromise are emblematic of the rise of the Judeo-Christian tradition that emphasized similarities over differences between Americans who could worship side by side as servicemen had proved possible during World War II.[117] Taken together, these new forms of advice literature demonstrate the extent to which intermarriage had become considerably more commonplace by 1960 than it had been three decades earlier.

Individuals involved in successful marriages across religion, ethnicity, and race shared firsthand accounts in 1939, 1941, and increasingly in the 1950s, which personalized the intermarriage experience for Jewish women. Two anonymous writers—one Jewish, the other Gentile—offered their perspectives on being married to a Gentile and a Jew, respectively, in the *Atlantic Monthly* in January and March of 1939. In "I Married a Jew," a non-Jewish wife described her marriage as "supremely happy." However, her contention that harmonious relationships between Jews and Gentiles could be accomplished was couched in calumnies against Jews and assimilatory rhetoric, weakening her very purpose. She contended that Jews were unsatisfactory citizens who should become less Jewish by throwing off "their dead and outmoded culture and traditions, their false pride of race"; "today it is America that is offering the children of Israel the greatest opportunity in history for absorption." According to this author, Hitler was "merely writing another page in history."[118] The author of "I Married a Gentile" advocated that husbands and wives should regard each other as individuals rather than as representatives of their races. He criticized the other author's reference to her husband's "Jewish hypersensitivity toward all criticisms of his race," and explained that his choice of a Gentile wife had everything to do with happiness and being at peace with her.[119] The emphases on absorption in the one article and on individualism in the other illustrate the coexisting priorities of assimilation and individual success over religious group cohesion and ethnic inheritance. In 1941 another *Atlantic Monthly* author elaborated on her intermarriage experience. Contrary to dire predictions attributed to "racial" differences, she learned that Jews had "the same virtues and vices as other people."[120] Written before World War II, the frank dismissal of antisemitic beliefs was progressive for its time.

Intermarrieds who wrote in the 1950s directed personal comments to the sociological studies (see the introduction) and mass media reports, as if to counter the negative reports with anecdotal evidence. An August 1951 article in *Woman's Home Companion* titled "My Mixed Marriage Was Happy" explained that the recipe for contentment lay in having a generosity of spirit so as to nurture whatever one's spouse held dear.[121] "For over forty years I've borne the semi-odium of having contracted a mixed marriage. I've squirmed, shrugged and almost writhed at times under the lash of talks, sermons, and occasional diatribes against this unquestionably serious defection," wrote one husband in a 1952 article, underscoring the persistent stigma of intermarriage. He argued that it was the propinquity provided by the secular and state universities that led to matrimony across faiths, not the proportion of Catholics in the total population.[122] After her 1952 marriage to a white drummer, a black blues singer was quoted in *Life* as saying that there was only one race, the human one. Regarding their raucous celebration, she commented: "All this is crazy. But we're happy, oh my, we're happy!"[123] "Our East-West Marriage Is Working" was the title of a December 1955 article arguing that marriages between American servicemen and Japanese brides stood a better chance of success because the couples knew from the start that they had to work for their happiness.[124]

Written after the American government incarcerated the West Coast Japanese American population during the war, this article suggested that Japanese ethnicity, like European ethnicity, no longer threatened America as both had done earlier in the century.[125] These accounts belie the existence of unhappy marriages, which certainly existed, but offered insider testimony to Jewish women that conflicted with "expert" opinions highlighting the pitfalls of intermarriage.

Antisemitism

Public commentary, personal testimonials, and fountains of advice made intermarriage less foreign, particularly to a Jewish woman seeking to free herself from the yoke of prejudice and the ghosts of antisemitism. Women who married "out" between 1930 and 1945 did so in the face of rising antisemitism, suggesting that Jew hatred could have unexpected social consequences. The nativism responsible for the immigrant quotas of the 1920s made descendants of Eastern Europeans cautious about displays of ethnicity.[126] Antisemitism increased during the Great Depression and peaked during the Second World War. The economic crisis, Protestant and Catholic demagogues, established Protestant fundamentalism, and widespread expression of anti-Jewish attitudes by respectable social and religious leaders culminated in violent physical attacks in Boston and other cities. Some Americans believed in an international Jewish conspiracy geared toward controlling the United States government.[127] Jew hatred permeated American society in the 1930s such that, in the words of the historian Leonard Dinnerstein, "Hitler's attacks on Jews as the root causes of the world's economic and social problems no longer seemed so outrageous to genteel bigots."[128] Some antisemites even claimed that Jewish influence over President Franklin D. Roosevelt was responsible for the "Jew Deal."[129] In the 1930s and early 1940s, Father Charles Coughlin, a priest, aired Nazi propaganda in his radio speeches, uncensored by the Catholic archdiocese.[130] An unknown number of American Jews modified or changed their names to better blend in. Hostility toward Jews continued to grow during the war years. In a November 1942 poll asking American high school students which group would be their last choice as a roommate, Jews fared the worst after Negroes, preceded by Irish, Protestants, Swedes, Catholics, and Chinese.[131] That same year 40 percent of Americans thought that Jews had too much power.[132] And in 1943 the Office of War Information found "widespread animosity toward Jews" in half of the forty-two states it surveyed.[133]

Social conditions remained tense for those women who married "out" during the postwar years. Actual antisemitism declined after World War II, and it became less socially acceptable to openly express anti-Jewish rhetoric. The archbishop of Boston Richard Cushing publicly condemned antisemitism and bragged that his own sister had married a Jew.[134] Although the interwar years had fostered the emergent Jewish ethnic community, the fact that Jewish and Gentile servicemen had fought alongside each other in Europe promoted the idea of an American national community in which Jews had full membership in the postwar period.[135] "Amnesia" may have encouraged some Jews to turn away from the war's atrocities, but it did not enable all American Jews to feel secure in a predominantly Gentile country. Memories of antisemitism convinced many Jews that it was still pervasive; Jewish history, personal experience, and the shadow of the Holocaust caused many Jews to overestimate the extent and depth of anti-Jewish fervor in the United States throughout the late 1940s and the 1950s. Public opinion surveys indicated a sharp decline in antisemitism since 1945, but most American Jews did not believe it was true.[136] Joseph R. McCarthy appeared on the political scene in 1950 as a popular anticommunist demagogue. The close connection between fascism and antisemitism in Europe and a belief that the rise of fascism in America would be disguised as anticommunism made many Jews fearful that they were vulnerable to the Great Red Scare.[137] Simultaneously the elimination of anti-Jewish real estate practices, country club membership, and resort restrictions helped to create opportunities for Jews and Gentiles to mingle more.[138] "Psychological insecurity," to quote Shapiro again, manifested itself in intermarriage for some Jewish women.[139]

Antisemitism, which some historians believe deterred Gentiles from marrying Jews,[140] may have actually influenced some women's decisions to marry non-Jewish men. Twelve out of fourteen of the women whose narratives are discussed in this chapter commented with vivid clarity about their personal experiences with antisemitism. From a young age, women were aware that being Jewish was negatively perceived by some Americans. The following examples illustrate that antisemitism played a memorable role in the lives of some women who intermarried. Sarah Pene, who was born in 1917, grew up in the West End of Boston and in Roxbury, Massachusetts. Sarah recalled her classmates throwing stones and snowballs at her because "I was a Jew."[141] Marilyn Rinalto was born in 1927 and grew up in Manhattan. A friend told Marilyn she couldn't play with her anymore after being taught in parochial school that Jews killed Christ.[142]

Ruth McBride, whose story was told through her son in *The Color of Water*, was born in Poland and immigrated to America in 1923 at the age of two. She recalled being compelled by law to attend an all-white school in the South and being taunted.

> It was a problem from the moment I started because the white kids hated Jews in my school. "Hey, Ruth, when did you start being a dirty Jew?" they'd ask. I couldn't stand being ridiculed. I even changed my name to try to fit in more. My real name was Rachel, which in Yiddish is Ruckla, which is what my parents called me—but I used the name Ruth around white folk, because it didn't sound so Jewish, though it never stopped the other kids from teasing me.[143]

This passage makes clear that neither she herself nor her classmates considered Ruth white. Antisemitism extended into women's adult years and affected their educational and employment opportunities. Harriet Mansfield remembered the complaint lodged by her college roommate's father in the late thirties or early forties: "I send you all the way East to go to college and you're rooming with a Jew?!"[144] Margaret Doherty remembered being told by prospective employers: "I'm sorry, we don't hire Jews."[145] Many such recollections suggest that discrimination was a significant part of intermarried Jewish women's consciousness.

Psychological theories help ground the connection between women's experiences with antisemitism and their decisions to intermarry. In their 1959 study, "Jews Who Intermarry," psychologists Maria and Daniel Levinson contended that antisemitism had provoked rejection and reinforced feelings of inferiority, adding to a desire for emancipation from parents. Self-doubts of those who intermarried were counteracted by an anti-ethnocentric ideology including an emphasis on individual worth apart from ethnic or other group membership.[146] Some women exhibited what one scholar called a "counterphobic attraction to Gentiles," perhaps out of a desire to identify with the non-Jewish population and proclaim that America was indeed safe for Jews.[147]

Jewish self-hatred was a factor in some Jewish women's intermarriages. According to the historian Sander Gilman, the concept of self-hatred began in late-nineteenth-century Germany and spread to the United States before and during the Holocaust as part of the rhetoric of race. The psychological model of Germans as monolithically German was undermined by the myth of American heterogeneity. "When applied to the American

Jewish experience," wrote Gilman, "it provided a working label for the sig-
nification of specific models of divergence, models that eventually turned
upon the ideological implication of 'Jewish self hatred.'"[148] The psychologist Irving Sarnoff in his research on personality found that the Jewish an-
tisemite displaced hostility toward himself and his family onto the Jewish
community, and thus the inclination to intermarry and assimilate, down-
playing Jewish identity.[149] About two-thirds of the women I interviewed
who married between 1930 and 1960 expressed unease with being Jewish,
and one admitted being antisemitic. Their comments reflect what Glenn
called a "vogue of Jewish self-hatred in post-world war II America."[150]
Some women intermarried out of discomfort with their own Jewishness.
Hetty Miller's sentiments and her 1952 choice of a Gentile spouse illustrate
Sarnoff's thesis. She commented: "I felt the Jewish people were for want
of a better word—I hate to say this—snotty. And I never felt comfortable
with them. Maybe I didn't like *myself* as a Jew so I didn't like other people
who were Jewish."[151] Hetty's self-loathing made marrying a coreligionist
unappealing. Another woman thought it was a compliment when someone mistook her for a Gentile. Alice Lawrence's antipathy for what she
termed the "ethnic manifestation" of Judaism—including an overemphasis
on clothes, cars, and money—made her pleased whenever someone told
her, "Oh, I didn't know you were Jewish. You don't *seem* it."[152] Alice's positive interpretation of this comment indicates her low opinion of being
Jewish. Intermarriage could be a salve as well as an exit route.

While far from being an actual antidote for antisemitism, scholars, popular writers, and the intermarried suggested that intermarriage reduced
discrimination. In a December 1939 article, a University of Pennsylvania
professor theorized that when a group married within itself, more prejudice against the group resulted. Conversely, as intermarriage increased,
so, too, did the degree of social acceptance between the two population
groups involved.[153] An anti-Zionist author argued vociferously in the January 1946 *Scientific Monthly* that intermarriage was the "best means" to
convince Gentiles that Jews were human beings with similar beliefs and
sentiments. He concluded, "Thus it is the most important task and almost
a *social mission* of the mixed marriage to bring the two population groups
together on an equal basis and fuse them also in a spiritual union."[154] The
author of a September 1941 *Atlantic Monthly* essay contended that she
broke through the "circle of myth and speculation" about Jews by marrying one. She discussed, and then discounted, negative characteristics
assigned to Jews, including clannishness, emotionalism, shrewdness, and

trickery. She explained her new insight with the statement: "Psychologically, I was a Gentile for twenty-six years. Now I am a Jew."[155] The author's intermarriage prompted her beliefs to shift from antisemitic to semitic. A popular magazine author noted that the problems caused by religious differences might someday be resolved, and that "some couples may even think they can bring that day nearer by marrying across the frontiers of faith."[156] Yvonne Evans experienced prejudice growing up in Waltham, Massachusetts, in the 1940s and intermarried in 1952. Yvonne concurred with her Presbyterian husband, who used to say, "The cure for antisemitism is intermarriage."[157] Though seemingly illogical, the idea is similar to recent efforts to build friendships between Israelis and Palestinians with the goal of peace in the Middle East. Harriet Mansfield explained why she thought that intermarriage was a good way to solve religious problems. "If you're married to a Jew, you're not going to be crusading against them."[158] Interfaith marriage may have reduced some individuals' antisemitism, but it is unlikely that the romantic notion of "love conquers all" had much influence on views held by people not immediately involved. Like racism, American antisemitism was systemic and structural rather than solely the work of individual antisemites.[159] Although none of the women intermarried with the purpose of combating antisemitism, marriage to a non-Jew appeared to some as a safety raft in an uncertain sea.

Intermarriage offered an individualistic and alternative path for some Jewish women who felt fortunate to be loved by a non-Jew in a discriminatory society. Living in an antisemitic environment could motivate people to intermarry; the insecurity antisemitism caused was allayed by having a Gentile spouse and, theoretically if not practically, acceptance in the non-Jewish world.[160] Total integration through intermarriage was one way for Jews to cope with the limitations they faced from the 1920s through the end of World War II.[161] Jews sometimes married non-Jews out of a desire for social security and acceptance by members of the Gentile group.[162] In 1940 the sociologist Uriah Zevi Engelman found that intermarriage had actually increased during the growth of the Nazi movement in Germany, when some Jews sought intermarriage to avoid the curtailment of ambitions and careers owing to antisemitic pressure.[163] The increase ended when Jewish-"Aryan" marriage was declared a crime by the "Law for the Protection of German Blood and Honor," one of the Nuremberg Laws of September 1935.[164] There has never been an anti-interreligious marriage law in the United States regarding marriage with a Jew to limit American Jewish women. Carolyn Jasper's determination to wed the man of her choice was not atypical. She remembered the Jewish quotas for college acceptance and the difficulty of career advancement. Carolyn remarked that as long as her husband was "willing" to marry her in 1945, she would not break it off no matter what her family did.[165] Her personal goal of escaping into the majority mainstream was stronger than her allegiance to her parents.

Intermarriage in the 1930s, 1940s, and 1950s provided a means to elude one's Jewish environment and a ticket to a more secure life of domesticity, while facilitating both flight from and connection to an oppressed past. Harriet Mansfield described her transition through marriage to a Congregationalist as follows: "I was suddenly out of that kind of intensely all-Jewish circle into what were more congenial, cooler, WASP Protestant circles."[166] She equated the change to a ticket up the social ladder, reflecting an individual case of what the sociologist Robert K. Merton termed "hypergamy" in 1941: "patterns of intermarriage wherein the female marries into a higher social stratum."[167] Two of the women interviewed were World War II refugees. Georgia Summer fled a childhood of antisemitism in Vienna in 1938. When asked whether personal persecution affected her decision to marry a non-Jew and how she chose to raise her children, Georgia responded: "Probably, yes . . . because in some ways I've wondered lately whether I was running away from all of this."[168] Getting married, settling into a home of her own for the first time, learning to cook, and starting a family—that is, fulfilling the prevalent domestic ideology— provided a safe haven and held more immediacy than Georgia's ties to Judaism. Born in Belgrade, Yugoslavia, in 1936, Paula Avante migrated to Italy during World War II, where strangers and the Church protected her family by including them in the Catholic community. After emigrating to the United States, she met and married an Italian Catholic in 1959. She liked that he was Catholic because it enabled an ongoing connection to the Church that saved her life.[169] Anti-Jewish sentiment, however, made complete escape impossible.

The tenacity of antisemitic cultural assumptions followed women into their married lives. In a 1939 article titled "The Shadow of Anti-Semitism," the male writer, whose name was withheld for "obvious reasons," described his Jewish wife's conversion to the Episcopalian faith and his fear for their children's future in what he considered a dangerously antisemitic society. He complained, "Whatever system of worship we may choose, the world regards me as a Christian and my wife as a Jewess."[170] Concern about the children of the intermarried suffering from antisemitism was prevalent. The authors of the 1948 book *Building a Successful Marriage* contended that Gentile prejudice against Jews stood in the way of successful inter-marriages by deterring the non-Jewish spouse from identifying with Jews as a group and by causing the Gentile concern about their child enduring discrimination.[171] Implicit in this contention is that intermarriage was best avoided. A 1943 letter describing a Gentile wife begging her husband not to reveal his Jewish identity for the sake of their children illustrates this subjective scenario.[172] One Christian mother, upon learning that her child planned to marry a Jew, blurted out "I don't want any Jewish grandchildren," an indication that prejudice continued into 1959.[173]

Antisemitism persisted when Lynne Ianiello wrote "Life on the Fence: The Jewish Partner in a Mixed Marriage Gets a Clear—and Painful—View of Prejudice" in September 1960. Ianiello, who identified in the article as a happily intermarried Jew, described the many instances when people with whom she interacted denigrated Jews without realizing she was one. Apparently her non-Jewish sounding last name, and the fact that she did not "look Jewish," made people think that she would not mind their antisemitic banter. They thought wrong.[174] The assumption that a woman was not Jewish if she did not have particular features or a typical Jewish last name illustrates how physical appearance and surnames were confounded with religious identity. Antisemitism may have encouraged women to intermarry while at the same time discouraging them from overtly identifying as Jewish.

Race and racism, both anti-black and anti-white, were more important than religion in interracial marriage. In the memoir *How I Became Hettie Jones,* the former Hettie Cohen described her 1958 marriage to the charismatic black writer Leroi Jones. At twenty-three, she left Laurelton, Long Island, for the bohemia that was Greenwich Village, entering the world of jazz music, poetry, and politics. Her own identity was ambiguous even before she fell in love: "Black/white was a slippery division for me."[175] As Hettie entwined her social life with a black man, she "was haunted by the problem of remaining a Jew, but I didn't know how to reinvent a Jewish woman who wasn't a Jewish wife." [176] Hettie was convinced that their interracial children would socially be black and that her family would effectively disown her: "And white I would be, because I knew the Jews—mine at least—would give me up."[177] Attending Yom Kippur services for the last time before intermarrying, Hettie begged forgiveness "for the sin of breaking off the yoke . . . for being someone these people could not influence, or hold, forgive me, but this is America . . . sometimes you have to go on the road."[178] Yet Jewishness clung to Hettie in racialized form: "I couldn't cease to think of myself as a Jew—a Semite really—I no longer felt Jewish, or sentimental about it."[179] When she auditioned for a play and left her sleeping daughter in the carriage, she had "Jewish second thoughts" and retrieved the baby.[180] Hettie's interracial marriage ultimately failed in 1965 when Leroi developed a high profile in the Black Power movement and literally shed his white wife.[181] Two people's commitment to make their own rules was not strong enough to win, either symbolically or practically, a country's battle over race.

Familial Reactions

For Jewish parents, memories of antisemitism and the Holocaust made the Gentile men their daughters married during the thirties, forties, and fifties members of "the enemy camp," in the words of Jerome Weidman's postwar novel.[182] Jewish parental concerns included that their intermarried child would become alienated from their family of origin, that the chance for happiness was slim, that latent antisemitism could erupt in crises, and that the future of Judaism and the Jewish people would be threatened if their grandchildren were raised as Christians.[183] The children of the intermarried consistently preoccupied the discourse about intermarriage from the 1930s on. The sociologist Ray Baber contended, in 1937: "Children are sometimes the *casus belli,* and sometimes the factor directly responsible for the reconciliation of opposing grandparents."[184] And experienced parents of newlyweds, according to the *New York Times Magazine* in 1960, evinced "grave concern . . . for the future children of mixed marriages." [185] That at least 70 percent of the children of mixed marriages were raised as non-Jews suggests that parents' fears were not baseless.[186] The loss to the Jewish population concerned Jewish demographers, even if it was not a central issue for women who intermarried. One 1943 source contended that if three children of an intermarried couple were raised as Christians, within three generations, one Jew who intermarried might be responsible for thirty-nine people "lost to Judaism!"[187] Many observers compared intermarriage to the Holocaust, suggesting that when American Jews intermarried they compounded Hitler's murder of two million Jewish children who should have lived to reproduce and replenish the Jewish population.[188] That the fertility of the Jewish population in the United States was barely sufficient to replace itself by the late 1950s contributed to alarm over the religious upbringing of the children of intermarriages.[189]

Although public opposition to intermarriage waned somewhat between 1930 and 1960, parental objection among Jews remained strong. A

November 1951 Gallup Poll based on a sample of 2,019 adults reported that 54 percent of respondents would not object to a son or daughter marrying a person of a different religious faith.[190] This information may be indicative of an evolving national perspective toward more tolerance of intermarriage, but national poll information is not conclusive proof that American parents of all religious backgrounds approved of it. "Disease," "ailment," "sickness," and "epidemic," were Jewish synonyms for intermarriage as late as 1958.[191] As one contemporary writer observed, Jewish families placed intermarriage in a similar category as cholera. They explained deploringly: "You can never tell when it will happen to you."[192] Equating intermarriage with an acute infectious disease connoted that it was an affliction as well as a *shande,* something disgraceful. By and large, endogamy remained a cultural if not a religious imperative. Parents' refusal to accept their children's proposed marriage prompted one Jewish-Gentile couple to attempt suicide. The newspaper headline read "Tragedy Mars Abie's Irish Romance," alluding to the 1927 novel (and 1928 film) about intermarriage titled *Abie's Irish Rose.*[193]

Although Jewish parents were more adamantly opposed, Gentile families were not altogether welcoming of intermarriage either. Acceptance of Jewish spouses by Gentile families was higher than acceptance of Gentile spouses by Jewish families, suggesting that Jewish parents were more resistant to intermarriage than were their Christian counterparts.[194] The results of a 1953 poll conducted by *Woman's Home Companion* showed that, in their sample, only 42 percent of Jewish mothers would approve their child intermarrying compared to 58 percent of Protestant mothers and 61 percent of Catholic mothers.[195] However, in 1953, the Catholic Archdiocese of Chicago disclosed a report that 54 percent of the Catholics and 75 percent of the Protestants questioned objected to a member of their family marrying a person of a different religion.[196] In 1957 one Catholic family actually sued a Lutheran family for allegedly enticing their Catholic son away from his faith to wed the Lutheran family's daughter.[197] Some women I interviewed experienced derisive comments from their families-in-law, including being referred to as "that Jew-girl he married" and a "White Jew."[198] The latter meant acceptable, relative to black people, in the white Christian community.

Tradition, consisting of racial and religious taboos, religious and group ties, motivated some Jewish parents to react a certain way to their children's intermarriages. Intermarriage was considered so unforgivable among some Jews that parents would urge against intermarriage in their wills, and even grieve a child who intermarried as if she were deceased.[199]

Abraham S. Rosenthal, a wealthy silk importer, stipulated before he died in 1938 that if any of his descendants married outside the Jewish faith they would forfeit their rights to their inheritance. He must have cringed in his grave when the law ruled on a technicality in favor of his great-grand-daughter in 1954. "Court Allows Heiress to Defy Will, Wed Outside Faith, Get Legacy," read the headline about Jean Lincoln Tanburn, the Vassar College graduate who intended to marry Donelson Morrison Kelley Jr.[200] That the *New York Times* placed the article on its front page suggests that the editor knew the decision would evoke controversy and deemed the story worthy of attention.

Familial reactions to Jewish women's intermarriages were negative for the majority of Jewish women I interviewed, perhaps because anti-intermarriage sentiment among Jewish families overpowered the domestic ideology encouraging women to wed. Ten out of fourteen of the women encountered opposition based on religious difference when they told their parents they planned to wed a non-Jewish man. Two women faced objections based on class, age, divorce, or how the woman met her betrothed. The anticipation of familial or communal disapproval sometimes inspired the women to avoid disclosing the news. Secrecy, manifested as elopement or concealment of having married, was a relevant factor in seven women's experiences. One mother did not tell the father of their child's intermarriage in 1950. Other parents disguised their offspring's intermarriage in 1956 as an in-marriage to avoid social judgment. One woman's parents did not express concern when she planned to intermarry, as her brother already had. And one woman's family was relieved that she would not end up an "old maid," illustrating how many Americans agreed with the experts that women who remained single would, in May's words, "be doomed to an unfulfilled and miserable existence."[201] Intermarriage remained a highly sensitive issue for most Jewish women and their families through 1960, as the following personal stories illuminate.

In some cases, parental reactions were sufficiently strong as to create long-lasting rifts between Jewish women and their families. Sarah Pene was the daughter of poor, Orthodox, Eastern European immigrants. She unintentionally became romantically involved with a non-Jew; she assumed he was Jewish because he worked in a Jewish bakery. When Sarah decided to wed her Italian Catholic sweetheart in 1938 she told him: "You have to turn Jewish if you want me to marry you because I don't know how I could live with a Gentile." He agreed and told Sarah's mother he intended to convert. She forbade the marriage, ordered him to go home, marry a nice Italian Catholic girl, and leave her daughter alone. Sarah married him secretly with the help of a Justice of the Peace. When Sarah's mother learned that Sarah had intermarried, she evicted her from the house and the two did not speak for three years.[202] When Carolyn Jasper's mother realized that her daughter intended to wed her Congregational boyfriend in 1945, their relationship deteriorated such that they did not talk to each other for about nine months. The two families were similar economically and socially, but both sides objected to the difference in religious background.[203] Ruth McBride remembered her relatives' reactions when she married a black man in 1942: "My family mourned me when I married your father. They said *kaddish* and sat *shiva*. That's how Orthodox Jews mourn their dead."[204] However, it was uncommon for a family to actually go to this extreme. Margaret Doherty's mother was told by an Orthodox rabbi to mourn her daughter as dead because Margaret had intermarried, but she insisted that her daughter was "very much alive!"[205] Multiple women remembered their mothers defying this mandate. Still, refusal to mourn one's child did not mean acceptance of their intermarriage.

Parents' concern about social stigmatization demonstrated that Jewish-Gentile intermarriage remained a serious taboo. The response of Ann Carlton's mother, a Conservative Jew, shows her disapproval: "Well, we won't disown you because who am I going to spite?" She was anxious about what other family members would think when Ann intermarried in 1956. Intermarriage was verboten, and to have a daughter intermarry reflected negatively on family members. Ann's brother said he *would* "disown" her, and her grandmother expressed interest in paying for her betrothed to be circumcised.[206] Alice Lawrence's father came to her college campus in 1960 with an amethyst ring and this guilt-loaded request: "Please do this for me; don't marry him." That her fiancé was physically disabled compounded the fact that he wasn't Jewish. They worried about what to tell their family and friends, Alice recalled: "I was treated as the black sheep of both my mother's and my father's extended families." She was not told that other cousins had intermarried, only that she had ruined her grandfather's life by marrying a Gentile and that she could never see him again, which she did not. After Alice wed a non-Jew, she did not see her mother for two years.[207] Hetty Miller's father and aunt tried to break off her interfaith relationship. She explained why they did this: "Jewish people just didn't intermarry; they felt very strongly—even though I wasn't brought up religiously—you just didn't intermarry."[208] It was assumed that Jews married Jews, period. Apparently diminished religiosity was sometimes irrelevant when it came to how parents felt about their offspring marrying outside the fold.

Strong Jewish group identification rather than religious fervor prompted parents to respond vehemently against their daughters' intentions of inter-marrying. Jacob Kohn, author of *Modern Problems of Jewish Parents,* was familiar with this popular contradiction. He wrote in 1932, "I have known men and women who have scarcely a shred of Judaism left, who never employ a Jewish phrase of any spiritual significance, but who in discuss-ing intermarriage will tell you that they cannot contemplate their children marrying a 'shegitz' or a 'shiksah.'"[209] He attributed the scorn of the Jew for the Gentile to centuries of oppression, and the use of disparaging terms for a non-Jewish man and a non-Jewish woman as an outdated ghetto de-fense mechanism against Jewish discontinuity. Harriet Mansfield's family typifies the inconsistency between parents who did not emphasize Jewish living to their daughter, yet responded with exaggerated negativity when she planned to intermarry. They never observed Shabbat. Nevertheless, her mother's initial response to Harriet's decision to wed, in her words, a "WASP New Englander," was emphatic: "Over my dead body!"[210]

Parental disapproval was forceful enough to encourage some women to wait to intermarry until their parents actually died. Hence death was not solely a hyperbolic threat; it had an intimate relationship with the timing of some women's intermarriages. Although individual conviction did not prevent Jewish women from marrying non-Jewish men, pressure from parents and communal criticism sometimes thwarted intermarriage plans, at least temporarily.[211] A 1946 study found that a higher proportion of the parents of the intermarried were deceased when their children wed than was the case among those who married coreligionists.[212] As one woman responded when asked how her family and her husband's family reacted to the couple's decision to wed: "Families like it fine, it's the mothers that cause all the problems and our mothers are dead."[213] Whether this was unfair mother bashing or an accurate indication of Jewish mothers' par-ticipation in their daughters' romantic decisions is difficult to say. Perhaps both are true. Six of the fourteen women included in this chapter had mothers who were deceased when they married Gentiles. Tamar Reynold met her Gentile beau right after high school. However, the couple did not wed until she was forty-nine, after a courtship of more than a quarter of a century. Tamar's mother vehemently opposed the relationship, so they waited until she died to marry.[214] Ultimately her mother could not prevent the marriage.

Jewish motherhood was socially constructed to be responsible for en-dogamy. "Who more than the Jewish woman carries the concern for the education of her child, and who lives through tragedy when her son or daughter brings an alien spouse into her home?" Rabbi David Kirshen-baum contended in 1958. "Who can bear the weeping and laments of the Jewish mother when she feels with motherly instinct the danger . . . a mixed marriage entails for her child and her family?"[215] Ann Carlton's mother internalized her social responsibility. "I haven't done a good job because you're not marrying somebody Jewish," she told her daughter.[216] Many of the stories of women who were Jewish when they married non-Jewish men highlight the significance of the mother's role in their daugh-ter's lives. Maternal influence and death could also affect a woman's reli-gious affiliation or fervor.

A mother's death could have a profound effect on a daughter's religious life. Ruth McBride formally became a Christian after her mother died. Her high school graduation had been held in a church, and as she ap-proached it she stepped out of the line of students. "I just couldn't go in-side that church. In my heart I was still a Jew. I had done some wrongs in my life, but I was still my parents' child."[217] She felt differently some years later. Although not yet married to her first husband (she married twice, both times to black men), Ruth decided it was time to give up her Jewish identity. She had not been present when her mother died and was filled with both grief and guilt. She began attending Metropolitan Church in Harlem, and the words of forgiveness eased her pain. Ruth recounted, "It helped me to hear the Christian way, because I needed help, and I needed to let Mameh go, and that's when I started to become a Christian and the Jew in me began to die. The Jew in me was dying anyway, but it truly died when my mother died."[218] When Sarah Pene, who kept absolutely kosher before she wed, accidentally ate a donut fried in animal fat while drinking a carton of milk, she thought she was going to die and recited the *Sh'ma*, the appropriate prayer. She awoke the next morning and thought some-thing must be wrong. "That's when I started having arguments with my mother about religion," Sarah remembered. She associated her own even-tual lessening of Orthodoxy to this experience and to her mother's death, *not* to her intermarriage.[219]

Death was also treated humorously to portray the unbearable pain a Jewish mother would endure if her daughter married a Gentile. The fol-lowing Jewish joke (one told by a Jew to a Jew and about a Jew)[220] ap-peared in a 1958 issue of *Midstream*:

A Jewish girl calls up her mother, and the following conversation ensues:
"Mama, I'm married."
"*Mazel Tov!* That's wonderful."
"But, mama, my husband is a Catholic."
"So? Not everyone is a Jew.
"But, mama, he's a Negro."
"What of it? The world has all kinds. We gotta be tolerant."
"But mama, he has no job."
"Nu, that's all right."
"But, mama, we have no place to stay."
"Oh, you'll stay right here in this house."
"Where, mama? There's no room."
"Well, you and your husband can sleep in our bedroom; Papa will sleep on the sofa."
"Yes, but, mama, where will *you* sleep?"
"Oh, don't worry about me, darling. As soon as I hang up I'm going to drop dead."[221]

This humorous piece depicts the coexisting tensions regarding plural-ism and intermarriage in postwar Jewish American culture. It also con-notes the mother's heightened significance relative to the father: she would be dead but he would just be sleeping. That the daughter in the joke calls her mother only *after* she married fits the secretive practice mentioned earlier. The new husband's unemployment is another negative factor. Fi-nally, that the non-Jewish husband is black emphasizes how far outside acceptable behavior the Jewish woman's marriage was according to con-ventional Jewish standards. Historically, in post World War II America, the organized Jewish attitude toward intermarriage was primarily condi-tioned by religious, not racial, considerations.[222] This may have been the case in theory, but the joke suggests that, in practice, a daughter's mar-riage to a black Gentile added insult to injury. Although intermarriage had become more commonplace in American society by 1960, the Jewish tradition of endogamy had not loosened its grasp on Jewish daughters.

Identity

After they disobeyed their parents and tradition by intermarrying, Jewish women who sought inclusion within a new fold usually chose Unitarianism over Catholicism or one of the strictly Protestant denominations. Though the numbers are too small to be conclusive, it is worth noting that of the fourteen women interviewed, one-third eventually found their way to the Unitarian Church and two-thirds continued to identify only as Jewish.[223] That most of the women did not take on their husband's religion is remarkable, given the contemporary pressure on American wives to be subordinate to their husbands, which increased during the postwar years.[224] None of the women's husbands converted to Judaism. Unitarianism presented an alternative to Christian religions that worshiped Jesus. Many Jewish women expressed strong reservations about the religious significance of Jesus, which in turn affected how they affiliated. For example, Harriet Mansfield was offended when her daughter came home from a Congregational Sunday School with a picture of Jesus. The family then joined the Unitarian Church, where there was an emphasis on diversity, inclusiveness, and acceptance rather than on the New Testament's "Son of God."[225]

Unitarian Universalism, the no-dogma, no-creed religion, offered something unique to Jewish women who married Christians. It enabled them to locate a religious middle ground with their spouses, one that did not accuse them of being Christ killers nor ask them to renounce their inherited faith and adopt another. Ann Carlton, who was born in 1933 and grew up near the Jersey Shore, commented that "it was very easy to become a Unitarian because I could still practice some of my Jewish things."[226] Unitarianism offered an acceptable compromise as well as unqualified acceptance of Jewish ethnic origins. "I don't think of myself as intermarried anymore," Ann declared, "because everybody has a different background in the Unitarian Church; so mine happens to be Jewish."[227] Despite many European connections, Unitarianism in North America was a domestic religious invention. The Unitarian Universalist historian Mark W. Harris writes, "Our history has carried us from liberal Christian views about Jesus and human nature to a rich pluralism that includes theist and atheist, agnostic and humanist, pagan, Christian, Jew, and Buddhist."[228] In New England, where many women eventually settled, Unitarianism had a long history, dating back before the Civil War, when Unitarians at Harvard developed a moral philosophy that extolled the virtues of individual conscience, a tradition that persisted into the twentieth century.[229] Unitarianism appealed to women's pluralistic sensibilities and their belief that all people were equal. Moreover, Unitarianism may be the only religion that actually validated interfaith marriages, as suggested by a 1991 pamphlet titled "Affirming Interfaith Marriages." The Unitarian Universalist community invited couples of diverse religious backgrounds and perspectives to contribute as equal members. This represented a sharp contrast to the Jewish and Christian religious communities that did not honor their differences.[230]

Unitarianism also allowed women to identify in multiple ways. The practice of dual identities reflects what psychologists describe as, "an attempt to synthesize a more pluralistic social identity in which specifically ethnic elements play a minor part."[231] Ann Carlton sent out an annual holiday mailing and had two versions, one Jewish and one Christian. The difference was that she would print "Happy Holidays" in blue for the Jewish relatives and something more specific to Christmas for the Christian family members. She kept a *pushke*, a small box for charity. Her *pushke* was a vestige of her religious and ethnic heritage, an ongoing expression of her Jewishness. Ann was considered the "Jewish authority" at her Unitarian church; she conducted the Seder for the Sunday School class and brought in Jewish food. However, growing up amid antisemitism caused her to resist full disclosure about the Jewish part of her identity. A lesson her mother taught Ann about race and religious identity held sway: "Everyone *knows* that blacks are black. Nobody knows that you're Jewish!" She explained, "I'll always *admit* that I'm Jewish *if* asked. But I don't come forward all the time and say that I am." Ann was concerned that people might view her differently because of her Jewish background, so she provided a nickname when she met someone, keeping her real name hidden.[232] Although Harriet Mansfield would put "Unitarian" on a hospital form, an example several women volunteered, she made this revealing statement about herself: "You can't take the Jewish apart from the Unitarian."[233] Harriet had a dual identity.

Being "Jewish" stuck with women, regardless of whether they intermarried or chose to identify otherwise. They all maintained some allegiance to the religious identity of their birth, however distant they grew or ran from it. Georgia Summer considered herself a Unitarian, as did her husband, but noted that her intermarriage would always be interfaith because the "outside world" would still see them as different from each other. Regarding her Jewishness, she observed:

> It's part of my background. I know this, and I appreciate it. On the other hand, I also appreciate what I've seen and what I've learned. One of the things the Church does most every year is they have a Seder to introduce some of the children and some of the families to the practice of the Seder. But I have this very wonderful memory of the very traditional Seders

that I saw in London and I don't want to go to this because I somehow don't think it's the real thing. Some of our neighbors when we were close invited us to their Seders and they didn't know what they were doing, frankly! And so I treasure that as part of my background, and I appreciate it, and I want to leave it there, that way.[234]

Yet when she visited her mother's gravesite in Vienna, sixty years after she had left Europe and many years after she married and became a Unitarian, she observed the Jewish tradition of placing a stone on top of the tombstone. "It felt right. *That* was comfortable," she explained.[235] Georgia's emphasis implies that her action and the related emotion were exceptions. Paula Avante disliked the narrow definitions others applied to Jews based on stereotypes and generalizations: "I didn't want to be identified as a Jewish girl. I wanted to be identified as somebody who had a very rich background." But she also avoided telling people her identity, preferring to remain inconspicuous. Still, being Jewish lingered deep within Paula.[236] Some women felt that their Jewishness was in their veins, a biological legacy whether they welcomed it or not.

"Still Jewish" was a double entendre for women who did not feel Jewish but believed that they were Jewish by descent and because of society's understanding of who is a Jew. Carolyn Jasper compared herself to college classmates who had grown up in observant homes. "I never considered myself a Jewish woman. But I never considered that I *wasn't* Jewish. I don't consider that I was ever a Jewish woman the way I think of it. I just . . . wasn't. But I *was* Jewish and obviously I am if you want to look at it that way because my parents were." Being Jewish was something that happened to her by virtue of her birth and had nothing to do with religious observance, whereas becoming a Unitarian was something she initiated. Carolyn was aware that other people still considered her Jewish, although she herself did not.[237] An experience relayed by Alice Lawrence epitomized being labeled a Jew despite having assumed a new religious identity. After attending a bar mitzvah she came home and told her husband: "I was the only person there who wasn't Jewish." He responded, "But you are." Though in her mind she was Unitarian, to others Alice was still Jewish. The Jewish label was socially constructed as permanent; it could not be erased by intermarriage or conversion.

Some Jewish women actually became "more Jewish" long after they intermarried. Several examples illustrate this point. Hetty Miller had been raised in a nearly secular household, intermarried, and, after experimenting with Hinduism and Bahai, became enamored of Hasidism. Her Jewish identity centered on having been "born Jewish," but she also yearned to go to Israel, collected Jewish books, and, as a retired person, moved into Jewish housing for the elderly and associated herself with Jewish people, something she had evaded earlier in life.[238] Harriet Mansfield's childhood was not religious, and she added "Jewish" to her self-identification long after her 1942 marriage. Once she became a socially secure octogenarian in the twenty-first century, she could "face up to the prejudices of the world. I would rather be identified with a minority group that is always under some criticism, so Jewish-Unitarian probably explains me better than just Unitarian."[239] Regardless of her intermarriage Sarah Pene pursued her lifelong desire to ascend to the *bimah* (a raised platform in a synagogue), and in 1998, when she was nearly eighty years old, she became a bat mitzvah.[240] The author Hila Colman, whose third marriage in 1945 was interfaith, became more Jewish when she and her family moved from New York City to a small Connecticut town where her son was the first Jew to enroll in the local school. She was, in her words: "A slice of good dark Jewish bread among a whole bunch of bland white bread eaters."[241] Jewish women's identities, therefore, were affected by intermarriage but also developed independent of it.

Jewish identity within intermarried women's sense of self was not solely a matter of religion or ethnicity or race but rather a complex mix of the three. The first could be changed, as some did when they intermarried, and the latter two were flexible yet tenacious. How women perceived themselves influenced the ways in which they identified. Roughly one-third of the women I interviewed ceased to identify actively as Jewish and yet maintained that being Jewish was part of their ethnic background. A small minority integrated their inherited Jewishness with their acquired non-Jewish affiliation. The majority insisted that they were and always would be Jewish by bloodline, implying that Jewishness was a racial trait as uncontrollable as one's DNA. In intermarriage, ethnic identity and religious identity were not distinct characteristics; instead, one often conditioned the other.[242]

Intermarriage and anti-Jewish associations, moreover, promoted a national identification. A movement toward a more "American" and less psychologically "Jewish" identity could be influenced by negative feelings, anxiety, and resentment toward Jews as a group.[243] Becoming what the historian Arthur Hertzberg termed a "general American" also contributed to women distancing themselves from actively cultivating Jewish identities.[244] Women who intermarried in the 1930s, 1940s, and 1950s demonstrated that they were fully integrated Americans who happened to be born Jewish. Although the effects of antisemitism fostered increased assimilation for some women whose ties to Judaism were tenuous, their personal trajectories illustrate how being Jewish continued to play a role in their lives, long after they had married non-Jews. The ways in which women retained or rejected their Jewish heritage and, in some cases, their self-defined Jewishness illustrates the subjective nature of the meaning of intermarriage.

Whether or not they maintained Jewish identities, women wanted their children to have some religious direction in life. A common concern expressed by the Jewish women who intermarried was that their children would be "neither fish nor fowl."[245] Seven of the Jewish women I interviewed raised their children as Unitarians, five as Jews, one as Catholic, and one had no children. Their choices demonstrate the influence of advice and periodical literature that encouraged training children in one religion rather than both or none whatsoever. That the majority of Jewish women I interviewed who intermarried before second-wave feminism did not raise Jewish children is not surprising for two reasons. First, because the egalitarian approach to marriage had not yet developed in practice. Second, women who perceived being Jewish as disadvantageous may have opted to protect their children from experiencing the prejudice that they had felt as children themselves.

Jewish women who grew up in secularizing households bemoaned knowing too little about Judaism to share it with their children. Harriet Mansfield lamented the void of knowledge about Jewishness and her ancestral heritage but was unable to regret not giving her children any Jewish training because, in her words, "I had nothing to give. I didn't grow up in a Jewish home . . . I didn't have the inheritance to pass on. I *wish* I had, really."[246] Her emphasis implies that Harriet might have raised her children with more knowledge of their Jewish background had her parents done more to educate her about Judaism. Another woman expressed stronger emotions: "I'm completely ignorant of a lot of things and I'm angry that my parents didn't teach me more."[247] Women who had the religious knowledge to give their children were in the minority. Those who had more religiously observant backgrounds raised their children as Jews. Sarah Pene, though she gave up keeping kosher after she intermarried in 1938, continued to belong to an Orthodox synagogue and raised her children as Jews. Her intermarriage notwithstanding, Sarah felt so strongly about her sons being Jewish that she told them she would only attend their weddings if they married Jewish girls.[248] She hoped, to no avail, that her kids would do as she said and not as she had done; one son married a Catholic woman and the other remained single.

Moreover, the gendered power dynamics within intermarriage played a significant role in women's choices of religious training for children. Women who entered into marriages during the 1930s, 1940s, and 1950s were schooled in contemporary methods of how to "catch a husband," including prioritizing men's needs, interests, and feelings.[249] Once married, the husband's preferences and careers often came first. For example, when Ann Carlton married in 1956, she gave up her goal of being a social worker and took a job as a payroll clerk to accommodate her husband's work hours.[250] Cold War tensions about security and expert opinions, including Freud's theory that a woman's anatomy was her destiny, reinforced traditional gender roles. The social emphasis on the differences between the sexes encouraged wives to be "womanly women," dependent on and subordinate to their "manly men."[251] Although some women discussed with their husband how they would keep their home and raise their children before they wed, many others did not address the issue until much later. Hetty Miller reflected on the lack of conversation with her spouse, "You didn't think of those things in those days. I didn't discuss anything with him."[252] Lack of discussion at the outset may have made it more difficult for women to suggest raising their children as Jews. Other contemporary research supported the idea that wives were prepared to adopt the religious stance that they and their husbands together considered best, rather than insist on raising children Jewish.[253] A 1958 letter from a Jewish woman asked a rabbi whether her daughter would be better off reared in her father's faith than in none, since he was disinclined to convert or have their daughter reared as a Jewess.[254] Her query reflects the larger trend of American wives making more adjustments than men by adopting their husband's preferences and changing their own desires to fit the marriage, as well as postwar Americans' determination to stay married illustrated by the decline in the divorce rate.[255]

Although Jewish women who intermarried were often prepared to yield regarding children's religious upbringing, not all women bowed to their husband's wishes wholeheartedly. Despite her earlier promise to raise their children Catholic, when Margaret Doherty's sons were born, she told her husband that they were not well enough to be circumcised in the hospital, although they were perfectly healthy. Eight days after each boy's birth, she took them to see her doctor, who also happened to be a *mohel,* and had her sons circumcised according to Jewish law. Margaret did this, she said, "just in case they wanted to be Jews later in life."[256] Paula Avante initially agreed to baptize her son because her brother-in-law insisted. However, since her husband was not willing to raise him as a Catholic, they were unable to find a priest to perform the baptism, which came as a huge relief to Paula.[257] Thus, whether or not they identified as Jewish, some women seemed to have reservations, however vague, about their offspring being something other than Jewish.

The Meaning of Intermarriage

Jewish women who intermarried during the years 1930 to 1960 did so within a culture that idealized heterosexual marriage and considered intermarriage taboo. They were not all on the fringes of Jewish life nor did every woman cease to identify as Jewish after she married a Gentile. The women who shared their stories represented immigrant, second- and third-generation Americans. Their particular generation, notably, did not always correlate with retention or rejection of a Jewish identity. For example, one second-generation woman self-identified as Jewish, whereas another woman, an immigrant, did not. The personal experiences of the individuals were more influential in this regard than their particular generation. Denomination at birth, however, did play a role; all the women I personally interviewed born to Orthodox families maintained Jewish identities, but not all those born to Reform or Conservative families did so.[258] Their backgrounds were as varied as the paths they took when they wed non-Jewish men. Some moved farther away from Jewish living, ceasing to observe the holidays they had celebrated in their youth. Others continued to practice their own forms of Judaism while married to Gentiles and raising their children either in their spouse's religion or a third alternative, Unitarianism. Some maintained or even increased their Jewish affiliations and raised Jewish children. Still others created dual identities, forging a connection between their Jewish pasts and their less-than-Jewish presents. Intermarried Jewish women's diverse histories illustrate the increasing individualism of American religious identity and practice.

Universal ideas and values held particular resonance; differences were downplayed or overlooked in lieu of forging a new future distinct from a past riddled with antisemitism and knowledge of the near annihilation of European Jewry. Marilyn Rinalto, who married in 1957, objected to the very idea of "Jewish values," insisting that values, love, and justice were neither Jewish nor Christian but universal.[259] For this reason, perhaps, Unitarianism presented an appealing compromise for many intermarried couples. The Holocaust itself did not affect women's marital choices but did influence their identities. Although Harriet Mansfied was aware that, had she lived in Germany, Auschwitz would have been her fate, this did not deter her from intermarrying and raising her children as Unitarians. As a senior citizen, however, her consciousness of her dogged plight motivated her to reclaim a Jewish identity—once she was safely ensconced in the American mainstream—in allegiance with all oppressed people.[260] This shift in identification may also illustrate the change in social consciousness from awareness during and after the war of the persecution and extermination of European Jews to when the mass murder was labeled "the Holocaust" by American scholars and journalists in the late 1960s.[261]

Women who embraced Unitarianism had strong views about religion and intermarriage. Georgia Summer commented: "What is important to me is the respect for other religions, for other people's way of thinking and not saying what I believe is right and what you believe is wrong."[262] Paula Avante suggested total amalgamation: "We have to become *one* people, more, all over the world. Religion . . . does *a lot* to divide people. I believe people *should* intermarry, I really do."[263] Knowledge of or experience with religious and racial bigotry encouraged women to seek neutral ground. The Unitarian Church provided such a "solution"—a word several women used repeatedly in describing their personal histories. However, one woman who rejected the idea of Jewish "chosenness" or peoplehood in favor of a more equal humanitarian approach to life also supported the State of Israel.[264] Ironically, the confidence in Jewish survival that accompanied the establishment of the Jewish nation in 1948 may have relaxed some Jews' sense of endogamous responsibility.[265]

There was also a crossover between spouses and their respective religious practices. Several women said that *they* wanted a Christmas tree and it was their non-Jewish spouses who objected.[266] The Gentiles they married sometimes participated in perpetuating at least a partially Jewish lifestyle. Sarah Pene's husband insisted that she continue practicing her "Jewish way." "I would do it anyway," she remarked, "but if it was starting to get dark on a Friday night and I hadn't lit the candles yet he'd say, 'Hey Goy! You've gotta light the candles!'"[267] He joked that she was more Gentile than he was. Ann Carlton's unconverted husband was always the one to dole out the Hanukkah *gelt,* to lead the Passover Seder, and to hide the *Afikomen.*

Christmas tree topped with Star of David cartoon. *U.S. Catholic* 55, no. 3 (March 1990): 37. Don Pract, artist. Courtesy of Anita Jackson-Hall.

When Ann's father died, her husband donned his *yamulke* to join the *minyan*, the ten (Jewish) men necessary to say the mourner's prayers.[268] Sometimes the Gentile husband initiated the decision that the children would be raised as Jews. Marilyn Rinalto, a second-generation Conservative Jew, married an Italian Catholic in 1957. When her husband proposed marriage, *he* suggested that their children and home be Jewish. When Marilyn suggested, one year, that they take their Jewish daughter to see the Christmas decorations in New York, her husband balked because it would confuse the child.[269] And Paula Avante's husband read prolifically about the Jewish religion, and, Paula admitted, he became more knowledgeable about it than she was.[270] According to these women, at no time did the non-Jewish husband attempt to deprive his wife of identifying or affiliating as a Jew. Quite the contrary, Gentile husbands were supportive of their wives' interest, to whatever degree, in maintaining their ancestral faith.

Whether or not marrying someone of another religion held much significance for a woman, the end of life sometimes suggested a return to one's religion of birth. Tamar Reynold, for whom intermarriage was a professed non-issue, remarked "Funny thing: you marry out of your religion and when you die, you want to be buried in your own religion."

Although she had buried her husband in his family plot in Cambridge, Massachusetts, Tamar, in her nineties when interviewed, wanted to be buried in a Jewish cemetery.[271] Although few women I interviewed actually commented on their own eventual demise, Tamar's observation seems to have been a prevalent irony among some intermarrieds. In her diatribe, *You Are a Jew and a Jew You Are!* Rebecca Mack told readers about a man who requested a *tallis* (a Jewish prayer shawl) on his deathbed. The story went as follows:

> A Jewish man who had forsaken his religion, his people; broken his parents' hearts; left everything behind him for the love of a Gentile girl; lived a Christian life for many years; raised his children to be Christians for the sake of his wife; yet at the very end of his life, during the last few moments, desired to die as a Jew and to be buried in a Jewish cemetery.[272]

Helena Rubinstein, the cosmetics mogul who intermarried in 1938 and maintained only a bare semblance of Jewishness as she built her beauty empire, was another example. She had a rabbi at her funeral.[273] The rabbi's presence was likely her request, as Rubinstein had "strong tribal instincts" and paid significant attention to the smallest of personal details, according to her obituary.[274] In the end, then, some intermarrieds returned to the Jewish fold.

Although the concerns of the organized rabbinate focused on whether rabbis should officiate, the underlying concern of those who spoke out against intermarriage continued to be the disintegration of the Jewish people. Jewish women who married Gentiles, at least those included here, both illustrate and defy common assumptions that intermarried individuals are "lost" to Judaism. In some cases, women sought a deeper connection with Jewish life by joining a temple or taking classes in Jewish subject matter. As their stories suggest, intermarriage was not the root cause of a lessening of Jewish self-identification for all women who married non-Jews. Some women, moreover, actually identified as "Jewish" *after* they intermarried, whereas they had avoided doing so previously. One woman made the profound point that perhaps Jewish communal concern should be focused elsewhere or, more accurately, on unaffiliated or nonpracticing Jews. Ann Carlton surmised that when it came to Jewish continuity, the people that were "*really* Jewish," that is, raised to be observant Jews who married other Jews, were not all perpetuating the religion either because many were Jews in name only.

The meaning of intermarriage for women who married at mid-century should be understood from the perspectives of the women themselves within their historical contexts. Their personal accounts demonstrate that intermarriage meant different things to different women. Some ceased to consider their marriages as mixed after many decades of matrimony, and others contended that their Jewish "background" or identity meant that their relationship with their husband would always be an intermarriage. Intermarriage for Ann Carlton was "a good compromise. I haven't given everything up but yet I've integrated and it's just sort of a nice marriage!" Those women who maintained strong Jewish identities continued to observe Jewish holidays and to believe in the importance of perpetuating the Jewish people. Women who changed how they self-identified, either by combining their Jewish identity with Unitarianism or becoming Unitarian, did so voluntarily. Women who identified as Jewish sometimes did so proactively, whereas others did so reactively, that is, they did not offer the information but would respond honestly if asked. For some, Jewishness remained an active part of their lives, something they *did*. For others, Jewishness was something they *were*, comparable to being a woman, an American, or having brown eyes. Those who explained Jewishness as an inherent part of themselves construed their religious identities in biological or racial terms. The two were not mutually exclusive, however, as Sarah Pene's comment illustrates, "I don't know if I was born that way or maybe it was instilled in me."[275] The different permutations of identity illustrate "the invention of ethnicity."[276] Further, although the ethnicity of some women in my sample may appear "symbolic," voluntary, and individualistic, this characteristic is vital to their Jewishness. As the sociologist Mary C. Waters explained, "what people believe a certain ethnic identity to be is important for the identity they consciously choose to become or choose to maintain."[277]

Ethnic inheritance and socialization mixed together, diluting some women's sense of being Jewish but augmenting others'. Women who intermarried and ceased to identify as Jews or to raise Jewish children integrated further into non-Jewish society, partly because of their premarital experiences and partly because of their unions with Gentiles. All the women manifested independence from the Jewish group by intermarrying, exhibiting the rising value of individual freedom. Those who proactively identified as Jewish after their intermarriage exhibited considerable initiative, given the time period. Women who continued to call themselves Jews after intermarrying Americanized rather than assimilated and devised their own personal expressions of Jewishness, illustrating the increasing malleability of modern religious identity. It is this latter group that inadvertently transformed one option of what it meant to be a Jewish woman in America: she who married "out" and yet remained "in" according to her own definitions, beliefs, and practices.

The history of Jewish women and intermarriage between 1930 and 1960 illustrates significant change over time. Intermarriage became a popularly discussed topic in American society compared to the first three decades of the century. Similarly public awareness of rising intermarriage rates, particularly among Catholics and Protestants, fueled increased attention from the religious bodies. The Jewish intermarriage rate, though still comparatively low, roughly doubled. Although Jewish parental opposition remained fierce, the general public's disapproval of interfaith marriage waned. Increasing secularism and more diversified opportunities for contact with non-Jews through peer socialization, higher education, employment, and the move to suburbia enabled more Jewish women to meet and marry Gentile men than earlier in the twentieth century. In addition, the unprecedented increase of antisemitism in the United States leading up to World War II, and its psychological aftermath, motivated some Jewish women to intermarry. And, unlike the celebrity women I discussed in the previous chapter whose Jewish identities became attenuated with time, some women who intermarried between 1930 and 1960 actually identified as more Jewish. The next chapter examines whether Jewish women would continue to intermarry when civil rights moved to the political foreground and women reorganized for equality.

3

Intermarriage Was A-Changin'

A Jewish woman is a person, she is not a toy.
He has no moral right to oppress and destroy.
You owe it to yourself, children and culture as well.
To rise from below and escape from your hell.

—Roberta Gootblatt, 1970

The decades of the 1960s and 1970s represent a turning point in intermarriage and Jewish women's history. In contrast to women earlier in the century, some of the women I discuss in this chapter who were Jewish when they married non-Jews actually became significantly *more* Jewish after they intermarried. They also defined on their own terms how they were Jewish and how they wanted to raise their children. Organized Jewish communities moved from being concerned about the increasing rate of intermarriage and what it portended for the future of the Jewish people to being alarmed about a full-scale crisis. As a result of social scientists' increased attention specifically regarding Jewish out-marriage, communal leaders held conferences, published books, and devised programs to address intermarriage more extensively and aggressively than ever before. American Jews had not fully confronted the issue of intermarriage earlier, largely because it affected a minority of Jews, but also because it represented a heady contradiction: the fulfillment of the quest for equality, on the one hand, and a threat to Jewish group existence, on the other.[1] By the early 1960s, and certainly by the time the National Jewish Population Study was published in 1972, that larger numbers of American Jews were marrying non-Jews became impossible to ignore. Communal scrutiny accelerated, lasting to the present. The reported two-to-one intermarriage ratio of Jewish men compared to Jewish women was believed by some to be narrowing, if not exaggerated.[2]

The liberalism, ecumenism, and feminism of the 1960s and 1970s created more leeway for Jewish women to intermarry and achieve greater independence within their marriages; ironically, these influences also allowed them to identify more proactively as Jews. Civil rights, less antisemitism, and legislation barring discrimination on the basis of sex brought Jewish women into greater contact with Gentile men and encouraged them to assert their religious and ethnic priorities. Cooperation and collaboration between organized religions similarly brought down fences separating one faith from another and fostering a more accepting approach to interfaith unions. The choice to intermarry for an increasing number of Jewish women was born out of the larger fight for women's right to decide for themselves what they wanted to do and who they wanted to become. The defection of women from Jewish marriage and their emergence from second-class citizenship allotted all women did not mean the demise of their identities as Jews. Gladys Rosen, a Jewish communal activist, asked in 1973: "Does self-realization as a human being demand the total abandonment of traditional roles or even their reversal?"[3] In the case of some Jewish women who intermarried in the 1960s and 1970s, self-realization meant the freedom to marry a Gentile man and still affirm their Jewish identity. Jewish identity, however, was often construed as cultural, tied to a people and a history, rather than explicitly religious.

The national rate of Jewish intermarriage increased dramatically between 1959 and 1984, provoking unprecedented polemical debate among scholars and Jewish communal activists. The proportion of Jewish persons who married non-Jews nearly tripled, from roughly 6 percent before the 1960s to 17.4 percent between 1961 and 1965, jumping to 31.7 percent for the years 1966 to 1972.[4] Eventually intermarried Jews outnumbered in-married Jews. Nationally, 51 percent of born Jews reportedly married non-Jews between 1975 and 1984.[5] A Boston community survey found a lower overall rate (7 percent of couples in 1965) but also found a significant increase in the rate of intermarriage when the marriage had occurred more recently: 20 percent of the unions with husbands thirty years old and younger were intermarriages.[6] This rate increased to 22 percent in 1975.[7] Demographers concluded that interfaith marriage was increasing rather steadily and was unlikely to stop. Comparatively still rare, interracial marriages involving a white, black, Native American, or Asian American comprised a mere 0.4 percent of all national unions in 1960 and increased only to 0.7 by 1970.[8]

Since organized Jewish life was based on the assumption that integration into American society and Jewish continuity through endogamy were compatible goals, the high incidence of marriages between Jews and non-Jews made intermarriage "the single most pressing problem confronting the organized Jewish community," according to one activist in 1979.[9] Social scientists, observing the steady increase in intermarriage and the simultaneous decline in Jewish fertility, issued dismal forecasts for the perpetuation of the Jewish people, though some scholars were more optimistic. For example, in 1978 the social scientists Samuel S. Liberman and Morton Weidfeld cited historian Salo Baron's argument that if there were five hundred first-rate Jewish scholars and fifty thousand good Hebraists, American Jewry would survive.[10] Members of the American rabbinates debated during the 1960s and 1970s whether Jewish continuity would be best served by the prevention of intermarriage or, to avoid alienation, the acceptance and inclusion of intermarried people within Jewish circles.

While Jewish communities deliberated on how best to deal with intermarriage, the attitudes of Jewish parents toward their children intermarrying shifted from forceful objection to accommodation, according to contemporary studies and the women I interviewed. Jewish families' historical objections to intermarriage remained relatively constant until the mid-1960s. For example, as late as 1964, a mother and father obtained a court order to keep one William Murray away from their daughter, Susan Abramovitz, on the grounds that he and his atheistic family "were leading the girl away from her home and religion."[11] However, in the face of widespread social integration of Jews and liberal democracy, the objections of Jewish families to their children's intermarriages began to wane. Although 26 percent of parents in the Boston area strongly opposed the intermarriage of their own child in 1965, 44 percent said that they would only try to discourage it; another 25 percent claimed that they would be neutral or accept the intermarriage, believing that it was the child's decision.[12] By 1975 strong opposition had declined to 14 percent and discouragement to 20 percent, while neutrality or acceptance had increased to 59 percent.[13] Thus, when in 1974 one woman responded to her future husband's suggestion that a Baptist minister perform their marriage rites with the words "you'll really kill my mother, I mean, here I am marrying a Goy in a church by a *Shvartse* (a less than neutral Yiddish term for a black person when used by an English-speaker)," she was only half joking. Her parents responded enthusiastically to the marriage.[14]

The patterns that emerge from a relatively small group of oral histories suggest what intermarriage meant to and for Jewish women. The oral history interviews conducted for this book illuminate the histories of some

Jewish women who intermarried and lived in the Boston area. This chapter integrates one-third of the narratives of women who married non-Jews with other historical sources to discuss three central themes: Jewish women's rebellion against a bourgeois Jewish lifestyle, the greater degree of autonomy they experienced in their intermarriages, and their increased attention to the Jewish plight and future. Social science studies also illustrate the heightened preoccupation with Jewish intermarriage and suggest how the women examined in this book resemble other 1960s and 1970s intermarrieds. Although one cannot generalize across time and place, it is possible to establish how some women's intermarriage experiences heightened their personal Jewish identities but also distanced them from Jewish communal life.

Jewish women who intermarried in the 1960s and 1970s reflect the changing composition of the intermarried population. Fourteen of the forty-three women I interviewed appear in this chapter, including three second-generation and eleven third-generation Americans. Most women had Reform or Conservative backgrounds, one was "Yiddish-Secular," and the majority were the grandchildren of immigrants from Eastern Europe. None was Orthodox. Their husband's religious affiliations included Roman Catholic, Congregational, Protestant-French Huguenot, Presbyterian, Buddhist, Episcopalian, Christian Science, and one Roman Catholic who converted to Judaism. The women intermarried between 1963 and 1979. At the time of these interviews, eight remained married, five were divorced, and one was widowed. Eight women were married for the second time: seven had divorced Jews and remarried Gentiles; one had intermarried the first time and then married a Jew. Ten women raised children who identified as Jewish, the children of two identified neither as Jewish or Gentile, and the children of two others were reportedly "both."

The rise in Jewish intermarriage and the impact of second-wave feminism during the 1960s and 1970s generated increased concern about Jewish group survival and, paradoxically, the growth of a specifically Jewish feminism among some women who married non-Jews. In this chapter I argue that although Jewish women may have married out with greater frequency, their resolve to retain their religious and ethnic heritage often grew stronger rather than weaker. Indeed, intermarriage actually accentuated some women's sense of being Jewish, despite predictions to the contrary. Moreover, women who continued to identify as Jews often insisted that their children were also Jewish, regardless of their having non-Jewish fathers. In the following pages I demonstrate how women illustrated greater consciousness about their Jewish connections, refashioning the traditional understanding of interfaith marriage in the process.

Consequences of Liberalism and Ecumenism

Thriving political and social liberalism in American society during the 1960s and 1970s facilitated the intermarriage of Jewish women with non-Jewish men by driving religious and racial prejudice, if not out of existence, at least much further underground. Outmoded legal distinctions based on race and religion became a significant step toward neutralizing social opposition to intermarriage. In 1962 the U.S. Supreme Court made prayer in public schools illegal; in 1964 the Civil Rights Act outlawed religious and racial discrimination; and the 1965 Voting Rights Act restored full citizenship to black Americans.[15] Such legislation suggested to all Americans that personal differences were to be mutually respected rather than cause for rejection. Criticism of intermarriage based solely on religious differences sharply contradicted social and political equality, which increasingly eroded the grounds for disapproving of interfaith unions (even when such disapproval still existed). Liberalism alone did not make intermarriage acceptable, but it laid the foundation for a new way of thinking that made objections to marriage outside the Jewish fold less convincing to more assimilated Jews.

Increased individualism combined with more liberal attitudes facilitated Jewish women's choices to marry non-Jews. The American ethos that emphasized individual will and personal fulfillment, as seen, for example, in the increase in recreational expenditures in the 1960s compared to the money spent on familial comfort in the 1950s, suggested to Jewish women that finding a decent person was more important than finding a coreligionist to wed.[16] Prospective mates could be selected based on character rather than religion; one's spouse should be judged in terms of respectability, goodness, and sincerity.[17] The American ethos also conflicted with the religious proscription against intermarriage, which expressed the will of the Jewish group and its law. "Cultural democracy," as the sociologist Milton Gordon argued in his influential 1964 work *Assimilation in American Life,* applied to individuals as well as groups: "the individual . . . should be allowed to choose freely whether to remain within the boundaries of communality created by his birthright ethnic group, to branch out into multiple interethnic contacts, or even to change affiliation to that of another ethnic group should he wish to do so as a result of religious conversion, intermarriage, or simply private wish."[18] The idea that Jews were "individuals with rights" not "members of communities with mutual duties" fueled a growing tension.[19] Arguments that intermarriage resulted in discord and unhappiness, rather than that it contradicted Jewish custom and law, illustrated the ethos of individualism. By objecting to intermarriage on the grounds of personal contentedness, one scholar observed in 1970, "parents acknowledge the primacy of individual choice when . . . they accept their children's intermarriages, rather than go into mourning, as was traditionally done."[20]

The direction of Jewish liberalism changed markedly during the 1960s and 1970s when it faced the conflicting goals of supporting civil rights and fostering Jewish mobility, fueling social conflict over intermarriage in the process. The politics of acculturation cut like a double-edged sword, according to the historian Marc Dollinger: "While it strengthened American Jews, giving them the drive to champion unpopular causes and establish themselves as guardians of liberal America, the politics of acculturation also erected strict barriers to Jewish liberal success." Cultural nationalism, inspired by the Black Power movement and the New Left's anti-Israel pronouncements after the 1967 Six-Day War, motivated Jewish liberals to champion Jewish causes.[21] Simultaneously the argument that became pervasive in the 1970s in favor of heightening Jewish reproduction to replenish the population devastated by the Holocaust protected male and heterosexual privileges. While Jewish liberalism supported the idea of full integration into American life, it also demanded the renewal of traditional Jewish communal life and the strengthening of the Jewish family.[22] The greater openness to intermarriage illustrated one of the contradictions of Jewish liberalism in that it directly conflicted with cultural nationalism on a personal level.

American indifference to or acceptance of intermarriage reflected a significant decline in antisemitism, increasing Jewish women's prospects for finding a spouse outside Judaism. Citing the growing rate of Jewish intermarriage since the mid-1960s, the historian Leonard Dinnerstein commented, "In human terms, the best indication of the decline of American antisemitism is the number of intermarriages that have occurred between Jews and Gentiles."[23] As prejudice against Jews abated, marrying Jewish women no longer threatened to diminish Gentiles' social status within their majority communities. Gentile attitudes reflected increasing acceptance of both Jews and intermarriage. According to the historian Edward Shapiro, "Between 1964 and 1981, Gentiles who would accept the marriage of a child to a Jew increased from 55 to 66 percent."[24] Further, in the words of the sociologist Marshall Sklare, intermarriage represented "the logical culmination of the quest for full equality," a powerful indication that discriminatory practices preserving social boundaries and restricting opportunity for Jews were essentially over.[25] The change reflected in public opinion polls suggests that approval of intermarriage between Jews and non-Jews had indeed markedly increased over time. Whereas, in 1951, 48 percent of Americans considered it acceptable for two people of different religions—Protestant, Catholic, or Jewish—to marry, 59 percent approved of marriage between Jews and non-Jews in June 1968; and this figure rose to 67 percent in 1972.[26] Although polls such as these may not be fully conclusive, the trend toward greater acceptance of intermarriage is obvious.

While the decline in antisemitism made intermarriage more plausible from the Gentile point of view, the antiwar and counterculture movements of these decades also made defying a homogeneous Jewish family more possible for Jews of both sexes who did not seek to marry coreligionists. The anti-Vietnam fervor that began with a small protest in New York in 1964 mushroomed into widespread public dispute of American policy, conscientious objection, and draft evasion after four student demonstrators were killed at Kent State University in Ohio in 1970.[27] If the American people could openly denigrate the government, certainly some Jewish women (and men) could defeat their parents' wishes and marry "out." The counterculture spirit that evolved beginning around 1966 attacked the traditional values, behavior, and personal relationships of most Americans. Moreover, many hippies, as many of the adherents of the countercultural mind-set were called, rejected the manicured suburban lifestyles and circumspect mores of their parents. Drugs and sexual permissiveness went hand in hand with the younger generation's lifestyle.[28] Among these socially turbulent times, when "Make Love, Not War" was a popular motto, marrying someone of a different religion became another of many ways to thwart social convention. A *New York Times* reporter observed in 1973 that, because of young Jews' proportionate overrepresentation in the counterculture, combined with rising rates of divorce and intermarriage, the Jewish family was "shaking in the winds of social change."[29]

American society's increasing openness to heterogeneity in the 1960s and beyond made marrying someone of a different religion, and even a different race, more feasible for Jewish women. The new hair styles and innovative dress produced by the counterculture, the expansion of higher education, the Civil Rights movement, the new ethnic consciousness, and the election of the first Roman Catholic president in 1960 all contributed to a greater tolerance of diversity.[30] In 1972 the Ethnic Heritage Studies Bill was passed, and a few years later the National Council of Teacher Education adopted new standards that made a strong commitment to multicultural education.[31] Religious experimentation with mysticism and Eastern religions likewise contributed to a broadening of behaviors that created social room for cross-faith and, to a lesser extent, cross-race alliances. The U.S. Supreme Court decision in *Loving* v. *Virginia* declared miscegenation laws unconstitutional in 1967, making it legal for Jewish white women to marry black men of whatever religion.[32] Legal, however, was not the same as socially approved.

Although in 1968 a thirteen-nation survey of attitudes toward interracial and interfaith marriages found Americans most opposed to interracial unions, interracial interfaith marriage was favored over unmarried cohabitation producing illegitimate children.[33] The preference of parents that their children marry outside their race rather than cohabitate outside of marriage illustrates a decline in racial prejudice, at least in theory, and constant disapproval of "living together." Although attitudes were not the same as actions, the 1975 Virginia Slims American Women's Opinion Poll suggested that a majority of Americans were more willing to have their daughters marry someone of a different racial background than to live with them outside of wedlock.[34] Moreover, bridging the racial divide remained less popular than crossing the religious line.[35] While the ethnic revival that began in the 1960s was infused with rhetoric about diversity and inclusion, it simultaneously reinforced white nationalism. As the historian Matthew Frye Jacobson argued, by reinventing America as a nation of immigrants, "the net effect of the Ellis Island epic has pitched decisively to the right: appeals to the romantic icon of yesterday's European immigrant—downtrodden, hard-working, self-reliant, triumphant—have shaped debates about everything from affirmative action and the welfare state to slavery reparation and contemporary immigration."[36] Thus it remained far easier for a Jewish white woman to marry a white non-Jew than a non-white Gentile. By the same token, whereas none of the women interviewed who intermarried before 1960 had interracial marriages, three of the fourteen women discussed in this chapter did; two married black men and one married a Japanese man.

Despite lingering racial prejudice and parental disapproval of cohabitation, casual living combined with the sexual revolution emboldened some Jewish women to meet and later marry non-Jewish, non-white men. Although national statistics are unavailable, a mid-1960s study by the sociologist Werner Cahman estimated that 70-80 percent of the white spouses of black men in the New York metropolitan area were Jewish women.[37] The historian Renee Romano acknowledges that the overly simplistic "forbidden fruit syndrome," black men asserting their masculinity and freedom through acquisition of white women, may have contributed to a gender gap in black intermarriage rates. There was no cultural stereotype that made black women and white (Jewish) men attractive to each other.[38] "Technical virginity" declined in importance and the proportion of women having premarital sex increased from 10 percent in 1958 to 23 percent in 1968. The courtship process also changed to include cohabitation for three times as many couples between 1970 and 1982.[39] Beth Jonah, a child care provider born in Boston in 1953, married a black man. "Well that was the '60s," she explained. "I met him hanging out in Harvard Square with the hippies." Beth was five months pregnant and felt coerced to get married (in 1976) by her parents and boyfriend. Her choices did not pass without comment; she remembers people driving by and shouting "Nigger Lover!"[40] Moreover, not all parents were as accepting as Beth's. In her novel *Meridien*, Alice Walker describes the anguish caused by a Jewish daughter's interracial choice: when the mother found her daughter at a black boyfriend's house, the mother's screams were heard "from three blocks away."[41] Although unplanned pregnancies did occur, the availability of oral contraception, the Pill, beginning in 1960 better enabled women to engage in sex without fear of pregnancy and to delay marriage, as an increasing number of Americans did. Beginning in 1960, the median age at marriage began to rise from its all-time low in 1956 of 20.1 for women and 22.5 for men, and by the late 1970s had reached its prewar level while the birthrate steadily declined. In 1979 the median age at first marriage was 22.1 for women and 24.4 for men.[42]

Karen Amai, born in Miami Beach in 1945, was a student at Boston University when she met her Japanese-American husband at the MIT bowling alley. Although she credited her parents with being "fairly open and liberal" in 1969, her father made the following chilling comment to her after she announced her plans to wed: "Remember Pearl Harbor."[43] That Karen lived in another part of the country than her parents who lived in the Southeast enabled her to shrug off her family's initial response and marry the man she loved. Living in the Northeast, in such liberal, multicultural Massachusetts neighborhoods as Porter Square, Cambridge, and what one woman referred to as "The People's Republic of Brookline," helps explain why this interracially married woman did not experience excessive prejudice. Karen's move north provided anonymity, and the culture of the 1960s encouraged her to experiment: "It was a very liberating experience," according to Karen, and really important at the time was "this idea that we're all the same and that it doesn't matter what your race or religion is and that the way to solve a lot of the conflicts and problems—because it was the Civil Rights movement we were just coming out of—was that people would intermarry."[44]

Jewish women's intermarriages exemplified the social trend of disregarding religious differences in interpersonal relationships. Carol Ferris earned a bachelor's and a doctorate degree at the University of Chicago, where she met her husband. She described that environment in the late 1960s as a "very liberal place" with people from all over the world, where a lot of "bonding" took place between Jews and non-Jews alike who were passionately antiwar. Carol, who considered herself a "maverick," speculated: "maybe before the 1970s it took this kind of avant-garde thinking and being and feeling not to give a damn."[45] Fran Rakefield considered herself part of the "love generation" that believed in going "beyond a little group of people and to love everyone, you know, to reach out to *all* kinds of people."[46] These women's statements illustrate the extent to which Jewish women lived and loved outside strictly Jewish society, facilitated by the American cultural emphasis on individual satisfaction over communal commitment.

Rising higher education matriculation, the relaxing of sex-role differentiation, and diminishing attendance at religious services and functions contributed further to Jewish women intermarrying. Between 1960 and 1973 the number of college students in the United States more than tripled, rising from three million to ten million, owing largely to the coming of age of the baby boomer generation.[47] The better educated American youth became, the less involved they were in religious institutional life and the more prone to interfaith relationships. In the decade after 1965 Protestant denominations experienced a 10 percent decline in membership; similarly Mass attendance by well-educated Roman Catholics declined as did synagogue membership by Jews.[48] In 1969 intermarriage was a "major campus topic"; Jewish university chaplains reported a sharp decline in counseling about sexual matters and a substantial rise in requests for advice about navigating intermarriage issues.[49] As of 1971 the proportion of Jewish women college students was nearly equal to that of Jewish men: 23.2 percent compared to 24.8 percent in the twenty-five- to twenty-

nine-year-old age group. Hence Jewish women were increasingly achieving their own educational success in university milieus where familial and
social restrictions limiting interactions with non-Jewish men were less
easily reinforced.[50] Meanwhile, student political activism also increased
significantly on campuses, first as part of the Civil Rights movement and
later in protests against the Vietnam War.

Similar to the intermarried Jewish women during the Progressive Era,
sharing a political worldview increasingly surpassed religion in importance for some Jewish women, making it still easier for them to marry
non-Jewish men. Jewish women who married non-Jews during the 1960s
might have disengaged from Judaism sufficiently to marry Christians with
similar politics; later, the women might decide whether and how they
wished to be Jewish. Their actions illustrate the "sovereign self" concept
described by the sociologists Steven Cohen and Arnie Eisen in their recent
book, *The Jew Within*: by drawing the activities and significance of their
Jewish group identity into the subjectivity of the individual, the meaning
of Judaism for these Jewish women transpired within the self.[51] The sociologist Andrew Greeley argued, in 1978, that young people made up their
minds about politics and religious affiliation simultaneously between the
ages of seventeen and thirty but that during the 1960s persons in this age
group suspended decisions about both until later.[52] Carol Ferris, who was
born in 1937 and married in 1968, reflected that countercultural thinking made marriage to an interesting man who shared her liberal politics
more important than marrying a fellow Jew. Carol described the social
scene in which she met her spouse: "We felt very bonded against an organization which would make war in Vietnam and so passions ran high."[53]
Fran Rakefield was born in 1945, grew up in New Jersey, attended graduate school in New York, worked as an editor, and married in 1976. She
recalled that peace and political views seemed "much more important
than religious things at the time."[54] This comment certainly suggests the
primacy of political, temporal priorities over religious ones.

Involvement in intellectual circles and political activities contributed to
making ideas and politics more significant than religious differences to
the intermarried women in my sample. Diane Endicott was born in up-
state New York in 1942 and taught elementary school both before and after marrying her second husband in 1974. She described the cultural context: "In the '70s you were intellectual, you weren't religious." Reflecting
on her decision to marry a non-Jew she pointed to the previous decade to
explain: "I think the '60s made life different . . . just opened up avenues

or made life . . . made issues less issue-like."[55] Ellen Kolokowski, born in Hartford, Connecticut, in 1943, got married, also for the second time, in 1973. She described how liberal thinking, integration between blacks and whites, the increase in divorce, and the increasing acceptability of intermarriage all contributed to how people found mates outside their own religion.

> Because you were meeting people more based on your political stance, your social stance, rather than *my life* of meeting people *through* the temple and *through* the youth group activities, and going to college and joining Hillel, and staying in that little circle. All of a sudden, it was open! You were *going* to rallies, you were *going* to the Arlington Street church because that's where the most radical, liberal stuff was happening. So, you weren't going there to pray; you were going there to meet the movers and shakers in the political world. And I think it was a *drastic* change (emphasis by respondent).[56]

Once political similarities brought Jewish women and Gentile men together, religious differences were insufficient to keep them apart.

While the social role of politics in American culture created new avenues for dialogue between individuals of different faiths, a turn toward a more ecumenical approach made intermarriage more tenable for Jewish women. In the early 1970s Jewish and Christian leaders began to collaborate in unprecedented ways. For example, a Roman Catholic college chaplain wrote the book *When a Christian and a Jew Marry* "with a Jewish perspective" by a Reform rabbi.[57] Similarly a write-your-own-wedding book was coauthored and co-edited by a rabbi, the Catholic dean of a women's college, and the Protestant marriage and family consultant of the National Council of Churches. The introduction highlights a couple's 1971 "ecumenical ceremony" that they wrote themselves, "combining Protestant and Catholic wedding prayers, Biblical verses and other devotional writings." The authors conclude with "Congratulations and Mazel Tov!" The book is a good illustration of the increasing social acceptability of interfaith marriages during the 1960s and 1970s. Only a brief caveat hints that Jewish law does not recognize interfaith marriages between Jews and Christians as religiously valid: "Needless to say, your wedding ceremony must be in accord with the requirements of your faith group and the laws of your state."[58] This advice ignores the fact that many Americans viewed religion as something individual prior to any organizational commitment.

For Americans, including intermarrieds, the local house of worship was not identical with *religion* according to Robert Bellah, "which has meaning that transcends the individual and the local congregation."[59]

Changes in the views of the Roman Catholic Church and other Christian denominations on intermarriage brought it a step closer to acceptability for all religious groups. In October 1958 Pope John XXIII sought to change the acrimony some Catholics fostered toward people of other faiths; he also sought to mend fences with other religions, calling for a new Vatican Council that would reexamine Church teachings on these issues. Pope John received representatives of the American Jewish Committee (AJC) and the Anti-Defamation League; he also deleted antisemitic pejoratives from prayers.[60] The New York Board of Rabbis later hailed Pope John for his efforts to join all faiths in pursuit of amity and understanding.[61] Later, in March 1966, Pope Paul VI liberalized the Church's stance on intermarriage by rescinding excommunication for a Catholic who married a non-Catholic before a non-Catholic clergyman. Pope Paul also gave local bishops the authority to determine whether the promise required of the non-Catholic partner to raise children as Catholics should be made in writing or verbally. The intermarried Catholic was considered to have an invalid marriage unless married in a Catholic ceremony, and the promise to raise all children in the Catholic faith continued to be exacted from the non-Catholic. However, these new changes did allow for greater interpretation.[62]

The Christian ecumenical movement that grew in the 1960s pointed out discrepancies between Catholic teaching and practice, and encouraged a more open attitude toward intermarriage that gained national attention.[63] The first wedding held at a Catholic Church to be jointly officiated by an Episcopal minister and a Catholic priest occurred in June 1964, generating the *Time* magazine headline "Toward Easier Mixed Marriage." A number of progressive Catholic bishops reportedly argued that marriage rules involved ecclesiastical law rather than divine sanction, and encouraged Rome to further revise canon law.[64] Five years later a Christian ecumenical weekly reported: "While falling short of recommending interfaith marriages as the ultimate solution to religious differences, a new set of guidelines issued by the Roman Catholic archdiocese of Boston does stress the positive aspects of such marriages."[65] The guidelines included interfaith premarital instruction and ceremony participation by both clergypersons, and respect for both parents' rights regarding children's religious education.

The spring of 1970 marked a pivotal juncture for intermarriage, at least within the Christian communities. On 29 April 1970 Pope Paul VI decreed that non-Catholic partners in intermarriages would no longer be required to promise to raise children as Catholics; the Catholic partner was only obligated to "do all in his power" to seek this outcome. Pope Paul also ruled that local bishops could grant dispensations from a Catholic ceremony. At the same time that liberalized Church laws made intermarriage more possible, papal opposition to married clergy and birth control was reinforced.[66] Although the Pope emphasized that the Church still discouraged mixed marriages and saw them as deterring Christian unity, his twenty-five-hundred-word document titled "Matrimonia Mixta" gave the impression that marrying a Catholic had become easier for a non-Catholic.[67] The very idea of Christian unity, however, focused almost entirely on Catholic-Protestant pairings who were "essentially one in Christ."[68]

According to social scientists analyzing 1960s and 1970s marriages, modern ecumenism contributed to the increase in intermarriage by lessening social concerns. Moreover, marriage was becoming increasingly secular. For example, a 1973 study of interreligious marriages in Indiana between 1962 and 1967 reported that although the growth of interfaith marriage was nothing new, "there is a lessening of religious constraint upon the marriages today."[69] Combined data from the 1973 through 1978 General Social Surveys conducted by the National Opinion Research Center found changes in intermarriage since the 1957 Current Population Survey by the Census Bureau. In addition to citing a significant increase in the extent of religiously mixed couples, the author found "no extremely strong barriers to religious outmarriage except among Jews" and a forceful ongoing trend toward secularization of the institution of marriage.[70] These analyses illustrate the perception among social scientists that religious institutions and extended families exerted less influence over interfaith marriage in the 1960s and 1970s than in the past. Beth Jonah's memory of her 1976 marriage ceremony illustrates how little religion figured into her thinking at the time. "It was just a Justice of the Peace in Brookline . . . and there were these two women in miniskirts and these little dogs yapping around and little orange trees in the apartment, and that's *all* I remember."[71]

From Concern to Crisis

The paths to intermarriage may have widened in the general American society in the 1960s and 1970s, but social science studies also contributed to rising alarm within the Jewish community regarding Jewish-Gentile marriages. Analyzing data about Jewish intermarriage in a large urban area (Greater Washington, D.C.) and a small-town Jewish community (in Iowa), the demographer Erich Rosenthal surmised in 1963 that the Jewish community was moving from acculturation to assimilation and amalgamation. "Acculturation" was favorable because it suggested that Jews could fully integrate in American society while maintaining their distinctiveness through endogamy; "assimilation" and "amalgamation" were negative because they signaled a loss of Jewish distinctiveness through blending with other ethno-religious groups. Moreover, Rosenthal gloomily concluded that since less than 30 percent of the children of intermarriage in Greater Washington identified as Jews, "intermarriage usually spells the end of belonging to the Jewish group."[72] Rosenthal's 1967 study of Jewish intermarriage in Indiana further substantiated his earlier claim that without large-scale immigration and a substantial rise in the birthrate to increase the size of the Jewish-Jewish marriage market, intermarriage would be an increasing threat to Jewish survival.[73] His work also cast doubt on the sociologist Will Herberg's 1950s religious endogamy theory known as "the return of the third generation," based on the historian Marcus Hansen's earlier thesis, and helped galvanize the organized Jewish community to support programs designed to investigate intermarriage in more depth.[74]

Jewish group cohesion and continuity became the primary Jewish communal concern regarding intermarriage beginning in the 1960s, evinced by an onslaught of studies and alarmist commentary about "disappearing" Jews. In 1963 the *American Jewish Year Book,* the standard reference regarding Jewish life, published Rosenthal's findings in its first full-length article on intermarriage.[75] "The Long Range Planning Project," the first study of the Jewish population of Greater Boston that included a chapter on intermarriage, was established in 1963, published its findings in 1967, and was followed by Boston community studies done in 1975, 1985, and 1995.[76] The activist Milton Himmelfarb took the contrarian view that, in light of rising intermarriage, proselytism was not "un-Jewish," and conversion could offset losses to the Jewish people.[77] Marshal Sklare clamored for more research about intermarriage at regular intervals and predicted that unless the "problem of intermarriage" produced a new consciousness about Jewish separatism and individual responsibility for collective longevity, the consequences for Jewish survival were "indeed ominous to contemplate."[78] He later excoriated rabbis who officiated at intermarriages, claiming that they legitimized them; this, he argued, struck "at the very

THE
VANISHING
AMERICAN JEW

Leaders fear threat to Jewish survival in today's "crisis of freedom"

■ New studies reveal loss of Jewish identity, soaring rate of intermarriage.
■ Judaism may be losing 70 percent of children born to mixed couples.
■ Because of low birthrate, Jews are "scarcely reproducing themselves."
■ Jews may fade from 2.9 to 1.6 percent of U.S. population by the year 2000.

"The Vanishing American Jew: Leaders Fear Threat to Jewish Survival in Today's 'Crisis of Freedom,'" *Look*, 4 May 1964, 42. Robert Lerner, photographer. Courtesy of Józef Topolski, Library of Congress.

core of Jewish group existence."[79] General interest magazines hammered the elevated concern documented by Rosenthal and expressed by numerous others into the mainstream press with articles such as "The Assimilators," "Judaism: A Threat to Survival," and "The Vanishing American Jew," publicizing the extent to which Jews were marrying non-Jews.[80]

Public discourse about Jewish intermarriage increased markedly in the mid- and late 1960s. On 13–14 February 1960 the Theodore Herzl Institute in New York convened the first conference on intermarriage. The intention was to bring together educators and rabbis as guardians of Jewish heritage, with sociologists as purportedly objective observers. The result was a published compendium of essays with disparate opinions about the scope of intermarriage, its causes and consequences, and prospective answers to the intermarriage "question."[81] The first monographs on intermarriage in more than forty years were also published.[82] *Intermarriage: Interfaith, Interracial, Interethnic,* by the Conservative rabbi and sociologist Albert I. Gordon, was hailed in 1964 as "the most careful, up-to-date, methodologically sound study of intermarriage in North America that exists." The psychologist Louis A. Berman's 1968 *Jews and Intermarriage: A Study in*

Personality and Culture was commended as "an important book because it insists on seeing intermarriage as the end product of cultural historical processes, not merely as the computerized, or lamented, or praised union" of individuals from different cities.[83] The conference and the lengthy book publications illustrate the extent to which intermarriage had become an issue of substantial debate among scholars of different disciplines.

Public discourse about intermarriage and Jewish continuity also became decidedly more polemical during the 1960s, with some observers contesting the dismal outlooks. A rabbi of the Society for the Advancement for Judaism in New York was quoted in 1964: "To have withstood Hitlerism and still create Israel, and to revitalize Hebrew and continue to maintain scholarship and philanthropy—this shows that the Jewish people are strong to survive. It is utterly premature to be morbid about intermarriage."[84] The sociologists Sidney Goldstein and Calvin Goldscheider conducted a 1966 study of the Jewish community in Greater Providence, Rhode Island. They found that although the rate of intermarriage was higher among the third generation than the first, conversion of the third-generation non-Jewish spouse to Judaism was also higher. Their finding that a majority of children of intermarried couples were actually raised as Jews contributed to their conclusion that, "the net effect of intermarriage on the overall size of the Jewish population may not be as serious as suggested by several other community studies."[85] Notwithstanding these positive perspectives, the argument that became pervasive in the 1970s was that the appropriate response to the Holocaust was increased Jewish reproduction, which intermarriage threatened at the very least.[86]

Although intermarriage continued to be a divisive issue, over time some communal leaders found ways to accept what they considered an undesirable situation. For example, in 1966 a Reform rabbi suggested that when a Gentile converted to Judaism prior to marrying a Jew it was a "mitzvah marriage." The mitzvah, generally understood to mean "good deed," was that the faith and identity of the Jew was sufficiently strong to convince the Gentile to become Jewish.[87] This positive take on intermarriage overlooked the possibility that some non-Jews converted simply in order to get married—"shot gun" conversions—and not because they truly embraced Judaism.[88] An Orthodox rabbi-professor bemoaned in 1965: "One changes one's faith with the same ease as one changes one's car."[89] In a 1967 paper, Abraham I. Shinedling, another rabbi, articulated what may have been the more common Reform position: "For in intermarriages there is always the hope for accretions to Judaism, and not always the fear of losses."[90] Shinedling disliked intermarriages, but he also thought they were inevitable in an ecumenical age and that opposition would be counterproductive.[91]

In the 1970s intermarriage moved from being a matter of concern to a crisis for the organized Jewish community, illustrated by two national studies and their by-products. Whatever optimism scholars and religious leaders had about the impact of intermarriage was checked, at least for some, by the first National Jewish Population Study (NJPS) sponsored by the Council of Jewish Federations and Welfare Funds in 1970. The NJPS found that 31.7 percent of Jewish persons marrying in the years 1966 to 1972 chose a non-Jewish spouse. This was a significant increase from 17.4 percent in 1961 to 1965, and ten times the percent of Jewish persons who intermarried in the 1930s.[92] Citing these findings, a rabbinic scholar named Kalman Packouz brought together parents, rabbis, and yeshiva students to convene the Intermarriage Crisis Conference in 1973; in 1976 he authored *How to Stop an Intermarriage: A Practical Guide for Parents*.[93] The American Jewish Committee sponsored a national study in 1976, citing the need to better understand the consequences of intermarriage and not just the rates and causes. Sociologists confirmed fears that intermarriage threatened Jewish continuity when they summarized the findings from this study in 1979: "Most non-Jewish spouses do not convert to Judaism; the level of Jewish content and practice in mixed marriages is low; only about one-third of the Jewish partners in such marriages view their children as Jewish; and most such children are exposed to little by way of Jewish culture or religion."[94]

Jewish intermarriage polemics appeared increasingly in the national press by the late 1970s, highlighting the dissension among communal leaders and raising questions about the alleged causes and consequences of Jewish–non-Jewish marriage. In contrast to the forecast that intermarriage weakened prospects for Jewish existence, the demographer Fred Massarik encouraged "rethinking the intermarriage crisis." He theorized that if two Jews married two non-Jews, and only one of the couples raised their children as Jews, just as many Jewish children would result as had the two Jews married each other.[95] Massarik's viewpoint is notable, as he was the scientific director of the NJPS in 1970-72. In December 1979 *USA Today* featured a two-page spread of the AJC's report, illustrating the other end of the spectrum by emphasizing intermarriage as a threat to the American Jewish community.[96] The editor of the *American Jewish Year Book* presented a third perspective in 1979. "It is not intermarriage which leads to assimilation," David Singer wrote, "but assimilation which leads to intermarriage."[97] Intermarriage was not the root of the problem threatening Jewish continuity but rather Jews' lack of synagogue attendance or Jewish organizational activity. If the norm for both in-married and intermarried Jews was noninvolvement, as the NJPS reported, there seemed little reason to differentiate between the two according to some scholars.[98]

The American rabbinates became more proactive in the 1960s and 1970s than ever before, demonstrating the Jewish community's heightened preoccupation with intermarriage. In 1962, after fifteen years of relative silence, the newly established Special Committee on Mixed Marriage made its first report to the Central Conference of American Rabbis (CCAR). The Reform committee summarized extant evidence about intermarriage and speculated: "What programs can we devise . . . that will inhibit Jewish-Gentile marriage in a free society? What can we as rabbis do to encourage mixed couples to identify with the synagogue and to raise their children as Jews?"[99] Clearly the CCAR was no longer solely focused on whether rabbis should officiate. Referring to biblical times, one CCAR member contended in April 1964, "Not since the days of Ezra has mixed marriage been as vexing an issue to Jewish religious leadership as it is to us in the United States today."[100] In 1972 the Committee on Mixed Marriage presented an in-depth discussion of intermarriage at the annual conference. On 19 June 1973 the CCAR adopted a resolution, with some ardent discord, that declared "its opposition to participation by its members in any ceremony which solemnizes mixed marriage." It also called upon its members to keep the temple doors open to people who had already intermarried, to assist in educating children as Jews, and to provide opportunity for conversion of the non-Jewish spouse.[101] Although the CCAR discouraged intermarriage and sought to stem its increase, its stance suggested an acceptance of the inevitability of Jewish-Gentile marriage in a free society.

Members of the Reform rabbinate, acknowledging a need for a response to the desire for rabbis' participation, launched a campaign in the late 1960s and early 1970s to make information available about colleagues who would officiate at Jewish-Gentile marriages. This movement stood in direct opposition to the official CCAR resolution against rabbis officiating.[102] It also recognized the growing number of intermarriages involving Jews who sought rabbinical involvement and the rabbis who believed it was better to officiate than to risk losing Jews through alienation or disillusionment about Judaism, "because of the spiritual insensibility of so many of our colleagues."[103] Rabbi David Max Eichhorn sent a letter to his CCAR colleagues on 3 June 1969, asking whether they officiated at marriages between a Jew and a non-Jew without requiring the non-Jew to convert, whether they would like the names of others who followed the same course, and whether they were willing to be included on such a list.[104] As of 1 August 1969 the list contained eighty-nine rabbis, and Eichhorn estimated that, based on his knowledge of other rabbis who were not listed, there were more than a hundred CCAR members who officiated at interfaith marriages without requiring conversion.[105] In 1970 Rabbi Irwin H. Fishbein founded the Rabbinic Center for Research and Counseling (RCRC) and assumed responsibility for Eichhorn's list, which, by the end of the century, grew to include three times the original number of rabbis. The RCRC was the "first organization established to promote research on intermarriage and to serve the needs of intermarrying and intermarried couples."[106]

The Conservative rabbinate's focus on preventing intermarriage suggests the extent to which the Jewish-Gentile marriage "problem" had grown across denominations. In April 1964 intermarriage was discussed for the first time at the annual convention of the Conservative Rabbinical Assembly. One rabbi argued that intermarriage was increasing and that, although the rabbinate and Jewish parents could not "re-create the ghetto," they ought to "re-create the mood of appreciation and respect for the uniqueness of Judaism" to thwart further defection. Other authors debated whether the intermarried Jew and "his family" should be welcome in the synagogue or sanctioned from membership.[107] Although the response to the discussion provoked the creation of a permanent commission to study how best to prevent intermarriage, it was not until fourteen years later that the intermarriage topic resurfaced at the Rabbinical Assembly.[108] A 1978 paper emphasized conversion as the alternative to attrition of Jews from Judaism, arguing that, although the commitment of some converts might be "watered down or minimal," other converts became far better Jews than the Jews they married. In either case, the author suggested, "we have saved the Jewish partner, and there is a chance for saving the children, the grandchildren, the great-grandchildren and all the generations of the future who will be retained within the Jewish people."[109]

Eventually joining with the Reform and Conservative rabbinates, the Orthodox Rabbinical Council of America decried intermarriage beginning in the 1960s and took action in the 1970s. According to its executive director Steven Dworken, the Council did not publish any decrees about intermarriage during the 1960s and 1970s.[110] However, Orthodox leaders were hardly silent on the topic. The two largest Orthodox Jewish organizations jointly issued a statement when intermarriage was proposed as a solution at the annual meeting of the American Council for Judaism, an anti-Zionist group, on 6 May 1961. The Rabbinical Council and the Union of Orthodox Jewish Congregations publicly criticized the British historian Arnold J. Toynbee for professing that more frequent intermarriage would break down "the traditional caste-barrier between Jews and non-Jews." The Orthodox leaders denied that such a barrier existed in American society, arguing instead that, "the Jewish prohibition against intermarriage is the basic guarantee of Jewish survival of that Judaism which Jews are perpetuating for the benefit of all mankind."[111]

Continuing the public assault on intermarriage, Orthodox leaders of the Rabbinical Court of America, established in 1960 to handle Jewish religious divorces, urged at a December 1963 press conference that all rabbinic groups forbid their members to perform intermarriages. Intermarriage threatened Judaism as well as other faiths, and it caused 42 percent of Jewish family breakdowns, the Court stressed.[112] The Union of Orthodox Jewish Congregations established a commission in 1965 to examine the factors that led Jewish college students to intermarry and to "combat the inducements to intermarriage."[113] And, in 1972, the Rabbinical Council voted to establish a National Commission on Jewish Survival to resist intermarriage and took the significant step of inviting Reform, Conservative, and "secularist" Jews "committed to Jewish survival" to participate in the commission.[114] Another Orthodox organization, the Committee for the Furtherance of Jewish Education, actually sued *Newsday* in 1973 for refusing to publish verbatim an advertisement that condemned intermarriage as "suicide, national and personal."[115] Use of the word "national" might seem to imply that fear of intermarriage was tied to Zionism. More likely, however, it was a reference to the Jewish people and not to the state of Israel. The establishment of Israel in 1948 and its impressive military victory in the 1967 Six-Day War may have lulled non-Orthodox Jews into a sense of security about group survival.[116]

While the rabbinates discussed intermarriage, the officiating debate played out in the popular and national press, raising public awareness about the increase in Jewish-Gentile marriage and the quarrels over rabbinic participation. Illustrating this point, in July 1971 *Newsweek* carried a story highlighting the tensions over whether rabbis should officiate at marriages between Jews and Gentiles, and the related politics within the rabbinates.[117] The CCAR's 1972 findings that 41 percent of Reform rabbis in the U.S. married Jews to Gentiles made national news.[118] "The

Intermarriage Rip-Off," a 1978 article in *Moment* magazine, focused on the economics involved when a rabbi officiated. Painting intermarriage as a "lucrative business," the author detailed the fees rabbis requested for their services and, in some cases, their lack of involvement with the couple prior to the ceremony.[119] However, interfaith couples seeking a rabbi faced other obstacles than simply expense and disinterest.

While highly cynical, "The Intermarriage Rip-Off" article accurately depicted the difficulty interfaith couples faced when trying to find a rabbi willing to officiate, and the potential consequence of refusal. Most rabbis were unwilling to officiate at intermarriages, as Jewish law assumes that marriage unites two people who subscribe to the "the religion of Moses and Israel," that is, who are Jewish. Rabbis also had to reconcile their personal involvement in an interfaith ceremony with Jewish prohibitions against exogamy.[120] For many rabbis, the challenges could not be surmounted. A woman cited in the article commented regarding their attempts, "they made us feel as if we were looking for a doctor to do an illegal abortion, not a rabbi to officiate at a wedding." The couple vowed never to enter a Jewish house of worship ever again.[121] Linda Nusbaum-Stark, a special education teacher born in 1953, searched a long time for a rabbi and encountered significant sarcasm along the way. She asked the representative of one temple, "Do you do mixed marriages?" Linda was disconcerted by what she considered to be a scornful response: "What, boy and girl?" Women who wanted a rabbi to perform the marriage ceremony and were unconcerned with the rabbi's reputation sometimes hired a "marrying Sam," a rabbi who would marry anybody.[122] Fran Rakefield remembered the frustration of having to "import a rabbi" from New York to Boston for her 1976 wedding.[123] Rabbi Samuel M. Silver's comment in his advice book, "I am one of those 'heretical' rabbis who performs weddings in tandem with Christian clergymen," illustrates that to officiate was still considered blasphemous in 1977.[124] However, heretical rabbis found favor with some Jewish women who asserted their wish for the participation of a Jewish officiant when they intermarried. Five of the fourteen women whose narratives are discussed in this chapter were determined to find a rabbi who would preside over their nuptials, and they did.

Feminism and Intermarriage

The second wave of feminism in the 1960s and 1970s increased negotiating power for Jewish women who intermarried by undermining the relationship between the sexes and the definition of marriage in American society. The findings of a 1960 University of Michigan study indicated that more egalitarian decision making between husbands and wives was on the rise, perhaps motivated by the discourse, in the 1950s, on domesticity and women's differences from men.[125] Betty Friedan's 1963 book, *The Feminist Mystique,* sold more than a million copies and has been credited with re-launching the American Feminist movement.[126] Title VII of the 1964 Civil Rights Act outlawed discrimination in public accommodations or employment on the basis of race, color, religion, national origin, or sex.[127] President John F. Kennedy issued Executive Order 10980 on 14 December 1961, establishing the Commission on the Status of Women to overcome employment discrimination while providing social services.[128] However, the refusal of the Equal Employment Opportunity Commission, in 1966, to consider a resolution to treat sex discrimination as seriously as race discrimination prompted Friedan and like-minded women to form the National Organization for Women (NOW). That organization sought an end to occupational segregation, income disparities, and discrimination in education and the professions, a national system of child care, and a fresh "concept of marriage" including "an equitable sharing of the responsibilities of home and children."[129] By 1967 the Women's movement became fragmented.[130] By then, however, the efforts of the 1960s to secure social and economic equality for women had laid an essential foundation for more change. Moreover, the proliferation of radical feminist groups by the end of 1969—twenty-five in Boston, thirty in Chicago, thirty-five in the San Francisco Bay Area, and fifty in New York—and an avalanche of hard-hitting rhetoric called for an end to women's subordination to men in the family structure.[131]

Prompting Jewish women to reevaluate the terms of their own relationships was feminist discourse that identified the differences between women and men as socially constructed, denounced patriarchy, and criticized traditional marriage as rendering women politically powerless.[132] Writers described how women were raised to accept dependency and were "programmed" for a passive role from an early age, when, in reality, they possessed the same assertive quality as men.[133] Shulamith Firestone, a Jewish founder of a pro-woman group called the Redstockings and just twenty-five years old when *The Dialectic of Sex,* her best-selling book on feminist theory was published in 1970, explained:

> Women, biologically distinguished from men, are culturally distinguished from 'human.' Nature produced the fundamental inequality—half the

human race must bear and rear the children of all of them—which was later consolidated, institutionalized, in the interests of men.[134]

Firestone's concept of "self-determination" and a woman's freedom to choose her own lifestyle appealed to women choosing their own marriage partners.[135] The idea of a "participatory democracy" that originated in the Students for a Democratic Society's New Left politics helped make personal relations, including marriage, a topic of analysis.[136] Critiques of marriage argued that marriage locked women into oppressive relationships where they had essentially no power, were exhausted physically, stereotyped emotionally and sexually, and atrophied intellectually.[137] One group went so far as to charge the Marriage License Bureau of New York with "fraud and malicious intent," claiming that the marriage contract legalized and institutionalized "the rape and bondage of women, both their internal (reproductive) and external (domestic labor) functions."[138] Thus, from the 1960s and 1970s on, marriage and women's roles within it, became less externally defined and more personally negotiable.

The new feminism that arose in the 1970s further encouraged Jewish women to become aware of the imbalances in their own lives and to assert themselves. Younger feminists sought not only sexual equality but also social revolution, a complete transformation of values, attitudes, behavior, and institutions. Kate Millet's *Sexual Politics,* published in 1970, advocated the elimination of sexism through the abolition of sex roles in order to liberate all women. The growth of the Women's Liberation movement stemmed from an increasingly widespread criticism of family and personal life, which struck at the heart of a large proportion of American women's oppression. Consciousness-raising groups, where women shared their personal experiences, led them beyond demands for equal rights externally to demands for equal power within their homes.[139] The feminist Pat Mainardi advocated that "participatory democracy begins at home," explaining that although women increasingly had careers, they were also still burdened with housework that men considered too trivial to do.[140] The goal of achieving parity within the home extended from domestic labor to other aspects of married life, including the religious orientation of the family unit.

A more malleable and egalitarian understanding of marriage enabled Jewish women to better formulate and articulate their religious preferences within their marriages. Marriage that was more democratic and defined by consent between the couple, rather than by the state, spread in popularity through the 1970s.[141] Although not all women were activists or participated in feminist discussion groups, *Ms.* magazine distributed the spirit of feminism far and wide. By 1973, the year after Gloria Steinem founded the magazine, *Ms.* had a subscription list of nearly two hundred thousand, and a poll showed that close to three-quarters of its readers were not members of feminist organizations.[142] Although most readers may not have identified as "feminists," the rapid increase in subscriptions indicated that many American women were eager to achieve greater equality in their personal lives. One of the very first issues in 1972 featured an article titled "How to Write Your Marriage Contract."[143] New books also appeared in the 1970s, advising women on how to create a unique wedding ceremony and offering suggestions on making their relationships more fulfilling. Equality was one book's moral keynote that deemed "enrichment of the individual identity of each partner" as more important than social roles and expectations.[144] Another example, *For Better, For Worse: A Feminist Handbook on Marriage and Other Options,* claimed to give women "new ways to look at your situation . . . to share concrete information as well as personal stories and suggestions for new ways of interacting."[145]

As feminism raised women's awareness of the potential to achieve greater parity with their husbands, women's increasing professional involvement in the labor force and the rising valuation of "women's work" outside the home meant more voting power within the familial structure. Once the strictly husband-provider and dependent-wife model of marriage began to break down, Jewish women were increasingly in a position to voice their opinions about how they wanted to self-identify and raise their children. Thirty percent of married women were in the labor force by 1960, twice the percentage in 1940. By 1970, 40 percent of all American wives and two-thirds of mothers with children younger than six were working outside the home.[146] The term "dual-career family," popularized in 1969, illustrated how American marriage had changed to include a wife and husband both taking their work and professional needs seriously. This significantly altered the idea that a wife's income was supplemental and that a woman's professional aspirations were subordinate to her husband's.[147] In 1975, 42 percent of Boston Jewish women age thirty to thirty-nine, and nearly three-quarters of Jewish women over age forty, worked outside the home.[148] All but one of the fourteen women interviewed for this book who intermarried between 1963 and 1979 earned an income during her marriage. In 1977 more than half of all mothers with school-age children, and more than a third of mothers with children younger than three years old, worked outside the home. Women who entered the employment marketplace who had tasted independence gained greater confidence and were less easy to satisfy.[149] During the decade after Congress passed the Equal Pay Act in 1963, 171,000 employees won $84 million in back pay, thanks to the "equal pay for equal work" legislation.[150] Perhaps this signaled to women of all religious and ethnic backgrounds that their labor, both inside and outside the home, was worth more than they had realized. Hence their opinions should also carry more weight.

Work and feminism influenced Jewish women in the late 1960s and 1970s similarly as they had been factors in the lives of Mary Antin, Rose Pastor Stokes, and Anna Strunsky Walling at the beginning of the century. Now that more women defied the traditional gender roles of full-time homemaker and could increasingly demand greater equality with their politically like-minded husbands, women were in a better position to shape their personal lives according to their own wishes without necessarily threatening their marriages. A major shift in women's attitudes toward work and family occurred from 1943 to 1971. The proportion of college women who would opt for full-time homemaking and volunteer activities declined dramatically; 62 percent of the women polled in 1971 indicated that they would definitely return to work after the birth of a child compared to 30 percent in 1943.[151] Moreover, women who worked were more liberal in their attitudes than women who did not and, according to one 1976 study, Jewish women appeared to be less accepting of women's traditional familial role expectations and responsibilities than either Catholic or Protestant women.[152]

In addition to the evolving institution of marriage and equal pay legislation that created room for all women advocating for themselves, that certain high-profile feminists were Jewish may have contributed to the effect of second-wave feminism on intermarried Jewish women. As the historian Joyce Antler points out in *The Journey Home,* many of the women involved in the feminist movements for rights and liberation in the 1960s and early 1970s were Jewish, though largely secular and unidentified.[153] Betty Friedan, Phyllis Chesler, and Letty Cottin Pogrebin, to name a few, experienced a reawakening of their Jewish identities through their work as feminists.[154] Further, the debut in 1976 of *Lilith,* a Jewish women's quarterly magazine, publicized the interrelationships between Jewish identity and feminism, serving as a catalyst for action on behalf of Jewish women.[155] The combination of feminism and Jewishness suggested to some women who married non-Jews that they, too, could achieve greater balance within their marriages and openly identify as Jews. Jewish feminists helped to reconfigure

Sally Priesand, the sole female rabbinical student at Hebrew Union College-Jewish Institute of Religion, in 1971 (Garrett Cope, photographer; courtesy of the Jewish Women's Archive and the American Jewish Archives).

what it meant to be a Jewish woman in America; this, in turn, allowed Jewish women who intermarried to choose how they wanted to be Jewish.

Jewish feminists expanded the boundaries of Jewish womanhood, which paved the way for Jewish women who married non-Jews to increasingly define themselves as Jews according to their own standards. Some women aspired to overthrow the patriarchy of traditional Judaism and claim their space on the *bimah*. For example, the Conservative feminist organization Ezrat Nashim sought full religious parity with Jewish men. Its members demonstrated at the Conservative Rabbinical Assembly in March 1972, after having been excluded from the official program of the annual meeting.[156] The entry of women as ordained clergy signaled a shift in the story of American religion.[157] On 3 June 1972 Sally Priesand became the first woman rabbi, symbolizing, in the words of the historian Pamela S. Nadell, "the fulfillment of women's emancipation within Reform Judaism."[158] These examples illustrate that Jewish women could claim new roles for themselves within Judaism. A woman's Jewishness could be accentuated to the extent of becoming a rabbi, deemphasized to the point of apparent irrelevance, or reinvented in what may appear as a secular vein.

Secularization theory, however, does not generally take into account the private realm. "Secularization," according to the historian Ann Braude, "can mean the same thing as feminization, a decline in religious efficacy in a public realm associated with men's activities, concurrent with persistent or increased influence in a private realm associated with women and the family."[159] Like the interracial couples whose lives Romano describes, the relationship between feminism and interfaith marriage exposes the ways in which boundaries traditionally known as "public" and "private" are socially constructed and change over time.[160]

Some women were repulsed by the patriarchy and turned away from Judaism, at least temporarily, and others urged their Jewish sisters to stake their claim to Jewishness lest non-Jewish feminists do it for them. Author, activist, and one of the founding editors of *Ms.*, Letty Cottin Pogrebin had disassociated from her Jewishness at age fifteen when she was not counted in the *minyan* that said *kaddish* (the Jewish mourners' prayer) for her own mother. When she later reconciled Judaism and feminism, Pogrebin claimed that being Jewish was irrelevant to her social and professional life up until 1975. Pogrebin's Jewish persona was reawakened when delegates at the first United Nations International Women's Decade Conference held in Mexico City passed a resolution that identified Jews as racist. This experience and the realization that some of her "sisters" were antisemites who supported the PLO slogan "Zionism is racism" made her see the importance of "being a public, affirmative Jew—even when ethnicity or religion 'didn't matter.'"[161] Pogrebin was among the thirteen women who, in 1976, initiated the first feminist Seder in the United States where participants forged Jewish identities consistent with feminist values.[162] She warned: "The Jewish woman who does not take possession of her total identity, and make it count for something, may find that others will impose upon her a label she does not like at all."[163]

The specifically Jewish feminism spoke directly to women of Jewish heritage, encouraging them to take ownership of their own lives and identities. Roberta Gootblatt, whose poem appears in the epigraph to this chapter, urged women to throw off the middle-class goal for Jewish women to become "a good cook and a terrific housewife," exposing Jewish women's oppression as the "property" of Jewish men, first fathers then husbands. Gootblatt wrote in 1970: "Hitler did outwardly to all Jews, male and female, what the Jewish male does inwardly to the Jewish woman. . . . Within that Jewish middle class, the women exist in a psychological concentration camp." Her shocking rhetoric, which was clearly influenced by Friedan's analogy of domesticity as the "comfortable concentration camp" in her *Feminine Mystique*, encouraged Jewish women to use their inner strength to gain a deeper understanding of being a Jew as a whole, self-liberated person.[164] Gootblatt did not propose exogamy; her criticism of Jewish men was about patriarchy and middle-class domesticity. Such discourse intended to alert Jewish women that the time had arrived to become "New Jewish Women" who identified positively as Jews *and* as women. Unlike the New Jewish Womanhood of the Progressive Era that combined labor, socializing, and political activism alongside men, New Jewish Women in the 1970s demanded equality with men. Incidentally a New Jewish Man has yet to emerge, as demonstrated by the current debate about the disappearance of Jewish men from organized religious life. Why women, more than men, find ways to understand their experiences and construct their identities through religion has yet to be understood.[165]

Jewish feminism played an important role in the relationship between intermarriage and Jewish women's influence on the contours of family life. While the structural barriers to intermarriage between Jewish women and non-Jewish men diminished, Jewish feminism encouraged Jewish women to retain, reclaim, or redefine their ethnic and religious heritage.[166] Awareness began to surface in the late 1970s that Jewish women responded to intermarriage differently than Jewish communal leaders previously thought. Although most observers continued to report that more Jewish men intermarried than Jewish women, they also incorporated gender in their analysis of endogamy's effects. For example, one social scientist suggested that a Jewish wife in an intermarriage was more likely to raise her children as Jews, illustrating the continued Jewish involvement of Jewish women who intermarried.[167] The Women's Liberation movement that extended the American ethos of self-fulfillment to women also enabled them to make more Jewish choices concerning their identities and their children. Reversing a historical trend, one rabbi projected in 1974 that many of the Jewish men who intermarried would be permanently lost to the Jewish community, whereas the majority of Jewish women would remain "proudly and loyally Jewish." Although personally opposed to intermarriage, he opined that, "the idealistic and determined young Jewish females of today, even those who marry out, are going to develop, during the years to come, into better and more devoted Jews than were or are many of their fathers and mothers."[168]

Jewish Rebels

The socially and politically turbulent decades of the 1960s and 1970s created significant alterations in the meaning of intermarriage to Jewish women in America. Three themes appear repeatedly throughout the fourteen oral history narratives that speak to this time period, capturing the major changes that occurred. These women questioned imposed values and criticized what they considered hypocritical, such as a lack of spirituality and pretentious concerns about appearances and social status, breaking free of cultural restraints and expanding their life experiences in the process. Indeed, hypocrisy was a frequent charge against organized religion in America in general and was particularly common among religious individualists.[169] They were more vocal and negotiated adamantly about including Jewish practices in their married lives, increasingly identifying passionately as Jewish. These intermarried women also voiced greater preoccupation about the past and the future, linking personal choices to the Holocaust and to the future of the Jewish people. These three unprecedented themes illustrate the evolving contour of intermarriage and provide the framework for the following analysis.

Some of these intermarried Jewish women charged their parents and their Jewish community with superficiality, illustrating one of the differences between baby boomers who rejected social boundaries and the preceding Cold War generation that upheld them.[170] According to Fran Rakefield, the Reform synagogue culture of her youth lacked "any feeling of religion or spirituality" and "the most important thing was the clothes you wore. I hated the whole scene."[171] In 1973 an administrator for the Jewish Student Press Service likewise complained that the "synagogues were stultifying," the "fashion show" gave Jewish youth reasons to reject bourgeois middle-class life and to leave the Jewish fold.[172] Olivia Barton, who was born in 1929 and became an artist before devoting herself entirely to motherhood, was thrown out of Sunday School for asking a facetious question about reading Hebrew right to left or top to bottom. She joined the temple youth group but quit after finding out that, allegedly, the Sisterhood tried to misappropriate her waitress earnings from a Brotherhood dinner.[173] Joan Marcus was born in 1940, grew up in a kosher home, and secretly dated a non-Jew in high school. Her parents received an anonymous letter informing them that she was seeing "a *Gentile* boy of *questionable* reputation," that is, one without money or familial status. Her father threatened not to send her to college if she continued to see the boy. Joan described her reaction: "I felt persecuted and I thought they were crazy. I thought they had shallow values."[174] Although Joan married a fellow Jew with radical political views in 1964, she divorced him shortly thereafter, and then remarried a Presbyterian in 1968.

Jewish women who intermarried in the 1960s found fault with what they considered parental inconsistency and hypocritical behavior. Nearly half the women discussed in this chapter described their decisions to intermarry as a form of rebellion against their parents. At a time when risk substituted for security and activism replaced adaptation, marrying the "other" represented an appealing act of subversion.[175] Amy Jacobson's family was not religious when she was growing up in Brooklyn, New York; they did not encourage Jewish education, nor did they attend synagogue. Yet, similar to the attitudinal phenomenon discussed in the previous chapter, her father was upset when she decided to marry a non-Jew.[176] "Yeah, my father was hypocritical," she remarked. Amy strove to differentiate her life from her parents' lives. Amy described the crux of her marriage to a non-Jew: "This marriage was about getting away from my family and getting away from, emotionally, from the Brooklyn environment. . . . And if I wanted to pick somebody who was *least* like anything that I knew in childhood, I did."[177] She was well aware that her actions were acts of resistance. Amy explained, "One of the reasons for this marriage seemed to be this rebellion against home." Without any formal religious background, being Jewish was about home, family, and environment, all of which Amy rejected when she intermarried. In the early 1960s Amy and her friends rebelled by going to Europe and then returned to the United States to rebel by intermarrying. Amy's marriage lasted less than four years.[178]

Several women rejected what they referred to as a Jewish ghetto mentality. Joan Marcus associated her parents' view about interdating with their fear that Jews had to stick together because there might be repercussions against Jews if they fraternized with non-Jews. She found this belief offensive and credited the times for allowing her to think more broadly: "We came out in the '60s and it opened our eyes. We were given an opportunity to break out of little small-town roots . . . and we thought, screw that."[179] Parental apprehension was part of a larger ideological framework of a generation that married during the Great Depression and war, not to mention greater antisemitism, and responded by turning inward for domestic security. Joan Marcus and Karen Amai experienced dating under different circumstances that dispelled Cold War notions about domestic containment and enabled them to reject Jewish familial security as the means to individual freedom and fulfillment.[180] Karen Amai's high school had an area known as "Little Jerusalem," where all the Jewish kids congregated. Her displeasure with what she considered clannish behavior and a constricting, cliquish milieu was ameliorated by her departure for Boston. Karen met people "who *weren't* Jewish, who weren't the same, who weren't from this identifiable, tight—and in some ways, I felt, stifling—group. It was very exciting to me to meet people from different countries and cultures, and backgrounds."[181] Karen's intermarriage ultimately fulfilled her desire to be free from what she felt was a confining Jewish-only group existence.

Rebellion against their parents and the Jewish community through intermarriage did not extinguish women's Jewish identities, nor did all Jewish women intermarry as an act of rebellion. In an important article on intermarriage and identity, the historian Deborah Dash Moore contextualized her thirty-year marriage to a non-Jew by illustrating the similarities between her Jewish childhood and her married life that included Shabbat dinners and synagogue affiliation. Moore stated: "Mine was not a rebellion, a rejection of parental values and mores, an act of conscious assimilation away from Judaism to American society."[182] Women identified as Jewish despite having intermarried, often conceiving of being Jewish in an ethnic or racial sense, in addition to or instead of religiously. A *New York Times* reporter observed in 1973 that the Jewish spouses in intermarriages had strong Jewish identities, "regardless of how they feel about religion per se."[183] Dora Maci was born in Boston in 1933, grew up in Revere, Massachusetts, became an English teacher, and married an Italian Catholic in 1969. Her family of origin was a combination of observant and assimilated Jews; they kept kosher at home but ate in restaurants, worked on Saturdays but not on Jewish holidays. Dora insisted on telling people she was Jewish, working it into casual conversations and identifying with fellow Jews; "'I'm one of you' is what I want people to know . . . I feel very tribal sometimes."[184] Tribalism, according to Cohen and Eisen, is the sense of familism (or peoplehood) expressed in special concern for other Jews; unflattering views of non-Jews, and positive images of themselves; Jews as different from others and sharing a common sensibility with each other.[185] Marsha Ember, born in 1943, became a speech therapist and married a black Baptist man in 1971. Identifying as Jewish, for her, was devoid of religion: "I identify really strongly as a Jewish woman, but it has *nothing* to do with religion. It really has to do with where I fit in history and the culture."[186] Apparently the disjoining of

Judaism and Jewishness did not lessen the fervor of Jewish women's identities. The combination of individualism and assimilation, political liberalism and feminism, changed the nature of Judaism in such a way that
women could effectively be culturally Jewish and religiously observant to
greater or lesser degrees according to their preferences.

Women who intermarried in the 1960s and 1970s were considerably
more adamant about their being Jewish, with few exceptions, than those
who intermarried earlier in the century. Jewish women who intermarried
emphasized repeatedly that their spouses were well aware of their wives'
Jewishness; it was an established fact. Carol Ferris, who married in 1968,
thought that her husband was pleased to have a Jewish wife. In her words,
"I felt cared for and I am a Jewish woman . . . and I felt that he accepted all
parts of me."[187] One woman who took her husband's non-Jewish last name
made sure that every person she met knew that she was Jewish.[188] Another explained that she kept her last name for reasons that went beyond
feminism: "I did *not* want a non-Jewish last name . . . Because I *am* Jewish and I wouldn't want people to think that I wasn't."[189] A third woman
remembered her aversion to names of non-Jewish origin: "I would *never*
want my name to be something like Murphy or Antonelli," she explained,
"I'm glad I'm not Christian."[190] Thus, though some Jewish women were
comfortable marrying a Gentile, they did not wish to be mistaken for one.
This intense objection to possibly being identified as a non-Jew marks a
significant change from some of the women discussed in chapter 2, who
intermarried at mid-century and did not proactively identify as Jewish,
only admitting that they were Jewish if asked.

Intermarriage could actually strengthen and accentuate a woman's Jewish cultural identity. Linda Friedman Shah, a Jewish woman who married
a Moslem in 1971, publicized her experience in the *New York Times*. "My
acquaintance with Islam has had the overwhelming effect of resurrecting
my own Semitism," she wrote, "something I never before knew was a part
of me."[191] Olivia Barton described the effect of having to educate her Episcopalian husband about being identified as "other"; her identity as a Jewish woman was strengthened. Moreover, she explained, "I'm *not* displeased
to be Jewish . . . it has enormous assets and . . . as a minority member, it
has made me perhaps more sensitive to other people's situations and has
helped me to sensitize those people who I feel *need* to be sensitized."[192]
Her narrative illustrates how some women identified as Jewish culturally,
in connection with a people, rather than religiously, involving Jewish texts
and active worship. Fran Rakefield summed up her experience: "Well, the

whole marriage heightened my sense of being Jewish. I mean, at the time that I got married, my sense of identity as a Jew was *totally* minimal. Over the marriage, I became more and more aware of being Jewish."[193] Her heightened Jewish identity led her to become more involved in the Jewish community than she had ever been before; she worked for a Jewish organization and accumulated Jewish colleagues. Rochelle Larkin, quoted in a 1973 *New York Times* article about Jewish-Gentile marriages, thought her Jewishness had "intensified and multiplied" since she married her black Roman Catholic husband.[194]

Although not widely recognized, the prospect that Jewish women could marry "out" and yet remain "in" did not go unnoticed. Rabbi James Rudin of the Interreligious Affairs Commission, a Reform organization, acknowledged in 1976 that Judaism's pull was stronger than previously believed and that Jews who intermarried were "more self-conscious about remaining Jewish these days." Inge Gibel, who participated in the AJC's 1976 study on intermarriage, summed it up as follows: "The trend has been for the Jewish partner to work harder at being Jewishly involved."[195] Linda Nusbaum-Clark enrolled in an "Introduction to Judaism" class with her husband so that he could gain knowledge about Jewish history and learn a little Hebrew. She remembered, "Actually, that's sort of what taught me enough Hebrew so I could go on and do my bat mitzvah. So it motivated *me*."[196] Hence, instead of becoming more distant from Judaism after intermarrying, some Jewish women became more proactive about being Jewish than they had been before they married a non-Jew.

Jewish women's involvement in political movements contributed to their increased power within their marital relationships and outspokenness about how they identified and wanted to raise their children. The legacy of President Kennedy's 1960 inaugural challenge, "Ask not what your country can do for you; ask what you can do for your country," inspired political activism and risk taking that extended into the personal lives of intermarried Jewish women.[197] Linda Nusbaum-Stark was more politically active than most women I interviewed, but she also illustrated the potential effects of activism on intermarriage. Linda attended Kent State University less than two years after the Ohio National Guard fatally shot four students protesting the dispatch of U.S. troops from Vietnam into Cambodia in 1970.[198] She raised money for Israel during the Yom Kippur War of 1973, participated in an anti-inaugural demonstration against President Richard Nixon in 1973, and organized campus speakers regarding the students who had been killed. By the time she married in 1978, Linda had

had a lot of practice articulating her point of view. She and her spouse discussed in advance that marriage would not be fifty-fifty when it came to religion. Their home would be Jewish. In Linda's words: "We wouldn't have a Christmas tree, we wouldn't have Christmas lights. And that was something he had to be able to live with." Linda tried to persuade her husband to take her surname, which was identifiably Jewish, but ended up hyphenating their names. "I made out like a bandit in this one. I did not give up very much," she boasted regarding the marital negotiation.[199]

Insecurity about being Jewish or a lack of Judaic knowledge affected some women who intermarried. For example, Diane Endicott disliked feeling that, as a Jew, she grew up outside the American mainstream. Staying home from school on Jewish holidays had made her cringe, whereas getting into elite social clubs as an adult made her feel connected to the mainstream. Her parents were upset when she chose not to circumcise her son so that he would resemble his father, and this disagreement pushed her away from her family of origin, from Judaism, and from Jewishness. Regarding her decision to eliminate her Jewish last name, Diane commented, "I wasn't confident enough to wear it, comfortably, and I think I will always wonder about that part of myself." Nevertheless, Diane insisted: "I was born Jewish and I'll die Jewish. I will always just be plain Jewish."[200] Diane remained adamantly Jewish despite her internal conflicts about her Jewishness.

Identifying as a Jewish woman was a sensitive journey for women who grew up without strong parental support for Jewish education. Amy Jacobson was always interested in religion and convinced her father to allow her to attend Hebrew School. As an adult, she immersed herself professionally in Jewish culture; "Now it's very clear to me why I've been working on Jewish stuff. . . . It was never a clear identity, and I always envied those people tremendously—and still do—who had learning and background and all of that. For those of us who didn't, it's not so easy."[201] Amy Jacobson, among other women, sought more Jewish education than her parents offered. Comparing her lack of Jewish schooling with her daughters, Linda Nusbaum-Stark commented, "My training was less than what my girls have had, by *half*."[202] Evidently Linda made sure her children received what she had missed, and Amy enriched her life by pursuing Jewish related work.

Even though most Gentile husbands supported their wife's Jewish identities and desire to raise Jewish children, some women wished that their husbands were Jewish. Judaism had always been important to Linda

Nusbaum-Stark and, regarding her husband, she said "I would've liked him to be Jewish."[203] She thought it would be unfair to ask him to convert, however, and was content with his declaration that he was a "Jew by association."[204] Trudy Melos did ask her husband if he would consider converting, and initially he refused. His willingness to learn, however, led to a course on Judaism. Twenty years after they first wed in 1979, Trudy's husband returned from attending Christmas Mass and announced, "I'm converting." Trudy's surprise was quickly replaced by sheer joy.[205] Her experience, however, was not common.

Despite feminism emboldening some women to take a stronger stand regarding Jewish identity and family practice, conversion to Judaism continued to be largely done by women, with relatively few Gentile men converting to match their Jewish spouse. In 1966 the sociologists Goldstein and Goldscheider found that in one out of every three cases of intermarriage between a non-Jewish female and a Jewish male the woman converted, whereas in only one out of six cases did the non-Jewish male married to a Jewish female convert.[206] Similarly, the 1970-72 NJPS found that whereas 27 percent of non-Jewish wives converted to Judaism, only 3 percent of non-Jewish husbands did so.[207] A 1978 study found that 66 percent of converts to Judaism were women.[208] The trauma of adult circumcision or the fact that most Jews would consider children of a Jewish mother and Gentile father as Jewish may have made conversion by Gentile husbands seem unnecessary.[209] Moreover, as Dru Greenwood, the director of the William and Lottie Daniel Department of Outreach and Synagogue Community of the Union of American Hebrew Congregations (the Reform movement), explains, conversion to Judaism is "a gendered phenomenon" in the United States with men tending to convert later in the life cycle than when they wed (if at all).[210] Not surprisingly, therefore, only one husband out of fourteen who married Jewish women between 1963 and 1979 had converted by the time of this study.

Women who did not want their husbands to convert to Judaism did want them to understand the nature and threat of antisemitism. Whether Ellen Kolokowski's husband became Jewish was not important as long as he respected that she was Jewish. Ellen felt that her husband's support when she pointed out prejudicial remarks against Jews became a bonding thread for the couple. Their common understanding of antisemitism made it their issue, rather than hers alone. That Ellen's husband cried when they viewed *Schindler's List,* Steven Spielberg's award-winning 1993 film about the Holocaust, suggested to her that "he really got it" on a visceral level.[211]

Women wanted their husbands to understand antisemitism because they were offended by it, even angry. Ellen did not consider it a compliment when someone told her, "You don't *look* Jewish." Moreover, Ellen felt that her in-laws' lack of understanding about not socializing on Yom Kippur or eating bread on Passover was antisemitic. "I have been married 27 years, and *really* and *truly* it's time they got onboard."[212] Olivia Barton equated antisemitism with sexism. "You either get it as a woman or you get it as [a Jew]," she declared, explaining that antisemitism infuriated her and that she had no patience for it.[213] Beth Jonah was hurt by antisemitic remarks that someone had made, but they did not make her wish that she was not Jewish. Instead, she considered the remarks a reflection on the commentator; "there was something defective with their thinking," she concluded.[214] Jewish women who intermarried in the 1960s and 1970s openly and vociferously condemned antisemitism; they did not seek to escape it or to find a "cure."

Holocaust Remembered, Future Pondered

The Holocaust and its historical aftermath linked individual Jewish women to the Jewish group despite their having married "out." The consequences of the Second World War had an emotional impact on some Jewish women who intermarried in the 1960s and 1970s, eroding the "group amnesia" that seemed to affect women who intermarried in the 1940s and 1950s, as discussed above.[215] Karen Amai, born in 1945, cared intensely about the Holocaust when she intermarried in 1969. Her preoccupation with this topic fostered a bond with her Japanese husband whose mother experienced internment during World War II; they related on the basis of both being minorities whose people had been threatened.[216] Similar to Jews in the 1940s, whose insecure status as white may have predisposed some to marry blacks, persistent feelings of being an "outsider" may have predisposed some women to marry interracially in the 1960s.[217] Another woman shuddered, "Had I been in a different place or time, it would've been *me* that went to the ovens."[218] Her realization illustrates awareness that intermarriage did not exempt her from the fate of Jewish people to whom, historically, she remained closely tied.

Jewish women's intermarriage experiences reflect the public consciousness about the Holocaust brought about by the Israeli abduction and trial of the Nazi war criminal Adolf Eichmann and new books published in the 1960s such as Raul Hilberg's *The Destruction of the European Jews* (1961),

Hannah Arendt's *Eichmann in Jerusalem* (1963), and Arthur Morse's *While Six Million Died* (1967). Morse's book provoked the question, "What did American Jews do in the years of the Holocaust?" which, according to the historian Jack Wertheimer, "haunted American Jews and inspired a new commitment to Jewish survival, succinctly expressed in the newly coined Jewish credo–'Never Again!'"[219] Although it is impossible to determine the extent to which Jewish women who intermarried followed Eichmann's trial or read these particular books, they were well aware of the mass deaths of their European coreligionists and often chose actions to counterbalance the loss of Jewish life.

Many of the Jewish women I interviewed who intermarried during the 1960s and 1970s made intimate connections between the Holocaust and their decisions to raise their children to be Jewish, unlike the Jewish women who married in the 1940s and 1950s. Beginning in the late 1940s, the human destruction of World War II was recognized many times over within Jewish circles. However, its influence on Jewish women's consciousnesses was delayed until after the 1967 Israeli War when the Holocaust emerged as "an icon of American Jewish identity," in the words of the historian Hasia Diner. Holocaust remembrance events that reached a broader audience combined with popular culture, such as the NBC television series *Holocaust* (1978) and the film *Schindler's List* (1993), contributed to making the Holocaust a significant element of American Jewish consciousness.[220] Dora Maci, who was born in 1933 and married in 1969, spoke at great length with her husband about the religious identity of a prospective child. "I said, the child has to be Jewish," she remembered asserting.[221] Dora explained that thoughts of those who perished seriously factored into her thinking about insisting that her child be raised Jewish. Raising children in any other religion was inconceivable, she told her husband, "I cannot take away from the numbers. I just can't do that."[222] Fran Rakefield felt extremely guilty about the Holocaust and the prospect of weakening Jewish survival by intermarrying and raising children with a non-Jewish father. "I did not want to let down the Jewish people by not continuing the race that was already so decimated," she explained. She felt she had done her duty by raising Jewish children.[223] Fran's use of the word "race" illustrates her perception of Jews as a distinct biological group.

It is striking that the narratives of some intermarried Jewish women reflect the racialized notions of Jewishness consistent with the pre-World War II period discussed in chapter 1, despite that the historical concept of "racial" Jewishness in common American understanding became intolerable after the Nazi atrocities.[224] Perhaps it illustrates a repercussion of antisemitism on conceptions of Jewish identity. A forty-something intermarried woman spoke out about the connection between her traumatic past and child rearing in the *National Jewish Monthly* in February 1965: "Maybe because Hitler killed my family I feel that by raising my children Jewish I can make up for it."[225]

Conceptions of Jewishness played important roles in some women's premarital discussions regarding children, even though politics figured more prominently than religion in their romantic lives. In the late 1960s and 1970s, the discussion of how children of intermarriage would be raised was frequently initiated *before* they wed rather than as children arrived, which was more often the case earlier in the century. Carol Ferris insisted that any future child she had with her prospective spouse would be Jewish, given the Jewish law of matrilineal descent and because that was her preference. Her finality on the issue suggests that there was no room for debate concerning her child's ethno-religious identity. Like Fran, Carol's understanding of Jewishness was primarily racial; it was in the blood.[226]

Some women's belief in "Jewish bloodlines" illustrates the tenacity of a racialized notion of Jewishness and the small role they ascribed Jewish education on conceptions of Jewish identity in America. Their assumption that Jewish identity was somehow passed down echoes the late-nineteenth-century rhetoric about race. According to the historian Eric Goldstein, "If the language of race was employed by Jews who sought to regulate social interaction with gentiles and to prevent intermarriage, it also helped those Jews who had given up affiliation with the Jewish community retain a sense of identity as Jews."[227] Carol did not intend to provide religious training, because she did not believe that being Jewish was associated with "organized religious beliefs."[228] For both Carol and Beth Jonah, who also supported matrilineal descent, their children's Jewish identity was disassociated from Jewish education. "It was important to me that my children have a strong Jewish identity," Beth explained, "[but] it wasn't *that* important to me that they have a very strong Jewish *education*."[229] These women did not, however, elaborate as to how their children would develop Jewish identities other than through awareness of their inherited bloodlines. Their narratives illustrate, in the words of Matthew Frye Jacobson, "how historical circumstances, politically driven categorization, and the eye of the beholder all conspire to create distinctions of race that are nonetheless experienced as *natural* phenomena, above history and beyond question."[230] Just as women in the previous century used racial terminology to define Jewishness once they experienced greater integration in the non-Jewish world, Jewish women who intermarried in the twentieth century did so as well when defining themselves and their children.[231]

Women who did not explicitly raise Jewish children expressed lingering concerns regarding antisemitism, distaste for all religions, and regret. For example, Joan Marcus never suggested raising their children as Jews because she had not wanted to impose on her husband; she knew he would have been uncomfortable having Jewish children. But when her grown daughter became an Episcopalian, Joan was upset that neither she nor her spouse had given their children anything of a spiritual nature from their own religious traditions.[232] Marsha Ember told her son about the history of Jewish holidays but steered clear of religious theology, professing a strong dislike for religion. She raised him to accept the differences in people, a lesson her mother had taught her, which she exemplified when she married interracially. Although Diane Endicott never took her son to temple, and felt that he would always be both Jewish and Christian, she regretted not enabling him to have a bar mitzvah. Moreover she told a detailed story about her son going to Hillel for Rosh Hashanah with a classmate. Diane reflected with a degree of awe, "My son is *very* aware of being Jewish and my hat's off to him as a person. I don't know where it came from, how it happened."[233] Clearly Diane was enthusiastic that her son was proactive about cultivating his Jewish identity, though she had not pursued Jewish education on his behalf.

The Jewish women I interviewed who intermarried following divorce usually wanted their children to marry Jews, regardless of whether their first husbands were Jewish or Gentile. Although her first marriage to a non-Jew lasted a mere three years and she subsequently remarried a Jew, Amy Jacobson wondered whether her daughters from her second marriage would model her first marriage for their own behavior.[234] She hoped they would marry Jews, but conceded that some interfaith couples raise children with stronger Jewish identities than Jewish-Jewish couples she knew. Dora Maci despaired that her daughter was not a more observant Jew and attended a Unitarian Church with her partner. She agonized over her son's suggestion that her own intermarriage made an interfaith relationship appealing to her daughter; "That just *killed* me," Dora said.[235] Trudy Melos remarried a non-Jew in 1979, but she insisted that her children marry Jews and gave them "a hard time" when they considered doing otherwise. Trudy's explanation for how she could oppose her children intermarrying when she herself had done so was the following:

> Because I felt that my first marriage, during which these children were created, that was a Jewish marriage and these children were Jewish and that's part of the Jewish people. My *second* marriage was done just for me. Pure selfishness. It had nothing to do with the community. It was for *me*. I met this guy, he's my best friend, we're going to have the rest of our lives together, and that's a done deal, you know. And to my kids, it's their turn now to produce Jewish children.[236]

The women's behavior, though seemingly contradictory, illustrates their belief in sustaining the Jewish people. They had done their portion, so to speak, and hoped that their children would follow suit.

Although some Jewish women worried that their own intermarriages would influence their children, nearly all who intermarried between 1963 and 1979 were concerned about their prospective grandchildren. Beth Jonah expected her biological grandchildren to be Jewish. Regarding her offspring she said, "I don't really have a preference for whether they marry Jews. I do feel strongly whether they bring up their children Jewish."[237] Fran Rakefield, who married a Presbyterian, had raised Jewish children primarily because she did not want to hurt her grandparents. Thinking ahead to her own future as a grandmother, she commented, "I'd feel really uncomfortable to have Catholic grandchildren."[238] Linda Nusbaum-Stark admitted that she could not look her children in the eye and implore they marry Jews when their own father was not Jewish. Yet, she had no reservations about expressing herself regarding grandchildren: "I really want my grandchildren to be Jewish, and I think it will be hard for me if they're not."[239] Jewish women who intermarried and wished for Jewish grandchildren understood that the religious fate of their descendants was beyond their control.

Intermarriage after Divorce

Complicating the widespread belief that religious intermarriage was likely to end in divorce, The experiences of Jewish women suggest that previous divorce sometimes led to intermarriage.[240] The divorce rate doubled in the United States between 1967 and 1977.[241] All the women's intermarriages between 1930 and 1960, discussed in chapter 2, were first marriages. In

contrast, eight of the fourteen women I interviewed who intermarried between 1963 and 1979 had divorced and remarried. In all but one case the
first marriage was to a Jew, which failed, and the second to a non-Jew. Erich Rosenthal's 1970 study, "Divorce and Religious Intermarriage," found
that a previous divorce led to subsequent intermarriage. Moreover, Jewish
intermarriages recorded a greater percentage of former marriages than did
marriages between two Jews.[242] The Jewish women I have discussed who
divorced Jews and remarried Gentiles in the 1960s and 1970s resemble
the Jews whose second marriages were exogamous in Rosenthal's study.
This suggests that women whose first marriage to Jews was unsuccessful
were not disinclined to remarry, but they may have been more inclined to
marry "out" the second time around.

Greater acceptance from Jewish family members multiplied along with
the increases in the rates of intermarriage and divorce during the 1960s
and 1970s. Ellen Kolokowski's father preferred that she remarry a Gentile than to remain a divorcée. She recalled that he was happy when she
remarried, "*Even* to a non-Jew!"[243] Sometimes parents prioritized their
daughters' happiness over their son-in-laws' religious background. Dora
Maci's parents accepted her non-Jewish husband, partly because he was
a good person and partly because they did not want her to be alone for
"the rest of her life" following a divorce with a Jewish man. Once Dora's
mother got to know her daughter's betrothed, she said, "Some people don't
need religion to be good," and he was one of them.[244] Diane Endicott's
parents empathized with their daughter's unfortunate experiences when,
after an initial divorce, the next man with whom she became romantically involved died. She described their response when she remarried a
Gentile: "I think they just were happy that I was happy and they liked
him *so* much that . . . it just didn't matter."[245] When Joan Marcus mustered
up the courage to tell her grandmother about her second husband, "Well
you know, Bubbie, he's not Jewish," she was surprised by the response. "It
happens," said the family matriarch.[246] The blasé response illustrates the
extent to which intermarriage had become less objectionable by the last
third of the century, even among older Jews. This is not to say that all
Jewish families wholeheartedly accepted Jewish women's intermarriages.
One woman recalled her Jewish sister-in-law's question about her Gentile
partner: "Well, do you think he can handle chopped liver?"[247] The comment was not intended, nor was it received, as a joke.

The attitudinal shift that occurred during the 1960s and 1970s influenced the ways in which Jewish parents responded to their daughter's

intermarriages. The emphasis on individual happiness and personal pre-
rogative contributed to what the sociologist Eugen Schoenfeld cited, in
1969, as a parental policy of "preferred endogamy" that replaced "compul-
sory endogamy." Parents continued to prefer that their daughters marry
a Jewish man but recognized that it was their choice whether they did.
Parents were also unlikely to sever relationships with their intermarried
children, unless they were Orthodox.[248] (Correlations between parental disapproval and lower rates of intermarriage, which fluctuated across
denominations, are discussed in chapter 4.) In January 1968 *PTA* magazine encouraged parents of children who intermarried to be "supportive,"
to "respect the conscience and faith of our child and of the one he or
she loves."[249] Jewish parents who were committed to the idea of equality
"regardless of race or religion," who believed that love was the basis of
marriage and that choosing one's own mate was an individual preroga-
tive, were hard-pressed to oppose a child's decision to intermarry. The
increased emphasis on self-fulfillment and the lifting of social bans restricting romantic love according to religion likely increased the rate of
intermarriage for Jewish women as well as men.[250] Liberalism and individualism similarly contributed to social acceptance of intermarriage.

The reality of increasing Jewish intermarriage in the latter half of the
century forced a reinterpretation of ideologies and social values beginning in the late 1960s. The exogamous person became more welcomed
to remain a part of the Jewish community, at least in a small-town, maintaining her position in the temple and other Jewish organizations.[251] The
softening of the Jewish stance toward intermarriage continued in the
1970s as a result of a new approach to responding to Jewish intermarrieds
in urban areas. Although opposition to intermarriage remained intense,
particularly among many Conservative and Orthodox Jews, some influential Jewish leaders, in the mid-1970s, began trying to keep those who intermarried "within Jewish cultural, religious, and family life," rather than
expelling them from the community. AJC officials emphasized that, while
they did not condone intermarriage, "a climate of acceptance" should replace the traditional rejection, which history had shown had done nothing
to stem an increase in intermarriages.[252] This new approach marked a significant change in the Jewish communal attitude toward intermarriage; it
also signaled the beginning of the Outreach-to-Intermarrieds movement
that gained momentum in the 1980s and 1990s, and that persists today.

Reform and Conservative synagogues were reportedly more open to
the participation of Jews who had intermarried, who were, in turn, more

likely to affirm their Jewish heritage. As one AJC researcher explained in 1976: "Thus a mother and her children who 30 years ago might have felt rejected and unwelcome in her temple or in her parents' home would more likely be accepted and encouraged these days." Even some Orthodox rabbis were reexamining their attitude toward non-Jews who sought conversion solely for the purpose of marrying a Jew rather than on religious grounds as required by *Halakhah*.[253] A study by sociologists Egon Mayer and Carl Sheingold, sponsored by the AJC and released in January 1979, documented how parents' attitudes toward their children's out-marriages had become less contentious than in earlier decades. "Though a majority of the parents were clearly opposed to their children's intermarriage, most were not strongly opposed; and approximately one-third were perceived by their children as neutral," Mayer and Sheingold reported.[254] Diminished disapproval from family members and the community meant less alienation from Jewish circles for Jewish women who intermarried.

However, the increased acceptance of intermarriage did not mitigate the loss, sadness, and loneliness some Jewish women experienced as a result of their 1960s and 1970s intermarriages. Olivia Barton was downcast about not sharing with her spouse a common background and appreciation of holidays. Her husband thought Passover was interesting in an academic sense, but he could not relate to her fond memories. Olivia explained, "In a peculiar way it makes me feel more remote from him to see that he can't really participate fully . . . he doesn't have the history, he doesn't remember the children's table, he doesn't remember the *matzoh* being hidden."[255] Different religious backgrounds meant his and her holidays. Linda Nusbaum-Stark was sad that she did not celebrate Shabbat more frequently while married. She elaborated, "Not that he's ever stood in my way, and in fact has encouraged me, but it's like my participation in his Christmas. It's *his* Christmas, this is *my* Shabbat."[256] Although Jewish women and their non-Jewish husbands celebrated each other's holidays, an unbridgeable cultural divide remained between them.

Some women who intermarried described what they considered specific Jewish social and cerebral qualities that were absent from their intermarried lives. Beth Jonah cited a special rapport when talking with other Jews, a common understanding of each other's mentalities, which was lacking in her dialogue with her non-Jewish partner.[257] Similarly Mavis Rue, after her intermarriage, felt the loss of what she called "Jewish energy" and "Jewish intelligence," ethnic qualities she ascribed to Jewish people.[258] Joan Marcus did not celebrate Jewish holidays with her Gentile husband once her children left home, and she felt an extreme sense of loss. "I *miss it* terribly, *terribly,*" she said between tears. "Despite all the crapola you get with Jewish families, and the harangue, and my mother doing the martyr thing whenever she would cook, I miss the familial gatherings that were warm and funny . . . I could have pursued it on my own but it was a lonely place to be."[259] Evidently Jewish women who intermarried paid unanticipated, and little recognized, costs.

Although intermarriage was not a panacea for women seeking self-actualization and marital bliss, the Civil Rights and counterculture movements and feminism during the 1960s and 1970s enabled Jewish women to play fundamental roles in how they identified and shaped their family life. Women did not defer to their husbands' religious affiliations nearly as much as they had in previous decades. Rather, most were steadfast in their belief that they would continue to identify strongly as Jewish women, and that their children and even their grandchildren would likewise be Jewish. Thus the Jewish women I interviewed did not seem to reflect Milton Gordon's 1964 theory of marital assimilation that "the minority group loses its ethnic identity in the larger host or core society, and identificational assimilation takes place."[260] Jewish women who intermarried in the 1960s and 1970s more closely resembled Marcus Hansen's "principle of third-generation interest." Eleven out of fourteen of the women were the granddaughters of immigrants. Modifying Hansen's 1938 "law" according to gender: what the daughter wishes to forget the granddaughter wishes to remember.[261]

The opposition to organized religion and religious education expressed by many women, however, is illustrative of what the sociologist Herbert Gans defined in 1979 as "symbolic ethnicity." According to Gans, third-generation Jews were less interested in their ethnic cultures and organizations, both sacred and secular, but still perceived themselves as Jewish; thus individual behavior expressed ethnicity, but it did not regulate daily life. Gans wrote:

> Because people's concern is with identity, rather than with cultural practices or group relationships, they are free to look for ways of expressing that identity which suits them best, thus opening up the possibility for voluntary, diverse, or individualistic ethnicity.[262]

Assessing women's involvement in religion requires that people expand their perception of power beyond the publicly recognized forms within religious institutions and religious bodies.[263] The next chapter examines whether Jewish women who intermarried in the 1980s and 1990s continued the trend of an individualistic resurgence of Jewishness, largely cultural rather than religious in nature, and how the organized Jewish communities became increasingly proactive in their response to the ever growing number of intermarriages.

4

Revitalization from Within

A woman and a Jew, sometimes more
of a contradiction than I can sweat out,
yet finally the intersection that is both
collision and fusion, stone and seed.
                    —Marge Piercy, *The Ram's Horn Sounding*, 1988

Between 1980 and 2004 the high degree of disaffiliation per-
meating American society enabled women of Jewish heritage to marry
men who frequently were not religious. The decrease in religious identification and observance among many Americans muted the differences
between young Gentile men and Jewish women. The proportion of adult
Americans among a nationally representative sample who indicated
membership in a religious institution declined from 61 percent in the
early 1970s and early 1990s to 54 percent in 2001, and the number who
did not subscribe to any religious identification more than doubled between 1990 and 2001.[1] People met each other in college, at their places
of employment, or through mutual friends and fell in love unimpeded
by stark distinctions between their beliefs and practices. Escalating national divorce rates simultaneously suggested that marriage was a gam-
ble regardless of whether one married within one's own religious group.
Paradoxically, as the Jewish women in my sample married, had children,
and became their family's spiritual guides, they also began to reclaim
their personal and communal ties to Jewish religion and culture. This
process caused turmoil for some women whose non-Jewish husbands
advocated Christmas as a "secular" holiday. As their narratives illustrate, the end of the twentieth century and the beginning of the twenty-
first continued the shift that began in the 1960s and 1970s, where most
Jewish women identified more strongly with their Jewish heritage not

despite their marrying non-Jewish men but actually *because* they married Gentiles.

Intermarriage between Jews and non-Jews became a common phenomenon to an unprecedented degree within the larger social context of the increased rate of marriages across lines defined by European ethnic ancestry in mainstream American society. Although surveys were criticized for their design and data collection or for how Jews were identified and who may have been missed, they did highlight an unmistakable rise in intermarriage over time.[2] A 1990 national survey of the Jewish population found that 52 percent of born Jews had intermarried between 1985 and 1990, a significant jump from the 32 percent rate seen between 1966 and 1972.[3] Another national survey in 2001 found that 47 percent of Jews (who were born and remained Jews) intermarried between 1996 and 2001, up from 43 percent between 1991 and 1995. Applying the broad definition of "born Jews" (those with at least one Jewish parent but not necessarily raised as Jewish), this same study, for the same time periods, yielded rates of 54 percent and 53 percent, respectively.[4] Three studies of the Boston Jewish community, however, found lower overall rates, as they had in 1965 and 1975, but again also found significant increases in the rate of intermarriage the more recently the marriage had occurred: 29 percent of the spouses of Jewish adults who married for the first time between 1981 and 1985 were not Jewish compared to 10 percent twenty years earlier; this figure increased to 34 percent between 1991 and 1995, and it increased again to 37 percent between 1998 and 2002.[5] These findings confirmed that American Jews were steadily becoming as exogamous as other ethnic groups.

The marriage patterns of the seven largest European ancestry groups likewise showed a marked increase among most white ethnic Americans born after 1950 compared to those born in 1920 or before. The percent of spouses not from the same ancestry group changed for the major ancestry groups as follows: Polish (from 47.8 to 82.3); Scots (from 74.2 to 85.2); Italian (from 40.7 to 75.0); French (from 78.9 to 77.4); Irish (from 53.7 to 60.0); German (from 50.9 to 49.7); and English (from 37.6 to 44.1). These numbers reflected a significant decline, by the end of the twentieth century, in the influence of ethno-religious origins on marriages between whites.[6] Analysis of 1980 census data allowed researchers to create the first comprehensive national portrait of ethnic and racial intermarriage in America that offered a representative sample of 226,000 of the 43.8 million American married couples in which both spouses were native-born. Richard D. Alba, then director of the Center for Social and Demographic analysis at the State University of New York at Albany, elaborated in a September 1986 paper that Jewish-Jewish marriages in the United States were "well below the in-marriage tendencies of eastern and central European groups and about on a par with those of the British and Irish, two of the weakest."[7] Hence nonimmigrant-generation Jews were considered along with other white ethnics from Western Europe to intermarry extensively. The increase in Jewish-Gentile marriages was paralleled by increases in other forms of interreligious marriages; for example, approximately half of Catholics married non-Catholics, mainly Protestants.[8] Although not as dramatic and comparatively still small, the increase in interracial marriage over the last four decades was likewise remarkable. Whereas in 1960 only 0.4 percent of all marriages were interracial, by 2000 this rate had multiplied five times to 2 percent of the total.[9]

As intermarriage across ethnic and religious lines became the norm in American society at large, Jewish communal concern over the marked increase of marriages between Jews and non-Jews meant that Jewish women who intermarried were considerably more visible defectors from the group than they had been earlier. Adding to this visibility was the finding of a 1980s study of Jews under the age of thirty in Los Angeles that even more Jewish women intermarried than Jewish men.[10] Thus, as the intermarriage rates for each gender converged, Jewish women who married non-Jews were no longer social exceptions. The 2000-2001 National Jewish Population Survey found that, overall, the intermarriage rates among men and among women were quite similar: 33 percent and 29 percent, respectively.[11] Hence Jewish women who intermarried became major "contributors" to what appeared on the surface as Jewish discontinuity. However, the documented rise in women's intermarriages did not result, as one might expect, in eliminating personal experiences of alienation and marginalization.

Even though, by the late twentieth century, intermarriage had become an "equal opportunity" for Jewish women as for Jewish men, all American women continued to encounter inequality in the workplace and in the home. Between 1975 and 1995 the rate of mothers of children less than six years of age who participated in the labor force increased by 60 percent.[12] Job segregation and disparity in salaries persisted, however. American women continued to work in predominantly stereotypical, female jobs such as clerical, sales, and service. In 1984 full-time women workers had median earnings of $14,479, whereas men's earnings were $23,218.[13] Even as the gender pay gap narrowed and women's incomes rose, most reports indicated that their leisure time decreased while men's increased.[14] In *The Second Shift* (1989), Arlie Russel Hochschild and Anne Machung found that, when one added paid labor to housework and child care, women worked approximately fifteen hours more each week than men.[15] To quote the feminist writer Elizabeth Janeway: "Women today don't have it all; they just do it all."[16] As I discuss in the following pages, intermarried Jewish women's domestic responsibilities actually gave them more control and influence over their families' lives than had the responsibilities been equally divided.

As discussed in chapters 2 and 3, the patterns that can be detected from a relatively limited number of oral histories enable an analysis of prevalent themes that shed light on what intermarriage meant to and for Jewish women at the end of the twentieth century. This chapter delves into the personal narratives of fifteen of the forty-three women interviewed to discuss three central themes: Jewish women's marriages to men without religious faith; the intensified identification and observance the women experienced as a result of their intermarriages and motherhood; and the ironic triple marginality they faced as intermarried Jewish women living in an American society where the dominant identity was Christian male, and in an organized Jewish community where "intermarriage" remained a dirty word. I argue in the following pages that some Jewish women's intermarriage experiences brought them closer to their religious heritage, rendered a new meaning of intermarriage in America, and transformed what it meant to be a "Jewish wife."

Jewish women who intermarried in the 1980s and 1990s, like their predecessors of the 1960s and 1970s, were usually not immigrants. Among the fifteen women discussed in this chapter who married between 1980 and 2000, only one was second-generation; eleven were third-generation, two were fourth-generation, and one was fifth-generation American. There was an almost equal proportion of women with Conservative Jewish backgrounds as Reform; some of them described their upbringing as "nonobservant Conservative" or "Secular Reform." One was Orthodox-Conservative, and two were raised as secular. The religious affiliation of their husbands' families of origin included: Roman Catholic, Episcopal, Greek Orthodox, Haitian Protestant, Methodist, Southern Baptist, and Unitarian. For eleven of the women, it was the first marriage; three intermarried twice; and one, after two previous marriages to Jewish men, had married a Gentile. All but one of the women remained married to a Gentile at the time of the interview. Twelve of the fifteen women had raised or were in the process of raising Jewish children, two were childless, and one was pregnant for the first time.

Jewish women who intermarried and became more committed to Judaism and to perpetuating Jewish values were living contradictions. All but two of the women discussed here were so-called Baby Boomers, born between 1946 and 1964 when the overall number of births in North America rose markedly.[17] In a 1982 book about women of the Baby Boom generation coming of age, Joanne Michaels wrote: "We are opening up to the stirrings within that propel us forward, while we try to square them with our beliefs."[18] Jewish women who intermarried illustrated this real need to navigate between seemingly incongruous variables: their love for non-Jewish men and their enlivened commitments to living as proud Jews in America. As Marge Piercy's 1988 poem, the epigraph to this chapter, articulates, being an intermarried Jewish woman was a weighty contradiction. Yet, as I will demonstrate, the dual commitment to both their heritage and their Gentile spouses inspired Jewish women to re-estimate the value of being Jewish, to better appreciate its significance, and to shape their married lives accordingly.

Influence and Confluence

Continuing the trend from earlier decades, the political liberalism and social freedom of most American Jews made it substantially easier for Jewish women to marry non-Jewish men in the 1980s and 1990s. The highest percentage of votes among Jews, more than any other group in 1984, went to the Democratic candidate Walter Mondale. Leonard Fein, the founder of *Moment* magazine and a former professor at Brandeis University, recognized that less than 10 percent of American Jews were religiously observant; in 1988 he argued that a commitment to economic and social justice could "serve as our preeminent motive, the path through which our past is vindicated, our present warranted, and our future affirmed."[19]

Sharing a political worldview with their prospective husbands was as important to Jewish women who intermarried in the last decades of the twentieth century as it was to those who married non-Jews during the 1960s and 1970s, as discussed in the previous chapter. Karla Matzman, who had been living in New Hampshire when she met her future husband in 1986, was convinced that their common social values were a stronger factor than their religious differences: "I remember thinking: 'Oh my gosh, he's a Democrat!'"[20] Her pleasure at his political affiliation and immediate attraction suggests that the man's vote for Mondale and vice-presidential candidate Geraldine Ferraro, the first woman on a national party ticket, held romantic appeal for the liberal-minded Jewish woman.[21] Some opined that while interfaith marriages were "Odd Couples," compatible political attitudes, hobbies, or career interests that usually first brought them together also helped sustain their relationship.[22]

While increasing political liberalism made intermarrying easier to do, the ethnic revivalism that began in the 1960s and 1970s encouraged Jewish women who married in the 1980s and 1990s to proudly claim their association with their ethnic group. Contextual factors such as America's involvement in an ignoble foreign war, racial violence, political assassinations, riotous confrontations on college campuses, and the Watergate scandal had weakened the ideology of a unitary American identity based on universalistic principles. It became, according to the historian Phillip Gleason, "highly functional for people to remember that they were really ethnic, simultaneously distancing themselves from responsibility for the defects of the American system."[23] The 1966 slogan "Black Power" was emulated by Chicanos and American Indians with Brown Power and Red Power movements, followed by white ethnic groups clamoring for attention. If black was beautiful, wrote the "new ethnicity" advocate Andrew Greeley in 1971, "then so is Irish, Polish, Italian, Slovenian, Greek, Armenian, Lebanese and Luxembourger."[24] The discourse on multiculturalism emphasized that descendants of immigrants had not assimilated into the mainstream to become unrecognizable as a distinct group. Rather, a new ethnic identity was formed, shaped by the group's distinctive experience in America.[25] The new place of honor that ethnic distinctiveness occupied was illustrated, for example, by ethnic festivals and parades, the elevation of ethnic cooking to a respected niche in American cuisine, and pins such as "Kiss Me, I'm Jewish" and "Dress British, Think Yiddish."[26]

The backlash against feminism in the 1980s, including the renewed glorification of the differences between women and men, encouraged Jewish women to marry Gentile men with whom they shared liberal political views and to identify as Jewish. The persistent theme of "family values" in the Republican political arena, the Supreme Court's upholding of the Hyde Amendment that denied public Medicaid funding for abortions, and the failure of the ratification of the Equal Rights Amendment (ERA) in June 1982 signaled the success of the New Right in American politics.[27] Phyllis Schlafley, a conservative who led the pro-family movement against the ERA was named one of the one hundred most important women of the twentieth century by the *Ladies' Home Journal.* According to one reporter, "within two decades" after Schlafley self-published her book on how to achieve a Republican win of the presidency in 1964, "she would bring people of all Christian denominations together to begin the profamily drive that put Ronald Reagan in the White House."[28] Schlafley's rhetoric was motivated by her belief that men and women were inherently different and that women's "power" came from remembering the "essential validity" of the old Protestant prayer about accepting what one could not change.[29]

While Schlafley became popular with some Gentile Americans, the voices and leftist politics of Jewish feminists involved in the women's liberation movement were far more likely to continue to resonate with Jewish American women who intermarried and navigated their identities. For example, Adrienne Rich's "Split at the Root: An Essay on Jewish Identity" discussed the feeling of inadequacy about being an assimilated Jew and rejected traditional Judaism's patriarchy in favor of identifying as a woman while simultaneously contending, "in 1982 Right Wing America, *I, too, will wear the yellow star.*"[30] The publication of *On Being a Jewish Feminist* in 1983 explored the ways in which women who wished to be both feminists and religious Jews could claim ownership of a Judaism that had historically excluded them; it signaled to Jewish women an alternative to Republican conservativism.[31] The Pulitzer Prize-winning journalist Susan Faludi, in her 1991 book *Backlash*, disputed myths about man shortages, an infertility epidemic, and accusations that the Women's movement created unhappy childless women. Faludi's definition of the agenda of feminism was simple: "It asks that women be free to define themselves—instead of having their identity defined for them, time and time again, by their culture and their men." In this, she spoke to the hearts and minds of some intermarried Jewish women.[32]

Moreover, the high visibility of a Jewish woman who intermarried, such as Kitty Dukakis, the wife of the Democratic presidential candidate who interrupted her campaign schedule in the fall of 1988 to observe Yom Kippur in Boston, illustrated that liberal politics and intermarriage were compatible bedfellows. Although one cannot know what Jewish women thought about Dukakis without direct commentary, she was a prominent example of an intermarried Jewish woman. According to *Time* magazine, Dukakis, who had the potential to become the first Jewish First Lady, "naturally stirs pride within her religious community" at the same time that she "personifies American Judaism's most vexing and divisive issue: intermarriage."[33]

Although the commitment to liberalism made verbalized parental disapproval of religious intermarriage increasingly rare, according to the women I interviewed, interracial marriage did not become widespread in the 1980s and 1990s. Parental disapproval of interfaith marriage sometimes correlated with lower rates of intermarriages, which also fluctuated across denominations. For example, among Reform Jewish families in Cleveland, 37 percent had at least one child who intermarried, and among Conservative families the rate was 31 percent compared to only 15 percent of Orthodox families.[34] Furthermore, of the fifteen women whose narratives about intermarriage are included in this chapter, only two experienced parental opposition, and one of these had to do not only with an interfaith union but also an interracial one. Becca Tamen, born in 1961, raised as a Reform Jew, married a Haitian Protestant man in 1987. She recounted: "There are a bunch of Jewish democrat liberals in my family and you don't even necessarily *say* certain things if you feel them; so I didn't get a lot of grief from people."[35] However, the fact that she was the only one of the fifteen Jewish women who married someone not of white European ancestry reflected a larger social pattern. In contrast to marriages across (white) ethnic and religious lines, marriages between whites of European ancestry and non-whites (Latinos, American Indians, Asians, and Blacks) remained uncommon. Nationally, nearly 99 percent of non-Latino whites married other non-Latino whites.[36] As another woman reflected: "I have a cousin who married a woman who is from the Dominican Republic and she is black, which was even worse than what I did!" a remark that clearly illustrates the extent to which race continued to be a stronger barrier to intermarriage than religion was through the end of the twentieth century.[37]

A Jewish woman married to a non-Jewish man fit the conservative political drive in the 1990s to preserve heterosexual marriage as the standard model, showing that liberalism had its limits. As interfaith marriage became more commonplace, legislation against same-sex marriage became more firmly rooted. This increased rigidity was similar to the time when laws that repealed bans on interracial marriage (the U.S. Supreme Court declared miscegenation laws unconstitutional in 1967) were followed by laws in which biological sex was more deeply embedded, which served to ban same-sex marriages.[38] The 1996 Defense of Marriage Act defined the words "marriage" and "spouse" in federal law to mean involving one woman and one man. Notwithstanding the constitutional rule that each state should accept the public acts of other states, the federal act also declared that no state would be required to acknowledge a same-sex marriage contracted in another state, such as in Hawaii, Alaska, or Vermont. The historian Nancy Cott wrote, "Where public authorities a century earlier had been primed to defend Christian-model monogamy from free love, interracial coupling, polygamy, self-divorce, and commercial sex, now the Congress found heterosexuality the crucial boundary to maintain."[39]

While public discourse on intermarriage took a backseat to politics about same-sex marriage, soaring national divorce rates in the 1980s and 1990s suggested to Jewish women that in-marriage was no more a guarantee of success than intermarriage. The American divorce rate hit its highest point in history in the early 1980s; in 1980 alone, there were 22.6 divorces per 1,000 married women age fifteen and older. An increase in divorce had been a long-term trend since the colonial period (1600-1775), but after remaining level for two decades following World War II, the divorce rate doubled between the mid-1960s and early 1980s. Although the rate declined modestly in the remaining years of the twentieth century, it was described as "leveling off at a high level." According to the National Marriage Project at Rutgers University, the chance of a marriage entered into in the year 2000 ending in divorce or permanent separation was very high: between 40 and 50 percent.[40]

New sociological reports that intermarriage more often led to divorce than in-marriage added to the larger picture of an overwhelmingly high national rate of divorce, without necessarily dissuading Jewish women from marrying a Gentile. Research in the 1950s suggested that interfaith couples did not have a higher than usual divorce rate and that it was impossible to generalize about interfaith marriage among Catholics, Protestants, and Jews, and about marital outcome.[41] Later research, however, demonstrated that when the wife and husband were not of the same Christian denomination, the likelihood of the marriage terminating in divorce was significantly higher.[42] More important for this book, research published in 1989 by the North American Jewish Data Bank, which analyzed the marital histories of 6,457 never-widowed, Jewish adults from nine cities around the United States between 1982 and 1987, found a divorce rate of 17 percent among those who married coreligionists and a rate of 32 percent among the intermarried. This finding confirmed that Jewish-Gentile intermarriages reflected the national picture of high levels of divorce; in the researchers' words, "the most significant predictor of divorce is intermarriage."[43] However much this data was embraced by advocates of endogamy, it is doubtful, given the persistent rates of exogamy, that Jewish women gave these reports much notice.

In fact, Jewish women in my sample seemed to be influenced more by the dynamics of their individual families of origin than they were by alarming statistics about intermarriage and marital instability. Penina Mintz Jennings maintained her long-held belief that she would marry "a Jewish doctor" just like her father. However, she reported that her parents' divorce, which occurred during her freshman year in college, illustrated that marrying someone of the same faith did not automatically make a great marriage: "My parents are just wonderful people and wonderful parents; they just were not a good couple." Thus the model of marital failure was a stronger influence on her than her original inclination to in-marry. She married a Catholic accountant in 1997.[44] Lisa Schiffman, the intermarried author of the 1999 national bestseller, *generation j,* a book about soul-searching post-Holocaust Jews, wrote: "Endogamy. In my grandmother's case, this rule turned out to be less than ideal." That her Jewish grandmother's Jewish husband deserted his wife less than a year after their marriage had been "blessed by a rabbi" and shortly after she gave birth to twins showed Lisa firsthand that endogamy was no guarantee of happiness.[45] The impression a parental intermarriage made was also significant, especially if it involved the female role model. Two women's Jewish mothers divorced their Jewish husbands and remarried non-Jews. When Hannah Noble's mother remarried a non-Jew, Hannah was "at a really formative age, twelve, and I think it made it really clear to me that it was completely fine to do that." Fulfilling the Midrash (commentary on Genesis) about Dinah going out like Leah, "As the mother, so her daughter," Hannah married a Methodist in 1992.[46] The influence of a parent's intermarriage on the Jewish women in my sample reflected national demographic data that Jewish adults who were the children of intermarriages were three times more likely to marry non-Jews themselves.[47]

Moreover, as in previous decades, intermarried Jewish women's experiences illustrate that whether a Jewish wife and a Gentile husband divorced was contingent upon factors unrelated to religion, disputing the notion that exogamy was the reason for divorce.[48] Of the fifteen women I discuss in this chapter, three were divorced at the time of the interview; two out of the three were presently remarried to non-Jews and the third was single (a divorcée). Like the women earlier in the century who parted ways with husbands for political reasons, Jewish women who separated from or divorced non-Jewish men likewise did so for secular reasons. One woman who intermarried in 1989, divorced, and intermarried again in 2000 explained that it was her first husband's infidelities involving prostitutes, phone sex, and Internet sex chat lines that contributed to the deterioration of her marriage.[49] Similarly, another woman who also intermarried twice believed that her first Gentile spouse had an affair, and that her second non-Jewish husband felt inadequate or insecure about her intensely close relationship with her family, which led to their divorce.

Although the prospect of divorce was not a deterrent to intermarriage, personal narratives about actual negative experiences with Jewish men are perhaps indicators of why some Jewish women intermarried. Penina Mintz Jennings had high hopes when she went to the Matzoh Ball, an annual Jewish singles' dance held on Christmas Eve, where she met a Jewish man whom she dated for several weeks. The pair planned to go on a ski weekend with another couple when, suddenly, her "Jewish darling boyfriend," as she called him, backed out and left her as a third wheel. The other man of the original foursome invited a Catholic friend to go on the trip; the new ski partner eventually became Penina's husband. Thus, despite all her good intentions to meet and marry a Jew, the Jewish man who initially thrilled her mother, "just wasn't a nice person," and, ironically, his inconsiderate action created the circumstance under which she met her non-Jewish spouse.[50] Likewise, Michelle Johns who was "pinned" by the Jewish man she dated for four years and had every hope of marrying was devastated when he broke off the engagement. The Gentile friend who consoled her over the loss of her Jewish sweetheart was the man she eventually married.[51] As these examples illustrate, personal histories behind intermarriage are multidimensional. Using stereotypes perpetuated by American culture and mass media about coreligionists to explain why Jewish women intermarried is to overgeneralize and, in the process, oversimplify the many layers of meaning and experience of intermarriage.[52]

Although these cases point out that it was the men's actions, not their Jewishness, that were detestable, the fact that Jewish women had unpleasant, and in one case extremely hurtful, experiences with Jewish men exemplified that not all Jews were good marriage material and, conversely, that not all Gentiles must be bad. Rachel Lyon, a Conservative Jew whose religious observance included buying kosher chickens, married and divorced two different Jewish men before remarrying a Gentile in 1998. She described her second husband, a Moroccan Jew, as an emotionally and physically abusive con artist who made her feel like a prisoner in her own home: "And you know what? It probably turned me off to foreign-born Jewish men."[53] She felt less negatively about her first husband than her second, but, after two failed Jewish marriages, it is not surprising that her third husband was a Gentile. Rachel's experience sheds light on both the idealized concept of the Jewish marriage and the invisible history of Jewish wives battered by Jewish husbands.[54] For women who grew up assuming that they would find happiness with congenial coreligionists, experiences to the contrary, opened wider the door to intermarriage.[55]

While a confluence of factors forged interfaith romances, internalized memories of antisemitism and feelings of alienation from non-Jewish society also fueled Jewish women's decisions to marry Gentile men in the late twentieth century, just as antisemitism and insecurity prompted some women to intermarry at mid-century. Bonnie Aaronson, an academician born in 1948 who intermarried in 1981, remembered the antisemitism in her high school that led to her being turned down for a pre–coming-out dance, "a *very* difficult experience." When asked how this event affected her subsequent dating experiences, Bonnie replied, "The net result was that I didn't want to date Jewish boys."[56] By the time she married, institutionalized exclusion from social events based on religious background was obsolete, but the damage to Bonnie had already been done.[57] Personal accounts of being Jewish and female in America published in the 1990s, such as the essays in *Daughters of Kings* edited by Leslie Brody, depicted how women's feelings of pride about being Jewish mingled with feelings of difference that were sometimes internalized as self-hatred and oppression. Women acknowledged being haunted by intergenerational stories of persecution, especially the Holocaust, and many had experienced firsthand the effects of ongoing antisemitism.[58]

Although the persistence of private experiences of antisemitism may have partially motivated more recent intermarriages, feelings of being different suggest that intermarriage provided the opportunity to claim participation in something that had been formerly denied to some Jewish women. Two of the women discussed in this chapter described their uncomfortable feelings of otherness while growing up Jewish and female in America. Brandy Simon stated three times during her interview, "I was a lot of people's first Jew," and she also recalled being singled out when she was in fifth grade and told by her teacher that she could not participate in the school Christmas play because she was Jewish. Brandy also remarked that the Chanukah presents she received from her parents were fewer than what her friends received as stocking stuffers.[59] Although she did not express a desire for more gifts (and gave her own children modest presents), the comparison suggests that she experienced a sense of material inequity while a child. Karla Matzman, who was one of four Jewish children in her high school (her sister was one of the others), resented the feeling of being different, of being apart from the rest of her peers. Regarding her 1990 intermarriage to a Protestant, Karla commented: "I get to have the best of both worlds."[60]

Popular literature portrayed the notion of Jewish women marrying non-Jewish men as a way to quench the flames of otherness in Gentile men's difference from their own coreligionists. In "The Joys of Goys," Melissa Schorr quipped: "I've tried to be a good Jewish girl. . . . I've Hilleled and B'naied. But . . . Lower me into a gold mine of dark, brooding Mount Sinai med students and, somehow, I'll sift out the three thick-necked, polo-shirted, beer-swigging Yalies in the corner." She further surmised, "Ultimately, I love Gentile men because they're the only species deluded enough to take one look into my eyes and see . . . exotica." Conversely, and illustrating Jews' elevated social status in late-twentieth-century American society, a self-proclaimed "American Shiksa" confessed: "I discovered Jewish men like I discovered books, in the library, tucked away in the dark corners of suburbia, reticent and wise and spouting words I had to look up in the dictionary." The use of self-deprecating humor in both these women's depictions of the opposite sex and religion suggest the ways in which the Jewish woman's attraction to Gentile men and the Gentile woman's attraction to Jewish men originated from their own ambivalence about themselves.[61] The aptly titled 1985 *Vogue* magazine article "I Married an Alien" described the appeal of marrying "out" to someone ambivalent about her own group: "To be alien among those clearly alien to oneself is a more comforting position than to be an alien among those alleged to be one's kin." The author, self-identified as an Irish Catholic who was ethnically Irish, Italian, and (patrilineally) Jewish, was reportedly happily married to "an Indiana WASP."[62] Thus some Jewish women overcame the ambivalence that stemmed from feelings of exclusion because of their difference not by seeking the insular comfort of their own group but by dating and marrying outside it. The possibility remained, however, that a Jewish woman who went "Goy Crazy," a recent book title, might eventually marry (or remarry) a Jewish man.[63]

Faith Married No-Faith

The reemergence and rise of secular Judaism during the last quarter of the twentieth century, previously written off as an ideology in the 1950s when there was an increase in synagogue construction and higher affiliation rates, facilitated Jewish women's intermarriages to men of little faith.[64] By 2001, according to the American Jewish Identity Survey (AJIS), nearly half the estimated 4.3 adults of the 5.2-5.3 million U.S. Jews regarded themselves as secular or somewhat secular in outlook.[65] The growing "un-synagogued" population reflected a broad trend in American religious life: between 1980 and 2002 the percentage of American adults who indicated that their religious preference was "none" steadily rose from 7 percent to 14 percent.[66] However, Jews were disproportionately represented in the number of Americans that claimed no religion. Adults of Jewish parentage constituted 3.8 percent of all American adults without religion in 2001, according to AJIS researchers, "while adults claiming Judaism as their religion constitute just 1.6 percent of Americans who claim a religion."[67] In response to the AJIS findings, the Center for Cultural Judaism opened in New York in the summer of 2003 to meet the needs of the large and rapidly increasing population of cultural, nonreligious Jews. The following December, the Center for Cultural Judaism, backed by Felix Posen, a millionaire philanthropist based in London, pledged ten million dollars to a Jewish education fund called Fund for Our Jewish Future, with the stipulation that half the money be allocated for teaching secular and unaffiliated Jews about Judaism from a cultural, nonreligious perspective.[68]

Continuing the trend from earlier in the century, secular Judaism's increasing popularity among American Jews enabled the intermarried women in my sample to separate Jewish culture from belief in God, and their Jewish identities from their interfaith marriages. "My religion is liberal politics!" articulated one woman I interviewed.[69] Her belief that discussing political and current events with her children was culturally "very Jewish" illustrates a way in which people could create a Jewish identity without religious belief or spiritual practice. Women who intermarried began to construct their own wedding ceremonies with language excluding God and focusing on the union between the couple. Two-thirds of the women discussed in this chapter who married in the 1980s and 1990s wrote their own wedding vows, entirely or in part. Karla Matzman, a software professional who married a Unitarian in 1990, described the couple's atheistic stance: "We have cultural ties, but neither of us is a big fan of the God concept. So that having God bless the relationship wasn't something that was important to either of us."[70] Brandy Simon, who wanted to have a Humanist chaplain officiate her 1989 wedding to a man raised as a Southern Baptist, but was ultimately married by a Justice of the Peace, emphasized that they were "very careful not to mention" God. Instead: "This wedding marks a public celebration of a private love." Held in the Boston Public Garden, the ceremony featured the 1976 song "Ships in the Night" by Bill Nelson of Be Bop Deluxe and the poem "I do, I Will, I Have" by Ogden Nash (1902-1971). The humorous poem gives barely a nod toward marriage as a sacred act with the line: "Just as I know that there are two Hagens, Walter and Copen, / I know that marriage is a legal and religious alliance entered into by a man who can't sleep with the window shut / and a woman who can't sleep with the window open."[71] Even when Gabriella Abrahms's 1992 wedding incorporated Jewish elements such as a *chuppah* (canopy), she did not want God to be mentioned. The registered dietician who married a Catholic told the presiding Unitarian chaplain: "This is between Donald and I."[72] American interfaith romance, with its emphasis on individualism and personal happiness, had eclipsed the desire for any divine involvement in an increasingly secular American Jewish culture.

Jewish women's experiences reflect the reported decrease in religious identification in American society, illustrated by their intermarriages with men of little or no religious faith.[73] Rather than marry Gentile men with strong attachments to the religious affiliations of their families of origin, most Jewish women in my sample married non-Jewish men who no longer perceived themselves as connected to a Christian denomination, were atheists, or had renounced their birth religion. One husband had not attended church in twenty-five years. Twelve of the fifteen women discussed in this chapter commented specifically about their husband's lack of religiosity in terms of observance, affiliation, and identity.[74] One woman succinctly described her husband's religious position as: "Zero. None. Anti."[75] Their depictions of their husbands clearly reflect their own interpretations; nevertheless, Jewish women's accounts of their husband's a-religiousness help to explain the ease with which these women married outside their own religious heritage, as well as the marital environments in which they often cultivated increasingly Jewish identities and practices for themselves and their children.

The Jewish women's statements about how unimportant religion was to their husbands suggest that the term "interfaith marriage" had become inaccurate by the end of the twentieth century. For example, Bonnie Aaronson married a man of Catholic background in 1981 whose family had left the Church around the time of the Vietnam War because they were upset that the Church did not oppose the war. She considered herself a practicing Jew married to "somebody who doesn't have any kind of religious observance or practice." Whenever someone asked if she was part of an interfaith couple, she responded: "No, I'm part of a faith/non-faith couple." Her statement raises an important point: if a Jewish woman married a non-Jewish man who had no religion, can they accurately be called an interfaith couple? The term "interfaith" has historically been applied to couples consisting of individuals of different religious and ethnic lineage, regardless of their religious connections or lack thereof; "faith/no-faith marriage" was, in many cases, a far more accurate description.

Jewish women took comfort in their Gentile husband's lack of non-Jewish religious zeal, perhaps because it reduced the differences between them. Zena Jethro, an affiliated Reform Jew, and her husband, who met in 1977 while undergraduates at Brown University, corresponded about their religious differences during the summer after their freshmen year and before they eventually married in 1984. In a letter dated 13 July 1978, Zena's then boyfriend professed his love and tried to assuage her concerns that their different backgrounds were an obstacle to their future happiness: "I am not religious, and really not Catholic. What I am is really an agnostic."[76] His lack of religiousness combined with his willingness to raise Jewish children was what enabled her to marry him. In Zena's words:

> The truth is my husband is probably as far as I could ever have gone in an interfaith marriage. Meaning: he has no faith. He is not Christian. He's not anything. He was raised Catholic. But religion means nothing to him, really. . . . He, because it didn't mean really anything to him and he found none of it threatening, was happy as a clam to have a Chanukah menorah, was, you know, fine with him to do all this stuff.[77]

That this couple discussed their religious differences at such young ages (she was nineteen and he was eighteen) illustrates how intensely Zena felt about the enduring role of Judaism in her life. Another example, Karla Matzman, who married a man with whom she shared political views and social values commented on their similarities: "It's kind of interesting, I think, from an intermarriage point of view, because from a basic-values—how you see the world—we're not an interfaith couple."[78] In these instances, Jewish women had not so much married out of their own faith as brought their Jewish backgrounds to relationships with men of little or no faith.

That Jewish women often were more religious than their husbands also reflected the national picture of gender and religion in American society. According to ARIS 2001, adult women were more likely than men to describe their outlook as "religious" (42 percent of women compared to

31 percent of men).[79] National survey research on prayer and health concerns by Anne McCaffrey of Harvard Medical School found that American women prayed more than men did.[80] Based on these findings, one can suppose that non-Jewish women who intermarried also tended to be more religious than the men they married, and some evidence supports this premise. A Jewish man married to a Unitarian woman who converted to Judaism and wanted to be a rabbi was quoted in *Newsweek* as saying that he and his wife perpetually negotiated the level of their family's religious observance: "Her faith is a resolute force, my secularism is a marshmallowy object."[81] In the same article, a Catholic wife strong-armed her Jewish husband into becoming a "better Jew," insisting after their 1992 wedding that he relearn what he had forgotten from Hebrew School.[82] Furthermore, the 1995 finding in a survey of interfaith families that women, both Jewish and non-Jewish, were more interested in Jewish outreach programs reinforces the idea that women who intermarried were more open to making religious connections than their male partners.[83] Based on ARIS, it is likely that women of other religions and ethnicities shared Jewish women's experiences of marrying men who had drastically less religious zeal. When I asked an acquaintance, a devout Catholic of Irish descent, what her husband's religious affiliation was, she responded: "He's an engineer."[84] Although purely anecdotal evidence, the remark suggests that Jewish women's marriages to less religious men were not unusual.

Normative or Calamitous?

Articles on intermarriage in the mainstream press and periodical literature in the 1980s and 1990s normalized interethnic and interfaith unions in American society while perpetuating the belief that intermarriage was still primarily the domain of Jewish men. For example, on 2 April 1990 *New York* magazine ran a cover story with the headline "Star-crossed: More Gentiles and Jews Are Intermarrying—and It's Not All Chicken Soup." The publicity for intermarriage that this particular article generated was indicative of how common intermarriage had become. Interweaving personal anecdotes, "Star-crossed" highlighted the interfaith marriages of well-known celebrity couples such as the Jewish designer Calvin Klein and Kelly Rector, Caroline Bouvier Kennedy (the daughter of the late president) and Edwin A. Schlossberg, and Laura Delano Roosevelt (a granddaughter of another late president) and Charles Henry Silberstein.[85] To the extent that celebrities raised public awareness and served as cultural

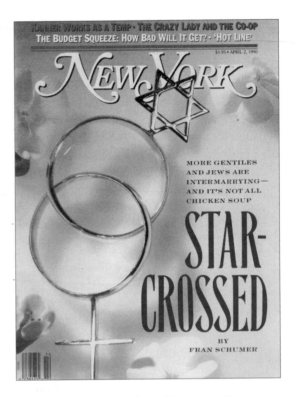

"Star-Crossed: More Gentiles and Jews Are Intermarrying—and It's Not All Chicken Soup," *New York* magazine, 2 April 1990, cover.

role models, this kind of media attention reinforced intermarriage as an American reality. New sociological research confirmed popular impressions by reporting that marriage across ethnic lines had become so common that only a quarter of American-born whites of non-Latino origin married someone with an identical undivided ethnic heritage.[86]

With the increase in intermarriage and lack of affiliation, some Catholic leaders began emphasizing that practicing dual religions was preferable to practicing neither. An article in *U.S. Catholic*, in June 1982, conceded: "Marriage between persons of two faiths . . . is not far from becoming the norm in today's church." Directors of family life for regional Catholic archdiocese were less concerned with whether both individuals shared the same faith than that "both have faith."[87] In September 1988 a priest enthusiastically emphasized interfaith marriage as an opportunity for Catholics and Jews to learn about each other's faith and to give children "the best of both traditions."[88] Underlying these opinions were concerns about the cumulative effect of secularism and declines in religious membership. If each individual maintained her or his own distinct religious ties within their intermarriage, theoretically if not in practice, neither group would suffer attrition. Instead, successful interfaith unions would be symbols of the "worldwide ecumenical movement," as one writer in *U.S. Catholic* suggestively endorsed in 1989.[89] Public discourse detailed that a Jew married to a Christian would, for example, light candles on Friday nights, and celebrate Chanukah *and* "a real old-fashioned Christmas with a big tree and presents and lots of food."[90] Celebrating both holidays could be, in one reverend's words, "an opportunity to affirm both traditions."[91]

The overall acceptance of intermarriage reflected in national opinion polls and a survey of Jews reporting that a majority of the American public and many Jews thought that intermarriage was acceptable illustrated the culture of individualism that surpassed in importance allegiance to a religious community. A Gallup Report in April 1983 found that 77 percent of the adults polled (among a national sample of 1,517) approved of marriage between Jews and non-Jews, a 10 percent increase in acceptance from a decade earlier. That three-quarters of the population accepted marriage across religious lines continued to be the case fifteen years later, reflected in a 75 percent approval rate in a November 1998 survey.[92] Although the Gallup statistics did not differentiate between the responses of Jews and non-Jews, a study of Jewish attitudes netted nearly identical results. In a 1990 report designed to assess attitudes toward intermarriage of American Jewish leadership and of "typical American Jews," 74 percent of respondents would have advised a Jewish young woman or man in her or his mid-thirties to marry a Gentile whom they loved rather than avoid intermarrying. A mere 5 percent would advise against the intermarriage, and 21 percent would advise that the Jewish person marry the Gentile, provided that the latter convert to Judaism.[93] The 2000 Annual Survey of American Jewish Opinion similarly found that 80 percent of respondents agreed that intermarriage was inevitable in an open society and only 39 percent would be pained if their child married a Gentile, findings that led researchers to conclude: "The Jewish taboo on mixed marriage has clearly collapsed."[94] That such a large percentage of the American population accepted intermarriage illustrated the decline of overt antisemitism and the extent to which Jews had become an accepted part of the American tapestry. The extent of Jewish acceptance demonstrated that the Jewish population had become American Jews rather than retaining their distinctiveness as Jewish Americans who married endogamously.

Acceptance did not mean communal approval, however, and while the mainstream press served to normalize intermarriage and members of Christian denominations touted "two faiths are better than none," the 1980s and 1990s marked a time of unprecedented panic among the organized Jewish communities who perceived intermarriage as calamitous.[95] Emblematic of the heightened concern about the loss of Jews through intermarriage was the debate over who is a Jew that reverberates today in academic, communal, and religious circles. According to traditional Jewish law, Jewish identity passed matrilineally. This had long meant that the children of a Jewish mother and a non-Jewish father would automatically be Jewish, whereas children born to a Jewish father and a non-Jewish mother would not be Jewish without conversion. At the end of 1979 Rabbi Alexander Schindler, president of the Union of American Hebrew Congregations, formally proposed that the child of a Jewish father and a non-Jewish mother be accepted as Jewish as long as the child was raised Jewish. The hope was that a redefined Jewishness would increase the number of Jews who would ensure Jewish survival.[96]

After much debate, the Reform movement made the historic decision to accept patrilineal descent, sharpening the distinctions between Jewish denominations in the process. This followed on the heels of a lesser-known decision of the Reconstructionist movement in 1968.[97] The resolution adopted on 15 March 1983 by the Reform rabbinate presumed Jewish descent regardless of which parent was Jewish and included that the child's Jewish status was "to be established through appropriate and timely public and formal acts of identification with the Jewish faith and people."[98] The resolution, passed by a three-to-one margin by the Central Conference of American Rabbis, was partly a response to the rising rate of intermarriage.[99] By making descent egalitarian, the Reform movement essentially declared that the children of all Jewish-Gentile marriages were Jewish, provided that the child lived a Jewish life. Conservative and Orthodox Jewish leadership, however, continued to uphold matrilineal descent. For example, denouncing the patrilineal descent decision as an illegal position was Orthodox Rabbi J. Simcha Cohen, who wrote in 1987: "It is without dispute . . . that the children of gentile mothers and Jewish fathers are categorized as gentiles. They are simply not Jews."[100] The lack of agreement had several inadvertent consequences, not least of which was to create different standards between denominations for who is a Jew.

Scholars of Jewish continuity have overlooked the most telling aspect of the patrilineal descent issue as it relates to gender. Concerns have

centered on a decline in conversion among non-Jewish spouses, resulting in less religious homogeneity within intermarried families and that
children of Jewish mothers and non-Jewish fathers, formerly considered Jewish by matrilineal descent, were delegitimized if they did not
"perform formal acts of identification."[101] However, if one sees that the
patrilineal descent decision is a product of the widespread belief based
on demographic research through the end of the 1980s that Jewish men
intermarried in greater numbers than Jewish women, a new interpretation is possible.[102] The perceived need by Reform leadership to legiti-
mize the children of Jewish fathers and non-Jewish mothers would not
have been necessary had it been evident that Jewish men who intermarried were upholding tradition by converting their children to Judaism.[103]
Coincidentally, the "disappearance" of Jewish men from lay leadership
positions in Reform congregations, with the exception of the office of
Temple president, and the difficulty of attracting them to the professional workforce in the Jewish community indicates that Jewish men
became less communally involved over time.[104] This phenomenon is not
particular to the Jewish community; regarding the identification of piety and femininity that has persisted in American religion, the historian
Ann Braude noted that "the strong association of clergy with men and
laity with women seems to have a chilling effect on the participation
of male laity."[105] Therefore, the decision to include as Jews children of
Jewish men married to Gentile women suggests that Jewish leadership
understood the meaning of intermarriage, at least implicitly, in highly
gendered terms. Although the decision strove to make Jewish descent
egalitarian, it also created a loophole for Reform Jewish men who intermarried while the active roles of Jewish women who intermarried and
raised Jewish children, discussed below, went unnoticed. It effectively reduced Jewish men's responsibility for playing active roles in raising Jewish children, for they could now claim that their children were equally
Jewish as those born to Jewish women, a child care responsibility that
was and continues to be gendered female.[106]

Seven years after the Reform movement's adoption of patrilineal descent fanned the flames of debate among and within the Jewish denominations, the release of the 1990 National Jewish Population Survey raised
communal concern about intermarriage and lack of conversion to Judaism by Gentile spouses to a historic new level by reporting that 52 percent of born Jews "who married, at any age, whether for the first time or
not, chose a spouse who was born a Gentile and remained so, while less

than 5 percent of these marriages include a non-Jewish partner who became a Jew by choice." That more than half the number of American Jews
chose to marry "out," combined with the finding that, since 1985, twice as
many Jewish intermarriages had been entered into than in-marriages, set
off sirens in every corner of organized Jewish communities about Jewish
survival.[107] The magnitude of change was indicated by the fact that, prior
to 1965, there had been five times as many marriages between two Jewish
spouses than between one Jewish and one non-Jewish spouse.[108] Hence,
although Jews had landed on America's shores more than three hundred
years earlier, it took only two decades for intermarriage to surpass marriage within Judaism. The international press reported on Jewish alarm;
"For American Jews," one concerned sociologist was quoted in *U.S. News
& World Report,* "intermarriage is the single greatest concern next to the
fate of Israel."[109]

The impact of the NJPS on the American Jewish communities' perception of intermarriage cannot be underestimated. In the words of
Jonathan Sarna, a professor at Brandeis University and one of the most
well respected observers of American Jewish history: "In the world of
American Jewish symbols, NJPS now stands for the challenge posed by
assimilation and rampant intermarriage. Thanks to its clarion call, the
eyes of American Jews have been opened."[110] Jewish intelligentsia convened from across academic disciplines, denominations, and communal
offices for the American Jewish Committee-Brandeis University Conference on Intermarriage in October 1990, which was followed by more fo-
rums in the 1990s dedicated to intermarriage.[111] Shortly after, and partly
based on papers from the conference, the William Petschek National
Jewish Family Center of the AJC published *The Intermarriage Crisis:
Jewish Community Responses and Perspectives,* including broad analyses
and policy recommendations.[112] Although the contributors differed in
their approaches to the topic and in their suggestions, a clear consensus emerged that resulted in the primary recommendation of the AJC's
statement on intermarriage:

> The American Jewish community must find sensitive ways to respond
> to intermarriage that can enhance Jewish identity and continuity. At the
> same time, it must be recognized that intermarriage cannot be under-
> stood or dealt with in isolation from the more general erosion of Jewish
> identity and practice that has taken place.[113]

Disagreement over how best to respond to intermarriage polarized the organized Jewish community and led to the forceful "outreach" versus "in-
reach" debate, which I discuss in the concluding chapter.

Birth of A Jewish Matriarch

Marrying a Gentile, combined with becoming a mother, heightened the
consciousness of most of the women interviewed regarding their Jewish identity and Judaism in general. Thirteen out of the fifteen women
discussed in this chapter who intermarried between 1980 and 2000 described intensified Jewish identities, increased religious practices, or both.
For example, when Bonnie Aaronson planned her 1981 wedding, she had
a very strong cultural and social identity as a Jew, but she was not a religious person. In the late 1980s, however, after Bonnie had two children,
she became actively involved in her temple and co-chaired a committee that created an alternative High Holiday service. Interviewed nearly
twenty years after she wed, Bonnie remarked, "I have changed pretty *dramatically* in terms of my Jewish practice and observance . . . in the course
of our marriage." Although Bonnie may have become "more Jewish" once
she became a mother regardless of whether she intermarried, representing
a typical American Jewish pattern, the extent of her change over time suggests that the paradox created by her marriage to a non-Jew significantly
fostered the development of her Jewish identity.[114] As Bonnie emphasized:
"*I* was the one that *cared.*"[115] Intermarried Jewish women's experiences
demonstrate the "tenacity of Jewishness" that Mayer identified in 1985 and
the continued revitalization of Judaism envisioned by Sarna in 2004.[116]

The juxtaposition of being Jewish while married to a non-Jew usually
heightened Jewish women's consciousness about being Jewish, and having
children while intermarried made the Jewish women I interviewed decidedly proactive about making Jewish connections, about observance, and
about Jewish education. The sociologist Susan Maushart argued, in her
1999 book, *The Mask of Motherhood,* that becoming a mother precipitated
an identity crisis for women that presented new opportunities for personal
growth and development.[117] Becca Tamen's description of how having children solidified her Jewish identity illustrates the impact of motherhood
on intermarried women: "I actually don't think I started as firmly thinking about myself as Jewish till I had kids, and then starting thinking about
religion and the future and what they would be and so what I needed

to be."[118] The experience of having a child also forced women to come to terms with the inadequacies of their own Jewish upbringing and to look for creative ways to teach their children (and themselves) about Jewish heritage. Hannah Noble remarked:

> It's really about the kids. It has really only begun to be important to me to—I really want to raise my kids with a really solidly Jewish identity and I want them to know more than I did, because I couldn't tell ya, when I got married, what Passover was about or Chanukah was about. I'd never been taught. And now I go to the Israeli bookstore on Harvard Street and just go *crazy* with books for my kids and toys in Hebrew, and so . . . .we're working on it.[119]

Thus, rather than the generations becoming assimilated to the point of no return over time, I found that, among my sample of intermarried Jewish women, those who intermarried in the 1980s and 1990s made increasingly sure, more so than their predecessors in the 1960s and 1970s, that their children received more Jewish religious and cultural education than they themselves had had. Bonnie Aaronson felt her parents had made a "big mistake" by not providing her with a religious education, a mistake she would not repeat as a mother raising Jewish children.[120] That some Jewish women who intermarried made significantly more commitments to Jewish education and observance for their children than their own Jewish-Jewish parents had done for them illustrates one way that Judaism continued to be revitalized by women who married "out." Whereas some women who intermarried in the 1960s and 1970s disassociated Jewish education from Jewish identity, women who intermarried at the end of the century were considerably more committed to Jewish identification through education. Women who intermarried in the 1980s and 1990s seemed less convinced than their predecessors that their children's Jewish identity was absolute; whether their children would be Jewish depended intimately on the choices these women made about Jewish education and lifestyle.[121] Coincidentally, through this process, the Jewish women themselves became more involved with Jewish beliefs and practices as they learned alongside their children. A poignant example was a woman who did not experience a Jewish rite of passage when she was thirteen and was seriously considering becoming a *bat mitzvah* with her daughter.[122]

The increased religiosity of intermarried Jewish women over time also reflected the national trend that people tend to become more religious as they age. According to the 2001 ARIS, the percentage of people who considered themselves to have a religious outlook increased with age as follows: 27 percent (age 18-34); 38 percent (age 35-49); 42 percent (age 50-64); 47 percent (age 65 and over).[123] In her study of adult mother-daughter relationships, the sociologist Debra Kaufman identified a pattern that appeared to be particular to the Jewish women in the sample; as Jewish mothers age, they tend to pursue their spiritual lives to a greater extent than they may have earlier when they had less time.[124] Similarly the coeditors of *Jewish Mothers Tell Their Stories* (2000) describe the Jewish identity of Jewish mothers as "fluid," "consisting of a continuing process of growth and change"; even women who continued to identify with the denomination or secular tradition of their parents experienced "an evolving inner consciousness and a maturing concurrent change in the external expression of their Jewishness."[125]

When Jewish women first met and fell in love with non-Jewish men, one's religiousness could sometimes be temporarily pushed aside so that the relationship leading to marriage was unimpeded by issues of distinction. Reflecting back on how little her religion meant to her when she fell in love with a non-Jewish man, Brandy Simon admitted that she convinced herself that her religious background was irrelevant: "I reduced its importance—much more than I would now if somebody asked me."[126] Overlooking or minimizing differences between Jewish women and Gentile men was preferable to drawing attention to them or anticipating difficulties that might arise because of them. One woman described her marriage to a Catholic as follows: "And with religion especially we did not want to acknowledge disagreement."[127]

A woman's Jewishness could be overlooked according to the speed with which the relationship moved, and then reinvigorated as the relationship progressed. Women who had been raised in less observant Jewish households, like Hannah whose parents considered her a religious fanatic for lighting Shabbat candles once she was married, were typically urged by their Gentile husbands, none of whom converted, to better educate themselves about Judaism to substantiate their claim to raising Jewish children. Gabriella Abrahms, for example, agreed to her husband's proposition that if she went to Friday night services every week for six months to learn more about the tradition she professed was so important to preserve, he would agree to send their son to Hebrew School.[128]

Evidence from periodical literature further illustrates that, by marrying outside their faith, Jewish women often became more interested in and more committed to Judaism than they might have otherwise. Writing in *Commonweal* about her intermarriage, Madeline Marget explained how fifteen years after she wed, she wanted to "stand up and be counted": "I find myself, lately, eager to declare myself as a Jew, and to return to the formal observance of the religion in which I was raised."[129] Whereas her husband was uncomfortable with organized religion in general, Eileen Ogintz confided, "I, on the other hand, have felt an increasingly stronger pull to Judaism."[130] Beth Levine, in an aptly titled article "The Forbidden Road Home," explained that although she intended to marry a fellow Jew and raise "nominally Jewish children," she would have been hard-pressed to explain what being a Jew meant. That changed when she married Bill Squier. Marrying a Gentile made her a more observant and knowledge-able Jew, and forced her to search her soul for answers to questions she had never thought to ask before. She wrote: "More so than anything else, marrying Bill has opened the door to my Jewish spiritual home."[131] Emily Blank married a Protestant minister, which set her on an even more extreme journey of educating herself about her Jewish faith, one that eventually led to her becoming a cantor with a pulpit.[132]

The experience of intermarriage heightening a person's awareness of and connection to a religious heritage is not limited to Jews or to women.[133] Periodical literature is replete with examples of intensified relationships with the religion and culture of one's childhood, or observations about this phenomenon. Ruth Mendelson was a Catholic woman who married a Jew after her first husband died, and she lived with both a crucifix and a mezuzah on her doorpost. She believed that her intermarriage had positively influenced her Catholicism: "I'm basically the same," she reflected, "but my faith's gotten richer."[134] Emily M. Brown, director of the Divorce and Marital Stress Clinic in Arlington, Virginia, noted in 1984 that coming into contact with a different way of life provided the contrast that enabled people to see what made them "American," for example.[135] Thus, when a Catholic married a non-Catholic or a Jew married a non-Jew, they could likewise better conceptualize and thereby strengthen their own Catholicness or Jewishness. As Steve Roberts commented about his thirty-three-year relationship with the ABC News political commentator Cokie Roberts in their coauthored book *From This Day Forward* (2000): "In a real sense, marrying a non-Jew made me more Jewish." Because Christian rituals were all around them, Roberts felt that he had to "work at the Judaism part."[136] A Catholic priest who encouraged "loving alienated Catholics and people of other or no religions" and who assisted at intermarriage ceremonies reported, in a September 1988 editorial, that couples told him that their interfaith marriages fostered increased devoutness.[137]

Although most women felt and acted more Jewish after they intermarried, those who did not were still Jewish by their own accounts, illustrating the belief that Jewish identity is inalienable.[138] In the case of the two exceptions, their Jewishness was an inseparable part of their identity that remained constant since having intermarried. Karla Matzman could have envisioned herself becoming a pioneering female rabbi—except that she could not reconcile Jewish law as commanded by God. Nevertheless, she would always be Jewish: "I am because it's inescapable. And whether I've lived any aspects of my life in a Jewish fashion or not, I would still be Jewish because I have this so ingrained in my identity that there is *no* possibility for me to consider myself anything else."[139] Karla's children attended the Workmen's Circle *Shule* (Yiddish for school), a secular Jewish educational program, on Sundays. This was one way in which she negotiated her own ambivalence about the existence of God with a sense of commitment to social justice and the maintenance of a Jewish cultural identity. Muriel Cypress realized that although her Jewishness had remained constant since 1996, her intermarriage, she said, "certainly has sort of defined me as being Jewish."[140] In addition, Muriel was the one person I spoke with who emphatically identified herself as a *Jewish* American rather than an American Jew, because she thought of herself as being more Jewish than American. Had she had children, she imagined that she would have become more religiously demonstrative. Ironically, people mistook Muriel for a non-Jewish Greek because she had taken her husband's last name when she wed, an accommodation an increasing number of women refused to make.

The issue of identity was connected to the legacy of the second-wave Women's Liberation movement that encouraged many Jewish women who came of age in the 1970s and 1980s and intermarried in the 1980s and early 1990s to keep their own surnames. This phenomenon illustrated the changing relationship between women and men in general, and, in particular, the increased assertiveness of Jewish women regarding their individual identities. The new trend in American marriage history of more women keeping their own surnames, which reflected the culture of individualism, was precipitated by public discourse encouraging women to determine what they wished to be named.[141] Although the issue of a woman not changing her name upon marriage had surfaced at the beginning of the century, as discussed in chapter 1, it took on more widespread acceptability toward the century's end. For example, in a questionnaire completed by more than three hundred women, 75 percent kept their own names.[142] Women who retained their names or created new ones with their husbands gained increasingly autonomous visibility and, in the process, overturned the convention that a woman must take her husband's name.[143] A *Boston Phoenix* writer, responding in 1992 to a question about why she did not take her husband's name, said: "For the same reason I didn't take his underwear. I mean, his name has as much to do with me as his Hanes do, right?" The article's illustration of a bride holding an automatic weapon certainly suggested that the modern woman who wed was no pushover.[144] By 2000, however, the percentage of women who kept their own name was in decline, perhaps reflecting a maturing of the gains won by the Women's Rights movement and that fewer women felt the need to make a statement. According to a Harvard study, whereas 23 percent of college-educated women kept their own name in 1990, 17 percent did so in 2000.[145]

Jewish women who kept their own surnames played active parts in this larger story of maintaining one's identity separate from one's husband in recent American women's history. Eight of the women discussed in this chapter kept their own surnames when they wed, five took their husband's name, one changed her name the first time she married but not the second, and one took her husband's name but continued to use her maiden name professionally. That more than half the women held onto their pre-married-life surnames illustrates that women identified with feminist theories about power and equality within married life. Zena Jethro, an attorney and writer who married a Catholic man in 1984 explained: "I kept my own name; that was a feminism thing."[146] The trend also shows that women who married when older, especially after spending several years in the workforce, were less inclined to trade in their professional identities. Zipora Ackerman, also an attorney, said, "It honestly never occurred to me to give up my name," when she married a Catholic in 1987 at the age of twenty-seven.[147] Melissa Sherman, a teacher who married an Episcopalian when she was twenty-nine, retained her family name because that was how people knew her professionally.[148]

More significant to this discussion, that a woman kept her family name also illustrated that the family name was an inherent part of her Jewish identity, one she could not suppress. One woman believed that her face appeared so Jewish that, "I can't see myself walking around in this life with a WASP name."[149] Another insisted: "I'm Gabriella Abrahms, always was, always will be. And that was really important to me to keep my Jewish identity through my name."[150] This intensified association between a woman's name and her Jewish identity was part of the historical context of Jewish feminism in which increasing numbers of women came forward to claim their religious and ethnic heritage.[151] As the feminist Letty Cottin Pogrebin wrote:

> No matter how 'un-Jewish' we are, no matter how unobservant, atheistic, disconnected to the Jewish community or the State of Israel, more and more women who were *born* Jewish are coming to believe they must deal with what that identity means to them and how they feel about other Jews and Jewish issues.[152]

Women determined what their Jewish identity meant to them while married to a non-Jew, a process that involved negotiation and compromise over time.

Women who kept their own names often agreed to have their children take their husband's names as part of the marital negotiation over religious identity. For example, Hannah Noble kept her own name for feminist reasons, but thought that since her husband was generous enough to give the children her religion that she would give them his name. Having, in her words, "healthy Jewish children" was all she cared about.[153] Women who had brothers also justified this decision by explaining that their husbands were the only male children in their families of origin, and therefore the responsibility for continuing the family name rested with them. Finally, women who did take their husband's name rationalized that they still won what was most important to them. One woman described the outcome of her bargaining with her husband over identity in this way: "I got the religion and he got the name."[154] Thus marrying a Gentile forced Jewish women to examine closely how they conceived of being Jewish, and what, if anything, was most important to them in terms of perpetuating Jewish life encompassing both religion and culture.

The relatively new social phenomenon of women raising children as Jews with less obviously Jewish surnames challenged an assumption that someone with a non-Jewish last name was unlikely to be Jewish, and perplexed some people in the process. For example, a story about life in the 1990s in the Catholic periodical *America* told of a woman who had to inform her obstetrician that he should not perform a circumcision on her son, because they planned to have a *bris*. The doctor, somewhat incredulous, asked, "Do you mean to tell me that Sean Patrick Quinn is Jewish?" The author quipped, "Welcome to the new millennium, doctor," and introduced another child: "Her name is Maggie Rosenbaum. She's Catholic."[155] In both cases, the children of an interfaith marriage were given their father's last name and their mother's religious identity. These examples further illustrate how the gendered relationship between intermarriage, child naming, and child rearing applied to women of different ethnic backgrounds.

The women in my sample who intermarried in the last decades of the twentieth century embraced the historically gendered notion of the Jewish woman as the "maternal keeper of the domestic flame of Judaism." Because Jewish women's roles were primarily confined to the home in nineteenth-century America, and therefore less fraught with the tension Jewish men experienced in a Christian-dominated society or impacted by substituting secular education for Torah study, they were able to maintain a level of ritual observance and spirituality. And, as the historian Paula Hyman has argued, "Jewish women acquired a new role that was ostensibly highly valued, the role of transmitters of Jewish culture to their children."[156] The deep roots of the Jewish cult of domesticity continued to influence the thoughts and actions of women in the contemporary period. Most of the Jewish women I interviewed who intermarried in the 1980s and 1990s believed that it was their responsibility to instill an understanding of Jewish history and culture, if not Judaism, in their children. Michelle Johnson imbued her view of women's roles with a sense of divine ordinance: "I think as a Jewish woman, I feel we have certain responsibilities to carry on what is given to us, the Torah, *all* of it. . . . The women are the ones in the family who are here to teach, to pass on to the family, to the kids. If we don't do it, it won't get done."[157]

Intermarriage in the 1980s and 1990s for the Jewish mothers in my study meant assuming the mantle of the religious head of the family while reinforcing traditional gender roles as the family communicators and event organizers. Like women of other ethnic backgrounds, Jewish women had greater ability than their husbands to control their children's religious socialization.[158] Although Melissa Sherman and her Episcopalian husband mutually agreed to raise Jewish children, the responsibility for holiday celebrations was Melissa's domain; for example, she led the Passover Seder, a role he declined to learn. Melissa described her position with regard to religious practice in her family perfectly with the words: "I'm the only expert."[159] The women I interviewed were highly aware of their unique roles as the planners and masters of ceremonies of holidays and rituals, and as the spiritual guides of their families. Penina Mintz Jennings surmised that she could not "coast," as she put it, because she had intermarried: "I am carrying more weight around here and with my family because [my husband] is looking to *me* on different holidays to show the way. So maybe that has made me stiffen my back a little bit and do some reading and learn how to carry the show, like maybe I wouldn't have to if I'd married someone else, someone who was Jewish."[160] Thus religious-related responsibilities were intermarried "women's work."

Intermarried Jewish women, like most American women, were caught between contemporary ideas about gender equality and the unyielding structural realities of family life that meant "more work for mother," such as keeping children well occupied and engaged with relatives.[161] Women's responsibilities for the family's religious direction mirrored their other domestic responsibilities, including researching child care options and finding appealing summer camps, Jewish or secular. Bonnie Aaronson remarked that although she located the information about synagogues and religious education programs in the area because she was the one who cared, her efforts were consistent with the gender-based division of labor in her marriage.[162] Women were largely the information gatherers, the social planners, and the communicators with extended family members. Thus their roles as the religious leaders of their families were extensions of their other gendered activities and workload. Remarking on her role regarding religion in her family, intermarried freelance writer Beth Levine commented, "This left me as captain of our family's spiritual ship."[163]

The influential role of Jewish women living in the Greater Boston Area did not, however, improve the odds for Jewish continuity when less than half of all children of intermarriage nationwide were raised as Jewish compared to a reported 96 percent of the children of in-married Jews.[164] The Jewish women in my sample who intermarried in the 1980s and 1990s for the most part raised Jewish children. Of the fifteen women discussed in this chapter, twelve were raising children to identify as Jewish, two were childless, and one was pregnant at the time of the interview. These women reflect the finding in the 2005 Boston Community Survey that "Jewish mothers, married to non-Jews, are near-universal in reporting that they raised their children as Jews." This phenomenon was actually documented earlier when the 1970-72 NJPS found that 98 percent of the children of Jewish mothers (whether by birth or by choice) were being raised as Jews compared to 63 percent of the children of Jewish fathers.[165] The 1990

NJPS found that of the children under age eighteen living in households with Jewish-Gentile parents, only 28 percent were being raised as Jewish. Forty-one percent were raised in a non-Jewish religion, and 31 percent were raised with no religious instruction. Whether the latter group would choose a Jewish identity was considered a key factor in determining the loss, or potential gains, to the Jewish population in the next generation. The authors noted that in-depth analysis was needed to determine how factors such as the gender of the Jewish parent affect the children's religious upbringing.[166] Similarly the 2000-2001 NJPS simply reported that 33 percent of the children in households with one non-Jewish spouse was being raised Jewish, a slight increase from 1990.[167]

The numbers about how many children of intermarried households were being raised Jewish vary by study and community. In Boston, the 2005 population survey found that the estimated proportion of children being raised Jewish was 60 percent, much higher than the national figure and figures in New York (30 percent in 2002) and Pittsburgh (36 percent in 2002), and on a par with the study of Bergen County, New Jersey (59 percent in 2001).[168] Although the exact percentages of children reared as Jews differs between studies, illustrating that qualitative and quantitative data sometime conflict, the consensus among scholars is that of those children raised as Jewish, a majority have Jewish mothers. Ironically, the question a three year old posed upon learning that she, her sister, and her mother but not her father were Jewish captures the gendered implications of intermarriage: "Do you have to be a girl to be Jewish?"[169]

Triple Marginality

Although Jewish women have made major inroads to equal status in mainstream American social and religious culture in the past twenty-five years, the intermarried Jewish woman remained the "Other" in three ways: she was a Jew in a Christian world, a woman in a male society, and a Jewish woman married to a Gentile man.[170] Prejudice against intermarried Jewish women illustrates the shifting focus of discrimination in American society: in the early twentieth century she was marginalized as a Jew; at mid-century, as a woman; and by the end of the century, for intermarrying. Scholars have argued that intermarriage became so normalized that preferential endogamy ceased to exist in American society at large.[171] However, and despite the passage of time, an anti-intermarriage bias continued to permeate the Jewish communities where intermarried

Jewish women lived. Anti-exogamy rhetoric has become hushed in wider circles but remains vocal within the creases of the Jewish fold, where individuals and organizations are deeply concerned about continuity.

The narratives of intermarried Jewish women illustrate the social stigma of intermarriage. Robin Elk, who married a lapsed Catholic in 2000 and worked as a schoolteacher at various Reconstructionist and Reform temples, felt that she no longer fit any of the acceptable categories of identification. By intermarrying, she ceased being a single woman and was also no longer considered "Jewish" by some; her identity became, simply, "intermarried."[172] Zena Jethro equated the experience of being labeled as intermarried with the narrow view some hold of gay people. When the question "Do you have a Christmas tree in your house?" was of the utmost importance to people she called the "Jewish establishment," that was a denial of the multifaceted nature of being intermarried, just as questions about why a woman would sleep with another woman reduced gay people to the single variable of sexual intercourse. She lamented: "But they have so many other parts of themselves, but that's *all* people can look at."[173] The need for the consciousness-raising groups of the 1960s and 1970s became more specialized, as intermarried Jewish women gathered together in the 1980s and 1990s. Some Jewish women in the Boston area who were married to nonreligious men started informal clubs to discuss their roles as the ones responsible for raising Jewish children, to share information, or, as one woman described it, to bring together "New York metropolitan-area Jewish women and their white-bread Midwestern husbands."[174]

Although, according to the women interviewed for this book, the label "intermarried" was an identity that members of the organized Jewish community imposed on them, many considered themselves Jewish first and foremost, and extended this definition to their family. Intermarried women who raised Jewish children denied that "intermarried" defined them or their families, refusing to be stereotyped in the process. Heidi Laker emphasized: "I feel strongly that I'm Jewish . . . Henry is not, but the family is and the kids are. They're not half one thing and half of something else; they're Jewish. . . . My family is a Jewish family; it is not an interfaith family."[175] The self-conceptions of intermarried Jewish women were contrary to how others saw them. Penina Mintz Jennings commented, "I basically see us living a Reform Jewish life . . . I don't walk around thinking of myself in an intermarriage. . . . I'd rather do something Jewish where we all feel comfortable rather than doing something labeled interfaith."[176] The women's insistence that their families were Jewish despite their husbands remaining unconverted Gentiles suggested that the women overlooked their husband's identities in favor of a unified familial front, which *they* labeled "Jewish"; the phrase "interfaith family" did not apply in their eyes. Some women, however, accepted the "interfaith" label as accurate, exemplified by their ambivalence about affixing a *mezuzah* on their doorpost. Their reluctance stemmed from feeling that theirs was not truly a Jewish home, and so the *mezuzot* remained in a drawer.[177]

The high percentage of Jewish intermarriage and communal hysteria about Jewish "decline," combined with the communal efforts to include the intermarried, had the paradoxical effect of increasing the visibility of Jewish women who married non-Jewish men in the 1980s and 1990s. That more than half of all American Jews were reportedly intermarried meant that intermarried Jewish women were among the "majority," heretofore unimaginable, and yet they were also emblematic of the perceived threat to Jewish continuity. More than half of the fifteen women discussed in this chapter experienced some instance of social alienation or marginalization after they intermarried, and this came from a wide range of sources including rabbis, Jewish friends, temple staff, and extended family members.

Jewish women who intermarried earlier in the century were seen as exceptions or rebels, but by the end of the century they were perceived as "decimators" of the Jewish people. In an address delivered at the May 1990 annual meeting of the AJC, David Belin poignantly emphasized the need for outreach:

> I am going to talk about the ultimate irony of Jewish history that will occur if we continue in our present path—that after having seen the world stand idly by while our ranks were decimated by the Holocaust, we American Jews today are, for all practical purposes, standing idly by while our ranks are being decimated as a result of intermarriage.[178]

In January 1999, the AJC issued a press release deploring a statement by the Israeli Orthodox Chief Rabbi Eliyahu Bakshi-Doron blaming Reform Judaism for assimilation and again drawing a comparison between intermarriage and the Holocaust. Criticism of Bakshi-Doron's statement was based on the view that such a comparison demeaned Holocaust victims and undermined the Jewish communal effort to emphasis the uniqueness of the Holocaust as a historical event.[179] Although refuting the idea that Reform Judaism was the cause of assimilation, the AJC did not explain, unequivocally, that intermarriage was not, in fact, the same as genocide.

The link between intermarriage, the Holocaust, and the end of American Jewry extended to Jewish women and Jewish men alike. The author Ellen Jaffe McClain, who sat on her temple's board of directors and attended Friday night services nearly every week, described how the release of the 1990 NJPS three months after she wed affected her social status: "Suddenly, married to a non-Jew, I was an enemy of the Jewish people."[180] Steve Roberts, mentioned above, wrote about his interfaith family's trip to Israel in the *New York Times*. His intermarriage was a lightning rod for personal attacks, and he received letters that read: "You are carrying out Hitler's work."[181]

In addition to the perception that intermarried Jewish women and men contribute to the decline in the Jewish population, it was commonly assumed by some Jewish clergy and scholars that those who intermarried had essentially forsaken their Jewish identity, that it was no longer important to them and would never be so. A Jewish woman told *Glamour* in 1983 about her difficulty arranging an ecumenical ceremony for herself and her Catholic fiancé. Regarding the dozen phone calls she made to rabbis: "Their attitude was very negative: 'If you really wanted to be Jewish, you wouldn't marry a gentile.' Some of them hung up on me before I even finished talking."[182] The association between intermarriage and a perceived lack of Jewish identity was so strong that Jewish women who intermarried had to convince people that they were indeed still Jewish.

Intermarried Jewish women were marginalized in different ways, sometimes explicitly, sometimes subtly. For some women, their most powerful memory was rejection from a rabbi. For example, Melissa Sherman twice experienced marginalization from the organized Jewish community, illustrating how these insults turned her away from one Jewish house of worship forever: "The first time was when my rabbi wouldn't marry us and the second time was when my parents asked us to bring my oldest daughter home for a naming at their temple. And their—my rabbi invited me up on the *bimah* with the baby and told my husband to sit in the congregation. And I was so upset by that, I never went back to that temple."[183] Melissa stated that the treatment her husband was subjected to at his own child's naming ceremony was analogous to the way women are treated by Orthodox Judaism when they are prohibited from reading from the Torah.

For other intermarried Jewish women, marginalization was more subtle, a part of the social landscape but no less painful. Whether by a pregnant pause or a raised eyebrow, women were made to feel that when someone learned they were intermarried, that person, in one woman's words, had to "reorder their worldview of you."[184] In one instance, while trying to arrange for her son's *brit milah* (ritual circumcision), Penina Mintz Jennings encountered what she called the "hairy eyeball" and silence from temple staff when she told them her non-Jewish sounding last name. The negative feeling this experience generated had a powerful impact. Penina explained: "Makes me feel like an outsider. Makes me feel like not quite one of the group."[185] The sad irony of Penina's experience is that she was made to feel uncomfortable and marginalized while actively seeking to fulfill one of the most sacred tenets of Judaism, a biblical commandment (Genesis 17:10). Similarly Heidi Laker, who was nominated to participate in a program in Israel for Jewish leaders, had to listen to someone condemn intermarriage at one of the first educational discussions.[186]

The Combined Jewish Philanthropies (CJP) in Boston acknowledged the contradiction between the high rates of intermarriage and the stigma attached to it that persisted to affect intermarried Jewish women and men. In response to negative experiences and widespread intermarriage within its constituency, the CJP created a Task Force on Intermarriage in the spring of 1996 to examine the barriers "perceived or otherwise" that alienated the intermarried from connecting with the Jewish community. At its first meeting, Task Force members recognized that prevailing communal attitudes made members of interfaith couples (both Jews and non-Jews) feel that they were "second-class citizens" or "pariahs." The progressive efforts of the CJP culminated in a January 1997 statement of intent about cultivating and promoting an environment in which the intermarried were "genuinely respected, valued and supported in their efforts to explore, affiliate with, and become integral members of the Jewish Community of Greater Boston."[187] Adding to this effort was InterfaithFamily.com, Inc., a nonprofit organization founded in 2001, whose mission is "to empower interfaith families to make Jewish choices for themselves and their children, and to encourage the Jewish community to be welcoming of interfaith families."[188] By 2004 anti-intermarriage rhetoric was a mixture of condemnation and balanced discourse, suggesting that what was unacceptable in Orthodox terms deserved attention from non-Orthodox denominations and resources from organizations such as the CJP.[189]

While the Jewish women in my sample and those described in published articles experienced bias against intermarriage in the public sphere, they also faced oppression inside their own homes. Despite their Gentile husbands' apparent lack of affinity for their religions of origin, the cultural divide between spouses, discussed in the previous chapter, grew wider as the majority of Jewish women reconnected with their own sense of being Jewish, and some Gentile husbands struggled to retain what, for them, was sometimes the one remaining connection to childhood memories: Christmas. Christmas was an annual reminder to intermarried Jewish women, and to all American Jews, that American culture was overwhelmingly Christian. "On no other day during the year," as one historian eloquently wrote, did they "so deeply feel the clash between the country they love and the faith they cherish."[190] For most intermarried Jewish women, the clash was threefold: between them and the men they loved, the country they called home, and the faith they cherished. Having a Christmas tree was the only thing Heidi Laker's husband wanted that had religious connotations, but she refused to have a tree in their home. Aware that her refusal caused him sadness, she explained why she could not bear the thought of having a tree: "because I think there is nothing that so much identifies a Jew as one's feelings about Christmas." Boiling just beneath the surface was Heidi's rejection of the view that Christmas was an "American holiday," an intense sentiment many Jewish women expressed.[191] A 1998 *Newsweek* author opined: "When is a tree not a tree? When you're Jewish and your husband wants a Christmas tree in your living room." Psychologically the Christmas tree was no benign symbol when it brought to mind two thousand years of persecution and stirred fears of annihilation.[192] The annual proliferation of advertising and material consumption proclaiming Christmas "America's Greatest Holiday" also made it impossible to ignore.[193]

Jewish women's narratives regarding Christmas reflected the larger trend of public discourse about how intermarrieds negotiated holiday celebrations. The 1980s and 1990s represented a period of unprecedented media coverage about a phenomenon that came to be commonly referred to as the "December Dilemma." This phrase signified the manifold tensions and decision making that intermarried couples faced regarding reconciling two different faiths at a particular time of the year. The term itself seems to have been first conceived by Rachel and the late Paul Cowan, a Jewish man and a Unitarian-turned-Jew-by-choice woman, who in 1987 co-authored the advice book *Mixed Blessings: Overcoming the Stumbling Blocks in an Interfaith Marriage.*[194] Strife over Chanukah and Christmas had caught public attention even before it had a name. The December 1982 issue of *Ladies' Home Journal,* for example, had a feature-length article

"Living on a Prayer: With Interfaith Unions on the Rise, It Takes More Than Just Love to Keep a Marriage Working—Especially around the Holidays," *Boston Magazine,* December 2000, 36.

about the "common clashes and strengths" of interfaith couples that began and concluded with how Jewish-Christian couples navigated the winter holidays.[195] But once the phrase was coined, press coverage increased with annual December headlines such as: "Whose holiday is it, anyway?" (*Glamour,* 1988), "Of Latkes and Lights" (*Newton Graphic,* 1992), "Interfaith Families Face 'December Dilemma'" (*USA Today,* 1996), and "Living on a Prayer" (*Boston Magazine,* 2000). By the dawn of the millennium, one could anticipate seeing as many articles in December about how Jewish-Gentile couples negotiated holidays as one might see menorahs in the windows and wreaths on the doors.

Some Jewish women paid a high emotional price for "coming out" as a committed Jew after they wed, particularly when their husbands were entirely disinterested in religion. For example, Bonnie Aaronson found it "very painful and very difficult to accept," when her husband declined to attend High Holiday services. Remembering how much she had wanted her husband to hear her when she had the honor of giving a talk at the Yom Kippur morning service, Bonnie explained: "I mean I sort of felt like it was, like I was, it was like I was coming out or something. It was like–it was just a really big thing for me, religiously, spiritually. And, you know, he wasn't there."[196] Bonnie's decision to speak at the Yom Kippur service signaled her transformation from a private Jew to a communally involved Jew, a deeply meaningful personal journey, something her husband evidently could not appreciate. Her use of the words "coming out" is analogous to the experiences of gays and lesbians in both the larger American society and as active members of the Jewish community in the past twenty-five years.[197] This comparison illustrates that, for some Jewish women, intermarrying and becoming "more Jewish" felt counter-cultural.

Although most Gentile husbands were significantly involved with their wives living a Jewish life, and indeed fostered the women's Jewishness and participated in raising Jewish children, most Jewish women in my sample, ironically and despite the positive qualities they described about their intermarriages, expressed sadness about not being married to a fellow Jew. Zena Jethro, for example, reported that her husband would attend a Jewish study group or events at their synagogue if she asked, but because that was not his first choice, she often went alone or with a friend. She was the one who brought religion into their home, and, once it was there, he supported it. Zena commented, "I initiate it, but he's on the train with me."[198] Heidi Laker also described that despite how flexible and accommodating her husband had been–"He is prepared to do everything I ask, short of becoming Jewish"–she experienced sadness that he did not really care about living a Jewish life. "It's clearly *my* thing that he goes along with," she said.[199]

Women's wistfulness about not being married to Jewish men, however, overlooks the likelihood that, had they married Jewish men, the Jewish men may have been equally disinterested in religious activities and that their Gentile husbands were effectively ambassadors of good will. Contemporary sociological studies of moderately affiliated American Jews have found, as I have, that women, as wives and mothers, are "more emotionally invested, physically present, and ultimately influential in conveying Jewish identity" and that, although exceptions do exist, men "do and care far less."[200] Hence, when religion was fundamentally important to the women, the difficulty of leading a Jewish life and of raising Jewish children depended less on whether the husband was actually Jewish than on whether he had any interest in faith at all.

But despite their anguish, the intermarried Jewish women in my sample insisted that they would not wish to be married to someone other than their Gentile husbands. Sadness about being alone or wishing their husband was Jewish did not mean that they regretted their decision to intermarry. Some women who intermarried in the 1980s and 1990s confessed that they would love their husbands to convert to Judaism, a significant change from women who intermarried in the 1960s and 1970s. This latter group was satisfied if their husbands simply understood antisemitism, provided they did so for the "right reason": that it was what the husband wanted and not just to please the wife. Women were quick to point out, however, that they considered it highly unlikely that their husband would convert to Judaism. Regardless of the wish that they had been cut from the same ethno-religious cloth, Jewish women placed their marital relationships with Gentile men before religious principle. Zena Jethro, for example, emphasized that she would intermarry all over again: "My *marriage* is more important than anything else. So if Judaism puts me in the position of making choices here, Judaism isn't going to win."²⁰¹

Jewish women's dual loyalties to their Gentile husbands and to identifying as Jews created a love triangle, one in which Jewish women would not give up their right to non-Jewish husbands for Judaism. Nor would they resist being actively Jewish for their Gentile husbands who encountered more Jewish religion and culture than they originally bargained for when they wed. Although women were active agents of free choice rather than mere subjects of stereotypes or social persecution, their feelings about difference and experiences with latent antisemitism made intermarriage more appealing than it otherwise might have been. At the same time, however, the convergence of feminism, age, and motherhood facilitated Jewish women's histories of personal growth toward feeling more Jewish, becoming more observant and more involved in their Jewish communities, and revitalizing Judaism from within their intermarriages, despite all prognoses to the contrary. While the pursuit of individual happiness and the simple act of falling in love led them to intermarry, Jewish women who married Gentiles at the end of the twentieth century maintained a deep and abiding allegiance to the Jewish people as an enduring entity. "I still consider myself, forever, a Jew," one woman wrote, "and this birthright, this primal identification with my tribe, carries a fierce desire to protect it against outsiders, even if the outsider is my husband."²⁰² As their personal narratives attest, Jewish women's increased awareness of, and attachment to, their Jewish identities, inspired largely by their intimate relationships with the Other, contributed to their assertiveness about the role of Jewish religion in their intermarried family lives and the upbringing of offspring.

Marrying someone of another faith cast women's Jewish identity into high relief and made the women more consciously Jewish than had they married endogamously. One woman decried the notion that intermarriage led to assimilation with a statement regarding her Jewish friends who married other Jews: "I'm doing *more* for the continuity of Judaism in this house with [her Gentile husband] than most of my Jewish girlfriends combined!"[203] Jewish women's identification with Judaism sometimes lay as if dormant during the dating and engagement period, a Sleeping Beauty awakened by the kiss of a Gentile husband and furthered by her concerns for her children. The evolution of Jewish women's identities illustrated the fluidity fostered by a culture of individualism as well as the personal meaning of religious identity that changed over the life course.[204] Some Jewish women's paradoxical relationships led them to develop themselves in ways they would never have explored without the influence of their Christian husband. Regarding her own intermarriage, Tirzah Firestone, raised as an Orthodox Jew, wrote: "For me, marrying 'the stranger' and becoming an outcast were, ironically, the necessary alchemical ingredients to my coming home to my Jewish roots, to becoming a rabbi, to standing in an honorable position of one who can help heal her people."[205] The majority of women who intermarried at the end of the twentieth century whose narratives filled this chapter debunk the myth that people who intermarried ceased to feel strongly about their Jewish identity. As this historical study has attempted to demonstrate, intermarriage may actually be a catalyst for a more clearly defined and meaningful Jewish identity and life.

Conclusion

We were a hybrid couple . . . We were an expression of love.
We were an expression of Judaism. We had to be, because I'm Jewish.
We, and others like us, were part of a Judaism that no one had yet
named.

—Lisa Schiffman, *generation j*, 1999

America's paradox of pluralism enabled the Jewish women in
my study to marry Gentile men while also forcing the women to determine in what ways they integrated into the American population and how
they retained their ethnic and religious heritage despite intermarrying.
As I have described, America's religious freedom, ethnic diversity, and
marital opportunities offered Jewish women the chance to choose their
own spouses and how they would self-identify. The meaning of religious
identity thereby became increasingly personal and individualistic, as it
did for many moderately affiliated American Jews.[1] The intrinsic struggle
between the selection of a Gentile husband and the maintenance of a Jewish self evolved over the past hundred or so years, as American women
gained more political rights and personal power within their marriages.
The democratic culture made blending into the mainstream possible, and
some Jewish women did when they intermarried, but it also increasingly
encouraged them to assert their Jewishness. As the literary scholar Ruth
R. Wisse, quoted in the introduction, observed: American Jews are in a
tough position: they have to accept America's generous welcome without
being obliterated by it.[2]

Jewish women who intermarried were in the toughest position of all,
because they brought America's hospitality into their hearts and beds. One
intermarried woman wrote in her autobiography: "I had signed on with a
man who was a ticket to freedom from my insular Jewish background.

Now I was fighting the very freedom he had brought me."[3] The increasing incidence of intermarriage between Jewish women and non-Jewish men symbolized the mutual love between Jews and America that signaled both freedom and challenge. The journalist Samuel G. Freedman wrote in 2004: "The thoroughgoing assimilation of postwar America, the emergence of Jewishness as just another brand of white ethnicity that can be halved or quartered, attests most profoundly to Oscar Wilde's aphorism to be careful what you wish for, because you might get it."[4] The intermarried Jewish women discussed in this book epitomized both the liberty to live as one wished and the challenge to define the meaning of being Jewish in a society where interfaith marriage, by the first years of the twenty-first century, had become "as American as apple pie."[5] Yet, their histories illustrate that intermarriage was not an adversary to Jewish continuity; rather, it was an opportunity for self-reflection and personal growth. In the words of the late Egon Mayer, sociology professor and director of the Center for Jewish Studies at the Graduate School of the City University of New York, intermarried women with accentuated Jewish identities "took advantage of cultural pluralism not by *blending* into the majority but by *absorbing*" Gentile members of the majority.[6] In addition, Sarah Coleman, an intermarried, third-wave Jewish feminist, pointed out that "in forming partnerships with non-Jews, we intermarrieds are spreading Jewish values and culture into the population at large."[7]

I wrote this book with the belief that Jewish women's intermarriage experiences were nuanced, and therefore that the gendered meaning of intermarriage was more complex than quantitative studies have suggested. I was also convinced that to understand the significance of intermarriage today, one needed to look at how its meanings and representations evolved over an entire century during which American women's lives and the status of Jews and of Judaism were affected by two world wars and several social movements. After analyzing a wide range of sources over time, I understood that intermarriage for Jewish women was not part of a linear continuum toward absolute assimilation. Indeed, quite the opposite was true.

Change over Time

The meaning and representation of gender and intermarriage changed dramatically over the twentieth century for Jewish women in America. Prior to the First World War, when the rate of Jewish intermarriage was at its lowest, the immigrant Jewish women Mary Antin, Rose Pastor, and Anna Strunsky intermarried and moved out of the Jewish fold and into the circles of their Gentile husbands and mainstream society. Although the few immigrant Jewish women whom we know intermarried between 1900 and 1929 did not explicitly renounce their Jewish identities, each joined her husband's larger nonsectarian sphere. These women shed much of their immigrant backgrounds as they fulfilled the American dream of romantic love through marriage. Antin and Strunsky experimented with other religions, yet that none of the women completely abandoned her Jewish identity in favor of a non-Jewish affiliation shows the ability of women to intermarry and remain Jewish. Thus, although they may have largely disappeared from Jewish immigrant life, they did not disappear as Jews. Moreover, that all three marriages dissolved because of political and economic disagreements with their spouses indicates that religious differences were not the cause of their unhappiness, as contemporary commentators had forecast.

Jewish women in the 1930s, 1940s, and 1950s similarly merged into the dominant culture through intermarriage, now with the aid of diminished religiosity, assimilation, and educational and employment opportunities. For the women in this book who married Gentile men in the face of rising antisemitism leading up to World War II and during the postwar years when the ghost of prejudice lingered psychologically, intermarriage provided a social escape from their ethno-religious group. Antisemitism may have deterred Gentiles from marrying Jews, but it also motivated some Jewish women to seek refuge with "the enemy." Women who intermarried between 1930 and 1960 were mostly second- and third-generation Americans who made a wider variety of choices concerning both identity and family religious life. Some Jewish women who intermarried during these three decades avoided overtly identifying as Jewish and raised children either in the religion of their spouse or as Unitarian. Others maintained their ties to their heritage and even identified as "more Jewish," a significant change from the beginning of the century. Whichever path of self-identification the women chose, they continued to be labeled as "Jewish" by others, even when the women considered themselves something else. Clearly the women who seemed to run from their Jewish community by intermarrying could not hide: being Jewish was inescapable.

Whereas their predecessors were sometimes influenced by prejudice in deciding who to marry and how to identify, the political liberalism, ecumenism, and feminism of the 1960s and 1970s enabled an increasing number of Jewish women to intermarry and, ironically, more proactively identify as Jews. These decades marked a critical turning point during which the Civil Rights movement encouraged people to overlook differences in religion and race, leading to greater communication between Jewish and Christian denominations and contributing to a spiked increase in the rate of Jewish intermarriage. The second-wave Feminist movement, many of whose leaders were Jewish women, also redefined marriage as an institution in which women could advocate for their equality to men and therefore their right to actively shape their family life. For the first time in history, the intermarried Jewish women I interviewed were considerably more outspoken about being Jewish and about raising Jewish children. Jewish women's heightened awareness of the Holocaust also made them feel connected to, and more invested in, the future of the Jewish people.

Jewish women who intermarried between 1980 and 2000 were among an unprecedented majority of Jews who married Gentiles, and yet their minority status became threefold: intermarried, Jewish, and living in a society where the dominant identity was Christian male. Escalated national divorce rates notwithstanding, the high degree of individualism in general American society combined with ethnic revivalism enabled women of Jewish heritage to marry men without religious faith and, paradoxically, to become considerably more Jewish once married. An increasing number of Jewish women retained their own names when they wed, reflecting a change in marriage customs as well as a determination to maintain a Jewish identity apart from their Gentile husband. Having children further accentuated women's Jewish identities and, while bearing the brunt of domestic responsibilities, made them more proactive about observance, education, and communal connections. Despite the greater number of intermarried Jews by the end of the century, Jewish women remained marginalized in a predominantly Christian and male-dominated society, where intermarriage was persistently scorned by the organized Jewish communities.

The intermarried Jewish women discussed in this book illustrate the gains some American women made toward equality with men, such as greater educational and employment opportunities, but also the tenacity of gendered behaviors regarding domesticity and religion. A comment in *People* magazine, in 2004, describing Howard Dean, the presidential hopeful that year, and his wife Judy, an intermarried Jewish woman and a physician, illustrates the disproportionate responsibilities American women continued to have relative to men: "He has his political thing, Judy has

Judith Steinberg and
Howard Dean, 1981
wedding photograph.
From *People* magazine,
26 January 2004, 57.

her doctor-mother thing."[8] The intermarried Jewish women whose personal papers I scoured and who told me their stories consistently had careers *and* more responsibility for child rearing and domestic religion than did their Gentile husbands. By voluntarily doing all the necessary planning and most of the physical labor involved in religious observance and cultural participation, Jewish women assumed responsibilities that in an allegedly post-feminist society one might hope would be equally shared between both parents. They thereby reinforced the social expectation that women are the purveyors of Judaism increasingly practiced in the home in addition to or instead of the synagogue. In this sense, the actions of intermarried Jewish women were no different than other ethnic women who brought their children to church or did most of the Christmas shopping.[9]

As their personal narratives illustrate, intermarried Jewish women, beginning in the 1960s and increasingly in the following decades, also initiated what I call a Jewish-feminist modus vivendi in which they were both the gatekeepers of, and door openers to, Jewish life for their families. Increasingly intermarried Jewish women determined the religious beliefs that entered their homes and the cultural practices that were initiated, reconnecting with traditions that sometimes fell by the wayside in the homes of their parents and grandparents.[10] The intermarried Jewish women in this book combined ethnicity and domesticity with assertiveness and ingenuity to create Jewish identities that were personally meaningful.[11] Reinventing and refurbishing their religious and ethnic heritage in ways that felt authentically Jewish, intermarried Jewish women sought opportunities to identify as Jews and inspire the Jewish identities of their children. If there is a silver lining in what scholars have called "the second shift," the working mother's role as primary caregiver and domestic overseer, it is the power of intermarried Jewish women to determine the religious orientation, activities, and communal involvement of their families. As Professor Susannah Heschel wrote in *Yentl's Revenge* (2001), a book about third-wave Jewish feminists:

> The real issue is not equality, but power. Who's in charge? Who defines Judaism. . . . The point of feminism is to create institutional structures and mental frameworks in which women act as their own authority, determining for themselves the nature of Jewishness that best expresses their identity. . . . The victory of feminism is that women are the authorities—not male rabbis, male-authored halakha (laws) or male-imaged divinities.[12]

Ethno-religious domesticity, indeed, all domestic labor, was underappreciated, and yet it had intrinsic value for intermarried women who sought to identify as more Jewish, not to mention its value in perpetuating the Jewish religion, culture, and people. More broadly, as the historian Ann Braude has argued, if "women's participation is viewed as a neutral or conceivably even as a positive contribution to a religious institution, then the story of American religion might have a very different shape."[13]

Although both the representation of intermarriage and the meaning of intermarriage to Jewish women changed to a great extent, members of the organized Jewish community, at the end of the twentieth century, referred to intermarriage in the same overtly negative terms as they had at the beginning of the century. That flyers about this book were repeatedly torn down from a public bulletin board at the Jewish Community Center in Newton, Massachusetts, demonstrates the persistently heated sentiments surrounding the topic of intermarriage. Thus, despite increased approval ratings in national surveys, those who intermarried continued to be stigmatized within Jewish circles. Prior to 1930, when between 2 and 3.2 percent of Jewish men and women married non-Jews, rabbinical organizations opposed intermarriage, and the Jewish press warned girls not to follow in the steps of Antin, Pastor, or Strunsky. By 1960 the intermarriage rate had doubled, and what had earlier been considered an aberration became a perceived threat to Jewish continuity. Despite an evolving trend toward greater national tolerance of intermarriage, religious endogamy remained a cultural imperative according to Jewish parents, most of whom reactive negatively to their daughter's intermarriage. By 1975, however, strong parental disapproval had declined to a minority, the result of Jewish political liberalism. As parents became less vocal about their opposition to intermarriage, the unprecedented rate of intermarriage, that by 1972 had increased to 32 percent and then jumped to 52 percent by 1990, provoked Jewish communal activists to sound the alarm about Judaism's potential demise. "From outrage to outreach," described the attitudinal shift for some, while others advised preventing intermarriage.[14]

Outreach versus In-reach

Highlighting the significance of a historical interpretation of the meaning and representation of intermarriage was the ongoing debate between those who advocated outreach in response to intermarriage and those who favored in-reach. Although the movement to counteract the impact of intermarriage on the size and quality of the Jewish community had begun more than a decade earlier, the intellectual aftermath from the 1990 NJPS sharpened the polemical discourse. Or, as one keen observer wrote: "Organized American Jewry has been freaking out every since."[15] Those supporting outreach and those favoring in-reach have historically argued different sides of the intermarriage coin; whereas the former contend that intermarriage is inevitable in modern times, the latter believe that intermarriage can be stemmed through intervention.[16] Outreach entailed welcoming intermarried couples into the Jewish community, making Judaism accessible ideally so that the non-Jewish spouse converted to Judaism, and encouraging couples to raise Jewish children. Some scholars believed that the extent of successful outreach by the organized Jewish communities would determine whether by the year 2020 the Jewish population would be shrunken and elderly or demographically balanced and growing.[17] Promoters of in-reach, on the other hand, argued that marriages between Jews and Gentiles could be prevented in the first place through more exposure to formal and informal Jewish education, trips to Israel, increased numbers of Jewish friends, and a greater fostering of positive Jewish identity. One in-reach proponent went so far as to suggest that, without continuous resistance to Jewish-Gentile marriage, the intermarriage rate could exceed 90 percent because of the minuscule Jewish population in the larger American society.[18] Although some Jewish scholars and communal professionals aligned themselves somewhere along the spectrum, particularly on the issue of the non-Jewish spouse converting, or encouraged a mixture of the two methods, individuals and organizations usually were vociferous over one or the other.

Organized outreach efforts that began twenty-five years ago to retain those who intermarried within the Jewish fold gained significant momentum as the twentieth century ended and the new millennium dawned. In 1979, the Reform movement had created a task force to study and develop a program of outreach to the intermarried, which in 1983 became the Commission on Outreach directed by Lydia Kukoff, a Jewish communal professional, and chaired by David Belin, an attorney and philanthropist. In 1988 Belin, believing that outreach also had a secular, cultural mission, created the Jewish Outreach Institute (JOI), a think tank that agitated for the community-wide inclusion of intermarried couples in Jewish life that cut across denominational and institutional boundaries. Over the next dozen years the JOI was transformed from a part-time, university-based research organization housed at the Graduate School of the City University of New York to a multi-service agency, sponsoring conferences, conducting public opinion surveys, and publishing a newsletter titled *The Inclusive* in addition to several major publications serving as resources for outreach professionals and the intermarried themselves.[19] The outreach intent of the Task Force on Intermarriage of the Combined Jewish Philanthropies in Boston led to funding for programs for the intermarried such as "A Taste of Judaism," "Yours, Mine, and Ours," and, in 2004, "And Baby

Makes Three," sponsored by the Union for Reform Judaism, formerly the Union of American Hebrew Congregations (UAHC). Whether or not these and similar efforts directly contributed to the 2005 finding that a majority of the children of intermarriage in Boston were being raised Jewish, they certainly did not hurt.[20]

Some outreach professionals, however, advocated a course that strongly emphasized but was not limited to the rhetoric of endogamy. Rabbi Eric Yoffie, president of the UAHC in 1997 and who had refused to officiate at a Jewish-Gentile marriage and only reluctantly referred a couple to one of the more than 40 percent of Reform rabbis who did officiate interfaith marriages, believed that more money should be allocated to outreach: "We can discourage intermarriage and still welcome the intermarried."[21] The Conservative movement's outreach commission, the Joint Commission on Conversion and Outreach, disbanded in 1998 after operating for less than four years because its rabbinic members determined that resources would be better spent promoting Judaism from within the faith than on handling intermarriage.[22] Conservative efforts toward including the intermarried in Jewish life would begin anew, but not until the fall of 2001. The Conservative Federation of Jewish Men's Clubs published a seventy-page booklet titled "Building the Faith: A Book of Inclusion for Dual-Faith Families," which was blessed by the Committee on Jewish Laws and Standards. The publication called for Conservative Judaism to do everything possible to "increase the involvement of intermarried families in Jewish communal life," but it also upheld the movement's prohibitions against intermarriage, rabbis officiating at mixed-marriage ceremonies, and non-Jewish participation in many aspects of synagogue life. Although some applauded the Conservative effort for combining opposition to intermarriage with compassion to the intermarried, others criticized that the apparent negative attitude toward intermarriage would turn away interfaith couples.[23] Hence one person's idea of "outreach" was another person's idea of "in-reach."

Meanwhile, advocates on the opposite side of the policy and programming debate argued that preventing intermarriage should be at the forefront of communal efforts. In a 1991 article Steven Bayme, then the AJC's national director of Jewish communal affairs, strongly argued for a multi-track approach, encouraging in-marriage, conversion, and continued outreach to intermarrieds for whom conversion was not currently possible. His priorities were clearest in this statement: "Intermarriage prevention ought not be sacrificed for the sake of outreach."[24] Bayme's well-intentioned desire to secure Jewish continuity was evident, as was his lack of interest in devoting resources to couples in which non-Jewish spouses may never want to convert. In a 1997 interview Bayme said, "Outreach poses a danger of becoming neutral toward mixed marriage."[25] He believed that the marked decrease in conversion rates among intermarried couples over the previous ten years was the result of the increased acceptance of intermarriage. His concern, therefore, was that outreach programs sent the complacent message to their constituents, namely, that intermarriage was acceptable even when the non-Jewish spouse did not convert so long as the children were raised Jewish.

Jewish activists who advocated allocating resources for in-marriage efforts cited Jewish education as an answer, if not *the* answer, to preventing intermarriage. The National Jewish Outreach Program, an independent nonprofit organization started in 1987 by an Orthodox rabbi, Ephraim Buchwald, which still operates, sought to provide "a basic Jewish education for every Jew in America."[26] According to Buchwald: "It is immoral to expend Jewish resources trying to convince a gentile to put on a yamulke . . . We have to repair the holes in our own boat before we begin welcoming people aboard."[27] Although the Orthodox Rabbinical Council of America did not alter its position that intermarriage was strictly forbidden under Jewish law, a 1990 study of the attitudes of American Jewish leadership found "a broad consensus among *all* three movements that the Jewish community ought to engage in a concerted effort to attract intermarried couples into the Jewish fold—an effort that represents a serious departure from tradition as far as the Orthodox are concerned."[28] However, attracting the intermarried to Jewish life took a back seat to advocating for the prevention of intermarriage when a group of twenty-five Jewish intellectuals, rabbis, lay leaders, and communal affairs professionals met at the offices of the American Jewish Committee and formed a new coalition in February 2001, later named the Jewish In-Marriage Initiative. One rabbi half-jokingly referred to Jewish-Gentile marriage as "the I-word," and others emphasized the need for Jewish leadership to more forcefully articulate that Jews must marry Jews if Judaism is to continue. The group also pinpointed the objective to make conversion a positive goal.[29]

The prospect of preventing intermarriage, which the scholars in this new group took so seriously, was scoffed at by others. For example, Egon Mayer, the founding director of the Jewish Outreach Institute, opined that fighting intermarriage in an open, democratic, pluralistic society was like opposing the weather: "You can't change it." He believed that intermarriage was a fact of life in America and that the determining factor of whether intermarriage threatened Jewish survival was not the Jewish-Gentile marriage itself but the way the organized Jewish community responded to it. Rather than viewing intermarriage as something pathological to be prevented, Mayer saw intermarriage "as a pattern emerging out of the reality of our normal lives as American Jews."[30] Mayer's views angered those attempting to refute the notion that intermarriage had become normative.[31] Withstanding the controversy his views generated, Mayer discouraged Jewish organizations from blaming the intermarried and the unaffiliated for their disaffection and encouraged them instead to "listen well" to Jewish individuals about what made their lives fulfilling; only in this way would Jewish community professionals truly understand the "target populations."[32] Illustrating the powerful legacy Mayer left when he died in January 2004, the Jewish Outreach Institute organized "Toward a New Definition of 'Outreach,'" the Egon Mayer Memorial Conference and the first national gathering for Jewish professionals serving unaffiliated Jews, held on 8-10 June 2004. The Boston meeting was sponsored and produced by a large number of Jewish foundations and collaboratively produced by multiple organizations. The new definition of outreach was the following: "to take Jewish community out to where the people are, rather than waiting for them to come to us." The JOI's multi-step method sought to reach out to the unaffiliated "*where they are*, both physically and metaphysically," to guide them to greater engagement with the organized Jewish community.[33]

At the same time that the organized Jewish community mounted interest in creating programs addressing intermarriage, the subject drew scarce attention from Christian denominations. The Catholic Archdiocese in Boston, for example, sponsored no programs specifically designed for interfaith couples, which was surprising given that half of all Catholics reportedly married non-Catholics. According to Kari Colella, the coordinator of the marriage ministry in the office of family and life, although pastors are instructed on how to respond to individual couples, no programs are designed for the individuals themselves.[34] This means, effectively, that no resources are available for a Catholic who marries a non-Catholic unless the couple knows a pastor with whom they can comfortably discuss interfaith issues. One writer in the Catholic periodical *America* argued that the paucity of guidance for Catholics married to non-Catholics threatened to produce children who were Catholic in name only and that the cost of ignoring intermarriage might one day make the phrase "disappearing Catholic" entirely appropriate.[35]

In contrast to the Catholic Church, the Presbyterian Church demonstrated the most assistance to Presbyterians and their non-Protestant spouses among the Protestant denominations. In the late 1990s its department of ecumenical and interfaith relations produced a pamphlet and resource guide on interfaith marriage intended for intermarried couples and their families, and for chaplains and pastoral counselors. The fifty-three-page guide outlined the theological frameworks of different religions, discussed challenges and opportunities for couples, and used case studies to illustrate the major issues involved in Presbyterian–non-Presbyterian marriage. Another booklet, *A Theological Understanding of the Relationship between Christians and Jews,* was an additional useful reference for Presbyterians, one that repented and repudiated the "teaching of contempt" of Jews and affirmed God's promise of land to "the people of Israel."[36] These publications indicated the willingness of the Presbyterian Church to confront the reality of intermarriage rather than ignore it as apparently other Christian denominations such as the Catholic Church preferred. However, the United Methodist Church, like the Presbyterian Church, its brethren Protestant denomination, did not initiate any outreach to, or programs designed for, interfaith couples.[37] According to Jay Rock, the coordinator for interfaith relations of the Presbyterian Church U.S.A. based in Louisville, Kentucky, the priority has been to help Presbyterians who were reticent to talk with someone "different" and to enable them to interact with the increasing numbers of non-Presbyterians living in their neighborhoods.[38]

The population differences may help to explain both the Jewish alarm about intermarriage and the related efforts to either bring the intermarried into the Jewish community or prevent intermarriage altogether, and the comparatively little concern among Christian communities. The total Jewish population in the United States was estimated at 5.2 million in 2000-2001, a census that defined a Jew in numerous ways: a person whose religion is Jewish or is Jewish and something else, or who has no religion but had a Jewish upbringing or at least one Jewish parent, or who has a non-monotheistic religion and a Jewish upbringing or at least one Jewish parent.[39] The Jewish population is roughly two percentage drops in the bucket of the total U.S. population which is estimated at 281.4 million people, according to the 2000 U.S. Census.[40] An overwhelming 83 percent of Americans identified as Christian in a July 2001 ABC News poll. Fifty-three percent of Americans identified as Protestant (either unaffiliated or belonging to a particular denomination) and 22 percent as

Catholic. Jews must have been considered part of the 4 percent that were classified in the category "All Non-Christian Religions."[41] Thus, for those who believed that the loss of Jewish identification and connection to the Jewish community would inevitably result from a Jew marrying a non-Jew, intermarriage posed an ominous threat. Yet many observers of Jewish life realized that, although intermarriage may be inevitable in a pluralistic democracy, Jewish persistence depended on welcoming those individuals who had married outside the group and their families. At least one Jewish voice suggested a way to satisfy both sides of the heated outreach/in-reach debate. When asked, by the *Jewish Week*, whether the Jewish community should prioritize outreach or in-reach, Elie Wiesel, Holocaust survivor and Nobel Peace Laureate, responded: "Both. We can do both. We have enough means, enough energy, and enough people to do both."[42]

Identity Politics

There is something unique about the increasing obsession of organized Jewish communities with intermarriage over the past two decades that involves the politics of identity. I use the laden phrase "identity politics" to mean a set of unifying claims about the meaning of experience to diverse individuals and the associated suggestion that a more authentic alternative exists to that experienced by some American Jews.[43] The patrilineal descent decision by the Reform Rabbinate, discussed in chapter 4, created a schism between those who accepted that the child of a Jewish father and a Gentile woman was Jewish and the Conservative and Orthodox branches of Judaism that did not. It is no coincidence that, with few exceptions, the advocates of outreach were predominately members of the Reform movement including Alexander Schindler, the past president of the Union of American Hebrew Congregations; David Belin, the creator of the Jewish Outreach Institute; Rachel Cowan, the first female convert rabbi; and Dru Greenwood, the director of the UAHC Department of Outreach—whereas the proponents of in-reach have been Conservative and Orthodox Jews. The answer to Jewish continuity, according to Jack Wertheimer, the late Charles S. Liebman, and Steven M. Cohen, depended on the Jewish community redirecting all its funding and programming "from the periphery to the core," that is, away from the intermarried and Jews-by-choice (born or converted) and toward those "dependable" members of the Jewish tribe who already were involved. Promoters of in-reach, rather than considering Jewish identity as socially constructed and personally chosen, argued that

Jewish identity was "natural."[44] The disagreements between the two camps resemble the nature versus nurture debate between biological determinists and behavioral scientists, as well as the conflict between feminists and conservatives. The biological descent issue, more recently, has contributed to myriad intense discussions: the creation of the Web site "half-jewish. net," blog postings, and the development of the colloquial term "cashew," meaning half Catholic, half Jewish.[45]

The promoters of outreach and of in-reach are essentially engaged in a political debate over the definition of a Jew and Jewish continuity; or, as one observer noted, "who determines how high the bar is in the bar mitzvah."[46] Wertheimer and colleagues used the 1990 NJPS to devise their own categories of Jewish engagement involving certain standards for synagogue attendance, charity, periodical subscriptions, visits to Israel, and home rituals. On this basis, they determined that 44 percent of American Jews were actively or moderately engaged. They argued, too, that these Jews were the "core of the future community," whereas those outside their categories, the people for which outreach efforts were designed, comprised the "lowest common denominator."[47] This perspective suggested that, to be a Jew who was valuable for the sake of Jewish continuity, a person had to fit the activists' notions of what made someone genuinely Jewish. Illustrating the opposite end of the spectrum were outreach advocates who widened the definition of Jewish identity, affirming that "a Jew is a person of Jewish descent or any person who declared himself or herself to be a Jew who identifies with the history, ethical values, culture, civilization, community, and fate of the Jewish people."[48]

Identity politics increasingly divided the American Jewish community and challenged scholars to search for new working definitions of a "Jew," particularly after the 1990 NJPS, a task that continues today. Whereas prior to World War II most Americans judged Jews as less than white, some Conservative and Orthodox Jews who advocate in-reach now judge cultural or secular Jews as less than Jewish. As the historian Deborah Dash Moore argued, "Plural metaphors of identity politics cannot compete with the demand for a single primary identity." The alarm about intermarriage and Jewish continuity, according to the viewpoint that Judaism is assigned by God rather than elective, threatened to reallocate resources toward a more conservative approach to Jewish life and away from, in Moore's continuing words "a confident liberal agenda that claimed for Jews an equal place at the American civic table all along."[49] In "Who's a Jew in an Era of High Intermarriage?" Joel Perlmann examined how different definitions of identity influence survey outcomes and suggested that surveys use the principle of self-identification rather than identification by religion.[50]

The outreach versus in-reach debate regarding intermarriage was analogous to the debate between those who believed that the U.S. Constitution was an evolving document that could be interpreted according to modern needs and strict Constitutionalists who considered that the framers' original intent was to faithfully adhere to the Constitution as written. The Torah commands: "The stranger that lives with you shall be to. you like the native, and you shall love him [or her] as yourself; for you were strangers in the land of Egypt. I am the Lord your God" (Leviticus 19:34). Rabbi Kerry M. Olitzky, JOI's executive director, believed that the idea of welcoming and loving the stranger, included in a section of the Torah called the Holiness Code and repeated more than thirty times, "sets the standard for Jewish behavior . . . and is emphasized even more frequently than are the laws of Shabbat or the laws of *kashrut* [Jewish dietary laws]."[51] For outreach advocates, the Torah was a *Torat Hayim*, a "living document," declaring that all people should be welcome in the Jewish community. One might argue that if not for people who interpreted laws long after they were originally written, neither blacks nor women would have the right to vote and public schools would still be segregated. Conversely, if the Torah were to be reinterpreted as accepting of intermarriage and the communal gates flung wide open, one might question whether Jews would continue to exist as a people apart.

In sharp contrast, Steven Bayme, currently the AJC's director of contemporary Jewish life department and a high-profile in-reach advocate, charged that the outreach exegesis of "welcoming and loving the stranger" was "radical deconstruction" of the ancient text and compromised religious ideals. In other words, the stranger, that is, the intermarried or the Gentile, could be loved but only "to the extent that they accept the norms of the community in which they live."[52] The assertion that, in order to be included in the Jewish community, one had to follow "norms" determined by someone else—precisely who is unclear—exemplified the exclusivity of the in-reach movement. The "radical deconstruction" accusation insists that the Torah's mandates against intermarriage, "You shall not intermarry with them" (Deuteronomy 7:3) should not be reinterpreted in light of high rates of intermarriage, and that the commandment to "welcome the stranger" should not be extended to interfaith couples who do not raise Jewish children in exclusively Jewish homes (i.e., *sans* Christmas tree). Bayme's use of words such as "sin" and "crime" in relation to intermarriage connote the strict *halakhic* view of exogamy as a terrible transgression.[53]

The idea of maintaining a status quo for Jewish identity and inclusion in the Jewish community veered uncomfortably close to suggesting the existence of Jewish essentialism; arguing against intermarriage within the American liberal ethos appeared racist to some scholars.[54] Although promoting endogamy is not in itself prejudicial, suggesting that one must marry a fellow Jew (or someone who converts to Judaism) in order to *be* Jewish is exclusionary. The anti-intermarriage platform seemed to categorize Jews along an earlier tribal line, "rather than a set of ideas that intentionally transcend race." As the author Douglas Rushkoff continued, "Jewish 'fidelity' became the reason to be Jewish, instead of the evermore attractive call to make the world a better place."[55] Whereas enemies of Jews had counted them for slavery, conversion, and extermination, post-modern activists counted Jews and warned against intermarriage as the ultimate destroyer of a population in which some people, those who intermarried, had become suspiciously "unfaithful." Although the Jewish leaders who advocated in-reach, encouraged in-marriage, and lobbied against intermarriage used exclusionary rhetoric, they did so because they were observant Jews with traditional views of who was Jewish, and they defined the Jewish community with solid instead of permeable boundaries. By arguing that Jews must remain separate from non-Jews to be Jewish, in-reach proponents were also saying that in order to "count" as Jewish, one must be just like them: married to a Jew. However, to the extent that one focuses on the high rate of Jewish intermarriage and the low percentage of children of intermarriage who are raised as Jews, their concern that modern American Jews might intermarry straight out of existence is understandable.

The suggestion that to be Jewish one had to remain distinct from all others denied the possibility that someone could intermarry and remain Jewish. To the extent that activists avoided or minimized the positive aspects of intermarriage, such as accentuated Jewish identities and children who were raised Jewish by one Jewish parent and one indifferent parent, in-reach advocates communicated a desire to keep the tribe purely Jewish, a notion that ignores thousands of years of Jewish intermarriage dating back to biblical times.[56] That "Jewish peoplehood" could actually include the intermarried was incomprehensible; how could one be intermarried and at the same time remain loyal to the Jewish people? Mik Moore, the former editor of *newvoices,* compared the late-twentieth-century opposition to intermarriage with Southern whites who opposed civil rights for blacks: "If the current intermarriage debate is really about continuity, and not miscegenation, then the focus should remain on the children of intermarriage and how they are raised."[57] Responding to critics who disqualified children of intermarriage as Jews, Edgar Bronfman, president of the World Jewish Congress and chairman of the Hillel International Board of Governors, remonstrated: "the whole concept of Jewish peoplehood, and the lines being pure, begins to sound a bit like Nazism, meaning racism."[58] The challenge, therefore, is how Jewish communities should respond to intermarriage in ways that promote Jewish continuity without alienating anyone who, if drawn closer, could actually make positive contributions.

As social scientists struggled to define a Jew and policy makers debated the effectiveness of outreach and in-reach, Jewish women who intermarried illustrated the fluid nature of identity, human free will, and social ascription. The preeminent theme of this book, as the title suggests, is that Jewish women who married non-Jewish men during the twentieth century considered themselves still Jewish in three ways: by birth, by label, and, for some, by cultural and religious practices. The intermarried Jewish women in this book illustrate what the sociologist Lynn Davidman discovered about Jews and what her colleague Wendy Cadge learned about Buddhists, namely, that they experienced their Jewish sense of self as "deriving both from the ascribed religious traditions of their birth and the identities they have achieved or chosen to adopt as adults in the United States."[59] Even more important for a historical study of intermarriage is that Jewish women who came of age at different historical periods confronted different social factors that influenced the development of their Jewish identity over the course of their intermarried lives. Thus these women exemplify the "connections and journeys" model of American Jewish identity proposed by the social psychologist Bethamie Horowitz. According to this model,

> Identity formation is the result of an ongoing process, rather than an entity which is fully acquired at some point in a person's lifetime. A person's Jewish identity can be conceptualized as both the cause and the consequence of choices made at certain points through a lifetime within particular milieus.[60]

By the end of the twentieth century, moreover, American women were vastly more comfortable asserting their Jewishness as a primary component of their identity. The actress Ellen Barkin, for instance, on the eve of

Jeanne Ross-Neuwirth, Mary Antin's great-granddaughter, her mother Anne Ross, and her Jewish children Eliana and Julia. Courtesy of Jeanne Ross-Neuwirth.

the new millennium, was asked by a popular women's magazine how she was going to ring in the New Year. Her response: "What new year? I'm Jewish, it's 5760." It is hard to imagine Lauren Bacall replying similarly in the 1950s.[61]

"Demography Is Not Destiny"

Just as the history of American women disproves Freud's statement that "anatomy is destiny," intermarried Jewish women's experiences demonstrate that, in the words of the sociologist Calvin Goldscheider, "demography is not destiny."[62] Looking at intermarriage and Jewish identity from a historical perspective underscores that Jewish women who intermarried remained Jewish and that their descendants may very well turn out to be Jewish as well. Only the benefit of hindsight regarding some of the earliest known cases of immigrant Jewish women who married Gentiles during the first decade of the twentieth century can discern the long-term consequences. Mary Antin's speculative words that appear in the epigraph to the first chapter of this book now seem prophetic. "What positive affirmation of the persistence of Judaism in the blood my descendants may have to make, I may not be present to hear," Antin wrote in her autobiography.[63] Both Antin's daughter and granddaughter married non-Jews. However, Antin's great-granddaughter, Jeanne Ross, married a Jewish man, Michael Neuwirth, and is raising her children as Jews. Thus, despite three consecutive generations of intermarriage, the direct descendant of a Jewish woman who intermarried chose to marry "in" and contribute to the size of the Jewish population.[64]

The phenomenon called "return in-marriage" adds an unexpected twist to the history of intermarriage. The sociologist Bruce Phillips, in his reexamination of intermarriage trends, wrote, "Finally, we must credit the inherent attraction of Judaism itself, which, as our findings have shown, consistently draws participants in mixed marriage families back into its fold. Adult children of mixed marriage, whom many observers of the Jewish scene have written off, make up a critical proportion of recent in-marriages."[65] The family history of Samuel Stein, an Orthodox Jewish man who married an Italian Catholic woman in the late 1940s, is a striking example of return in-marriage. Stein told his wife when their first child was born that she was the mother and could raise "her children any way she wanted," which was an unusual accommodation for a man to make at that time. The Stein's three children were raised as practicing Catholics. However, after fifty-one years of marital happiness, Stein reported in 2001: "Incidentally, our three children all got married to Jewish partners and became Jews."[66] Thus no one, no matter how sophisticated the methodology or the technology, can predict with certainty the Jewish future and all its permutations. Regarding the Jewish past, one can at least draw some conclusions. To the excellent question raised by Pamela S. Nadell and Jonathan D. Sarna in their anthology *Women and American Judaism,* "Is women's history also the history of American Judaism?" I answer unequivocally, reflecting on my own examination of intermarried Jewish women, yes.[67]

Using gender as a category of analysis and with the benefit of hindsight, the gloomy forecasts about Jewish continuity may be overstated, at least regarding intermarried Jewish women. In 1997 the Harvard Law School professor Alan Dershowitz argued that if trends of intermarriage, assimilation, and fertility continued apace, "American Jewry–indeed, Diaspora Jewry–may virtually vanish by the third quarter of the twenty-first century."[68] My analysis, as a historian and not a fortune-teller, is confined to the past. But looking at the trajectory of the hundred-year history of intermarried Jewish women, it is clear that although more Jewish women have married "out" over time, they have also, contrary to all prognoses, increasingly ventured more deeply "in." Therefore, it is reasonable to speculate that Jewish women will continue to marry Gentile men and, paradoxically, to contribute to a renaissance of Jewish religious and cultural identity formation and practice from within their intermarriages.

In writing these last words in the summer of 2008, my hope is that this book will broaden the historical understanding of gender and intermarriage in the twentieth century. It has broadened mine.

Afterword

Although scholarly and personal interest in the concept and practice of intermarriage generated a substantial volume of literature, much more work needs to be done in this field. Titles referring to the "stranger" abound, including Ellen Jaffee McClain's *Embracing the Stranger* (1995), Gabrielle Glaser's *Strangers to the Tribe* (1997), and Anne C. Rose's *Beloved Strangers* (2001). Yet, very little has been written about who the stranger is, what makes a person "strange," and how that person experiences intermarriage. To truly understand Jewish-Gentile marriage, an examination of the Gentiles involved in Jewish intermarriages would seem important in order to draw a two-sided historical picture. If, in the words of the Australian poet Harold Stewart, one must embrace the stranger to find one's true self, surely scholars need to devote attention and resources to discerning the views and experiences of the "Other." One might begin by exploring the meaning of intermarriage to non-Jewish women who married Jewish men.[1] Similarly historical inquiry into the intermarriage experiences of Gentile men is needed. Jim Keen, a Christian father raising Jewish children with his Jewish wife, offers some personal insights in his book *Inside Intermarriage: A Christian Partner's Perspective on Raising a Jewish Family* (2006). Jewish foundations, of course, may not wish to spend limited funds on research about non-Jews, and the Christian denominations have thus far shown less interest in understanding Christian-Jewish intermarriage than Jewish organizations; hence the responsibility falls to independent scholars and academicians working on their own initiatives.

In addition to the need for research on the intermarriage experiences of non-Jewish women, historical analyses of Jewish men who intermarried are scarce. Though brief reference is frequently made to Hollywood moguls who married non-Jewish women, studies are needed to explore what intermarriage meant to "ordinary" Jewish men who married "out"? How did intermarriage influence their ethno-religious identities, and what roles did Jewish men play in shaping their families' spiritual lives? Whether one studies women or men, using gender as a category of analysis is critical to advancing knowledge about intermarriage in America. It is telling that the majority of households that volunteered to participate in a multiyear, longitudinal study of intermarriage conducted by researchers at the Center for Judaic Studies and Contemporary Jewish Life at the University of Connecticut were Jewish females rather than males.[2] Researchers must ask what it is about the relationship between the sexes and Jewish identity that encourages more Jewish women to participate and more men to abstain. And how does this gender imbalance influence the findings?

Finally, among other topics one might pursue is a comparative analysis of the advice literature generated over the years on the issue of intermarriage. Given the scope of this book, I call attention to only a handful of guides published earlier in the twentieth century. From the 1980s on, a plethora of new advice books appeared: *Mixed Blessings* (1987); *Happily Intermarried* (1988); *122 Clues for Jews Whose Children Intermarry* (1988); *The Intermarriage Handbook* (1988); *Celebrating Our Differences* (1994); *Mixed Matches* (1995); *Celebrating Interfaith Marriages* (1999); *Guess Who's Coming to Dinner* (2000); *What to Do When You're Dating a Jew* (2000); *The Guide to Jewish Interfaith Family Life* (2001); *The Complete Idiot's Guide to Interfaith Relationships* (2001); and *Making a Successful Jewish Interfaith Marriage* (2003). The titles alone suggest that the language of intermarriage has changed significantly and beckons interested students to dig deeper.

May all those who believe, as I do, that there is more to learn about the relationship between gender and intermarriage roll up their sleeves and get to work.

Appendix

TABLE 1
American Jewish Persons Intermarrying by Time Period[1]

1900–1920	2.0%
1921–1930	3.2%
1931–1940	3.0%
1941–1945	6.7%
1946–1950	6.7%
1951–1955	6.4%
1956–1960	5.9%
1961–1965	17.4%
1966–1972	31.7%

TABLE 2
Gentile Identity of Spouse for "Born Jews" by Year of Marriage[2]

Before 1965	9%
1965–1974	25%
1975–1984	44%
1985–1990	52%

TABLE 3
Intermarried American Jews by Year Marriage Began[3]

Before 1970	13%
1970–1979	28%
1980–1984	38%
1985–1990	43%
1991–1995	43%
1996–2001	47%

TABLE 4
Variations in Intermarriage by Age and Gender[4]

Age	Women	Men
Under 35	37%	47%
35-54	37%	37%
55+	16%	24%

TABLE 5
Third of Children of Currently Intermarried Jews Being Raised Jewish[5]

Intermarried Women	Intermarried Men
47 % of children	28 % of children

TABLE 6
Ninety Young Adult Children of the Intermarried[6]

Jewish Parent	Encouraged Children to Identify with Jewish Religion
Mother	77%
Father	45%

TABLE 7
How Forty-six Intermarried Women Raised Children Changed over a Century[7]

Year of Marriage	Total Women	Women w/Children	Children Jewish	Children Not Jewish	Children "Both"
Before 1910	3	2	0	2	0
1938–1960	14	13	5	8	0
1963–1979	14	14	10	2	2
1980–2000	15	12	12	0	0

Notes

INTRODUCTION

1. Hannah Noble, interview by author, tape recording, Brookline, Mass., 9 January 2001.

2. See Melanie Fogell, "No-Woman's Land: Jewish Women and Intermarriage" (M.S. thesis, University of Calgary, April 1997) for a contemporary, primarily descriptive discussion of the experiences of ten Canadian Jewish women who married non-Jews. The only previous scholarship by a historian focused on Jewish-Gentile intermarriage treats gender (and race) as an immutable category of analysis. See Paul Spickard, "Jewish Americans," in *Mixed Blood: Intermarriage and Ethnic Identity in Twentieth-Century America*, pt. 3 (Madison: University of Wisconsin Press, 1989), 161–231. For an earlier history, see Anne C. Rose, *Beloved Strangers: Interfaith Families in Nineteenth Century America* (Cambridge, Mass.: Harvard University Press, 2001).

3. Throughout my text, except where it appears in quotations, I capitalize the word "Gentile" to create a semiotic balance with the word "Jew," which is always capitalized.

4. For a discussion of intermarriage from the beginning of Jewish history to the nineteenth century, see Ephraim Feldman, "Intermarriage Historically Considered," *Yearbook of the Central Conference of American Rabbis* 19 (9–16 November 1909): 271–307. Lila Corwin examined some of the early sociologists and their work in "The Sociological Love Affair with Intermarriage" (paper presented at the Sixth Biennial Scholars' Conference on American Jewish History, Washington, D.C., June 6–8, 2004).

5. Julius Drachsler, *Intermarriage in New York City: A Statistical Study of the Amalgamation of European Peoples* (New York: Columbia University Press, 1921), 7. See also *Democracy and Assimilation: The Blending of Immigrant Heritages in America* (New York: Macmillan, 1920).

6. Bessie Bloom Wessel, "Comparative Rates of Intermarriage among Different Nationalities in the United States," *Eugenical News* 15 (1930): 106; Reuben B. Resnik, "Some Sociological Aspects of Intermarriage of Jew and Non-Jew," *Social Forces* (October 1933): 97; Ray Baber, "A Study of Mixed Marriages," *American Sociological Review* 2, no. 5 (October 1937): 710; James H. S. Bossard, "Nationality

and Nativity as Factors in Marriage," *American Sociological Review* 4, no. 6 (December 1939): 798; J. S Slotkin, "Jewish-Gentile Intermarriage in Chicago," *American Sociological Review* 7, no. 1 (February 1942): 35–39; Ruby Jo Reeves Kennedy, "Single or Triple Melting-Pot? Intermarriage in New Haven, 1870–1940" *American Journal of Sociology* 49, no. 4 (January 1944): 332; idem, "Single or Triple Melting-Pot? Intermarriage in New Haven, 1870–1950," *American Journal of Sociology* 58, no. 1 (July 1952): 56; Barron, "The Incidence of Jewish Intermarriage in Europe and America," 13; Milton Barron, *People Who Intermarry: Intermarriage in a New England Industrial Community* (Syracuse: Syracuse University Press, 1946), 179, 194 (Barron found only one Jewish-Gentile intermarriage in Derby, Connecticut, in 1940, involving a Jewish female, apparently an exception [163, 178]); Will Herberg, *Protestant-Catholic-Jew: An Essay in American Religious Sociology* (Garden City, N.Y.: Anchor Books, Doubleday, 1955), 37; and U.S. Bureau of the Census, "Married Couples by Religion Reported for the United States: Civilian Population, March 1957" in *Current Population Reports, Population Characteristics* series P-20, no. 79 (Washington, D.C., 2 February 1958): 8, table 6. For an international perspective for the period 1901–1929, see Uriah Zevi Engelman, "Intermarriage among Jews in Germany, USSR, and Switzerland," *Jewish Social Studies* 2, no. 2 (1940): 166, 172, 176.

7. Kennedy, "Single or Triple Melting-Pot? Intermarriage in New Haven, 1870–1940"; idem, "Single or Triple Melting-Pot? Intermarriage in New Haven, 1870–1950"; Herberg, *Protestant-Catholic-Jew.* An exception was John L. Thomas, "The Factor of Religion in the Selection of Marriage Mates," *American Sociological Review* 16, no. 4 (August 1951): 487–491. Thomas found that Roman Catholics married non-Catholics at a higher rate than suggested by Kennedy and others, and believed that the single-melting-pot hypothesis was more valid.

8. The meaning of the word "assimilationists" differs in usage by immigration historians and Judaic studies scholars. Historians studying the broad range of American history usually use the word "assimilationists" to refer to individuals who supported the idea that immigrants should "melt" into the majority culture and the majority people. Although this would create a blended people, the emphasis is on the dominant culture swallowing up the newcomers and is therefore nativist in principle. This is the conventional use of the term. Scholars focusing on American Jewish history mean something quite different by the term. According to Steven Cohen, assimilationists are those who "perceive and project large-scale erosion of Jewish life as they understand it." The more pessimistic view estimates a huge decline in the number of American Jews and the more moderate envisions a polarized Jewish population, "a culturally active and passionate minority, and a largely uninvolved and apathetic majority." See Steven Cohen, *American Assimilation or Jewish Revival?* (Bloomington and Indianapolis: Indiana University Press, 1988), 1–2.

9. Calvin Goldscheider and Alan Zuckerman, *The Transformation of the Jews* (Chicago: University of Chicago Press, 1984), 225.

10. Egon Mayer and Carl Sheingold, *Intermarriage and the Jewish Future: A National Study in Summary* (New York: American Jewish Committee, Institute of Human Relations, 1979), 33.

11. Richard D. Alba, "Jewish-Christian Marriages and Conceptions of Assimilation," paper presented at the Double or Nothing? Jewish Families and Mixed Marriage conference sponsored by the Hadassah-Brandeis Institute and the Cohen Center for Modern Jewish Studies, Waltham, Mass., 26 April 2004. I am grateful to Professor Alba for sharing his written remarks with me. See also Richard D. Alba and Victor Nee, *Remaking the American Mainstream: Assimilation and Contemporary Immigration* (Cambridge, Mass.: Harvard University Press, 2003).

12. Recent scholarship points out that a fundamental problem of what the scholar Monisha Das Gupta called the "ethnicity paradigm," how U.S. scholars have theorized ethnic identities by framing the incorporation of different groups in terms of assimilation or cultural pluralism, was "its inability to account for culture as power relations between genders" (Monisha Das Gupta, "'What Is Indian about You?': A Gendered, Transnational Approach to Ethnicity," *Gender and Society* 11, no. 5 (October 1997): 573.

13. Carl N. Degler, *At Odds: Women and the Family in America from the Revolution to the Present* (New York: Oxford University Press, 1980), 29; Joan Wallach Scott, *Gender and the Politics of History* (New York: Columbia University Press, 1988), 48.

14. Shelly Tenenbaum, "Good or Bad for the Jews? Moving Beyond the Continuity Debate," *Contemporary Jewry* 21 (2000): 91–97.

15. Julius Drachsler calculated that 1.17 percent of New York City Jews (immigrants, second- and third-generation) intermarried in the years from 1908 through 1912. See Drachsler, *Democracy and Assimilation: The Blending of Immigrant Heritages in America* (New York: Macmillan, 1920), 122, 123, 128, 130, 143, 250, and Table F; Fred Massarik et al., *National Jewish Population Study: Intermarriage, Facts for Planning* (New York: Council of Jewish Federations and Welfare Funds, 1971), 10. These figures indicate the percentages of Jewish persons who intermarried by time period. Available online from the Mandell L. Berman Institute, North American Jewish Data Bank, at http://www.jewishdatabank.org.

16. If one applies a definition of "born Jews," a category that includes non-Jews who had at least one Jewish parent and were raised in a non-Jewish religion, the intermarriage rate among those married in 1985–90 was 52 percent, 53 percent in 1991–95, and 54 percent in 1996–2000. Laurence Kotler-Berkowitz et al., *The National Jewish Population Survey 2000–01: Strength, Challenge and Diversity in the American Jewish Population* (New York: United Jewish Communities, 2003),

16–17. Available online from the Mandell L. Berman Institute, North American Jewish Data Bank, at http://www.jewishdatabank.org.

17. "Just Between Ourselves Girls," *The Hebrew Standard*, 14 April 1905 (emphasis in original).

18. Milton Gordon, *Assimilation in American Life: The Role of Race, Religion, and National Origins* (New York: Oxford University Press, 1964), 80.

19. Alan M. Dershowitz, *The Vanishing American Jew: In Search of Jewish Identity for the Next Century* (New York: Little, Brown, 1997; first Touchstone edition, 1998), 42.

20. Ruth R. Wisse, "American Jewry through the Lens of NJPS," Session at Thirty-fifth Annual Conference of the Association for Jewish Studies, 21 December 2003, Boston, Mass.

21. Steven M. Cohen and Arnold M. Eisen, *The Jew Within: Self, Family, and Community in America* (Bloomington: Indiana University Press, 2000), 184.

22. Ibid., 2–3.

23. Kotler-Berkowitz et al., *The National Jewish Population Survey, 2000–2001*, 3–4, 18.

24. Linda J. Sax, *America's Jewish Freshmen: Current Characteristics and Recent Trends among Students Entering College* (University of California, Los Angeles: Higher Education Research Institute, June 2002), 54–55.

25. Pearl Beck, *A Flame Still Burns: The Dimensions and Determinants of Jewish Identity among Young Adult Children of the Intermarried*, Jewish Outreach Institute, June 2005. Available online from the Jewish Outreach Institute, at http://joi.org/flame.

26. Sylvia Barack Fishman, *Double or Nothing: Jewish Family and Mixed Marriage* (Hanover, Mass.: Brandeis University Press, 2004), 85–87, 70. Fishman's finding is based on 254 interviews with men, women, and children (including 68 intermarried, 36 in-married, and 23 conversionary couples).

27. E-mail communication from Laurence Kotler-Berkowitz, NJPS Research Director at United Jewish Communities, via Sherry Israel, 5 January 2006. The 2000–2001 NJPS reported that 33 percent of the children in households with one non-Jewish spouse were being raised Jewish, a slight increase from 1990. The data from Kotler-Berkowitz are based on the randomly selected children of all currently intermarried Jews who are being raised as Jewish, 38 percent of children; the 33 percent in the NJPS was based on a multiple response analysis of all children in the household. See Kotler-Berkowitz et al., *The National Jewish Population Survey, 2000–2001*, 18. See also Bruce Phillips, "American Judaism in the Twenty-first Century," in *The Cambridge Companion to American Judaism*, ed. Dana Evan Kaplan (Cambridge: Cambridge University Press, 2005), 401–402, Table 5; and Leonard Saxe et al., *The Boston Community Survey: Preliminary Findings* (Waltham, Mass.: Steinhardt Social Research Institute, Brandeis University, for Combined Jewish Philanthropies of Boston, November 2006), 12. Available online

from the Mandell L. Berman Institute, National Jewish Data Bank, at http://www.jewishdatabank.org.

28. Shaye D. Cohen, *The Beginnings of Jewishness: Boundaries, Varieties, Uncertainties* (Berkeley: University of California Press, 1999), 242.

29. Jonathan D. Sarna, "Intermarriage in America: The Jewish Experience in Historical Context," paper presented at the "Double or Nothing? Jewish Families and Mixed Marriage" conference sponsored by the Hadassah-Brandeis Institute; and the Cohen Center for Modern Jewish Studies, Waltham, Mass., 26 April 2004), 1; and Cohen, *The Beginnings of Jewishness*, 266.

30. Christine Hayes, *Gentile Impurities and Jewish Identities: Intermarriage and Conversion from the Bible to the Talmud* (New York: Oxford University Press, 2002), 13.

31. Ibid., 32.

32. M. Qiddushin 3:12 and M. Yevamot 2:5; M. Yevamot 7:5 and T. Qiddushin 4:16. Cited and explicated by Cohen, *The Beginnings of Jewishness*, 273–280, 282–283.

33. Although Jubilees is certainly a lesser-known work than Genesis, penned during the Second Temple era and read today by only a few scholars, I include it to trace the origins of ancient thought regarding gender and intermarriage using the sources available to the modern scholar. See *The Book of Jubilees* 30:7–8).

34. Also unthinkable was the prospect that Dinah could generate Jewish progeny. However, according to one Torah commentary, Dinah gave birth to a daughter Asenath who married her uncle (Dinah's brother) Joseph with whom she had two children, Efraim and Menasseh; Asenath's two sons received their grandfather Jacob's blessing and tribal lands in Israel. *Pirkê De Rabbi Eliezer*, translated and annotated with an introduction and indexes by Gerald Friedlander (New York: Hermon, 1970 [1916]), 272; *Pirkê D'Rabbi Eliezer*, 38; "Biblical Personalities: Dinah," Congregation Emanu-el of the City of New York; available at http://www.emanuelnyc.org/bulletin/archive/60.html (accessed 8 July 2004). I am grateful to Marsha P. Mirkin for calling my attention to this interpretation of the Torah.

35. For scholars who refer to Dinah's experience as rape, see Marsha Mirkin, *Women Who Danced by the Sea: Finding Ourselves in the Stories of Our Biblical Foremothers* (New York: Monkfish, 2004); Cohen, *The Beginnings of Jewishness*, 123. Shechem's love is also evident in the phrase "his soul did cleave unto Dinah." Biblical references to Dinah can be found in Genesis 34:1–27. Jewish Publications Society Bible, available at http://www.sacred-texts.com/bib/jps/gen034.htm (accessed 6 July 2004). A Midrashic interpretation by Rabbi Hunia of the wording about how Dinah's brothers "took her out of Shechem's house," explained: "When a woman is intimate with an uncircumcised person, she finds it hard to tear herself away" (Genesis Rabbah 80:11). *Midrash Rabbah, Genesis*, trans. Rabbi Dr. H. Freedman, 3rd ed. (London: Soncino, 1961 [1939]), 743. Also cited in Eric Kline

Silverman, "The Cut of Wholeness: Psychoanalytic Interpretations of Biblical Circumcision," in *The Covenant of Circumcision: New Perspectives on an Ancient Jewish Rite*, ed. Elizabeth Wyner Marks (Hanover: University Press of New England, 2003), 55. For an exceptional interpretation of Dinah's intermarriage, see, too, Anita Diamant, *The Red Tent* (New York: Picador, 1997), 179–204.

36. Cohen, *The Beginnings of Jewishness*, 254.

37. Ibid., 253–255.

38. Ibid., 264. See also Ephraim Feldman, "Intermarriage Historically Considered," *Yearbook of the Central Conference of American Rabbis* 19 (9–16 November 1909): 281–282.

39. Cohen, *The Beginnings of Jewishness*, 269.

40. Ibid., 266.

41. The word "house" is used to signify both the literal home and as a metaphor for tribe or people.

42. Barron, *People Who Intermarry*, 194. Barron found only one Jewish-Gentile intermarriage in Derby, Connecticut, in 1940, that of a Jewish female and apparently an exception (163, 178). For an international perspective of the period from 1901 to 1929, see Uriah Zevi Engelman, "Intermarriage among Jews in Germany, USSR, and Switzerland," *Jewish Social Studies* 2, no. 2 (1940): 166, 172, 176.

43. Jewish men married Catholic and Protestant women nearly twice as frequently as Jewish women married Catholic and Protestant men, according to a 1937 study including 130 Jewish-Gentile marriages in New York City; see Baber, "A Study of Mixed Marriages," 710. In 40 out of 59 intermarriages in Stamford, Connecticut, as of 1938, the Jewish partners were male; see Koenig, "The Socioeconomic Structure of an American Jewish Community," in *Jews in a Gentile World*, ed. Isacque Graeber and Steuart Henderson Britt (1942), 235–237; cited in Barron, "The Incidence of Jewish Intermarriage in Europe and America," 12. In a 1949 study, the husband was the Jewish partner in twenty out of twenty-five cases; see "Faith and Mixed Marriage," *Newsweek* 33, 31 January 1949, 64. A 1956 study of the Jews of Greater Washington found that twice the number of Jewish husbands had non-Jewish wives than Jewish wives had non-Jewish husbands; see Erich Rosenthal, "Studies of Jewish Intermarriage in the United States," in *American Jewish Yearbook 1963*, vol. 64 (New York: American Jewish Committee, 1963), 17.

44. Jacob Rader Marcus Center of the American Jewish Archives, Cincinnati Campus, Hebrew Union College, Jewish Institute of Religion.

45. Julius Drachsler, *Intermarriage in New York City: A Statistical Study of the Amalgamation of European Peoples* (New York: Columbia University Press, 1921), 27. For a 1943 example of a Jewish man who changed his name to "pass" and married an unsuspecting Gentile woman, see *A Bintel Brief: Sixty Years of Letters From the Lower East Side to the Jewish Daily Forward*, compiled, edited, and with an introduction by Isaac Metzker, foreword and notes by Harry Golden (Garden City, N.Y.: Doubleday 1971), 170–172.

46. Rosenthal, "Studies of Jewish Intermarriage in the United States," 16.

47. Pastoral Psych. Seminar Poll Results by Larry Cross and Dean Olson, Abraham I. Shinedling Papers, Jacob Rader Marcus Center of the American Jewish Archives, Cincinnati Campus, Hebrew Union College, Jewish Institute of Religion, series A, correspondence, box 2, folder 2, intermarriage. The document states that results were taken from the *American Jewish Yearbook 1963*, vol. 64 (New York: American Jewish Committee, 1963), 17, 37.

48. One hypothesis was that men resisted family pressure against intermarriage because of their greater license in mate selection. Jacob Rader Marcus, "A Survey of Intermarriage in Small Mid-Western Towns," conducted by his students at Hebrew Union College, spring 1944, Jacob Rader Marcus Center of the American Jewish Archives, Cincinnati Campus, Hebrew Union College, Jewish Institute of Religion.

49. Claris Edwin Silcox and Galen M. Fisher, *Catholics, Jews, and Protestants: A Study of Relationships in the United States and Canada* (New York: Harper and Brothers, 1934; reprint, Westport, Conn.: Greenwood, 1979), 266, 270.

50. Barron, "The Incidence of Jewish Intermarriage in Europe and America," 8. Regarding sexual relations initiated by males and females' activities as more circumscribed, see also Robert K. Merton, "Intermarriage and the Social Structure: Fact and Theory," *Psychiatry: Journal of the Biology and the Pathology of Interpersonal Relations* 4, no. 3 (August 1941): 373–374.

51. For a thoughtfully written interpretation of the original text, see Pearl Elman, "Deuteronomy 21:10–14: The Beautiful Captive Woman," *Women in Judaism: A Multidisciplinary Journal* 1, no.1 (1997). Available at http://www.utoronto.ca/wjudaism/journal/vol1n1/v1n1elma.htm (accessed 5 January 2005).

52. Louis A. Berman, *Jews and Intermarriage: A Study in Personality and Culture* (New York: Thomas Yoseloff, 1968), 94.

53. Barron, "The Incidence of Jewish Intermarriage in Europe and America," 8.

54. Toby Shafter, "The Fleshpots of Maine: Portrait of a Down-East Jewish Community," *Commentary* 7, January 1949, 63.

55. Keren Hadass, *A Marriage Guide for Jewish Women: Especially Prepared for the American Jewish Woman* (New York: author, 1941).

56. Whereas only 0.1 of the 4.5 percent of intermarriages involved a Jewish woman in Providence, for example, 10 percent of women and 14 percent of men of Jewish religious origin intermarried according to the 1964 NORC data. See Arnold Schwartz, "Intermarriage in the United States," *American Jewish Year Book* 71 (1970): 110. The Providence data to which Schwartz refers is from Sidney Goldstein and Calvin Goldscheider, "Social and Demographic Aspects of Jewish Intermarriage," *Social Problems* 13, no. 4 (spring 1966): 389. According to Rabbi David Max Eichhorn, Jewish brides outnumbered Jewish grooms 52 percent to 48 percent in the 680 intermarriages he performed from January 1963 to April 1974 (*Jewish Intermarriages: Fact and Fiction* [Satellite Beach,

Fla.: Satellite Books, 1974], 64–65). See also David M. Eichhorn, "Comments on 'Who Is a Jew,'" *Reconstructionist,* 6 December 1968, 19; quoted in Arnold Schwartz, "Intermarriage in the United States," *American Jewish Year Book* 71 (1970): 109–110.

57. "Marriage Israeli Style," *Newsweek* 77, 21 June 1971, 59.

58. Rela Mintz Geffen, "Intermarriage and Conversion," *Jewish Women in America: An Historical Encyclopedia* (New York: Routledge, 1998), 669–672.

59. Fred Massarik et al., *National Jewish Population Study: Intermarriage, Facts for Planning* (New York: Council of Jewish Federations and Welfare Funds, 1971), 1.

60. I make this statement about Conservative-secular and American-Israeli intermarriage based on the experiences of Jews I know personally who are married to Jews with different educational and cultural backgrounds. Regarding distinctions among Jews and the view that a marriage between a Russian Jew and a German Jew was an intermarriage, see Edwin Friedman, "The Myth of the Shiksa," *Ethnicity and Family Therapy* (New York: Guilford, 1996), 514; cited in Mary C. Waters, *Ethnic Options: Choosing Identities in America* (Berkeley: University of California Press, 1990), 103.

61. Regarding generations as cultural constructions, see Werner Sollors, *Beyond Ethnicity: Consent and Descent in American Culture* (New York: Oxford University Press, 1986), 208–236.

62. Throughout this book, except where it appears in quotations, I spell "antisemitism" without a hyphen as a generic term for Jew-hatred, rather than "anti-Semitism," which suggests that the word "Semite" is a real or natural racial category. See "What's in a Hyphen?" by Shmuel Almog, *SICSA Report: Newsletter of the Vidal Sassoon International Center for the Study of Antisemitism* (summer 1989). Available at http://sicsa.huji.ac.il/hyphen.htm (accessed 4 January 2005).

63. Locating these interviewees was accomplished in several different ways. Advertisements were placed in publications that attracted attention from both the religiously affiliated and the unaffiliated. In lieu of some print publications whose classified rates are prohibitive, electronic bulletin boards and mailing lists were used to target more local populations, such as the regional organization of the Unitarian Universalist Association Mass Bay District. I submitted a call for participants to select synagogues and churches, the JCC in Newton, and the YWCA in Boston with the request that it be included in their newsletters and displayed on their bulletin boards. I also posted flyers in senior centers, coffeehouses, ice cream parlors, and supermarkets in order to diversify the potential respondents. And I conducted snowball sampling by asking respondents to refer me to other intermarried women they knew; if they provided several names, I contacted the individual socially located farthest away to further diversify the sample.

64. Lynn Davidman, *Motherloss* (Berkeley: University of California Press, 2000), 10.

65. Werner Sollors, ed., *The Invention of Ethnicity* (New York: Oxford University Press, 1989), xiii–xv.

66. I refer here to Richard D. Alba's useful conception of ethnic identity; see his *Ethnic Identity: The Transformation of White America* (New Haven, Conn.: Yale University Press, 1990), 25. Regarding "flux and choice in American ethnicity," see Waters, *Ethnic Options*, 16–17.

67. The intermarriage of Nina Tumarkin, professor of Russian history at Wellesley College, and Harvey Cox, an eminent Christian theologian, is a high-profile example of a Jewish woman married to a religious man. See Harvey Cox, *Common Prayers: Faith, Family, and a Christian's Journey through the Jewish Year* (Boston: Houghton Mifflin, 2001). Some evidence suggests that, in many Israeli marriages between Jewish women and Muslim men, the women converted to Islam and their children were largely raised as Muslims. However, despite their conversions and willingness to raise their children as Muslims, some women were despised by their Arab neighbors and called "Dirty Jew." "Marriage Israeli Style," *Newsweek* 77, 21 June 1971, 59; e-mail from Philip Silverman to author, 15 December 2000, "Intermarried Jewish-Arab Families Caught in Ideological Crossfire," n.d. Limore Racin's work, "Porcupine Kisses: Jewish Women in Israeli Jewish and Arab Couples," Ph.D. diss., University College London, 2006, sheds more light on these issues. For a discussion of the "tenacity of Jewishness," see Egon Mayer, *Love and Tradition: Marriage between Jews and Christians* (New York: Schocken Books, 1985), 153–176.

68. Regarding women creating meaningful identities that are authentic albeit non-halakhic, see Ellen M. Umansky, "Beyond Androcentrism: Feminist Challenges to Judaism," *Journal of Reform Judaism* 37, no. 1 (winter 1990): 30.

CHAPTER 1. IMMIGRANT JEWESSES WHO MARRIED "OUT"

1. Emma Lazarus, "The New Colossus" (1883). Available from Liberty State Park: The Statue of Liberty and Ellis Island, http://www.libertystatepark.com/emma.htm (accessed on 12 August 2004). See also "Exhibit: Woman of Valor," Jewish Women's Archive, "JWA—Emma Lazarus—Introduction," http://www.jwa.org/exhibits/wov/lazarus/el9.html (accessed 22 June 2008).

2. Julius Drachsler calculated that 1.17 percent of New York City Jews (immigrants, and second- and third-generation) intermarried in the years 1908 through 1912. Although some marriages probably went undetected because of name changes, it is likely that the number of immigrant Jewesses who intermarried prior to 1930 was still small (*Democracy and Assimilation: The Blending of Immigrant Heritages in America* [New York: Macmillan, 1920], 122, 123, 128, 130, 143, 250, and Table F; Fred Massarik et al., *National Jewish Population Study: Intermarriage, Facts for Planning* (New York: Council of Jewish Federations and Welfare Funds, 1971), 10.

3. Erich Rosenthal, "Trends of the Jewish Population in Germany, 1910–1939," *Jewish Social Studies* 6 (1944): 233–273; cited in Marion Kaplan, *Between Dignity and Despair: Jewish Life in Nazi Germany* (Oxford: Oxford University Press, 1998), 240.

4. *A Bintel Brief: Sixty Years of Letters From the Lower East Side to the Jewish Daily Forward,* Compiled, edited and with an introduction by Isaac Metzker, foreword and notes by Harry Golden (Garden City, N.Y.: Doubleday, 1971), 10, 12.

5. Celia Silbert, "Intermarriage on the East Side," *The American Jewish Chronicle* 1, no. 15 (18 August 1916): 456–457. Harvard University Microfilm Collection, Cambridge, Mass.

6. An exhaustive analysis of intermarriage as discussed in the Yiddish-language press is beyond the scope of this chapter. Such a study, however, may turn up additional evidence about the meaning of intermarriage within the immigrant community during the early twentieth century. See, for example, Letter, *Jewish Daily Forward,* 22 January 1921. Heartfelt thanks to Mae Shafter Rockland Tupa for her perceptive translation of this Yiddish letter and the response to it.

7. Hannah Stein, "Beatrice Fairfax on the East Side's Love-Lorn," *The Day,* 29 March 1925, Sunday English Section.

8. I am grateful to an anonymous reviewer for this significant point regarding gender and sexual relations. See also Joseph Kleinman, "The Problem of Choosing a Wife," *The Day,* 13 January 1924, Sunday English Section.

9. Leah Morton, pseudonymous for Elizabeth Gertrude Stern, *I Am a Woman—and a Jew* (New York: J.H. Sears, 1926). For an insightful analysis about Stern and *I Am a Woman—and a Jew,* see Aviva F. Taubenfeld, "Rough Writing: Ethnic Authorship in the Age of Theodore Roosevelt (Elizabeth Stern, Jacob Riis, Israel Zangwill, Peter Dunne, James Weldon Johnson), Ph.D. diss., Columbia University, 2003. See, too, Ellen M. Umansky, "Representations of Jewish Women in the Works and Life of Elizabeth Stern," *Modern Judaism* 13 (1993): 165–176. I am indebted to Laura Browder, whose book, *Slippery Characters: Ethnic Impersonators and American Identities* (Chapel Hill: University of North Caroline Press, 2000), brought Umansky's article to my attention.

10. "A Jewish Woman," *New York Times Book Review,* 13 March 1927, 12.

11. *The Boston Transcript,* cited in *The American Hebrew,* 3 December 1926, 209.

12. Ellen K. Rothman, *Hands and Hearts: A History of Courtship in America* (New York: Basic Books, 1984), 248.

13. Golden, *A Bintel Brief,* foreword and notes 44–45.

14. Susan Glenn, *Daughters of the Shtetl: Life and Labor in the Immigrant Generation* (Ithaca, N.Y.: Cornell University Press, 1990), 210, 238, 39.

15. Alice Kessler-Harris, *Out to Work: A History of Wage-Earning Women in the United States* (Oxford: Oxford University Press, 1982), 186; Kathryn Cullen-DuPont, *The Encyclopedia of Women's History in America* (New York: Da Capo, 1998), 171.

16. Carl Degler, *At Odds: Women and the Family in America from the Revolution to the Present* (Oxford: Oxford University Press, 1980), 28, 357–359, 471.

17. "Rates for Husbands on the Increase: Price for Desirables Now Run as High as $25,000, So the East Side Schatchens Say," *New York Times*, 16 January 1910, C10.

18. Sydney Stahl Weinberg, *The World of Our Mothers: The Lives of Jewish Immigrant Women* (Chapel Hill: University of North Carolina Press, 1988), 205.

19. Elizabeth Ewen, *Immigrant Women in the Land of Dollars: Life and Culture on the Lower East Side, 1890–1925* (New York: Monthly Review Press, 1985), 230.

20. Nancy Cott, *Public Vows: A History of Marriage and the Nation* (Cambridge, Mass.: Harvard University Press, 2000), 3.

21. L. R. McCabe, "Poor Girls Who Marry Millions," *Cosmopolitan* 41, July 1906, 250.

22. Rothman, *Hands and Hearts*, 245.

23. Riv-Ellen Prell, *Fighting to Become Americans: Jews, Gender, and the Anxiety of Assimilation* (Boston: Beacon, 1999), 71.

24. Glenn, *Daughters of the Shtetl*, 157.

25. See Weinberg, *World of Our Mothers*, 128; Glenn, *Daughters of the Shtetl*, 157; Cott, *Public Vows*, 150–151; Ewen, *Immigrant Women*, 228, 250.

26. Anzia Yezierska, "The Miracle," in *Hungry Hearts* (New York: Signet Classic, 1996 [1920]), 93.

27. Prell, *Fighting to Become Americans*, 68.

28. According to the historian Linda Gordon, the European sex theorists Havelock Ellis, Edward Carpenter, and Ellen Key influenced "a radical shift in sexual attitudes" between 1910 and the First World War that considered sexual liberation to be dependent on women's sexual liberation and their opportunities for independent, full lives. By the 1920s, the belief that sexual indulgence and birth control could be mutually inclusive, and that sexual activity and reproduction were not necessarily so, achieved mass acceptance. See Linda Gordon, *Woman's Body, Woman's Right: Birth Control in America* (New York: Penguin Books, 1974), 186–187, 190, 192.

29. Barbara Easton, "Feminism and the Contemporary Family," in *A Heritage of Her Own, ed.*, with an introduction by, Nancy F. Cott and Elizabeth H. Pleck (New York: Simon and Schuster, 1979), 561–562; Charlotte Perkins Gilman, *Women and Economics: A Study of the Economic Relation between Men and Women as a Factor in Social Evolution* (Boston: Small, Maynard, 1898).

30. Alix Shulman, *To the Barricades: The Anarchist Life of Emma Goldman* (New York: Thomas Y. Crowell, 1971), 161, 163.

31. Christine Stansell, *American Moderns: Bohemian New York and the Creation of a New Century* (New York: Henry Holt, 2000), 1–2.

32. "Inter-Marriage: A Sermon Suggested by Elias Tobenkin's 'God of Might,'" 11 April 1925, Ferdinand M. Isserman Papers, Series B. Sermons and Addresses,

Subseries 1, General, box 11, folder 3, American Jewish Archives, Cincinnati, Ohio. "Just Between Ourselves Girls," *Hebrew Standard,* 14 April 1905.

33. "Just Between Ourselves Girls," *Hebrew Standard,* 14 April 1905; "Intermarriage," *Hebrew Standard,* 21 April 1905.

34. Hal May, ed., Contemporary Authors: A Bio-Bibliographic Guide to Current Writers in Fiction, General Nonfiction, Poetry, Journalism, Drama, Motion Pictures, Television, and Other Fields (Detroit: Gale Research, 1986), 118:22. Passenger Lists of Vessels Arriving at Boston, Mass., 1891-1943 (Waltham, Mass.: National Archives) T843, microfilm roll 10, vols. 16-17, 1 January-30 June 1894.

35. City of Boston, Registry Division, Certified Copy of Record of Marriage No. 4500, Recorded 8 October 1901. Antin's marriage license lists her age as eighteen. But this, and subsequent correspondence, I believe, was probably the propagation of a lie falsifying her age by two years. My understanding is based on a detailed analysis of a passage in the original manuscript of *The Promised Land* that was excised from the published book. See Keren R. McGinity, "The Real Mary Antin: Woman on a Mission in the Promised Land," *American Jewish History* 86:3 (September 1998): 291. See also Werner Sollors, introduction to *The Promised Land* by Mary Antin (1912) (New York: Penguin Books, 1997), xxvii-xxviii. For a different interpretation that claims Antin was born in 1883 rather than 1881, see Allan Mazur, "Mary Triumphant," in *A Romance in Natural History* (Syracuse, N.Y.: Garret, 2004), 139-143. See also Mary Antin to Israel Zangwill, 16 March 1902, in *Selected Letters of Mary Antin,* ed. Evelyn Salz (Syracuse, N.Y.: Syracuse University Press, 2000), 37. Ultimately, without a copy of Antin's birth certificate, her true age eludes all researchers.

36. Allan Mazur, "Amadeus and Mary," in the pre-published manuscript for *A Romance in Natural History* (Syracuse, N.Y.: Garret, 2004), chap. 4, p. 2. I am grateful to Professor Mazur of Syracuse University for generously sharing his work with me.

37. Arthur Antin (Mary Antin's nephew) to the author, 16 April 2001.

38. ChaeRan Y. Freeze, *Jewish Marriage and Divorce in Imperial Russia* (Hanover, Mass.: Brandeis University Press, University Press of New England, 2002), 16-17.

39. Clara Antin interview by Henry Laskowsky, 1972; cited in Mazur, "Amadeus and Mary," in the pre-published manuscript for *A Romance in Natural History,* chap. 4, p. 4.

40. Mary Antin to Israel Zangwill, 8 October 1901, *Selected Letters of Mary Antin,* ed. Evelyn Salz (Syracuse: Syracuse University Press, 2000), 37.

41. Antin, *The Promised Land* (Boston and New York: Houghton Mifflin, 1912), 247.

42. Jonathan Sarna, *The Jews of Boston: Essays on the Occasion of the Centenary (1895-1995) of the Combined Jewish Philanthropies of Greater Boston,* ed. Jonathan Sarna and Ellen Smith (Boston: Combined Jewish Philanthropies of Greater Boston, 1995), 14.

43. Mary Antin, *The Promised Land,* 331.

44. Sam Bass Warner Jr., *Province of Reason* (Cambridge, Mass.: Belknap Press of Harvard University Press, 1984), 26.

45. Antin, *The Promised Land,* 330.

46. Oscar Handlin, foreword to *The Promised Land* by Mary Antin (1912) (Boston: Houghton Mifflin, 1969), x.

47. Magdalena Zaborowska contended that Antin abandoned Judaism for Quakerism. Significant new evidence, however, suggests that it was Antin's contemporary, Anna Strunsky, who joined the Quaker Society of Friends. Magdalena Zaborowska, *How We Found America: Reading Gender through East European Immigrant Narratives* (Chapel Hill: University of North Carolina Press, 1995), 54.

48. Mary Antin to John and Minnie Grabau, 23 December 1905; cited in Mazur, "Amadeus and Mary," in the pre-published manuscript for *A Romance in Natural History,* chap. 4, p. 22. According to Mazur, Antin's letters to John Grabau are in the possession of his granddaughter, Janet McKellar.

49. Jonathan D. Sarna, review of *The Family Letters of Louis D. Brandeis,* ed. Melvin I. Urofsky and David W. Levy (Norman: University of Oklahoma Press, 2002); also in *Modern Judaism* 25, no. 1 (2005): 99-101. See also Anne Roiphe, "Christmas Comes to a Jewish Home," 21 December 1978, *New York Times,* C1; and idem, *Generation without Memory: A Jewish Journey in Christian America* (New York: Linden Press/Simon and Schuster, 1981), 125-126.

50. Mary Antin, "God and His World," in *Ford Hall Folks, A Magazine of Neighborliness* 3, no. 3 (1 November 1914): 1-2; and Mary Antin Papers, American Jewish Historical Society, Waltham, Mass. (cited, hereafter, as Antin AJHS).

51. Abraham Cronbach, "Autobiography," *American Jewish Archives* 11, no. 4 (April 1959): 41.

52. Susan Koppelman, "Mary Antin," in *Dictionary of Literary Biography Yearbook: 1984* (Detroit: Gale Research, 1984), 230.

53. Arthur Antin (Mary Antin's nephew) to the author, 16 April 2001.

54. "Steps from Synagogue to Church: The Way of the Wealthy Jewish Family, Which Passes from Reform Judaism to Apostacy," *The Day,* 13 October 1923, front page.

55. Werner Sollors, "Letter from Mary Antin to Mary Austin, March 11, 1925," in *RSA Journal* 7:111.

56. Mary Antin, "House of the One Father," in *Common Ground* (spring 1941): 36.

57. Antin, "House of the One Father," 37-38.

58. Mary Antin to Louis Lipsky, December 1905, in Salz, *Selected Letters of Mary Antin,* 41.

59. Antin, "House of the One Father," 41.

60. Eric L. Goldstein, *The Price of Whiteness: Jews, Race, and American Identity* (Princeton, N.J.: Princeton University Press, 2000), 168. Goldstein points to popular literature, including *Salome of the Tenements* (1923) by Anzia Yezierska,

I Am a Woman—and a Jew (1926) by Leah Morton (Elizabeth Stern), and *The Disinherited* (1929) by Milton Waldman.

61. Matthew Frye Jacobson, *Whiteness of a Different Color: European Immigrants and the Alchemy of Race* (Cambridge, Mass.: Harvard University Press, 1998), 176-177.

62. Eric Arnesen, "Whiteness and the Historians' Imagination," *International Labor and Working-Class History* 60 (fall 2001), 5-6. Arnesen cites Jacobson, *Whiteness of a Different Color,* 1. See also Elazar Barkan, *The Retreat of Scientific Racism: Changing Concepts of Race in Britain and the United States between the World Wars* (Cambridge: Cambridge University Press, 1992); and Ian F. Haney Lopez, *White by Law: The Legal Construction of Race* (New York: New York University Press, 1996), xiii-xiv, 155.

63. Barbara J. Fields, "Whiteness, Racism, and Identity," *International Labor and Working-Class History* 60 (fall 2001): 51. Fields cites Jacobson, *Whiteness of a Different Color,* 11.

64. Goldstein, *The Price of Whiteness,* 51.

65. Julian Morgenstern, "American Judaism Faces the Future," *American Hebrew* (New York), 22 September 1922, 502. Cited in Goldstein, *The Price of Whiteness,* 174-175.

66. Goldstein, *The Price of Whiteness,* 165.

67. Antin, *The Promised Land,* 277.

68. Mary Antin, "Malinke's Atonement," in *Atlantic Monthly* 108.3 (1911): 303.

69. Ewen, *Immigrant Women,* 39.

70. Antin, *The Promised Land,* 33.

71. See, for example, Rose Cohen, *Out of the Shadow: A Russian Jewish Girlhood on the Lower East Side* (Ithaca, N.Y.: Cornell University Press, 1995 [1918]), 201.

72. Rothman, *Hands and Hearts,* 249, 287. See also Barbara Miller Solomon, *In the Company of Educated Women* (New Haven, Conn.: Yale University Press, 1985), 121.

73. Solomon, *In the Company of Educated Women,* 47, 58.

74. Kessler-Harris, *Out to Work,* 124; Glenn, *Daughters of the Shtetl,* 86-87; Antin, *The Promised Land,* 253.

75. Solomon, *In the Company of Educated Women,* 62.

76. Ibid., 76-77.

77. Pamela S. Nadell, introduction to *From Plotzk to Boston* by Mary Antin, 1899 (New York: Wiener, 1986), xiii.

78. Koppelman, "Mary Antin," 227.

79. Mazur, "Amadeus and Mary," in the pre-published manuscript of *A Romance in Natural History,* chap. 4, p. 3.

80. Mary Antin to Israel Zangwill, 16 March 1902, in Salz, *Selected Letters of Mary Antin,* 38. Mazur's book, *A Romance in Natural History,* brought Antin's self-identification as "Frau Professorin" to my attention.

81. Mary Antin to Louis Lipksy, December 1905, in Salz, *Selected Letters of Mary Antin*, 41.

82. Warner, *Province of Reason*, 29. See also Mary Antin, *They Who Knock at Our Gates: A Complete Gospel of Immigration*, with illustrations by Joseph Stella (Boston: Houghton Mifflin, 1914).

83. Mazur, "Mary Triumphant," in the pre-published manuscript for *A Romance in Natural History*, chap. 5, pp. 17-18.

84. Salz, introduction to *Selected Letters of Mary Antin*, xiii; Elizabeth Anne Ross to author, e-mail communication, 1 September 2004. According to Ms. Ross, Josephine Antin attended boarding school beginning at the age of seven, which would have been around the year 1914.

85. Elizabeth Anne Ross, telephone interview by author, 14 October 1996.

86. Mazur, "Crisis at Columbia," in the pre-published manuscript for *A Romance in Natural History*, chap. 7, p. 13.

87. Koppelman, "Mary Antin," 231.

88. Grabau's professorship was terminated in 1918. For a detailed discussion of the circumstances surrounding his career at Columbia and his dismissal, see Mazur, "Crisis at Columbia," in the pre-published manuscript for *A Romance in Natural History*, chap. 7, pp. 7-12.

89. Abraham Cronbach, "Autobiography," *American Jewish Archives* 11, no. 1 (April 1959): 40.

90. Stansell, *American Moderns*, 254.

91. Arthur Antin (Mary Antin's nephew) to author, 16 April 2001.

92. Elizabeth Anne Ross, telephone interview by author, 29 October 1996.

93. Elaine Showalter, introduction to *These Modern Women: Autobiographical Essays from the Twenties* (New York: Feminist Press, City University of New York, 1979; 1989), 13; Elaine Tyler May, *Great Expectations: Marriage and Divorce in Post-Victorian America* (Chicago: University of Chicago Press, 1980), 2.

94. Mary Antin to Rosemary Antin, 31 January 1946, Antin AJHS.

95. Allan Mazur, *A Romance in Natural History: The Lives and Works of Amadeus Grabau and Mary Antin* (2004), 212-217.

96. "Miss Mary Antin, Wrote Noted Book: Russian Jewish Immigrant Who Won Acclaim Here with Her 'Promised Land' Dies at 67," *Special to the New York Times*, 18 May 1949, 27; Elizabeth Anne Ross, telephone interview by author, 14 October 1996. Note: Antin was born in June 1881 and died the month before her 69th birthday. The age indicated in the *New York Times* reflected the misconception that she was two years younger based on an earlier falsification by her father. See Keren R. McGinity, "The Real Mary Antin: Woman on a Mission in the Promised Land," *American Jewish History* 86:3 (September 1998): 291.

97. I discuss the influence of immigrant Jewish women who intermarried on popular culture elsewhere. See Keren R. McGinity, "Forbidden Fantasy: How Popular Culture Made Interfaith Romance a 'Man's World,'" work in progress.

98. Rose Pastor Stokes Papers, Yale University, group 573, box 1, folder 5 (hereafter, RPS Yale).

99. Stansell, *American Moderns,* 34-35.

100. Arthur Zipser and Pearl Zipser, *Fire and Grace: The Life of Rose Pastor Stokes* (Athens: University of Georgia Press, 1989), 1.

101. "Just Between Ourselves, Girls," *Jewish Daily News,* English Department, 12 August 1903.

102. I am indebted to Lynn Davidman for this insight.

103. James Boylan, *Revolutionary Lives: Anna Strunsky and William English Walling* (Amherst: University of Massachusetts Press, 1998), 55.

104. Rose Harriet Pastor, "The Views of a Settlement Worker: A Talk with J. G. Phelps Stokes," *Jewish Daily News,* 19 July 1903.

105. Zipser and Zipser, *Fire and Grace,* 13.

106. Stansell, *American Moderns,* 61.

107. Deborah Hertz, *Jewish High Society in Old Regime Berlin* (New Haven, Conn.: Yale University Press, 1988; reprint, Syracuse, N.Y.: Syracuse University Press, 2005), 207-208.

108. Pastor Stokes, quoted in *I Belong to the Working Class: The Unfinished Autobiography of Rose Pastor Stokes, ed.* Herbert Shapiro and David L. Sterling (Athens: University of Georgia Press, 1992), 99-100.

109. Pastor Stokes, *I Belong to the Working Class,* 4.

110. Ibid., 96.

111. James Graham Phelps Stokes to his mother Helen Louisa and father Anson, March 1905. Cable from mother to son, Columbia University Archives, Special Collection, Butler Library; cited in Zipser and Zipser, *Fire and Grace,* 34.

112. Pastor Stokes, *I Belong to the Working Class,* 100.

113. Zipser and Zipser, *Fire and Grace,* 176, 181.

114. *Philadelphia Evening Telegram,* n.d., 1905, clipping in Box 75, Columbia University; cited in Zipser and Zipser, *Fire and Grace,* 37.

115. "J. G. Phelps Stokes to Wed Young Jewess," *New York Times,* 6 April 1905.

116. James Graham Phelps Stokes to mother, 12 April 1905; and Zipser and Zipser, *Fire and Grace,* 36, 43.

117. *New York Sun,* 7 April 1905; *Philadelphia Press,* 8 April 1905; cited in Zipser and Zipser, *Fire and Grace,* 36.

118. Helen Louisa Stokes to Anson Phelps Stokes Jr., 15 April 1905; Anson Phelps Stokes Jr. to Helen Louisa Stokes, 20 April 1905; Anson Phelps Stokes Jr. Papers, Yale; cited in Stanley Ray Tamarkin, "Rose Pastor Stokes: Portrait of a Radical Woman, 1905-1919" (Ph.D. diss., Yale University, 1983), 23, 25.

119. Rothman, *Hands and Hearts,* 275.

120. Zipser and Zipser, *Fire and Grace,* 44.

121. Pastor Stokes, *I Belong to the Working Class,* 104-105.

122. Prell, *Fighting to Become Americans,* 70; Zipser and Zipser, *Fire and Grace,* 44.

123. "East Side's Poetess Is Now Mrs. Stokes: Wedding of Miss Pastor and Rich Settlement Worker," *New York Times,* 19 July 1905, 7.

124. "Attacks the Stokeses: Jewish Paper Fears Their Influence among Jewish Children," *New York Times* 20 July 1905, front page.

125. Stansell, *American Moderns,* 63.

126. Nancy B. Sinkoff, "Education for 'Proper' Jewish Womanhood: A Case Study in Domesticity and Vocational Training, 1897-1926," *American Jewish History* 77, no.4 (June 1988): 594-595.

127. "Attacks the Stokeses: Jewish Paper Fears Their Influence among Jewish Children," *New York Times,* 20 July 1905, front page.

128. *New York Evening Telegram,* 11 April 1905; *Jewish Independent,* December 1996; cited in Zipser and Zipser, *Fire and Grace,* 40-41.

129. Michael Cook, "The Debates of the Central Conference of American Rabbis on the Problem of Mixed Marriage: 1907-1968," Term Paper, 1969, 4. American Jewish Archives, Cincinnati, Ohio.

130. Cook, "Debates of the Central Conference of American Rabbis," 5-6. Cook cites someone by the name of Rabbi Mandel Silver, but the first and last names were misspelled.

131. Cook, "Debates of the Central Conference of American Rabbis," 9-10. Also see *Year Book of the Central Conference of American Rabbis,* 19, for the convention proceedings, November 9-16, 1909.

132. Jenna Weissman Joselit, *The Wonders of America: Reinventing Jewish Culture, 1880-1950* (New York: Hill and Wang, 1994), 27-28, 32-33.

133. Rothman, *Hands and Hearts,* 288-294.

134. "Inter-Marriage: A Sermon Suggested by Elias Tobenkin's 'God of Might,'" 11 April 1925; Ferdinand M. Isserman Papers, Series B, Sermons and Addresses, Subseries 1: General, Box 11, Folder 3. American Jewish Archives, Cincinnati, Ohio.

135. James Graham Phelps Stokes to Helen Louisa Stokes, 21 April 1905, JGPS Papers, Yale University; cited in Tamarkin, "Rose Pastor Stokes," 149.

136. Zipser and Zipser, *Fire and Grace,* 41.

137. Ibid., 118.

138. Ibid., 230.

139. Alice Preston, "The Things for Girls," *Ladies' Home Journal,* March 1905, 26. Cited in Rothman, *Hands and Hearts,* 262-263.

140. Alice Kessler-Harris, *Women Have Always Worked: A Historical Overview* (Old Westbury, N,Y,: Feminist Press, 1981), 42.

141. Rothman, *Hands and Hearts,* 265.

142. Lillian Baynes Griffin, "Mrs. J. G. Phelps Stokes at Home," *Harper's Bazaar* 40, September 1906, 796-797.

143. Pastor Stokes, *I Belong to the Working Class,* 98.

144. Cott, *Public Vows,* 3

145. Weinberg, *World of Our Mothers,* 212.

146. Tamarkin, "Rose Pastor Stokes," 202.

147. Mari Jo Buhle, *Women and American Socialism, 1870-1920* (Urbana: University of Illinois Press, 1983), 191-192.

148. Pastor Stokes diary, January 9, 1913. RPS Yale, Group 573 Box 12, Folder 1.

149. Pastor Stokes, *I Belong to the Working Class*, 131-132.

150. Zipser and Zipser, *Fire and Grace*, 92; Carl N. Degler, introduction to *Women and Economics: A Study of the Economic Relation between Men and Women as a Factor in Social Evolution* by Charlotte Perkins Gilman (Boston: Small, Maynard and Company, 1898; New York: Harper Torchbook, 1966), xxix.

151. Rose Pastor Stokes to Butler Davenport, 4 September 1914. Call/accession number A/S874. Schlesinger Library, Radcliffe Institute, Harvard University.

152. Zipser and Zipser, *Fire and Grace*, 170-173.

153. Pastor Stokes, *I Belong to the Working Class*, 148.

154. Zipser and Zipser, *Fire and Grace*, 189, 197.

155. Buhle, *Women and American Socialism*, 320.

156. Mark Naison, *Communists in Harlem during the Depression* (Urbana: University of Illinois Press, 2005), 322.

157. Susan Ware, *Modern American Women: A Documentary History* (Belmont, Calif.: Wadsworth, 1989), 100.

158. Zipser and Zipser, *Fire and Grace*, 122-123; Buhle, *Women and American Socialism*, 291-292.

159. Pastor Stokes diary, 20 or 30 March 1914, RPS Yale, additions 1984, group 573, box 13, folder 1.

160. Pastor Stokes diary, 27 March 1915, RPS Yale, additions 1984, group 573, box 13, folder 1.

161. Herbert Shapiro and David L. Sterling, eds., *I Belong to the Working Class: The Unfinished Autobiography of Rose Pastor Stokes* (Athens: University of Georgia Press, 1992), ix-xvii.

162. L. R. McCabe, "Poor Girls Who Marry Millions," *Cosmopolitan* 41, July 1906, 250.

163. Pastor Stokes, *I Belong to the Working Class*, 82.

164. Ibid., 148-149.

165. Alice Kessler Harris, "Organizing the Unorganizable: Three Jewish Women and Their Union" in *Labor History* 17, no. 1 (winter 1976): 8 n. 9.

166. My idea that Pastor's marriage outside the Jewish immigrant community actually strengthened her ties to her class is an extrapolation from Linda Gordon's contention that radical women who rejected marriage, the traditional family, and propriety of dress and behavior made greater class unity possible. Gordon, *Woman's Body, Woman's Right*, 198.

167. Zipser and Zipser, *Fire and Grace*, 24.

168. Ibid., 298.

169. Ibid., 305.

170. Boylan, *Revolutionary Lives*, 6-8. Boylan's book gives the year 1877 as Anna's birth year (3, 270), but the publication information and other sources list 1879. I use 1877 to be consistent with her primary biographer.

171. Emma Goldman, *Living My Life*, Vol. 1 (New York: Knopf, 1931), chap. 18 (available at http://dwardmac.pitzer.edu/Anarchist_Archives/goldman/living/living 1_18.html [accessed 24 August 2004]); Boylan, *Revolutionary Lives*, 10.

172. Boylan, *Revolutionary Lives*, 16.

173. Ibid., 94-95.

174. Anna Strunsky to Elias Strunsky, undated fragment, box 5, Huntington Library, San Marino, California; cited in Boylan, *Revolutionary Lives*, 95.

175. Mother to Anna Strunsky, 15 February 1906, box 4, Huntington Library, San Marino, California; cited in Boylan, *Revolutionary Lives*, 103.

176. Boylan, *Revolutionary Lives*, 6.

177. Elias Strunsky to Anna Strunsky, 15 February 1906, Anna Strunsky Walling Papers, Yale University, box 11, folder 153, reel 10 (cited, hereafter, as ASW Yale).

178. 1926 Letter in Golden, *A Bintel Brief*, 147-148.

179. 1926 Letter, in ibid., 149-150.

180. I am indebted to Howard Chudacoff for this insight.

181. William English Walling to his parents, 29 January 1906; Cable from Willoughby Walling to William English Walling, 17 February 1906; William English Walling to parents, 17 February 1906; another 1906 letter, undated (ASW Yale, box 19, folder 266). English may have reduced Anna's age by two years; if indeed she was born in 1877 (and not 1879) she would have been 28 when he wrote the letter to his parents. If English's letter is to be trusted, other sources must not be.

182. John Higham, *Strangers in the Land: Patterns of American Nativism 1860-1925* (New York: Atheneum, 1965 [1955]), 73-75.

183. Anna Strunsky to Willoughby Walling, 23 March 1906, ASW Yale, box 13, folder 194, reel 13.

184. Rothman, *Hands and Hearts*, 275.

185. Anna Strunsky to Rosalind Walling, April 1906, ASW Yale, box 13, folder 194, reel 13.

186. Rosalind Walling to Anna Strunsky and William English Walling, April 1906, ASW Yale, box 13, folders 189-199, reel 13.

187. Rothman, *Hands and Hearts*, 283.

188. Stansell, *American Moderns*, 7.

189. "They Were in Love: Friend Pays Tribute to Jack London," *New York World Telegraph*, n.d. ASW Yale, box 37, folder 435.

190. Anna Strunsky Walling to her family, 1 July 1906, ASW Yale, box 11, folder 153, reel 10.

191. Untitled, undated essay signed "Anna Strunsky Walling," ASW Yale, box 34, folder 414, loose pages.

192. Emma Goldman, "Marriage and Love," cited in Blanche Wiesen Cook, "Female Support Networks and Political Activism," in *A Heritage of Her Own*, ed., and with an introduction by, Nancy F. Cott and Elizabeth H. Pleck (New York: Simon and Schuster, 1979), 432.

193. Goldman, *Living My Life*, chap. 18.

194. Anna Strunsky Walling to her family, 1 July 1906, ASW Yale, box 11, folder 153, reel 10.

195. Although Pastor's ceremony was more elaborate, she similarly disregarded its import: "I literally ran up the aisle and down again, I was told. Perhaps I did. It was something disagreeable to be gone through with, quickly" (Pastor Stokes, *I Belong to the Working Class*, 104).

196. Judge Ben B. Lindsey and Wainwright Evans, *The Companionate Marriage* (Garden City, N.Y.: Garden City Publishing, 1929 [1927]), xx-xxi.

197. Anna Strunsky Walling to her in-laws, 29 July 1906, ASW Yale, box 13, folder 194, reel 13.

198. Boylan, *Revolutionary Lives*, 225.

199. Anna Strunsky Walling to Rosalind Walling, 21 December 1918, ASW Yale, box 14, folders 200-209, reel 14.

200. Christmas (1948) and Easter (n.d.) cards from Georgia Walling to Anna Strunsky Walling, ASW Yale, box 13, folders 189-199, reel 13.

201. Boylan, *Revolutionary Lives*, 10, 33.

202. Strunsky Walling diary, 11 July 1906, ASW Yale, diary #4-1, 1906, box 23, folder 302.

203. Strunsky Walling diary, 21 October 1906, ASW Yale, diary #4-1, 1906, box 23, folder 302.

204. Strunsky Walling diary, 3 September 1906, ASW Yale, diary #4-1, 1906, box 23, folder 302.

205. May, *Great Expectations*, 137-138.

206. Boylan, *Revolutionary Lives*, 228-229, 263-264.

207. Degler, *At Odds*, 28; Nancy F. Cott, *The Bonds of Womanhood: 'Woman's Sphere' in New England* (New Haven, Conn.: Yale University Press, 1977), 200-201.

208. Strunsky Walling diary, 25 or 28 October 1906, ASW Yale, diary #4-1, 1906, box 23, folder 302.

209. Strunsky Walling diary, 12 September 1916, ASW Yale, diary #5, box 23, folder 303.

210. Untitled, undated essay signed "Anna Strunsky Walling," ASW Yale, box 34, folder 414, loose pages.

211. Lucy Stone, who married in 1855, was the first woman to retain the use of her maiden name for all purposes, not just as a stage or authorial name, to symbolize her individual accomplishments and personhood. See Louis Filler, "Lucy Stone," in *Notable American Women, 1607-1950: A Biographical Dictionary*, Vol. 3, P-Z, ed. Edward T. James et al. (Cambridge, Mass.: Belknap Press of Harvard

University Press, 1971), 387-388; Leslie Wheeler, ed., *Loving Warriors: Selected Letters of Lucy Stone and Henry B. Blackwell, 1853 to 1893* (New York: Dial, 1981), 3 (cited in Susan J. Krupper, *Surnames for Women: A Decision-Making Guide* [Jefferson, N.C.: McFarland, 1990], 11); "Lucy Stone League," Available at http://www.lucystoneleague.org (accessed 22 June 2008).

212. "Scorns the Name of Wife/Mrs. Walling Wants to Be Known as Anna Strunsky, Though Married," *Chicago Daily News*, 1 December 1906.

213. Anna Strunsky Walling to Rosalind and Willoughby Walling, 26 February 1908, ASW Yale, box 13, folder 195 (reel #13); cited in Boylan, *Revolutionary Lives*, 125.

214. Stansell, *American Moderns*, 274.

215. Anna Strunsky Walling to Rosalind Walling, 23 April 1909, ASW Yale, box 13, folder 195; cited in Boylan, *Revolutionary Lives*, 160.

216. I am borrowing here from the title of May's book, *Great Expectations: Marriage and Divorce in Post-Victorian America.*

217. Prell, *Fighting to Become Americans*, 24-25, 36, 40.

218. "Just Between Ourselves, Girls," *The Hebrew Standard*, 14 April 1905.

219. "Intermarriage," *The Hebrew Standard*, 21 April 1905.

220. Jacobson, *Whiteness of a Different Color*, 176.

221. "Judaism—Religion or Race?" *The Day*, 23 August 1924, front page.

222. Intermarriage pledge, signed 22 December 1918, by a couple married by Rabbi Leo M. Franklin, Detroit, Mich., American Jewish Archives, Cincinnati, Ohio. Other extant pledges appear to be signed by a Jewish man and a non-Jewish woman. Hence such promises were sought regardless of the gender of the Jew who intermarried.

223. Anonymous, "My Jewish Wife," in *Menorah Journal* 16, no. 5 (May 1929): 456-461.

224. Goldstein, *The Price of Whiteness*, 175-176.

225. McGinity, "Forbidden Fantasy: How Popular Culture Made Interfaith Romance a 'Man's World,'" work in progress.

226. Cott, *Public Vows*, 8, 151.

227. Showalter, *These Modern Women*, 7.

228. Weinberg, *World of Our Mothers*, 220.

229. Ewen, *Immigrant Women*, 190.

230. Showalter, *These Modern Women*, 4.

231. Emma Goldman wrote of Strunsky in her autobiography, "Anna thought that the American woman would establish her right to liberty and privacy, once she secured the vote. I did not agree with her" (*Living My Life*, chap. 18).

232. Showalter, *These Modern Women*, 10.

233. Untitled, undated essay signed "Anna Strunsky Walling," ASW Yale, box 34, folder 414, loose pages.

234. Mary Antin Grabau to Theodore Roosevelt, 2 August 1913 (Cambridge, Mass.: Harvard University Government Documents) film A88, series 1, reel 179.

Theodore Roosevelt Papers, Presidential Microfilm (Washington, D.C.: Library of Congress, 1967).

235. Mazur, "Mary Triumphant," in the pre-published manuscript for *A Romance in Natural History*, chap. 5, p. 23.

236. Buhle, *Women and American Socialism,* 320-321; June Sochen, *Herstory: A Woman's View of American History* (New York: Alfred, 1974), 295.

237. Stansell, *American Moderns,* 258-259, 262.

238. Cott, *Public Vows,* 165.

239. Higham, *Strangers in the Land,* 324.

CHAPTER 2. INTERMARRIAGE IN AN AGE OF DOMESTICITY

1. Eugen Schoenfeld, "Intermarriage and the Small Town: The Jewish Case," Journal of *Marriage and the Family* 31, no. 1 (February 1969): 61; Sidney Goldstein and Calvin Goldscheider, "Social and Demographic Aspects of Jewish Intermarriages," *Social Problems* 13, no. 4 (spring 1966): 390.

2. Ruth Milkman, *Gender at Work: The Dynamics of Job Segregation by Sex during World War II* (Urbana and Chicago: University of Illinois Press, 1987), 28, 99; Glenna Matthews, *"Just a Housewife: The Rise and Fall of Domesticity in America* (New York: Oxford University Press, 1987), 198-199.

3. Marion Kaplan, *Between Dignity and Despair: Jewish Life in Nazi Germany* (Oxford: Oxford University Press, 1998), 76.

4. Fred Massarik et al., *National Jewish Population Study: Intermarriage, Facts for Planning* (New York: Council of Jewish Federations and Welfare Funds, 1971), 10. These figures indicate the percentages of Jewish persons who intermarried by time period.

5. "Holmes Says Love Overcomes Mixed Marriage Difficulties," *New York Times,* 26 January 1931, 13.

6. Dorothy Barclay, "Mixed-Religion Marriage Called Difficult to Sustain," *New York Times,* 2 April 1957, 60.

7. Renee C. Romano, *Race Mixing: Black-White Marriage in Postwar America* (Cambridge, Mass.: Harvard University Press, 2003), 3, 123-124.

8. Susan Ware, *Modern American Women: A Documentary History* (Belmont, Calif.: Wadsworth, 1989), 239.

9. Samuel C. Heilman, *Portrait of American Jews: The Last Half of the 20th Century* (Seattle: University of Washington Press, 1995), 26-27, 44.

10. Schoenfeld, "Intermarriage and the Small Town," 62. This remained the case until the rate of intermarriage exceeded 30 percent in the late 1960s, when alienating the intermarried could create an appreciable loss to the sustenance of the Jewish community.

11. Milton Barron, *People Who Intermarry: Intermarriage in a New England Industrial Community* (Syracuse, N.Y.: Syracuse University Press, 1946), 332.

12. Barbara Adams, interview by author, tape recording, Brookline, Mass., 30 August 2001.

13. Massarik et al., *National Jewish Population Study*, 10; "Conference on Intermarriage and Jewish Life," 13 and 14 February 1960, in Werner J. Cahnman, ed., *Intermarriage and Jewish Life: A Symposium* (New York: Herzl Press and the Jewish Reconstructionist Press, 1963), 11; Thomas B. Morgan, "The Vanishing American Jew," *Look* 5, May 1964, 42-46.

14. Arthur Hertzberg, *The Jews in America: Four Centuries of an Uneasy Encounter: A History* (New York: Columbia University Press, 1997), 259.

15. Henry L. Feingold, *A Time for Searching: Entering the Mainstream, 1920-1945* (Baltimore, Md.: Johns Hopkins University Press, 1992), 90.

16. Jenna Weissman Joselit, "The Jewish Home Beautiful," in *The American Jewish Experience,* ed. Jonathan D. Sarna (New York: Holmes and Meier, 1997 [1986]), 238.

17. Harriet Mansfield, interview by author, tape recording, Littleton, Mass., 17 April 2001.

18. Jonathan Sarna, ed., *The American Jewish Experience* (New York: Holmes and Meier, 1997 [1986]) 197, 217.

19. Feingold, *A Time for Searching*, 93.

20. Ibid., 96.

21. Mavis Rue, interview by author, tape recording, Brookline, Mass., 15 February 2001.

22. Deborah Dash Moore, *At Home in America: Second Generation New York Jews* (New York: Columbia University Press, 1981), 47, 80, 110. Feingold, *A Time for Searching*, 88, 97.

23. Feingold, *A Time for Searching*, 89.

24. Claris Edwin Silcox and Galen M. Fisher, *Catholics, Jews, and Protestants: A Study of Relationships in the United States and Canada* (New York: Harper and Brothers, 1934; reprint, Westport, Conn.: Greenwood, 1979), 242.

25. Margaret Doherty, interview by author, tape recording, Winthrop, Mass., 26 September 2001.

26. Lizabeth Cohen, *Making a New Deal: Industrial Workers in Chicago, 1919-1939* (Cambridge: Cambridge University Press, 1990), 147.

27. Hetty Miller, interview by author, tape recording, Newton, Mass., 12 February 2001.

28. Hasia Diner and Beryl Lieff Benderly, *Her Works Praise Her: A History of Jewish Women in America from Colonial Times to the Present* (New York: Basic Books, 2002), 294.

29. Ibid., 296.

30. Carolyn Jasper, interview by author, tape recording, Newton, Mass., 13 March 2001.

31. Howard Chudacoff, *The Age of the Bachelor: Creating an American Subculture* (Princeton, N.J.: Princeton University Press, 1999), 70.

32. Diner and Benderly, *Her Works Praise Her*, 279.

33. Hertzberg, *The Jews in America*, 259.

34. Jacob Rader Marcus, *The American Jewish Woman, 1654-1980* (New York: Ktav, 1981), 132. The year 1937, rather than 1934, is cited by Ruth Jacknow Markowitz in *My Daughter, the Teacher: Jewish Teachers in the New York City Schools* (New Brunswick, N.J.: Rutgers University Press, 1993), 21. Markowitz contends that this figure is undoubtedly low because it failed to include private schools and evening class students.

35. Alice Lawrence, interview by author, tape recording, Belmont, Mass., 11 January 2001.

36. Helene Schwartz Kenvin, "Playing the Kosher Card: Pembroke in the late 1950s, from a Jewish woman's point of view," *Brown Alumni Magazine*, September/October 2003, 31. I am grateful to Ms. Kenvin for sharing the unedited version of her article with me.

37. Mirra Komarovsky, "Cultural Contradictions and Sex Roles," *American Journal of Sociology* 52, no. 3 (November 1946): 184-185, 188-189.

38. Ware, *Modern American Women*, 240.

39. Feingold, *A Time for Searching*, 127.

40. Ware, *Modern American Women*, 239; Beth S. Wenger, *New York Jews and the Great Depression: Uncertain Promise* (New Haven, Conn.: Yale University Press, 1996), 62. See also, Milkman, *Gender at Work*, 28.

41. Rosalind Rosenberg, *Divided Lives: American Women in the Twentieth Century* (New York: Hill and Wang, 1992), 126.

42. Ware, *Modern American Women*, 239-240. Between 1940 and 1960 the percentage of married women who worked doubled from 15 percent to 30 percent; however, most wives worked to increase the family budget, not to change "domestic power relations" (Rosenberg, *Divided Lives*, 157).

43. Milkman argues that the "boundaries between 'women's' and 'men's' work changed location, rather than being eliminated" during the wartime economic mobilization, affecting manufacturing the most but transforming the entire occupational structure. After the war, the prewar division of labor was reconstructed, eliminating the potential for "an enduring transformation in the sexual division of labor" (Milkman, *Gender at Work*, 49-50, 99-101).

44. Ibid.

45. Marilyn Rinalto, interview by author, tape recording, Quincy, Mass., 27 March 2001. According to Deborah Dash Moore, increased Jewish-Gentile contact among teachers fostered separation in the 1920s (*At Home in America*, 101). Ms. Rinalto's experience suggests that by 1957, when she intermarried, Jewish and Gentile teachers were less segregated.

46. Tamar Reynold, interview by author, tape recording, Boston, Mass., 10 February 2001.

47. Yvonne Evans, interview by author, tape recording, Lexington, Mass., 23 March 2001.

48. Georgia Summer, interview by author, tape recording, Sharon, Mass., 20 March 2001.

49. Barbara Adams, interview by author, tape recording, Brookline, Mass., 30 August 2001.

50. Ellen K. Rothman, *Hands and Hearts: A History of Courtship in America* (Cambridge, Mass.: Harvard University Press, 1987), 287; Rosenberg, *Divided Lives*, 147.

51. Harriet Mansfield, interview by author, tape recording, Littleton, Mass., 17 April 2001.

52. Hetty Miller, interview by author, tape recording, Newton, Mass., 12 February 2001.

53. Leonard Dinnerstein, *Antisemitism in America* (New York: Oxford University Press, 1994), 105, 131, 150; Rosenberg, *Divided Lives*, 131.

54. Elaine Tyler May, *Homeward Bound: American Families in the Cold War Era* (New York: Basic Books, 1999 [1988]), xviii; Rosenberg, *Divided Lives*, 147-148.

55. Gary Gerstle, *American Crucible: Race and Nation in the Twentieth Century* (Princeton, N.J.: Princeton University Press, 2001), 8, 126-127.

56. Yvonne Evans, interview by author, tape recording, Lexington, Mass., 23 March 2001.

57. Hertzberg, *The Jews in America*, 290-291.

58. Michael E. Staub, *Torn at the Roots: The Crisis of Jewish Liberalism in Postwar America* (New York: Columbia University Press, 2002), 8-9. Staub cites Edward S. Shapiro, *A Time for Healing: American Jewry since World War II* (Baltimore, Md.: Johns Hopkins University Press, 1992), 3; Peter Novick, *The Holocaust in American Life* (Boston: Houghton Mifflin, 1999) 1; and Irving Howe, *World of Our Fathers* (New York: Harcourt, Brace, Jovanovich, 1976), 627.

59. Hasia R. Diner, *The Jews of the United States, 1654-2000* (Berkeley: University of California Press, 2004), 264.

60. Shapiro, *A Time for Healing,* 125.

61. Ibid., 143.

62. Moore, *At Home in America,* 85, 254 n. 33; *The Forward,* 4 July 1926, as translated and quoted by the *Jewish Daily Bulletin,* 7 July 1926.

63. May, *Homeward Bound,* xviii.

64. James H. S. Bossard, "Residential Propinquity as a Factor in Marriage Selection," *American Journal of Sociology* 38, no. 2 (September 1932): 219-224; Ruby Jo Reeves Kennedy, "Premarital Residential Propinquity and Ethnic Endogamy," *American Journal of Sociology* 48, no. 5 (March 1943): 580-584; John L. Thomas,

"The Factor of Religion in the Selection of Marriage Mates," *American Sociological Review* 16, no. 4 (August 1951): 491.

65. Marshall Sklare, *Jewish Identity on the Suburban Frontier: A Study of Group Survival in the Open Society* (Chicago: University of Chicago Press, 1979 [1967]), 270-271. Sklare's observation is pertinent to Jewish women meeting Gentile men, although it should be noted that interfaith marriage was not predominantly the case in Lakeville.

66. Carolyn Jasper, interview by author, tape recording, Newton, Mass., 13 March 2001.

67. Rothman, *Hands and Hearts*; cited in Chudacoff, *The Age of the Bachelor*, 71.

68. Louis L. Mann, "Intermarriage: As a Practical Problem in the Ministry," *Central Conference of American Rabbis* 47 (25-30 May 1937): 315-317, 322-323.

69. Solomon B. Freehof, "Report on Mixed Marriage and Intermarriage," *Central Conference of American Rabbis* 57 (24-28 June 1947): 161, 159. Use of the term "mixed marriage" is significant because the conference differentiated between "mixed marriage," meaning a marriage between a Jew and an unconverted Gentile, and "intermarriage," referring to a marriage between a Jew and a Gentile who converted to Judaism.

70. Freehof, "Report on Mixed Marriage and Intermarriage," 178-179.

71. Scott Shpeen, "Intermarriage and the Rabbinate: A Reform and Conservative Perspective as Reflected in the *Proceedings of the Rabbinical Assembly* and the *Yearbook of the Central Conference of American Rabbis*," history paper, Jacob Rader Marcus Center of the American Jewish Archives, Cincinnati Campus, Hebrew Union College, Jewish Institute of Religion, 1982.

72. Rabbi Jan Kaufman to author, electronic mail, 19 April 2002.

73. Rabbi Steven Dworken, Executive Vice President of the Rabbinical Council of America, telephone conversation with author, 25 April 2001. Rabbi Dworken confirmed that nothing regarding intermarriage has been published by the Orthodox rabbinate. He also stated that the rabbinate's files are too disorganized for research purposes.

74. Morton Sontheimer, "Would You Approve Your Child's Marrying a Protestant? A Catholic? A Jew?" *Woman's Home Companion* 80 (March 1953).

75. "Rabbi Opposes Intermarriage," *New York Times*, 23 November 1931, 17:5.

76. Mordecai M. Kaplan, *Judaism as Civilization*, enl. ed. (New York: Thomas Yoseloff, 1957 [1934]), 418; cited in Moshe Davis, "Mixed Marriage in Western Jewry: Historical Background to the Jewish Response," *Jewish Journal of Sociology* 10, no. 2 (December 1968): 182.

77. Davis, "Mixed Marriage in Western Jewry," 181-182.

78. "Reply to Catholics on Mixed Marriage," *New York Times*, 28 March 1932, 17:1.

79. "The Perils of Mixed Marriages," *Literary Digest* 113 (23 April 1932): 20. For a discussion of both sides of the debate, see also "Mixed Marriages," *The*

Commonweal 15 (13 April 1932), 646-647; "Mixed Marriages; Reply," *The Commonweal* 16 (25 May 1932), 102.

80. Ernest Groves, "The Problem of the Mixed Marriage," *Ladies' Home Journal* 58, June 1941, 92-93.

81. "Interfaith Marriages," *Time* 53, 31 January 1949, 64.

82. "Faith and Mixed Marriage," *Newsweek* 33, 31 January 1949, 64; "Interfaith Marriages," *Time* 53, 31 January 1949, 64.

83. "Mixed-Marriage Conflicts," *Newsweek* 34, 18 July 1949, 47. See also Judson T. Landis, "Marriages of Mixed and Non-Mixed Religious Faith," *American Sociological Review* 14, no. 3 (June 1949): 401-407.

84. Bernard Bamberger, "Plain Talk About Intermarriage," *The Reconstructionist* 15, no. 16 (16 December 1949), 10.

85. "Rabbinical Unit Hits Conversion of Jews," *New York Times*, 31 January 1950, 18.

86. David Kirshenbaum, *Mixed Marriage and the Jewish Future* (New York: Bloch, 1958), vii.

87. The study also found that one out of five Lutherans married Roman Catholics and close to one-fifth married non-Church members. The percentage of Lutherans that married Jews and other non-Protestants was "very small," according to the authors. See James H.S. Bossard and Harold C. Letts, "Mixed Marriages Involving Lutherans—A Special Report," *Marriage and Family Living* 18, no. 4 (November 1956): 308; James H.S. Bossard and Eleanor Stoker Boll, *One Marriage, Two Faiths: Guidance on Interfaith Marriage* (New York: Ronald Press, 1957), 56.

88. Thomas, "The Factor of Religion in the Selection of Marriage Mates," 491.

89. "Presbyterians Get Marriage Caution," *New York Times*, 23 May 1950, 32:1.

90. "Mixed Marriage Scored," *New York Times*, 1 November 1954, 30:1.

91. "Baptists See Peril in Mixed Marriage," *New York Times*, 22 June 1951, 28:6.

92. "Cushing Decries Moral Softness," *New York Times*, 13 March 1956, 24:2. See also "More Mixed Marriages," *Time* 58, 19 November 1951, 95, regarding the study by the Jesuit sociologist Father John L. Thomas.

93. "Catholics Assail Mixed Marriages: Family Life Meeting Fears Threat to Faith and Training of Children," *New York Times*, 15 March 1956, 35:5.

94. David R. Mace, "The Truth about Mixed Marriages," *Woman's Home Companion* (July 1951), 36, 43-44. See also "Should Persons of Different Faiths Marry?" *Reader's Digest* 59 (October 1951), 31-33.

95. Shapiro, *A Time for Healing*, 159-160.

96. Edwin S. Gaustad, ed., *A Documentary History of Religion in America since 1865*, 2d ed. (Grand Rapids, Mich.: Eerdmans, 1993), 431-432.

97. Shapiro, *A Time for Healing*, 159.

98. Ibid., 162-163.

99. Jonathan D. Sarna, *American Judaism: A History* (New Haven, Conn.: Yale University Press, 2004), 323-324.

100. Will Herberg, "The 'Triple Melting Pot': The Third Generation: From Ethnic to Religious Diversity," *Commentary* 20, no. 2, August 1955, 106-108.

101. Shapiro, *A Time for Healing*, 162.

102. Eugene D. Fleming and George Walsh, "Mixed Marriages," *Cosmopolitan* (November 1956), 72-73, mentions the works of Will Herberg, Judson Landis, and James Pike; Barclay, "Mixed-Religion Called Difficult to Sustain," *New York Times*, 2 April 1957, 60; James Bossard and Eleanor Boll are cited in J. H. Pollak, "Do Interfaith Marriages Work?" *McCall's* 84 (June 1957), 37ff.

103. Judson Landis, and James Bossard and Eleanor Boll are cited in Carl Bakal, "The Risks You Take in Interfaith Marriage," *Good Housekeeping* (July 1959), 62-63, 97-98, 100 (emphasis in original).

104. For example, the 1926 film production *The Cohens and Kellys* portrays a Jewish woman marrying an Irish Catholic man. Later, Jewish Marc Dreiser marries Protestant Erica Drake in the novel *Earth and High Heaven* (1944), and in *The Young Lions* film (1958) the Jewish man wins the approval of a ninth-generation American woman. A discussion of popular culture is necessarily limited here. My gender analysis of intermarriage in popular culture across the twentieth century is a separate work (in progress).

105. Rebecca E. Mack, *You Are a Jew and a Jew You Are!* (Jersey City, N.J.: n.p., 1933). The publication date and city were gleaned from the bibliographies of other works. A search for more background about this publication was fruitless. Mack is not included in *The Jewish Woman in America: An Historical Encyclopedia*, nor is she listed in reference works about Jewish American women writers.

106. Jacob J. Weinstein, "The Jew and Mixed Marriage," *The Reconstructionist* 7, no. 10 (27 June 1941), 9. Rabbi David Kirshenbaum similarly faulted Jewish girls' material expectations for intermarriage. See also Kirshenbaum, "The Jewish Daughter and Mixed Marriages" in idem, *Mixed Marriage and the Jewish Future*, 73.

107. Riv-Ellen Prell discusses the image of Jewish wives as demanding and obsessed with the indulgent consumption associated with Americanization before World War II and 1950s suburbia in her book, *Fighting to Become Americans: Jews, Gender, and the Anxiety of Assimilation* (Boston: Beacon, 1999), 119-120, 123, 127, 173, 176.

108. Groves, "The Problem of the Mixed Marriage," 93.

109. George Lawton, "Should Those of Different Faiths Marry?" *Senior Scholastic* 42 (8 March 1943), 35.

110. Deborah Dash Moore, *GI Jews: How World War II Changed a Generation* (Cambridge, Mass.: Belknap Press of Harvard University Press, 2004), 121.

111. "Pamphlet on Mixed Marriage," *New York Times*, 16 March 1954, 24:4. Algernon D. Black, *If I Marry Outside My Religion* (New York: Public Affairs Committee, March 1954).

112. "Felix Adler," Brooklyn Society for Ethical Culture, available at http://www.bsec.org/reference/ethicalculture/history/felix.html (accessed 27 June 2008).

113. "The Ethical Culture Gift," *The Day,* 18 October 1924, front page.

114. "The Ethical Society of Boston," pamphlet (n.d.).

115. James Pike, *If You Marry Outside Your Faith: Counsel on Mixed Marriages* (New York: Harper and Brothers, 1954), 30, 102-105, 11. Thrice married, each time to women of different backgrounds, Pike was a Roman Catholic who became an agnostic before becoming a bishop in the Episcopal Church, which likely influenced his advice to select one religious affiliation. Michael Lampen, "Bishop James Pike: Visionary or Heretic?" *Grace Online: Life from a Spiritual Perspective,* available at http:///www.gracecathedral.org (accessed 27 June 2008).

116. Bossard and Boll, *One Marriage, Two Faiths,* 156-163.

117. Moore, *GI Jews,* 121-123.

118. "I Married a Jew," *Atlantic Monthly* 163, no. 1 (January 1939): 40, 43, 44, 46.

119. "I Married a Gentile," *Atlantic Monthly* 163, no. 3 (March 1939): 321, 323, 326.

120. Frances Strauss, "The Intermarriage," in "Americans: Jews and Christians," *Atlantic Monthly* 168, no. 3 (September 1941): 292.

121. Lenora Mattingly Weber, "My Mixed Marriage Was Happy," *Woman's Home Companion* 78 (August 1951): 8 and 11.

122. J.D. Smith, "Why They Marry Others and Subsequent Results," *Catholic World,* 176, October 1952, 46-50. Smith disagrees with Thomas, "The Factor of Religion in the Selection of Marriage Mates," 487-491.

123. "'Just Crazy . . . We're Happy,'" *Life* 33, 1 December 1952, 89.

124. Hugh F. O'Reilly, "Our East-West Marriage Is Working," *American Mercury* 81 (December 1955): 17-19.

125. Gerstle, *American Crucible,* 188, 195-196.

126. Cohen, *Making a New Deal,* 54.

127. Dinnerstein, *Antisemitism in America,* 105.

128. Ibid., 105, 107.

129. Ibid., 109.

130. Ibid., 117, 132.

131. Ibid., 131.

132. Gerstle, *American Crucible,* 196.

133. Dinnerstein, *Antisemitism in America,* 136.

134. Jonathan A. Sarna, "The Jews of Boston in Historical Perspective," in *The Jews of Boston: Essays on the Occasion of the Centenary (1895-1995) of the Combined Jewish Philanthropies of Greater Boston,* ed. Jonathan Sarna and Ellen Smith (Boston: Combined Jewish Philanthropies of Greater Boston, 1995), 12-13.

135. Moore, *At Home in America,* 13-14; Gerstle, *American Crucible,* 251.

136. Shapiro, *A Time for Healing,* 28-31; Gerstle, *American Crucible,* 251.

137. Shapiro, *A Time for Healing,* 33-35.

138. Hershel Shanks, "Jewish-Gentile Intermarriage: Facts and Trends," *Commentary* 16, no. 4, October 1953, 375.

139. Shapiro, *A Time for Healing*, 29.

140. Ibid., 43; Dinnerstein, *Antisemitism in America*, 241.

141. Sarah Pene, interview by author, tape recording, Winthrop, Mass., 16 January 2001.

142. Marilyn Rinalto, interview by author, tape recording, Quincy, Mass., 27 March 2001.

143. James McBride, *The Color of Water: A Black Man's Tribute to His White Mother* (New York: Riverhead Books, 1996), 80.

144. Harriet Mansfield, interview by author, tape recording, Littleton, Mass., 17 April 2001.

145. Margaret Doherty, interview by author, tape recording, Winthrop, Mass., 26 September 2001.

146. Maria H. Levinson and Daniel J. Levinson, "Jews Who Intermarry: Sociopsychological Bases of Ethnic Identity and Change," *YIVO Annual of Jewish Social Science* 12 (1958/1959): 125.

147. Aaron Hass, *In the Shadow of the Holocaust: The Second Generation* (Ithaca, N.Y.: Cornell University Press, 1990; reprint, Cambridge: Cambridge University Press, 1996), 110.

148. Sander L. Gilman, *Jewish Self-Hatred: Anti-Semitism and the Hidden Language of the Jews* (Baltimore, Md.: Johns Hopkins University Press, 1986), 286, 304, 307-308.

149. Irving Sarnoff, "Identification with the Aggressor: Some Personality Correlates of Anti-Semitism among Jews," *Journal of Personality* 20 (1951): 199-218; cited in Louis A. Berman, *Jews and Intermarriage: A Study in Personality and Culture* (New York: Thomas Yoseloff, 1968), 69.

150. Susan A. Glenn, "The Vogue of Jewish Self-Hatred in Post-World War II America," *Jewish Social Studies: History, Culture, Society* 12, no. 3 (spring/summer 2006): 95-136. I am grateful to Susan Glenn for sharing her page proofs with me.

151. Hetty Miller, interview by author, tape recording, Newton, Mass., 12 February 2001.

152. Alice Lawrence, interview by author, tape recording, Belmont, Mass., 11 January 2001.

153. James H. S. Bossard, "Nationality and Nativity as Factors in Marriage," *American Sociological Review* 4, no. 6 (December 1939): 792.

154. George Wolff, "The Social Significance of Jewish-Christian Marriage," *Scientific Monthly* 62, no. 1 (January 1946): 96-97 (emphasis in original).

155. Strauss "The Intermarriage," 290-291.

156. Mace, "The Truth about Mixed Marriages," 44.

157. Yvonne Evans, interview by author, tape recording, Lexington, Mass., 23 March 2001. See also Ferdinand M. Isserman, "Intermarriage, Assimilation–Are these cures for anti-Semitism, if not, what is?" 15 December 1933, Ferdinand M. Isserman Papers, Jacob Rader Marcus Center of the American Jewish Archives,

Cincinnati Campus, Hebrew Union College, Jewish Institute of Religion, series B, sermons and addresses; subseries 1, general, box 13, folder 6.

158. Harriet Mansfield, interview by author, tape recording, Littleton, Mass., 17 April 2001.

159. Romano, *Race Mixing*, 291.

160. John E. Mayer, "Intermarriage Patterns: A Hypothesis," *Sociology and Social Research* 45, no. 2 (January 1961): 190-191; cited in Berman, *Jews and Intermarriage*, 70.

161. Diner, *The Jews of the United States*, 223.

162. Reuben B. Resnik, "Some Sociological Aspects of Intermarriage of Jew and Non-Jew," *Social Forces* (October 1933): 99.

163. Uriah Zevi Engelman, "Intermarriage among Jews in Germany, USSR, and Switzerland," *Jewish Social Studies* 2, no. 2 (1940): 166.

164. Kaplan, *Between Dignity and Despair*, 42, 74.

165. Carolyn Jasper, interview by author, tape recording, Newton, Mass., 13 March 2001.

166. Harriet Mansfield, interview by author, tape recording, Littleton, Mass., 17 April 2001.

167. Robert K. Merton, "Intermarriage and the Social Structure: Fact and Theory," *Psychiatry: Journal of the Biology and the Pathology of Interpersonal Relations* 4, no. 3 (August 1941): 364.

168. Georgia Summer, interview by author, tape recording, Sharon, Mass., 20 March 2001.

169. Paula Avante, interview by author, tape recording, Wellesley, Mass., 11 January 2001.

170. "The Shadow of Anti-Semitism," *The American Magazine* 128 (November 1939): 29.

171. Judson T. Landis and Mary G. Landis, "Mixed Marriages," in idem, *Building a Successful Marriage* (New York: Prentice Hall, 1948), 150.

172. *A Bintel Brief: Sixty Years of Letters From the Lower East Side to the Jewish Daily Forward*, compiled, edited and with an introduction by Isaac Metzker, foreword and notes by Harry Golden (Garden City, N.Y.: Doubleday, 1971), 170-172.

173. Bakal, "The Risks You Take in Interfaith Marriage," 100.

174. Lynne Ianniello, "Life on the Fence: The Jewish Partner in a Mixed Marriage Gets a Clear—and Painful—View of Prejudice," *ADL Bulletin* 17 (September 1960): 3, 8.

175. Hettie Jones, *How I Became Hettie Jones* (New York: Grove, 1990), 34.

176. Ibid., 37.

177. Ibid., 53.

178. Ibid., 62.

179. Ibid., *175*.

180. Ibid., *155*.

181. Ibid., 218.

182. Shapiro, *A Time for Healing*, 28.

183. Ira Eisenstein, "Intermarriage," *Jewish Information* 7, no. 2 (1969): 49.

184. Ray Baber, "A Study of Mixed Marriages," *American Sociological Review* 2, no. 5 (October 1937): 712.

185. Phyllis Ehrlich, "When the Marriage Is 'Interfaith,'" *New York Times Magazine*, 24 July 1960, 52.

186. Erich Rosenthal, "Studies of Jewish Intermarriage in the United States," in *American Jewish Yearbook 1963*, vol. 64 (New York: American Jewish Committee, 1963), 53. See also Ira Eisenstein, "Intermarriage," 52.

187. Roland G. Gittelsohn, "Should We Intermarry?" in *Modern Jewish Problems* (Cincinnati: Union of American Hebrew Congregations, 1943), 89.

188. Diner, *The Jews of the United States*, 308.

189. Erich Rosenthal, "Jewish Fertility in the United States," in *American Jewish Yearbook 1961*, vol. 62 (New York: American Jewish Committee, 1961), 25.

190. Gallup Poll, 11-16 November 1951, by the Gallup Organization. I am grateful to Sarah Dutton, Deputy Director of Surveys at CBS News, for this information.

191. Kirshenbaum, *Mixed Marriage and the Jewish Future*, vii-ix.

192. Toby Shafter, "The Fleshpots of Maine: Portrait of a Down-East Jewish Community," *Commentary* 7, January 1949, 63.

193. Gittelsohn, "Should We Intermarry?" in *Modern Jewish Problems*, 85. The newspaper clipping was from "several years ago."

194. J. S. Slotkin, "Adjustment in Jewish-Gentile Intermarriages," *Social Forces* 21, no. 2 (December 1942): 227. See also Gittelsohn, "Should We Intermarry?" 87-88.

195. Sontheimer, "Would You Approve Your Child's Marrying a Protestant? A Catholic? A Jew?" 31.

196. "Catholic Poll Split on Mixed Marriages," *Special to New York Times*, 18 July 1953, 14:6.

197. "Faith, Love, and Money," *Time*, 1 July 1957, 54.

198. Margaret Doherty, interview by author, tape recording, Winthrop, Mass., 26 September 2001; Marilyn Rinalto, interview by author, tape recording, Quincy, Mass., 27 March 2001.

199. Resnik, "Some Sociological Aspects of Intermarriage of Jew and Non-Jew," 99.

200. "Court Backs Will Restricting Faith," *New York Times*, 9 May 1953, 22:3; "Court Allows Heiress to Defy Will, Wed Outside Faith, Get Legacy," *New York Times*, 17 February 1954, 1:1.

201. May, *Homeward Bound*, 22, 89.

202. Sarah Pene, interview by author, tape recording, Winthrop, Mass., 16 January 2001.

203. Carolyn Jasper, interview by author, tape recording, Newton, Mass., 13 March 2001.

204. McBride, *The Color of Water*, 2.

205. Margaret Doherty, interview by author, tape recording, Winthrop, Mass., 26 September 2001.

206. Ann Carlton, interview by author, tape recording, Littleton, Mass., 17 April 2001.

207. Alice Lawrence, interview by author, tape recording, Belmont, Mass., 11 January 2001.

208. Hetty Miller, interview by author, tape recording, Newton, Mass., 12 February 2001.

209. Jacob Kohn, "The Jewish Family and the Danger of Intermarriage," in *Modern Jewish Problems: A Study in Parental Attitudes* (New York: Women's League of the United Synagogue of America, 1932), 113-114.

210. Harriet Mansfield, interview by author, tape recording, Littleton, Mass., 17 April 2001.

211. Shanks, "Jewish-Gentile Intermarriage: Facts and Trends," 374.

212. Barron, *People Who Intermarry*, 315.

213. Yvonne Evans, interview by author, tape recording, Lexington, Mass., 23 March 2001.

214. Tamar Reynold, interview by author, tape recording, Boston, Mass., 10 February 2001; Town Clerk's Office, Brookline, Mass., certified copy of marriage record no. 220; respondent's cousin, telephone interview by author, 25 February 2001.

215. Kirshenbaum, *Mixed Marriage and the Jewish Future*, 13.

216. Ann Carlton, interview by author, tape recording, Littleton, Mass., 17 April 2001.

217. McBride, *The Color of Water*, 158.

218. Ibid., 217-218, 235.

219. Sarah Pene, interview by author, tape recording and post-interview notes, Winthrop, Mass., 16 January 2001.

220. Bernard Rosenberg and Gilbert Shapiro, "Marginality and Jewish Humor," *Midstream* 4, no. 2 (1958): 72.

221. Ibid., 73.

222. Israel Bettan, "Response: The Marriage of a Negro Boy to a Jewish Girl," *Central Conference of American Rabbis: Annual Convention* 64, no. 4 (January 1954): 38.

223. An explanatory note is necessary. Because participation in this research was on a self-selected basis, a woman who converted to Christianity may have chosen not to participate and therefore have been inadvertently excluded.

224. Rosenberg, *Divided Lives*, 151-155; May, *Homeward Bound*, 85.

225. Harriet Mansfield, interview by author, tape recording, Littleton, Mass., 17 April 2001.

226. Ann Carlton, interview by author, tape recording, Littleton, Mass., 17 April 2001.

227. Ibid.

228. Mark W. Harris, *Unitarian Universalist Origins: Our Historic Faith*; available at http://www.uua.org/info/origins.html.

229. Daniel Walker Howe, *The Unitarian Conscience: Harvard Moral Philosophy, 1805-1861* (reprint; Middleton, Conn.: Wesleyan University Press, 1988; Cambridge, Mass.: Harvard University Press, 1970), 302-304.

230. Thomas R. Goldsmith, "Affirming Interfaith Marriages," UUA Pamphlet Commission Publication, 1991.

231. Levinson and Levinson, "Jews Who Intermarry," 109.

232. Ann Carlton, interview by author, tape recording, Littleton, Mass., 17 April 2001.

233. Harriet Mansfield, interview by author, tape recording, Littleton, Mass., 17 April 2001.

234. Georgia Summer, interview by author, tape recording, Sharon, Mass., 20 March 2001.

235. Georgia Summer, interview by author, tape recording and post-interview notes, Sharon, Mass., 20 March 2001.

236. Paula Avante, interview by author, tape recording, Wellesley, Mass., 11 January 2001.

237. Carolyn Jasper, interview by author, tape recording, Newton, Mass., 13 March 2001.

238. Hetty Miller, interview by author, tape recording, Newton, Mass., 12 February 2001.

239. Harriet Mansfield, interview by author, tape recording, Littleton, Mass., 17 April 2001.

240. Sarah Pene, interview by author, tape recording, Winthrop, Mass., 16 January 2001.

241. Hila Colman, telephone interview by author, 17 October 2006. Interview by author, tape recording, West Acton, Mass., 11 November 2006.

242. Barron, *People Who Intermarry*, 305.

243. Levinson and Levinson, "Jews Who Intermarry," 121.

244. Hertzberg, *The Jews in America*, 261.

245. See "The Shadow of Anti-Semitism," in *The American Magazine* 128 (November 1939): 90. See also Weinstein, "The Jew and Mixed Marriage," 6.

246. Harriet Mansfield, interview by author, tape recording, Littleton, Mass., 17 April 2001.

247. Hetty Miller, interview by author, tape recording, Newton, Mass., 12 February 2001.

248. Sarah Pene, interview by author, tape recording, Winthrop, Mass., 16 January 2001.

249. May, *Homeward Bound*, 105.

250. Ann Carlton, interview by author, tape recording, Littleton, Mass., 17 April 2001.

251. Rosenberg, *Divided Lives*, 151-154; May, *Homeward Bound*, 85.

252. Hetty Miller, interview by author, tape recording, Newton, Mass., 12 February 2001.

253. Levinson and Levinson, "Jews Who Intermarry," 110.

254. Joseph Brandriss, "I am Jewish—My Husband is Catholic," *The Jewish Spectator* 23 (1958): 15.

255. Andrew J. Cherlin, *Marriage, Divorce, Remarriage* (Cambridge, Mass.: Harvard University Press, 1981) 25; cited in May, *Homeward Bound*, 165.

256. Margaret Doherty, interview by author, tape recording, Winthrop, Mass., 26 September 2001.

257. Paula Avante, interview by author, tape recording, Wellesley, Mass., 11 January 2001.

258. An exception was Ruth McBride, the subject of *The Color of Water*, who was born into an Orthodox family but did not maintain a Jewish identity.

259. Marilyn Rinalto, interview by author, tape recording, Quincy, Mass., 27 March 2001.

260. Harriet Mansfield, interview by author, tape recording, Littleton, Mass., 17 April 2001.

261. Kirsten Fermaglich, "'The Comfortable Concentration Camp': The Significance of Nazi Imagery in Betty Friedan's *The Feminine Mystique* (1963)," *American Jewish History* 91, no. 2 (June 2003): 207, 231.

262. Georgia Summer, interview by author, tape recording, Sharon, Mass., 20 March 2001.

263. Paula Avante, interview by author, tape recording, Wellesley, Mass., 11 January 2001.

264. Georgia Summer, interview by author, tape recording, Sharon, Mass., 20 March 2001.

265. Kirshenbaum, *Mixed Marriage and the Jewish Future*, 124.

266. The women who insisted on having a Christmas tree over their husband's objections include Barbara Adams (married 1956); Ann Carlton (married 1956); and Paula Avante (married 1959).

267. Sarah Pene, interview by author, tape recording, Winthrop, Mass., 16 January 2001.

268. Ann Carlton, interview by author, tape recording, Littleton, Mass., 17 April 2001.

269. Marilyn Rinalto, interview by author, tape recording, Quincy, Mass., 27 March 2001.

270. Paula Avante, interview by author, tape recording, Wellesley, Mass., 11 January 2001.

271. Tamar Reynold, interview by author, tape recording, Boston, Mass., 10 February 2001.

272. Mack, *You Are A Jew*, 32.

273. Patrick O'Higgins, *Madame: An Intimate Biography of Helena Rubinstein* (New York: Viking, 1971), 288.

274. "Helena Rubinstein Dies Here at 94," *New York Times*, 2 April 1965, front page.

275. Sarah Pene, interview by author, tape recording, Winthrop, Mass., 16 January 2001.

276. Werner Sollors, ed., *The Invention of Ethnicity* (New York: Oxford University Press, 1989).

277. Mary C. Waters, *Ethnic Options: Choosing Identities in America* (Berkeley: University of California Press, 1990), 130.

CHAPTER 3. INTERMARRIAGE WAS A-CHANGIN'

1. Marshall Sklare, "Intermarriage and Jewish Survival," *Commentary* 49, no. 3, March 1970, 52.

2. Fred Massarik et al., *National Jewish Population Study: Intermarriage, Facts for Planning* (New York: Council of Jewish Federations and Welfare Funds, 1971), 1; Rela Geffen Monson, "The Case of the Reluctant Exogamists: Jewish Women and Intermarriage," *Gratz College Annual of Jewish Studies* 5 (1976): 125; David Max Eichhorn, *Jewish Intermarriages: Fact and Fiction* (Satellite Beach, Fla.: Satellite Books, 1974), 64-65; Arnold Schwartz, "Intermarriage in the United States," *American Jewish Year Book* 71 (1970): 110. The Providence data to which Schwartz refers is from Sidney Goldstein and Calvin Goldscheider, "Social and Demographic Aspects of Jewish Intermarriage," *Social Problems* 13, no. 4 (spring 1966): 389.

3. Nadine Brozan, "The Jewish Family: The Ties That Bind Are Being Loosened," *New York Times*, 9 February 1973, 40.

4. Massarik et al., *National Jewish Population Study*, 10.

5. Barry A. Kosmin et al., "Highlights of the CJF 1990 National Jewish Population Survey" (New York: Council of Jewish Federations, 1991), 14; Sidney Goldstein, "Profile of American Jewry: Insights from the 1990 National Jewish Population Survey," *American Jewish Year Book, 1992* (May 1993): 126.

6. Morris Axelrod, Floyd J. Fowler Jr., and Arnold Gurin, *A Community Survey for Long Range Planning: A Study of the Jewish Population of Greater Boston* (Boston: Combined Jewish Philanthropies, 1967), 168-169, table 15.2.

7. Floyd J. Fowler Jr., *1975 Community Survey: A Study of the Jewish Population of Greater Boston* (Boston: Combined Jewish Philanthropies, 1975), 67, table 5.16.

8. Cited in Renee C. Romano, *Race Mixing: Black-White Marriage in Postwar America* (Cambridge, Mass.: Harvard University Press, 2003), 3. Available at

http://www.census.gov/population/socdemo/race/interractab1.txt. 9. David Singer, "Living with Intermarriage," *Commentary* 68, no. 1, July 1979, 48.

10. Samuel S. Lieberman and Morton Weinfeld, "Demographic Trends and Jewish Survival," *Midstream* 24, no. 9 (November 1978): 19.

11. "Atheist's Son Marries Girl He Was Forbidden to See," *New York Times,* 22 June 1964, 53; "Prayer-Case Woman Ruled in Contempt," *New York Times,* 23 July 1964, 56.

12. Axelrod et al., *A Community Survey for Long Range Planning* (1967), 169-170, table 15.3

13. Fowler, *1975 Community Survey,* 67, table 5.17.

14. Diane Endicott, interview by author, tape recording, Cambridge, Mass., 25 January 2001.

15. Edwin S. Gaustad, ed., *A Documentary History of Religion in America since 1965,* 2nd ed. (Grand Rapids, Mich.: Eerdmans, 1993), 581; Irwin Unger and Debi Unger, eds., *The Times Were a Changin'* (New York: Three Rivers, 1998), 5.

16. Elaine Tyler May, *Homeward Bound: American Families in the Cold War Era* (New York: Basic Books, 1999 [1988]), 198; Howard Chudacoff, *The Age of the Bachelor: Creating an American Subculture* (Princeton, N.J.: Princeton University Press, 1999), 266.

17. Eugen Schoenfeld, "Intermarriage and the Small Town: The Jewish Case," *Journal of Marriage and the Family* 31, no. 1 (February 1969): 63.

18. Milton Gordon, *Assimilation in American Life: The Role of Race, Religion, and National Origins* (New York: Oxford University Press, 1964), 263.

19. *Marriage, Sex, and Family in Judaism*, ed. Michael J. Broyde (Lanham, Md.: Rowman and Littlefield, 2005), 215.

20. Arnold Schwartz, "Intermarriage in the United States," *American Jewish Year Book* 71 (1970): 117.

21. Marc Dollinger, *Quest for Inclusion: Jewish and Liberalism in Modern America* (Princeton, N.J.: Princeton University Press, 2000), 4, 220, 226.

22. Michael E. Staub, *Torn at the Roots: The Crisis of Jewish Liberalism in Post-war America* (New York: Columbia University Press, 2002), 243-244, 275-276.

23. Leonard Dinnerstein, *Antisemitism in America* (New York: Oxford University Press, 1994), 241.

24. Edward S. Shapiro, *A Time for Healing: American Jewry since World War II* (Baltimore, Md.: Johns Hopkins University Press, 1992), 43.

25. Marshall Sklare, "Intermarriage and the Jewish Future," *Commentary* 37, no. 4, April 1964, 51-52; idem, "Intermarriage and Jewish Survival," 52.

26. Gallup Polls, November 1951, June 1968, and October 1972 by the Gallup Organization. I am grateful to Sarah Dutton, Deputy Director of Surveys at CBS News, for this information.

27. Unger and Unger, *The Times Were a Changin',* 283-285.

28. Ibid., 158–159

29. Brozan, "The Jewish Family," 40.

30. Jack Wertheimer, "The Turbulent Sixties," in *The American Jewish Experience*, ed. Jonathan Sarna (New York: Holmes and Meier, 1986), 338.

31. Patricia K. Brown, "The 1980s: Decade for Ethnic Studies?" *History Teacher* 12, no. 3 (May 1979): 359-360.

32. Peggy Pascoe, "Race, Gender, and Intercultural Relations: The Case of Interracial Marriage," *Frontiers* 12, no. 1 (1991): 11.

33. "U.S. Found Most Opposed to Interracial Marriage," *New York Times,* 10 November 1968, 123.

34. Alex Bontemps, "National Poll Reveals Startling New Attitudes," *Ebony* 30, September 1975, 144.

35. Albert Gordon's study of 5,407 college students found receptivity to all forms of intermarriage, *except* interracial. See Albert I. Gordon, *Intermarriage: Interfaith, Interracial, Interethnic* (Boston: Beacon, 1964), 38.

36. Matthew Frye Jacobson, *Roots Too: White Ethnic Revival in Post-Civil Rights America* (Cambridge, Mass.: Harvard University Press, 2006), 8-9.

37. Werner Cahnman, "The Interracial Jewish Child," *Reconstructionist* 33 (1967): 7-12. Cited in Romano, *Race Mixing,* 123-124.

38. Romano, *Race Mixing,* 234-235.

39. Beth L. Bailey, *From Front Porch to Back Seat: Courtship in Twentieth-Century America* (Baltimore, Md.: Johns Hopkins University Press, 1988; paperback edition, 1989), 142; Ellen K. Rothman, *Hands and Hearts: A History of Courtship in America* (Cambridge, Mass.: Harvard University Press, 1987), 307, 310.

40. Beth Jonah, interview by author, tape recording, Brookline, Mass., 17 January 2001.

41. Alice Walker, *Meridien* (Orlando: A Harvest Book, Harcourt), 167.

42. Rothman, *Hands and Hearts,* 287; May, *Homeward Bound,* 198; Andrew J. Cherlin, *Marriage, Divorce, Remarriage,* rev. ed. (Cambridge, Mass.: Harvard University Press, 1992 [1981]), 9-10, fig. 1-1; Estimated Median Age at First Marriage by Sex: 1890 to Present, Table MS-2, U.S. Census Bureau, Internet release date: September 15, 2004. www.census.gov/population/socdemo/hh-fam/tabMS-2.pdf

43. Karen Amai, interview by author, tape recording, Cambridge, Mass., 9 February 2001.

44. Ibid.

45. Carol Ferris, interview by author, tape recording, Cambridge, Mass., 2 February 2001.

46. Fran Rakefield, interview by author, tape recording, Newton, Mass., 7 January 2001.

47. Unger and Unger, *Times Were A Changin',* 57-58.

48. Wertheimer, "The Turbulent Sixties," 337.

49. Irving Spiegel, "Rabbis Call Intermarriage a Major Campus Topic," *New York Times,* 18 December 1969, 41.

50. Monson, "The Case of the Reluctant Exogamists," 124. Cites NJPS 1971.

51. Steven M. Cohen and Arnold M. Eisen, *The Jew Within: Self, Family, and Community in America* (Bloomington: Indiana University Press, 2000), 183-184.

52. Andrew M. Greeley, "Religious Musical Chairs," *Society* 15, no. 4 (May/June 1978): 54.

53. Carol Ferris, interview by author, tape recording, Cambridge, Mass., 2 February 2001.

54. Fran Rakefield, interview by author, tape recording, Newton, Mass., 7 January 2001.

55. Diane Endicott, interview by author, tape recording, Cambridge, Mass., 25 January 2001.

56. Ellen Kolokowski, interview by author, tape recording, Cambridge, Mass., 28 December 2000.

57. Ronald Luka, *When a Christian and a Jew Marry* (New York: Missionary Society of St. Paul the Apostle, 1973).

58. Mordecai L. Brill, Marlene Halpin, and William H. Genné, *Write Your Own Wedding*, rev. ed. (Piscataway, N.J.: New Century, 1985 [1973]), 15, 17-18.

59. Robert N. Bellah et al., *Habits of the Heart: Individualism and Commitment in American Life* (New York: Harper and Row, 1985), 226.

60. Leonard Dinnerstein, *Antisemitism in America* (New York: Oxford University Press, 1994), 167.

61. "Board of Rabbis Hails Pope John: Pontiff's Emphasis on Unity of All Faiths Is Cited," *New York Times,* 9 June 1963, 71.

62. "Mixed Decision," *Newsweek* 67, 28 March 1966, 86.

63. See, for example, Elsie Gibson, "Dialogue on Marriage, *The Christian Century* 82, 10 March 1965, 297-300; Ladislas M. Örsy, "Mixed Marriages," *America* 117, 9 September 1967, 242-245; Rev. J. Robert Coleman, "Children in Mixed Marriages," letter, *America* 117, 14 October 1967, 398; Mrs. Robert P. McCabe, "How Protestants See the 'Promises,'" letter, *America* 117, 18 November 1967, 589-590; idem, "'Mixed Marriage' Retreat," letter, *America* 118, 29 June 1968, 812-813; John T. Catoir, "Promises in a Mixed Marriage," *America* 120, 12 April 1969, 446-449; Leo M. Croghan, "Marriage Law and Real Life," *America* 121, 25 October 1969, 352-355.

64. "Toward Easier Mixed Marriage," *Time* 84, 17 July 1964, 56.

65. "Boston Archdiocese Accents Positive Ecumenism in Mixed Marriages," *Christian Century* 86, 4 June 1969, 768.

66. "Behind Pope's Decree on Marriages," *U.S. News & World Report* 68, 11 May 1970, 77.

67. Ibid.; "Easier on Mixed Marriages," *Time* 95, 11 May 1970, 77; "How to Marry a Catholic," *Newsweek* 75, 11 May 1970, 79.

68. McCabe, "'Mixed Marriage' Retreat," 812.

69. Thomas P. Monahan, "Some Dimensions of Interreligious Marriages in Indiana, 1962-67," *Social Forces* 52, no. 2 (December 1973): 203.

70. Norval D. Glenn, "Interreligious Marriage in the United States: Patterns and Recent Trends," *Journal of Marriage and the Family* 44, no. 3 (August 1982): 557, 564.

71. Beth Jonah, interview by author, tape recording, Brookline, Mass., 17 January 2001.

72. Erich Rosenthal, "Studies of Jewish Intermarriage in the United States," in *American Jewish Yearbook 1963*, vol. 64 (New York: American Jewish Committee, 1963), 52-53.

73. Erich Rosenthal, "Jewish Intermarriage in Indiana," in *American Jewish Yearbook 1967*, vol. 68 (New York: American Jewish Committee, 1967), 263-264.

74. Will Herberg, *Protestant-Catholic-Jew* (Garden City, N.Y.: Anchor Books, Doubleday, 1956), 43-46; cited in Rosenthal, "Studies of Jewish Intermarriage in the United States," 53; "Mixed Marriages with Jews Rising: Rate among 3d Generation Is 12 Times That in First," *New York Times*, 13 October 1963, 78.

75. Sklare, "Intermarriage and Jewish Survival," 52.

76. Morris Axelrod, Floyd J. Fowler, and Arnold Gurin, *A Community Survey for Long-Range Planning: A Study of the Jewish Population of Greater Boston* (Boston: Combined Jewish Philanthropies, 1967); Floyd J. Fowler Jr., *1975 Community Survey: A Study of the Jewish Population of Greater Boston* (Boston: Combined Jewish Philanthropies, 1975); Sherry Israel, *Boston's Jewish Community: The 1985 Demographic Study* (Boston: Combined Jewish Philanthropies of Greater Boston, 1987); Sherry Israel, *Comprehensive Report on the 1995 Demographic Study* (Boston: Combined Jewish Philanthropies of Greater Boston, 1997).

77. Milton Himmelfarb, "The Vanishing Jews," *Commentary* 36, no. 3, September 1963, 249-250.

78. Sklare, "Intermarriage and the Jewish Future," 52.

79. Sklare, "Intermarriage and Jewish Survival," 56, 51; see also "Letters from Readers, *Commentary* 49, no. 6, June 1970, 4-14.

80. "The Assimilators," *Newsweek* 62, 7 October 1963, 97; "Judaism: A Threat to Survival," *Time* 83, 17 January 1964, 41; Thomas B. Morgan, "The Vanishing American Jew," *Look*, 5 May 1964, 45.

81. *Intermarriage and Jewish Life: A Symposium*, ed. Werner J. Cahnman (New York: Herzl Press and Jewish Reconstructionist Press, 1963), 11.

82. Julius Drachsler, *Democracy and Assimilation: The Blending of Immigrant Heritages in America* (New York: Macmillan, 1920).

83. Herbert Gezork, President, Andover Newton Theological School, "In My Opinion . . .," review of *Intermarriage: Interfaith, Interracial, Interethnic* by Albert Gordon (Boston: Beacon, 1964), back cover; David Polish, "When—and Why—People of Different Faiths Wed," review of *Jews and Intermarriage: A Study in Personality and Culture* by Louis A. Berman, *Chicago Sun Times*, n.d., Abraham Feldman Papers, series A: correspondence, subseries 1: general, box 5, folder 4,

Jacob Rader Marcus Center of the American Jewish Archives, Cincinnati Campus, Hebrew Union College, Jewish Institute of Religion.

84. Rabbi Alan Miller quoted in Morgan, "The Vanishing American Jew," 45.

85. Goldstein and Goldscheider, "Social and Demographic Aspects of Jewish Intermarriage," 398-399.

86. Staub, *Torn at the Roots,* 243.

87. Allen Maller, "Mixed or—Mitzvah Marriage," *Jewish Spectator*, March 1966, 8.

88. David Polish, "The Problem of Intermarriage—Will Moderation Help?" *Central Conference of American Rabbis* 11, no. 44 (January 1964): 36.

89. John Cogley, "Easy Conversion Scored by Rabbi: Mixed Marriage Often Is Behind Change of Faith," Orthodox Professor Says," *New York Times,* 19 July 1965, 29.

90. Abraham I. Shinedling, "On the Problem of Intermarriage," 19 April 1967, Abraham I. Shinedling Papers, Jacob Rader Marcus Center of the American Jewish Archives, Cincinnati Campus, Hebrew Union College, Jewish Institute of Religion.

91. Ibid. Shinedling believed that Judaism had more to gain by rabbis agreeing to officiate, and more to lose if they refused. His opinion reflected the view that opposing intermarriage was unrealistic and that doing so was counterproductive because it would disillusion couples about Judaism.

92. Massarik et al., *National Jewish Population Study,* 1.

93. Kalman Packouz, *How to Stop an Intermarriage: A Practical Guide for Parents* (Jerusalem: Intermarriage Crisis Conference, 1976).

94. Egon Mayer and Carl Sheingold, *Intermarriage and the Jewish Future: A National Study in Summary* (New York: American Jewish Committee, 1979), 3, 30.

95. Fred Massarik, "Rethinking the Intermarriage Crisis," *Moment*, June 1978, 29.

96. "Intermarriage Threatens American Jewish Community," *USA Today* 108, 10-11 December 1979.

97. Singer, "Living with Intermarriage," 53. For the response to Singer's article, see "Letters," *Commentary* 68, no. 6, December 1979, 6, 10, 12.

98. Samuel S. Lieberman and Morton Weinfeld, "Demographic Trends and Jewish Survival," *Midstream* 24, no. 9 (November 1978): 13.

99. Eugene Mihaly et al., "Report of the Special Committee on Mixed Marriage," Central Conference of American Rabbis (1962).

100. Albert S. Goldstein, "The Magnetic Attraction of Mixed Mating," *Central Conference of American Rabbis* 12, no. 45 (April 1964): 14. See also, for example, Charles E. Shulman, "Mixed Marriage, Conversion, and Reality," *Central Conference of American Rabbis* 11, no. 44 (January 1964): 27-32; and Jakob J. Petuchowski, "Realism about Mixed Marriages," *Central Conference of American Rabbis* 13, no. 55 (October 1966): 34-38, 41.

101. Herman E. Schaalman et al., "Mixed Marriage," *Central Conference of American Rabbis* 82 (12-15 June 1972): 66-91; Irwin H. Fishbein, "Minority Report," CCAR Report of Committee on Mixed Marriages, *Central Conference of American Rabbis* (19 June 1973): 64-67.

102. Eichhorn, *Jewish Intermarriages*, 128.

103. David Max Eichhorn to CCAR Colleagues, 1 August 1969, Jacob Rader Marcus Center of the American Jewish Archives, Cincinnati Campus, Hebrew Union College, Jewish Institute of Religion; Judy Klemesrud, "Jewish-Gentile Marriages: As Numbers Grow, So Does Debate," *New York Times*, 25 June 1973, 38.

104. David Max Eichhorn to CCAR Colleagues, 3 June 1969, Jacob Rader Marcus Center of the American Jewish Archives, Cincinnati Campus, Hebrew Union College, Jewish Institute of Religion.

105. David Max Eichhorn to CCAR Colleagues, 1 August 1969, Jacob Rader Marcus Center of the American Jewish Archives, Cincinnati Campus, Hebrew Union College, Jewish Institute of Religion.

106. Irwin Fishbein to author, electronic mail, 30 September 2001; "Home Page," Rabbinic Center for Research and Counseling, available at http://www.rcr-conline.org.

107. Albert I. Gordon, "Intermarriage," "Discussion"; Max J. Routtenberg, "The Jew Who Has Intermarried"; and Wilfred Shuchat, "The Intermarried Jew and Synagogue Membership," *Proceedings of the Rabbinical Assembly* 28, 19-23 April 1964 (New York: Rabbinical Assembly, 1964), 172, 173, 244-254.

108. Scott Shpeen, "Intermarriage and the Rabbinate: A Reform and Conservative Perspective as Reflected in the *Proceedings of the Rabbinical Assembly* and the *Yearbook of the Central Conference of American Rabbis*" (history paper, Jacob Rader Marcus Center of the American Jewish Archives, Cincinnati Campus, Hebrew Union College, Jewish Institute of Religion, 1982), 4.

109. Judah Nadich, "Mixed Marriage," *Proceedings of the Rabbinical Assembly* 40, 26-30 March 1978 (New York: Rabbinical Assembly, 1978), 94.

110. Rabbi Steven Dworken, Executive Vice President of the Rabbinical Council of America, telephone conversation with author, 25 April 2001.

111. William G. Weart, "Toynbee Predicts Gains by Judaism: Historian Assails Zionism as Akin to Anti-Semitism," *New York Times*, 7 May 1961, 37; Irving Spiegel, "Orthodox Jews Attack Toynbee: Leaders of 2 Bodies Score Stand on Intermarriage," *New York Times*, 12 May 1961, 60.

112. Irving Spiegel, "Orthodox Rabbis Warn Jews on Intermarriage: Threat to All Major Faiths Seen in Rising Trend: Practice Found Contributing to Family Breakdowns," *New York Times*, 20 December 1963, 27.

113. Irving Spiegel, "Orthodox Jews Move to Halt Trend toward Intermarriages," *New York Times*, 28 October 1965, 31.

114. Edward B. Fiske, "Rabbis Are Upset by Assimilation: Orthodox Council to Set Up Panel on Jewish Survival," *New York Times*, 25 June 1972, 25.

115. "Jews Sue Newsday over a Disputed Ad, *New York Times,* 10 April 1973, 34.

116. Thomas B. Morgan makes the point about the establishment of Israel lulling Jews into a sense of security about group survival, in "The Vanishing American Jew," *Look,* 5 May 1964, 45. I extend this theory to include the 1967 Six-Day War, which occurred before the Orthodox organization issued its complaint against *Newsday.*

117. "Mixed Marriage Feelings," *Newsweek* 78, 5 July 1971, 52.

118. George Dugan, "Study Finds that 41% of U.S. Reform Rabbis Marry Jews to Non-Jews," *New York Times,* 15 June 1972, 13.

119. Dannel Schwartz, "The Intermarriage Rip-Off," *Moment,* July/August 1978, 62-63.

120. Broyde, *Marriage, Sex, and Family in Judaism,* 248.

121. Schwartz, "The Intermarriage Rip-Off," 62-63.

122. Linda Nusbaum-Stark, interview by author, tape recording, Needham, Mass., 11 January 2001.

123. Fran Rakefield, interview by author, tape recording, Newton, Mass., 7 January 2001.

124. Samuel M. Silver, *Mixed Marriage between Jew and Christian* (New York: Arco, 1977), 95.

125. Marilyn Yalom, *A History of the Wife* (New York: Harper Collins, 2001), 366-367; Nancy Cott argues convincingly that the 1950s discourse was, paradoxically, a factor that enabled heightened women's awareness of inequalities in their personal lives, which created the potential for change in the 1960s; Nancy F. Cott, *The Bonds of Womanhood: "Woman's Sphere" in New England, 1780-1835,* 2nd rev. ed. (New Haven, Conn.: Yale University Press, 1997 [1977]), xxvii.

126. Yalom, *A History of the Wife,* 370.

127. Susan Ware, *Modern American Women: A Documentary History* (Belmont, Calif.: Wadsworth, 1989), 331.

128. John F. Kennedy, Executive Order 10980; available at http://www.lib.umich.edu/govdocs/jfkeo/eo/10890.htm.

129. Rosalind Rosenberg, *Divided Lives: American Women in the Twentieth Century* (New York: Hill and Wang, 1992), 189-190.

130. Sara Evans, *Personal Politics: The Roots of Women's Liberation in the Civil Rights Movement and The New Left* (New York: Vintage Books, 1979), 195.

131. Rosenberg, *Divided Lives,* 204.

132. I refer here to patriarchy in its wider definition, described by Gerda Lerner as: "the manifestation and institutionalization of male dominance over women and children in the family and the extension of male dominance over women in society in general" (*The Creation of Patriarchy* [New York: Oxford University Press, 1986], 239).

133. Evelyn Leo, "Dependency in Marriage: Oppression in Middle-Class Marriage," in *Voices from Women's Liberation*, ed. Leslie B. Tanner (New York: Mentor, 1970), 236; "Lilith's Manifesto," Women's Majority Union, Seattle, Wash., 1969, in *Sisterhood Is Powerful: An Anthology of Writings from the Women's Liberation Movement*, ed. Robin Morgan (New York: Vintage Books, 1970), 592.

134. Shulamith Firestone, *The Dialectic of Sex: The Case for Feminist Revolution* (New York: Farrar, Straus and Giroux, 2003 [1970]), 184. Rosenberg identifies Firestone as a founder of Redstockings in *Divided Lives*, 204.

135. Firestone, *The Dialectic of Sex*, 185-187, 214.

136. Rosenberg, *Divided Lives*, 195.

137. Beverly Jones and Judith Brown, "Toward a Female Liberation Movement," in Tanner, *Voices from Women's Liberation*, 400.

138. "The Feminists *vs.* The Marriage License Bureau of the City of New York," in *Sisterhood is Powerful: An Anthology of Writings from the Women's Liberation Movement*, ed. Robin Morgan (New York: Vintage Books, 1970), 602-603.

139. Evans, *Personal Politics*, 214-15, 217.

140. Pat Mainardi, "The Politics of Housework," *Redstockings* (1970). Reprinted in Tanner, *Voices from Women's Liberation*, 336-342; also available at "The Classical Feminist Writings Archive Page," http://www.cwluherstory.com/CWLUArchive/polhousework.html (accessed 19 October 2004).

141. Nancy F. Cott, *Public Vows: A History of Marriage and the Nation* (Cambridge, Mass.: Harvard University Press, 2000), 208.

142. Rosenberg, *Divided Lives*, 202, 211.

143. Ibid., 202.

144. Khoren Arisian, *The New Wedding: Creating Your Own Wedding Ceremony* (New York: Vintage Books, 1973), 12.

145. Jennifer Baker Fleming and Carolyn Kott Washburn, *For Better, For Worse: A Feminist Handbook on Marriage and Other Options* (New York: Scribner's, 1977), 10.

146. Yalom, *A History of the Wife*, 366, 371; Cott, *Public Vows*, 204.

147. Rhona Rapoport and Robert Rapoport, "The Dual Career Family," *Human Relations* 22 (1969): 3-30; cited in Yalom, *A History of the Wife*, 380.

148. Sylvia Barack Fishman, *A Breath of Life: Feminism in the American Jewish Community* (New York: Free Press, 1993), 83.

149. Paul C. Glick of the U.S. Census Bureau; cited in Jon Norheimer, "The Family in Transition: A Challenge from Within," *New York Times*, 27 November 1977, 74.

150. Rosenberg, *Divided Lives*, 184-185.

151. Mirra Komarovsky, "Cultural Contradictions and Sex Roles: The Masculine Case," *American Journal of Sociology* 78, no. 4, Changing Women in a Changing Society series (January 1973): 883.

152. Judith Porter and Alex A. Albert, "Attitudes toward Women's Role: Does a 'Jewish Subculture' Exist in America?" *Gratz College Annual of Jewish Studies* 5 (1976): 132-133.

153. Joyce Antler, *The Journey Home: Jewish Women and the American Century* (New York: Free Press, 1997), 260.

154. Ibid., 259, 283-84,

155. "Lilith's Legacy," *Reform Judaism* 31, no. 4 (summer 2003), 78; available at http://www.lilith.org.

156. Jacob Rader Marcus, *The American Jewish Woman, 1654-1980* (New York: Ktav, 1981), 157; Pamela S. Nadell, *Women Who Would Be Rabbis: A History of Women's Ordination, 1889-1985* (Boston: Beacon, 1998), 170.

157. Ann Braude, "Women's History *Is* American Religious History," in *Retelling U.S. Religious History*, ed. Thomas A. Tweed (Berkeley: University of California Press, 1997), 88, 102.

158. Nadell, *Women Who Would Be Rabbis*, 168. The first Conservative woman rabbi, Amy Eilberg, was ordained in May 1985. The question of Orthodox women rabbis remains. See Nadell, *Women Who Would Be Rabbis*, 214, 220.

159. Ann Braude, "Women's History *Is* American Religious History," 95-96.

160. Romano, *Race Mixing*, 9-10.

161. Antler, *The Journey Home*, 283. Letty Cottin Pogrebin, *Deborah, Golda, and Me: Being Female and Jewish in America* (New York: Doubleday, 1991), 149-161. "Miriam's Cup: Biography of Letty Cottin Pogrebin," miriamscup.com, available at http://www.miriamscup.com/PogrebinBiog.htm.

162. "At our seder," Pogrebin wrote, "we do not praise good girls and polite ladies; we honor rebellious women" (*Deborah, Golda, and Me*, 119-122; "Miriam's Cup: History," available at http://www.miriamscup.com/HistoryFirst.htm [accessed 20 October 2004]).

163. Pogrebin, *Deborah, Golda, and Me*, 154.

164. Roberta Gootblatt, "The Star of Silence," in Tanner, *Voices from Women's Liberation*, 329-331; idem, "Me, Myself, and the Middle-Class Jew," in ibid., 334-335; Kirsten Fermaglich, "'The Comfortable Concentration Camp': The Significance of Nazi Imagery in Betty Friedan's *The Feminine Mystique* (1963)," *American Jewish History* 91, no. 2 (June 2003): 205-232.

165. Ann Braude, "Women's History *Is* American Religious History," 107.

166. Without recognizing the positive potential of feminism, at least one sociologist, in 1976, accurately predicted that the impact of the Women's movement would contribute to an increase in the intermarriage rate of Jewish women. See Monson, "The Case of the Reluctant Exogamists," 124-125.

167. Massarik, "Rethinking the Intermarriage Crisis," 33, 29.

168. Eichhorn, *Jewish Intermarriages*, 66.

169. Bellah et al., *Habits of the Heart*, 234.

170. May, *Homeward Bound*, xxvi.

171. Fran Rakefield, interview by author, tape recording, Newton, Mass., 7 January 2001.

172. Nadine Brozan, "The Jewish Family: The Ties That Bind Are Being Loosened," *New York Times*, 9 February 1973, 40.

173. Olivia Barton, interview by author, tape recording, Lexington, Mass., 10 January 2001.

174. Joan Marcus, interview by author, tape recording, Lexington, Mass., 27 January 2001.

175. May, *Homeward Bound*, xxvi.

176. Jacob Kohn, "The Jewish Family and the Danger of Intermarriage," in *Modern Jewish Problems: A Study in Parental Attitudes* (New York: Women's League of the United Synagogue of American, 1932), 113-114.

177. Amy Jacobson, interview by author, tape recording, Brookline, Mass., 27 February 2001.

178. Ibid.

179. Joan Marcus, interview by author, tape recording, Lexington, Mass., 27 January 2001.

180. May, *Homeward Bound*, xxvi, 203.

181. Karen Amai, interview by author, tape recording, Cambridge, Mass., 9 February 2001.

182. Deborah Dash Moore, "Intermarriage and the Politics of Identity," *The Reconstructionist* 66, no. 1 (fall 2001): 44-45.

183. Judy Klemesrud, "Jewish-Gentile Marriages: As Numbers Grow, So Does Debate," *New York Times*, 25 June 1973, 38.

184. Dora Maci, interview by author, tape recording, Winthrop, Mass., 1 March 2001.

185. Cohen and Eisen, *The Jew Within*, 103-104.

186. Marsha Ember, interview by author, tape recording, Brookline, Mass., 25 January 2001.

187. Carol Ferris, interview by author, tape recording, Cambridge, Mass., 2 February 2001.

188. Ellen Kolokowski, interview by author, tape recording, Cambridge, Mass., 28 December 2000.

189. Fran Rakefield, interview by author, tape recording, Newton, Mass., 7 January 2001.

190. Marsha Ember, interview by author, tape recording, Brookline, Mass., 25 January 2001.

191. Linda Friedman Shah, "Khalid and Linda, Together," *New York Times*, 20 February 1975, 33.

192. Olivia Barton, interview by author, tape recording, Lexington, Mass., 10 January 2001.

193. Fran Rakefield, interview by author, tape recording, Newton, Mass., 7 January 2001.

194. Klemesrud, "Jewish-Gentile Marriages," 38.

195. Kenneth A. Briggs, "Jews Said to Ease View on Marriage: Study Finds an Increasing Attempt to Keep Jewish Partner in the Community," *New York Times,* 15 May 1976, 29.

196. Linda Nusbaum-Stark, interview by author, tape recording, Needham, Mass., 11 January 2001.

197. May, *Homeward Bound,* 195.

198. Unger and Unger, *The Times Were a Changin',* 285.

199. Linda Nusbaum-Stark, interview by author, tape recording, Needham, Mass., 11 January 2001.

200. Diane Endicott, interview by author, tape recording, Cambridge, Mass., 25 January 2001.

201. Amy Jacobson, interview by author, tape recording, Brookline, Mass., 27 February 2001.

202. Linda Nusbaum-Stark, interview by author, tape recording, Needham, Mass., 11 January 2001.

203. Ibid.

204. Ibid.

205. Trudy Melos, interview by author, tape recording, Brookline, Mass., 28 January 2001.

206. Goldstein and Goldscheider, "Social and Demographic Aspects of Jewish Intermarriage," 396.

207. My focus here is on the gender differential involved in conversion *into* Judaism, with non-Jewish women converting more often than non-Jewish men. It is worth noting, however, that although conversion *out* of Judaism was minimal, Jewish men converted out with greater frequency than Jewish women did, according to demographers. See Massarik et al., *National Jewish Population Study 1971,* 5.

208. Steven Huberman, "New Jews: The Dynamics of Religious Conversion" (Ph.D. diss., The Heller School, Brandeis University, 1978), 75; cited in Dru Greenwood, "Conversion to Judaism: A Gendered Phenomenon" (working paper, Hadassah International Research Institute on Jewish Women, September 2002), 1 n. 5. I am grateful to Dru Greenwood for sharing the draft of her HIRIJW paper with me.

209. Monson, "The Case of the Reluctant Exogamists," 124.

210. Greenwood, "Conversion to Judaism."

211. Ellen Kolokowski, interview by author, tape recording, Cambridge, Mass., 28 December 2000.

212. Ibid.

213. Olivia Barton, interview by author, tape recording, Lexington, Mass., 10 January 2001.

214. Beth Jonah, interview by author, tape recording, Brookline, Mass., 17 January 2001.

215. Arthur Hertzberg, *The Jews in America: Four Centuries of an Uneasy Encounter: A History* (New York: Columbia University Press, 1997), 290-291

216. Karen Amai, interview by author, tape recording, Cambridge, Mass., 9 February 2001.

217. Romano, *Race Mixing*, 124.

218. Marsha Ember, interview by author, tape recording, Brookline, Mass., 25 January 2001.

219. Jack Wertheimer, "The Turbulent Sixties," in *The American Jewish Experience*, ed. Jonathan Sarna (New York: Holmes and Meier, 1986), 338.

220. Hasia R. Diner, *The Jews of the United States, 1654-2000* (Berkeley: University of California Press, 2004), 334, 332.

221. Dora Maci, interview by author, tape recording, Winthrop, Mass., 1 March 2001.

222. Ibid.

223. Fran Rakefield, interview by author, tape recording, Newton, Mass., 7 January 2001.

224. Matthew Frye Jacobson, *Whiteness of a Different Color: European Immigrants and the Alchemy of Race* (Cambridge, Mass.: Harvard University Press, 1998), 176-177.

225. Evelyn Lauter, "Some 'Mixed Marrieds' Speak for Themselves," *National Jewish Monthly*, February 1965, 8.

226. Carol Ferris, interview by author, tape recording, Cambridge, Mass., 2 February 2001.

227. Eric L. Goldstein, "Different Blood Flows in Our Veins": Race and Jewish Self-Definition in Late Nineteenth Century America," *American Jewish History* 85, no. 1 (March 1997): 29-55.

228. Carol Ferris, interview by author, tape recording, Cambridge, Mass., 2 February 2001.

229. Beth Jonah, interview by author, tape recording, Brookline, Mass., 17 January 2001.

230. Jacobson, *Whiteness of a Different Color*, 199; emphasis in the original.

231. Goldstein, "Different Blood Flows in Our Veins," 29-55.

232. Joan Marcus, interview by author, tape recording, Lexington, Mass., 27 January 2001.

233. Diane Endicott, interview by author, tape recording, Cambridge, Mass., 25 January 2001.

234. Amy Jacobson, interview by author, tape recording, Brookline, Mass., 27 February 2001.

235. Dora Maci, interview by author, tape recording, Winthrop, Mass., 1 March 2001.

236. Trudy Melos, interview by author, tape recording, Brookline, Mass., 28 January 2001.

237. Beth Jonah, interview by author, tape recording, Brookline, Mass., 17 January 2001.

238. Fran Rakefield, interview by author, tape recording, Newton, Mass., 7 January 2001.

239. Linda Nusbaum-Stark, interview by author, tape recording, Needham, Mass., 11 January 2001.

240. Erich Rosenthal, "Divorce and Religious Intermarriage: The Effect of Previous Marital Status upon Subsequent Marital Behavior," *Journal of Marriage and the Family* 32, no. 3 (August 1970): 435.

241. Jon Norheimer, "The Family in Transition: A Challenge from Within," *New York Times,* 27 November 1977, 1.

242. Rosenthal, "Divorce and Religious Intermarriage," 435.

243. Ellen Kolokowski, interview by author, tape recording, Cambridge, Mass., 28 December 2000.

244. Dora Maci, interview by author, tape recording, Winthrop, Mass., 1 March 2001.

245. Diane Endicott, interview by author, tape recording, Cambridge, Mass., 25 January 2001.

246. Joan Marcus, interview by author, tape recording, Lexington, Mass., 27 January 2001.

247. Olivia Barton, interview by author, tape recording, Lexington, Mass., 10 January 2001.

248. Schoenfeld, "Intermarriage and the Small Town," 64. Schoenfeld does not differentiate between denominations in his study. However, it is likely that relationships between Orthodox families and their intermarried children were more severely strained than Conservative or Reform families and their children.

249. Elizabeth Genné and William Genné, "Married Life . . . for Better or Worse: Interfaith Marriages," *PTA Magazine,* January 1968, 18.

250. Erich Rosenthal, "Intermarriage among Jewry: A Function of Acculturation, Community Organization, and Family Structure," in *Movements and Issues in American Judaism: An Analysis and Sourcebook of Developments since 1945,* ed. Bernard Martin (Westport, Conn.: Greenwood, 1978), 274-275.

251. Schoenfeld, "Intermarriage and the Small Town," 63.

252. Kenneth A. Briggs, "Jews Said to Ease View on Marriage: Study Finds an Increasing Attempt to Keep Jewish Partner in the Community," *New York Times,* 15 May 1976, 29; Kenneth Briggs, "Change Is Found in Jewish Views of Intermarriage: More Positive Attitude Is Reported in New Study," *New York Times,* 24 January 1979, 33.

253. Briggs, "Jews Said to Ease View on Marriage," 29.

254. Mayer and Sheingold, *Intermarriage and the Jewish Future,* 12.

255. Olivia Barton, interview by author, tape recording, Lexington, Mass., 10 January 2001.

256. Linda Nusbaum-Stark, interview by author, tape recording, Needham, Mass., 11 January 2001.

257. Beth Jonah, interview by author, tape recording, Brookline, Mass., 17 January 2001.

258. Mavis Rue, interview by author, tape recording, Brookline, Mass., 15 February 2001.

259. Joan Marcus, interview by author, tape recording, Lexington, Mass., 27 January 2001.

260. Gordon, *Assimilation in American Life,* 80.

261. Marcus Hansen, "The Problem of the Third Generation Immigrant," Augustana Historical Society Publications (Rock Island, Ill.: Augustana Historical Society, 1938), 5-20; cited in Werner Sollors, *Beyond Ethnicity: Consent and Descent in American Culture* (New York: Oxford University Press, 1986), 214-216.

262. Herbert J. Gans, "Symbolic Ethnicity: The Future of Ethnic Groups and Cultures in America," in *Theories of Ethnicity: A Classical Reader,* ed. Werner Sollors (New York: New York University Press, 1996), 434-435.

263. Braude, "Women's History *Is* American Religious History," 91.

CHAPTER 4. REVITALIZATION FROM WITHIN

1. Although Gallup polls in 2000 and in 1980 showed that a consistent proportion of the population, 57 percent, thought religion was "very important," I believe that identification and membership are better measurements of religious engagement. See Gallup Poll, conducted 24-27 August 2000, telephone interviews with a national adult sample of 1,019; Gallup Poll (AIPO), conducted 15-18 August 1980, personal interviews with a national adult sample of 1,600. I am grateful to Sarah Dutton, Deputy Director of Surveys at CBS News, for the Gallup information. See, too, Barry A. Kosmin, Egon Mayer, and Ariela Keysar, *American Religious Identification Survey* (New York: Graduate Center of the City University of New York, 2001; reissued New York: The Center for Cultural Judaism, 2003), 10-11, 13-15, Exhibit 1: "Self Described Religious Identification of U.S. Adult Population 1990-2001"; and Exhibit 2: "Reported Household Membership in Church, Temple, Synagogue, or Mosque for Selected Religious Groups." ARIS cites aggregated survey data about a sample of 1,481 American adults from the General Social Survey 1972-1994, National Opinion Research Center, University of Chicago. ARIS is available online at http://www.gc.cuny.edu/studies/aris_index.htm. Lastly, for more recent data, see *U.S. Religious Landscape Survey* (Washington, D.C.: Pew Forum on Religion & Public Life, 2008), "Summary of Key Findings,"

5. Based on interviews with more than thirty-five thousand Americans age eighteen and older, the *Landscape Survey* finds that the number of people who say they are unaffiliated with any particular religion is more than double the number who say they were not affiliated as children. This survey is available online, at http://religions.pewforum.org/.

2. Calvin Goldscheider, "Are American Jews Vanishing Again?" *Contexts* 2 (winter 2003): 18-24; Editorial, "The 52% Fraud," *Forward*, 12 September 2003; Jason Nielsen, "Long-awaited Population Study Offers Mixed Verdict," *Jewish Advocate*, 12-18 September 2003; Calvin Goldscheider, "Why the Population Survey Counts," *Forward*, 11 October 2002: 11.

3. Barry A, Kosmin et al. *Highlights of the CJF 1990 National Jewish Population Survey* (New York: Council of Jewish Federations, 1991), 14; Fred Massarik et al., *National Jewish Population Study: Intermarriage, Facts for Planning* (New York: Council of Jewish Federations and Welfare Funds, 1971), 10.

4. Laurence Kotler-Berkowitz et al. *The National Jewish Population Survey 2000-01: Strength, Challenge and Diversity in the American Jewish Population* (New York: United Jewish Communities, 2003), 16-17.

5. Sherry Israel, *Boston's Jewish Community: The 1985 Demographic Study* (Boston: Combined Jewish Philanthropies of Greater Boston, 1987), 58; and Sherry Israel, *Comprehensive Report on the 1995 Demographic Study* (Boston: Combined Jewish Philanthropies of Greater Boston, 1997), 114; Morris Axelrod, Floyd J. Fowler Jr., and Arnold Gurin, *A Community Survey for Long-Range Planning: A Study of the Jewish Population of Greater Boston* (Boston: Combined Jewish Philanthropies, 1967), 168-169, table 15.2; Floyd J. Fowler Jr., *1975 Community Survey: A Study of the Jewish Population of Greater Boston* (Boston: Combined Jewish Philanthropies, 1975), 67, table 5.16. Leonard Saxe et al., *The 2005 Boston Community Survey: Preliminary Findings* (Waltham, Mass.: Steinhardt Social Research Institute, Brandeis University, for Combined Jewish Philanthropies of Boston, November 2006), 11. Available online from the Mandell L. Berman Institute, North American Jewish Data Bank, at http://www.jewishdatabank.org.

6. The majority from the two largest ancestry groups, English and Germans, did not marry outside their ethnic groups partly because of larger numbers of potential partners and their concentration. See Richard Alba, "Intermarriage and Ethnicity among European Americans," in *Jewish Intermarriage and Its Social Context*, ed. Paul Ritterband (New York: Jewish Outreach Institute and the Center for Jewish Studies, Graduate School of the City University of New York, 1991), 5-8. Material cited here was originally taken from the author's book, *Ethnic Identity: The Transformation of White America* (New Haven: Yale University Press, 1990).

7. The normalization of inter-ethnic marriage occurred despite the fact that the census did not provide information about people's religion because the findings were part of a larger trend that included interfaith marriage patterns. See Richard D. Alba and Reid M. Gordon, "Patterns of Ethnic Marriage in the United

States," *Social Forces* 65, no. 1 (September 1986): 213. See also Richard D. Alba, quoted by Glenn Collins in "A New Look at Intermarriage in the US," *New York Times*, 11 February 1985, C13.

8. Richard Alba, "Intermarriage and Ethnicity among European Americans," 8.

9. Renee C. Romano, *Race Mixing: Black-White Marriage in Postwar America* (Cambridge, Mass.: Harvard University Press, 2003), 3.

10. Bruce Phillips, "Los Angeles Jewry: A Demographic Portrait," *American Jewish Year Book* 86 (1986): 145-147, 153, and 177-178; cited in Jonathan D. Sarna, "Reform Jewish Leaders, Intermarriage, and Conversion," in *Journal of Reform Judaism* 37, no. 1, issue 148 (winter 1990): 3.

11. Although the ratio of intermarriage as it correlated to gender fluctuated with age, with men under the age of thirty-five and above the age of fifty-five more likely to have intermarried than women in the same age bracket, equal proportions of women and men intermarried in the thirty-five through fifty-four age bracket. See Laurence Kotler-Berkowitz et al. *The National Jewish Population Survey 2000-01*, 17.

12. Susan Maushart, *The Mask of Motherhood: How Becoming a Mother Changes Everything and Why We Pretend It Doesn't* (New York: New Press, 1999), 182. See also Susan Ware, *Modern American Women: A Documentary History* (Belmont, Calif.: Wadsworth, 1989), 375; Elaine Showalter, introduction to *These Modern Women: Autobiographical Essays from the Twenties* (New York: Feminist Press at the City University of New York,1989 [1979]), 25.

13. Ruth Milkman, *Gender at Work: The Dynamics of Job Segregation by Sex during World War II* (Urbana: University of Illinois Press, 1987), 153; Ware, *Modern American Women*, 376.

14. Rosalind Rosenberg, *Divided Lives: American Women in the Twentieth Century* (New York: Hill and Wang, 1992), 247.

15. Arlie Russell Hochschild and Anne Machung, *The Second Shift: Working Parents and the Revolution at Home* (New York: Viking Penguin, 1989); cited in Maushart, *The Mask of Motherhood*, 184.

16. Elizabeth Janeway quoted in Rosenberg, *Divided Lives*, 255.

17. "Baby Boom Generation Factoids," *It Seems Like Yesterday*, Available at http://www.itseemslikeyesterday.com/1998_fall/factoids.asp (accessed 12 May 2004).

18. Joanne Michaels, *Living Contradictions: The Women of the Baby Boom Come of Age* (New York: Simon and Schuster, 1982), 27.

19. Leonard Fein, *Where Are We? The Inner Life of America's Jews* (New York: Harper and Row, 1988), 199; cited in Edward S. Shapiro, *A Time for Healing: American Jewry since World War II* (Baltimore, Md.: The Johns Hopkins University Press, 1992), 219-221.

20. Karla Matzman, interview by author, tape recording, Arlington, Mass., 12 January 2001.

21. "Geraldine Ferraro," *A History of the American Suffragist Movement*, available at http://www.suffragist.com/gf.htm.

22. Georgia Witkin-Lanoil, "Odd Couples," *Health* 18 (September 1986): 77.

23. Phillip Gleason, "American Identity and Americanization," *Harvard Encyclopedia of American Ethnic Groups*, ed. Stephan Thernstrom, Ann Orlov, and Oscar Handlin (Cambridge, Mass.: Belknap Press of Harvard University Press, 1980), 54-55.

24. Andrew M. Greeley, *Why Can't They Be Like Us? America's White Ethnic Groups* (New York: Dutton, 1971), 191.

25. Nathan Glazer and Daniel Patrick Moynihan, *Beyond the Melting Pot: The Negroes, Puerto Ricans, Jews, Italians and Irish of New York City*, 2nd ed. (Cambridge, Mass.: MIT Press, 1970 [1963]); cited in Alba, *Ethnic Identity*, 18. See also Michael Novak, *The Rise of the Unmeltable Ethnics: The New Political Force of the Seventies* (New York: Macmillan, 1971).

26. Alba, *Ethnic Identity*, cover photograph, 2, 310; "Kiss Me, I'm Jewish" pin in author's possession.

27. Marilyn Yalom, *A History of the Wife* (New York: Harper Collins, 2001), 389-390; Ware, *Modern American Women*, 424; Nancy Cott, *Public Vows: A History of Marriage and the Nation* (Cambridge, Mass.: Harvard University Press, 2000), 13.

28. Karla Dial, "Founding Mother," *Citizen*, November 2002, cover story. Also see "Phyllis Schlafley bio," Eagle Forum, at http://www.eagleforum.org/misc/bio.html.

29. Phyllis Shlafley, *The Power of the Positive Woman* (1977); cited in Ware, *Modern American Women*, 446-453.

30. Adrienne Rich, "Split at the Root: An Essay on Jewish Identity" (1982), in idem, *Blood, Bread, and Poetry* (New York: Norton, 1986), 122-123.

31. Susannah Heschel, ed., *On Being a Jewish Feminist* (New York: Schocken Books, 1995 [1983]).

32. Susan Faludi, *Backlash: The Undeclared War against American Women* (New York: Crown, 1991), xxiii, 3.

33. "The Intermarriage Quandary: Can U.S. Judaism afford to say yes? Can it afford not to?" *Time* 132, 3 October 1988, 82.

34. Steven Bayme, "To Condone or Not to Condone—Is That the Question?" *Comment & Analysis*: 2, no. 4, November 1991, 2-3.

35. Becca Tamen, interview by author, tape recording, Cambridge, Mass., 17 January 2001.

36. Richard Alba, "Intermarriage and Ethnicity among European Americans," 5-8. Material in the paper I cite was originally taken from the author's book, *Ethnic Identity*. Alba used the word "Hispanic"; I replaced "Hispanic" with "Latino," the term more commonly used today to refer to people whose ancestors came from Mexico, Cuba, Central America, and South America, rather than the Iberian Peninsula that includes Spain and Portugal.

37. Zena Jethro, interview by author, tape recording, Lexington, Mass., 8 January 2001.

38. Peggy Pascoe, "Race, Gender, and Intercultural Relations: The Case of Interracial Marriage," *Frontiers*, 12, no. 1 (1991): 11.

39. Cott, *Public Vows*, 218-220.

40. *The State of Our Unions 2000: The Social Health of Marriage in America, The National Marriage Project* (New Brunswick, N.J.: Rutgers University, 2000), 25-26, figure 5.

41. Jerold S. Heiss, "Interfaith Marriage and Marital Outcome," *Marriage and Family Living* 23, no. 3 (August 1961): 229, 233.

42. Harold T. Christensen and K. Barber, "Interfaith versus Intrafaith Marriage in Indiana," *Journal of Marriage and the Family* 29 no. 3 (August 1967): 461-469; Howard M. Bahr, "Religious Intermarriage and Divorce in Utah and the Mountain States," *Journal for the Scientific Study of Religion* 20, no. 3 (1981): 251-261; Tim B. Heaton, Stan I. Albrecht, and Thomas K. Martin, "The Timing of Divorce," *Journal of Marriage and the Family* 47, no. 3 (August 1985): 631-639; cited in Barry A. Kosmin, Nava Lerner, and Egon Mayer, *Intermarriage, Divorce and Remarriage among American Jews 1982-1987* (New York: North American Jewish Data Bank, CUNY Graduate Center, 1989), 4.

43. Something that deserves further analysis is that women who intermarried had a divorce rate higher than men who intermarried: 38 percent compared to 25 percent (Kosmin, Lerner, and Mayer, *Intermarriage, Divorce and Remarriage among American Jews 1982-1987*, 1).

44. Penina Mintz Jennings, interview by author, tape recording, Newton, Mass., 4 January 2001.

45. Lisa Schiffman, *generation j* (New York: HarperSanFrancisco, 2000; HarperCollins, 1999), 19.

46. *Midrash Rabbah, Genesis*, trans. Rabbi Dr. H. Freedman, 3rd ed. (London: Soncino, 1961 [1939]), 735; Judith R. Baskin, *Midrashic Women: Formations of the Feminine in Rabbinic Literature* (Hanover, Mass.: Brandeis University Press, 2002), 149; "Outgoing Woman," *Genesis 34:1-2*, Chabad.org Parshah, available at http://www.chabad.org/parshah/article; Hannah Noble, interview by author, tape recording, Brookline, Mass., 9 January 2001.

47. Kotler-Berkowitz et al., *The National Jewish Population Survey 2000-01*, 18.

48. Sylvia Barack Fishman, *Double or Nothing: Jewish Family and Mixed Marriage* (Hanover, Mass.: Brandeis University Press, 2004), 44-45. Fishman contended: "Jewish mixed-married households are twice as likely to end in divorce as Jewish inmarried households," and that, of American families, "interfaith households are three times more likely to end in divorce as families in which both parents share the same faith." She continued, "For years, parents of mixed-married couples have accused Jewish communal leaders who articulate a principled preference for endogamy of contributing to the marital friction of mixed-married

households through their intransigence and insensitivity. The ARIS data, however suggest that religious differences themselves contribute to great spousal tensions. Marital problems within mixed marriage probably arise from internal—rather than external—sources." The statistical estimates are not confirmed by the original sources Fishman cited, the 1990 National Jewish Population Survey and the 2001 American Religious Identification Survey. More exhaustive research unearthed a *USA Today* article from 5 December 2002 that compared mixed-married divorce to same-faith divorce. Arielya Keysar, a demographer and the coauthor of both reports, could not confirm the statistics for the 1990 NJPS and stated that ARIS did not publish divorce rates for mixed-faith versus same-faith couples. Information about marital status and religious composition of couples was given to Cathy Grossman, the *USA Today* reporter who requested that the researchers cross-tabulate their findings for the purposes of her article. Keysar further clarified that the data required more in-depth analysis, namely, by age, gender, and more specific religious groups, something that *USA Today* did not address and that she might do in the future. Ariela Keysar to author, e-mail communication, 12 April 2004; Cathy Grossman to author, e-mail communication, 4 May 2004.

49. Brandy Simon, interview by author, tape recording, Brookline, Mass., 23 January 2001.

50. Penina Mintz Jennings, interview by author, tape recording, Newton, Mass., 4 January 2001.

51. Michelle Johnson, interview by author, tape recording, Brookline, Mass., 5 January 2001.

52. For a discussion about the relationship between stereotypes and Jewish intermarriage, see Fishman, *Double or Nothing*, 29, 109. See also Ellen Jaffe McClain, *Embracing the Stranger: Intermarriage and the Future of the American Jewish Community* (New York: Basic Books, 1995).

53. Rachel Lyon, interview by author, tape recording, Brookline, Mass., 18 January 2001.

54. For an important discussion of how Jewish wife beating was traditionally downplayed in favor of an idealized concept of the Jewish family, see Mimi Scarf, "Marriages Made in Heaven? Battered Jewish Wives," in *On Being a Jewish Feminist*, ed. Susannah Heschel, rev. ed. (New York: Schocken Books, 1995 [1983]), 51-64.

55. Zipora Ackerman, interview by author, tape recording, Newton, Mass., 19 January 2001; Muriel Cypress, interview by author, tape recording, Brookline, Mass., 5 January 2001.

56. Bonnie Aaronson, interview by author, tape recording, Brookline, Mass. 24 January 2001.

57. Regarding the paradox of declining antisemitism and Jews' continuing fears about its increase, Leonard Dinnerstein has remarked: "Jews have an acute sensitivity to oppression, and their two thousand year history in Christian lands, the Holocaust, and the annual ADL [Anti-Defamation League] figures listing

antisemitic incidents remind Jews that they are still vulnerable" (*Antisemitism in America* [New York: Oxford University Press, 1994], 243).

58. I am indebted to Orna Teitelbaum, who was kind enough to bring this book to my attention and to share her copy of it with me. Leslie Brody, ed., *Daughters of Kings: Growing Up as a Jewish Woman in America* (Boston: Faber and Faber, 1997), 8-9. See also Letty Cottin Pogrebin, *Deborah, Golda, and Me: Being Female and Jewish in America* (New York: Doubleday, 1991), 218-222.

59. Brandy Simon, interview by author, tape recording, Brookline, Mass., 23 January 2001.

60. Karla Matzman, interview by author, tape recording, Arlington, Mass., 12 January 2001.

61. Meghan Daum, "The Goy Next Door: Confessions of an American Shiksa," *Gentleman's Quarterly* 66, July 1996, 132-135; Melissa Schorr, "The Joys of Goys," *Gentleman's Quarterly* 66, December 1996, 70.

62. Mary Gordon, "I Married an Alien," *Vogue* 175, May 1985, 193.

63. Melissa Schorr, *Goy Crazy* (New York: Hyperion, 2006).

64. For a nuanced discussion of the postwar revival of institutional Judaism and the temporary collapse of secular Judaism, see Jonathan D. Sarna, *American Judaism: A History* (New Haven, Conn.: Yale University Press, 2004), 274-275.

65. Egon Mayer, Barry A. Kosmin, and Ariela Keysar, *American Jewish Identity Survey 2001* (New York: Graduate Center of the City University of New York, 2001; reissued, New York: Center for Cultural Judaism, 2003), 6; Kotler-Berkowitz et al., *The National Jewish Population Survey 2000-01*, 2; Cathy Lynn Grossman, "Cultural Movement Kindles Interest of Secular Jews," *USA Today*, 28 September 2003.

66. General Social Survey, National Opinion Research Center, University of Chicago, available at http://www.norc.uchicago.edu/projects/gensoc.asp; Carl W. Brown, research assistant, Roper Center for Public Opinion Research, University of Connecticut, e-mail communication to Sarah Dutton, Deputy Director of Surveys at CBS News, forwarded to author, 21 December 2004. The GSS figures mirror those in the *American Religious Identification Survey 2001*: 14 percent of American adults specified "no religion" in 2000 compared to 8 percent in 1990 (ARIS, 13). I am indebted to Ms. Dutton for this national survey information and for her experienced analysis of an "upstick in the percentage who say 'none.'" Data published in 2008 show that the trend continues and has increased slightly to 16.1 percent. See *U.S. Religious Landscape Survey*, 5.

67. Mayer, Kosmin, and Keysar, *American Jewish Identity Survey 2001*, 10.

68. Joe Berkofsky, "Donor Offers $10 Million to Fund, but with Secular Strings Attached," *InterfaithFamily.Com* 131, 9 April 2004, Internet. Reprinted from a *Jewish Telegraphic Agency* article dated 2 December 2003.

69. Brandy Simon, interview by author, tape recording, Brookline, Mass., 23 January 2001.

70. Karla Matzman, interview by author, tape recording, Arlington, Mass., 12 January 2001.

71. Brandy Simon, interview by author, tape recording, Brookline, Mass., 23 January 2001.

72. Gabriella Abrahms, interview by author, tape recording, Brookline, Mass. 2 January 2001.

73. See the first paragraph in the introduction to this volume.

74. There were three exceptions: a Greek Orthodox husband who continued to participate in the Hellenic community; a husband who attended church with his family of origin who were devout Irish Catholics; and a second Irish Catholic husband who wore a crucifix as a symbol of his ongoing commitment to his faith.

75. Rachel Lyon, interview by author, tape recording, Brookline, Mass., 18 January 2001; Heidi Laker, interview by author, tape recording, Newton, Mass., 26 January 2001.

76. Letter to Zena Jethro, July 1978. I am grateful to Zena Jethro for preserving and sharing this intimate correspondence.

77. Zena Jethro, interview by author, tape recording, Lexington, Mass., 8 January 2001.

78. Karla Matzman, interview by author, tape recording, Arlington, Mass., 12 January 2001.

79. Kosmin, Mayer, and Keysar, *American Religious Identification Survey*, 20, exhibit 4 "Outlook of U.S. Adult Men & Women: Religious and Secular." See, too, "Gender," *U.S. Religious Landscape Survey*, 62–64.

80. William J. Cromie, "One-third of Americans Pray for Their Health," *Harvard University Gazette*, 13 May 2004, cover story.

81. David Brooks, "Living Room Crusaders," *Newsweek* 130, no. 24, 15 December 1997, 55.

82. Jerry Adler, "A Matter of Faith," *Newsweek* 130, no. 24, 15 December 1997, 52.

83. Egon Mayer and Ron Miller, *The 1995 Survey of Interfaith Families* (New York: Jewish Outreach Institute, 1995), 4. Mayer and Miller found that, "Jewish respondents with non-Jewish spouses are generally more apt (40%) to be interested in learning about Jewish outreach programs than non-Jewish respondents (28%) with Jewish spouses. Women are somewhat more interested in learning about Jewish outreach programs than are men. Non-Jewish women are about twice as likely to be interested in learning about Jewish outreach programs than non-Jewish men (the sex associated differential is much smaller among Jewish men and women). Interest among the intermarried *with children* rises to nearly 45%."

84. Thanks to Nancy Seward for granting permission to include her comment.

85. Fran Schumer, "Star-Crossed: More Gentiles and Jews Are Intermarrying," *New York* 23, 2 April 1990, 32-38.

86. Glenn Collins, "A New Look at Intermarriage in the U.S.," *New York Times*, 11 February 1985, C13.

87. Lou Jacquet, "Interfaith Marriage: Two Faiths Are Better Than None," *U.S. Catholic* 47, June 1982, 49.

88. Henry Fehren, "How Odd of God," *U.S. Catholic* 53, September 1988, 42.

89. Robert T. Reilly, "How Interfaith Couples Make the Most of Their Differences," *U.S. Catholic* 54, May 1989, 28.

90. See Evelyn Kaye, "Interfaith Marriage: Is It Getting Any Easier?" *Glamour* 78, March 1980, 88; Stanley N. Rosenbaum, "Marriage in a Two-Faith House," *Christian Century* 98, no. 34, 28 October 1981, 1109; Horizons, "Behind Rise in Mixed Marriages," *U.S. News & World Report* 100, 10 February 1986, 71.

91. Eileen Ogitz, "A Marriage of Two Faiths," *Ladies' Home Journal* 105, December 1988, 26.

92. Gallup Poll, April 1983, by the Gallup Organization. *Washington Post*/Kaiser Family Foundation/Harvard Values Survey, November 1998. I am grateful to Sarah Dutton, Deputy Director of Surveys at CBS News, for this information.

93. Egon Mayer, *Intermarriage and the Attitudes of American Jewish Leadership: The Issues and the Controversies* (New York: Jewish Outreach Institute, 1990), 1.

94. *2000 Annual Survey of American Jewish Opinion*, Conducted for the American Jewish Committee by Market Facts, Inc. 14-28 September 2000, 3, 5. See also Rahel Musleah, "Jewish Jeopardy," *Reform Judaism* 30, no. 1 (fall 2001): 18-24; Gustave Niebuhr, "Marriage Issue Splits Jews, Poll Finds," *New York Times*, 31 October, 2000, A18; Ami Eden, "Jews Accepting of Intermarriage, Wary of Public Faith, Surveys Find," *Forward*, 3 November 2000, 1, 14; Francine Klagsburn, "Survey Says Intermarriage Is Okay," *Moment*, April 2001, 21.

95. Jacquet, "Interfaith Marriage: Two Faiths Are Better Than None"; Steven Bayme, "The Changing Face of American Jews," *USA Today* 121, no. 2570, November 1992, 86ff. Also see Irving Kristol, "Why Religion Is Good for the Jews," *Commentary* 98, no. 2, August 1994, 19-21; and "Letters from Readers: The Jewish Future," *Commentary* 98, no. 5, November 1994, 2, 4-11.

96. David Weinberger, "Embracing the Child of a Jewish Father," *Maclean's* 93, January 1980, 43.

97. Sarna, *American Judaism*, 322-323. Sarna notes that Reconstructionism comprised less than 2 percent of the American Jewish population, which might explain why the 1968 decision received little attention.

98. Central Conference of American Rabbis, "Resolution of the Status of Children of Mixed Marriages," adopted March 15, 1983, mimeograph; cited in Egon Mayer, *Love and Tradition: Marriage between Jews and Christians* (New York: Schocken Books, 1985), 267.

99. Kenneth L. Woodward, "A New Definition of Who Is a Jew," *Newsweek* 101, 28 March 1983, 50.

100. Rabbi J. Simcha Cohen, *Intermarriage and Conversion: A Halakhic Solution* (Hoboken, N.J.: Ktav, 1987), 3, 83.

101. Shapiro, *A Time for Healing*, 241; Fishman, *Double or Nothing*, 128.

102. For sources that reiterate the higher percentage of Jewish men that intermarried than Jewish women, see for example, U.O. Schmelz and Sergio DellaPergola, "The Demographic Consequences of U.S. Jewish Population Trends," *American Jewish Yearbook*, vol. 83 (New York: American Jewish Committee and the Jewish Publication Society, 1983), 161; Mayer, *Love and Tradition*, 266.

103. Though not specific to children, two sources regarding conversion to Judaism as historically gendered, mentioned in chapter 3, with more women converting to Judaism than men, are worth citing. The 1990 NJPS supports the idea there is a bias toward more females being "Jews by choice," who have converted to Judaism or who self-identify as Jews: in the 30-50 age bracket, two-thirds of the Jews by choice are women (Kosmin et al., *Highlights of the CJF 1990 National Jewish Population Survey*, 8). For a personal look at eleven Jewish-Gentile couples through the eyes of a woman with Jewish roots, raised as a Christian, who married a Jew and became a Jew-by-choice, see Gabrielle Glaser, *Strangers to the Tribe: Portraits of Interfaith Marriage* (Boston: Houghton Mifflin, 1997).

104. Rabbi Keith Stern, "A Taste of Heneini," 20 May 2004, Temple Beth Avodah, Newton Mass. See also Bethamie Horowitz, Pearl Beck, and Charles Kadushin, *Power and Parity: Women on the Boards of Major American Jewish Organizations* (Mayan, 1997), which found that among the forty-one "coed" organizations studied, only five had female presidents; and Shaul Kelner et al., *Recruiting and Retaining a Professional Work Force for the Jewish Community* (Maurice and Marilyn Cohen Center for Modern Jewish Studies and the Fisher-Bernstein Institute for Leadership Development in Jewish Philanthropy, Brandeis University, February 2004): "Paradoxically, in spite of the inequities [e.g., barriers to advancement and salary gaps] women face, the field disproportionately relies upon female labor, and finds it hard to attract men" (7-8). For more about gender equity issues in the Jewish community, see Shifra Bronznick, Didi Goldenhar, and Marty Linsky, *Leveling the Playing Field: Advancing Women in Jewish Organizational Life* (Cambridge, Mass.: Advancing Women Professionals and the Jewish Community, and Cambridge Leadership Associates, 2008); and Sylvia Barack Fishman and Daniel Parmer, *Matrilineal Ascent/Patrilineal Descent: The Gender Imbalance in American Jewish Life* (Waltham, Mass.: Maurice and Marilyn Cohen Center for Modern Jewish Studies and Hadassah–Brandeis Institute, Brandeis University, 2008).

105. Ann Braude, "Women's History *Is* American Religious History," in *Retelling U.S. Religious History*, ed. Thomas A. Tweed (Berkeley: University of California Press, 1997), 103.

106. In her work on interfaith families, Jane Kaplan found that many times a Christian woman married a Jewish man who was "not very active in Judaism" and "the Christian woman was often actually the catalyst for the family to lead a more Jewish life." This illustrates how Christian intermarried women were saddled with the responsibility of raising Jewish children. See Jane Kaplan, *Interfaith*

Families: Personal Stories of Jewish-Christian Intermarriage (Westport, Conn.: Praeger, 2004), xiv.

107. Kosmin, et al. *Highlights of the CJF 1990 National Jewish Population Survey*, 14.

108. Sidney Goldstein, "Profile of American Jewry: Insights from the 1990 National Jewish Population Survey," Occasional Papers No. 6, May 1993, *American Jewish Yearbook 1992*, vol. 92 (New York: Council of Jewish Federations, 1993), 127.

109. Egon Mayer quoted in "Behind Rise in Mixed Marriages," *U.S News & World Report* 100, 10 February 1986, 70.

110. Jonathan D. Sarna, "The Secret of Jewish Continuity," *Commentary* 98, no. 4, October 1994, 55.

111. "Intermarriage into the 21st Century: Our Choices and Our Challenges," coordinated and cosponsored by Jewish Family & Children's Services, UAHC, and United Synagogue of Conservative Judaism, and featured guest speaker Egon Mayer, 20-21 October 1991; Forum on Intermarriage, sponsored by the Social Planning and Allocations Committee of the Combined Jewish Philanthropies, February 1996; "Intermarriage from the Inside—Experiences and Responses," Brin Forum, sponsored by the Benjamin S. Hornstein Program in 1995; "Report on the Task Force on Intermarriage," Combined Jewish Philanthropies, Boston, January 1997, 3.

112. Steven Bayme et al. *The Intermarriage Crisis: Jewish Communal Perspectives and Responses* (New York: American Jewish Committee, 1991).

113. "American Jewish Committee Statement on Intermarriage," adopted by the Board of Governors, 2 May 1991, in Bayme et al., *The Intermarriage Crisis.*

114. It is common wisdom in the American Jewish community that, once Jews have children, synagogue membership rises (Amy Sales, Associate Director, Center for Modern Jewish Studies, Brandeis University, e-mail communication to author, 14 December 2004). For a humorous depiction of this phenomenon, see Woody Allen's film *Deconstructing Harry* (1997), in which Demi Moore portrays a fictitious ex-wife who, soon after her son was born, "became Jewish with a vengeance." Thanks to Lee Sanderson for introducing me to this particular cinematic moment.

115. Bonnie Aaronson, interview by author, tape recording, Brookline, Mass. 24 January 2001.

116. Mayer, *Love and Tradition*, 153-176; Sarna, *American Judaism*, 374.

117. Maushart, *The Mask of Motherhood*, xix.

118. Becca Tamen, interview by author, tape recording, Cambridge, Mass., 17 January 2001.

119. Hannah Noble, interview by author, tape recording, Brookline, Mass., 9 January 2001.

120. Bonnie Aaronson, interview by author, tape recording, Brookline, Mass. 24 January 2001.

121. My study suggests that the argument made by Steven M. Cohen and Arnold M. Eisen that "because today's Jews believe that Jewish identity is inalienable, i.e., that they will always remain Jewish no matter what choices they make" does not extend to intermarried Jewish women's perceptions about the Jewish identity of their offspring (*The Jew Within: Self, Family, and Community in America* (Bloomington: Indiana University Press, 2000), 185.

122. Hannah Noble, interview by author, tape recording, Brookline, Mass., 9 January 2001.

123. Kosmin, Mayer, and Keysar, Exhibit 5 "Outlook of Older & Younger U.S. Adults: Religious and Secular," *American Religious Identification Survey*, 21.

124. Debra Renee Kaufman and Gail Melson, "Prime Time Parenting: Adult Mother-Daughter Relationships," paper presented by Debra Kaufman at the Eastern Sociological Society, Boston, 9 March 2002. E-mail communication to author, 24 March 2004.

125. Rachel Josefowitz Siegel, Ellen Cole, and Susan Steinberg-Cohen, eds., *Jewish Mothers Tell Their Stories: Acts of Love and Courage* (New York: Haworth, 2000), 7.

126. Brandy Simon, interview by author, tape recording, Brookline, Mass., 23 January 2001.

127. Madeline Marget, "Madeline & Ernie: Honoring What We Do Not Share," *Commonweal* 115, 23 September 1988, 492.

128. Gabriella Abrahms, interview by author, tape recording, Brookline, Mass. 2 January 2001.

129. Marget, "Madeline & Ernie," 492.

130. Eileen Ogitz, "A Marriage of Two Faiths," *Ladies' Home Journal* 105, December 1988, 22-24.

131. Beth Levine, "The Forbidden Road Home," *Reform Judaism* 30, no. 1 (fall 2001): 22-23.

132. Emily Blank, "How Marrying a Protestant Minister Made Me a Better Jew," *InterfaithFamily.Com* 131, 4 April 2004, available at http://InterfaithFamily.com/article/issue131/blank.phtml.

133. For a discussion about whether individuals of different backgrounds actually became more religious in equal measure or simply identified more vigorously, see Jerry Adler, "A Matter of Faith," *Newsweek* 130, no. 24, 15 December 1997, 52. For an example of a Jewish man who bought a menorah and began lighting Chanukah candles for the first time in his adult life when his fiancé wanted a Christmas tree, see Paula Span, "Whose Holiday Is It, Anyway? For Interfaith Couples, 'Tis the Season for Having to Choose," *Glamour* 86, December 1988, 76, 82, 84.

134. Ruth Mendelson quoted by Robert T. Reilly, "How Interfaith Couples Make the Most of Their Differences," *U.S. Catholic* 54, May 1989, 28.

135. Carole Bodger, "The Challenges of Cross-Cultural Marriage," *Glamour* 82, May 1984, 361.

136. Cokie Roberts and Steve Roberts, *From This Day Forward* (New York: William Morrow, 2000), 111-112.

137. Henry Fehren, "How Odd of God," *U.S. Catholic* 53, September 1988, 42.

138. Cohen and Eisen, *The Jew Within*, 185.

139. Karla Matzman, interview by author, tape recording, Arlington, Mass., 12 January 2001.

140. Muriel Cypress, interview by author, tape recording, Brookline, Mass., 5 January 2001.

141. *Booklet for Women Who Wish to Determine Their Own Name* (Barrington, Ill.: Center for a Woman's Own Name, 1974).

142. Susan J. Krupper, *Surnames for Women: A Decision-Making Guide* (Jefferson, N.C.: McFarland, 1990), 1, 6.

143. Sharon Lebell, *Naming Ourselves, Naming Our Children: Resolving the Last Name Dilemma* (Freedom, Calif.: Crossing Press: 1988), 9, 64-65.

144. Sharon Brody, "A Name Is Just a Name . . . Or Is it?" *The Boston Phoenix*, 3 July 1992, section 2, 4-6.

145. Alvin Powell, "A New Comfort Zone? Fewer Women Keeping Names on Marriage," *Harvard Gazette*, 26 August 2004.

146. Zena Jethro, interview by author, tape recording, Lexington, Mass., 8 January 2001.

147. Zipora Ackerman, interview by author, tape recording, Newton, Mass., 19 January 2001.

148. Melissa Sherman, interview by author, tape recording, Brookline, Mass., 5 January 2001.

149. Karla Matzman, interview by author, tape recording, Arlington, Mass., 12 January 2001.

150. Gabriella Abrahms, interview by author, tape recording, Brookline, Mass. 2 January 2001.

151. See, for example, Susan Weidman Schneider, *Jewish and Female: Choices and Changes in Our Lives Today* (New York: Simon and Schuster 1984; reprint, 1985); and Janet Carnay et al., *The "New Woman Collective," The Jewish Women's Awareness Guide: Connections for the 2nd Wave of Feminism* (New York: Biblio Press, 1992; reprint, 1993).

152. Pogrebin, *Deborah, Golda, and Me*, 219.

153. Hannah Noble, interview by author, tape recording, Brookline, Mass., 9 January 2001.

154. Penina Mintz Jennings, interview by author, tape recording, Newton, Mass., 4 January 2001.

155. Terry Golway, "Life in the '90s," *America* 180, no. 6 (27 February 1999): 6.

156. Paula E. Hyman, *Gender and Assimilation in Modern Jewish History: The Roles and Representation of Women* (Seattle: University of Washington Press, 1995), 27, 153-154. For a discussion of European Jewish women as cultural transmitters

and "domestic Judaism," see Marion Kaplan, *The Making of the Jewish Middle Class: Women, Family, and Identity in Imperial Germany* (New York: Oxford University Press, 1991), 64-84.

157. Michelle Johnson, interview by author, tape recording, Brookline, Mass., 5 January 2001.

158. Norval D. Glenn, "Interreligious Marriage in the United States: Patterns and Recent Trends," *Journal of Marriage and the Family* 44, no. 3 (August 1982): 564; Edwin H. Friedman, "The Myth of the Shiksa," in *Ethnicity and Family Therapy*, ed. Monica McGoldrick, John K. Pearce, and Joseph Giordano (New York: Guilford, 1982), 503; Fishman, *Double or Nothing*, 85; Kaplan, *Interfaith Families*, xiv.

159. Melissa Sherman, interview by author, tape recording, Brookline, Mass., 5 January 2001.

160. Penina Mintz Jennings, interview by author, tape recording, Newton, Mass., 4 January 2001.

161. Maushart, *The Mask of Motherhood*, 207. I borrowed this phrase from Ruth Schwartz Cowan's book, *More Work for Mother: The Ironies of Household Technology from the Open Hearth to the Microwave* (New York: Basic Books, 1983).

162. Bonnie Aaronson, interview by author, tape recording, Brookline, Mass. 24 January 2001.

163. Levine, "The Forbidden Road Home," 23.

164. Kotler-Berkowitz et al. *The National Jewish Population Survey 2000-01*, 18.

165. Saxe et al., *The 2005 Boston Community Survey*, 12; Massarik and Chenkin, "U.S. National Jewish Population Survey"; cited in Goldstein, "Profile of American Jewry: Insights from the 1990 National Jewish Population Survey," 125.

166. Kosmin et al. *Highlights of the CJF 1990 National Jewish Population Survey*, 16.

167. Kotler-Berkowitz et al. *The National Jewish Population Survey 2000-01*, 18.

168. Saxe et al., *The 2005 Boston Community Survey*, 12; Ira Sheskin, *The 2001 Jewish Community Study of Bergen County and North Hudson* (Teaneck, N.J.: UJA Federation of Bergen County and North Hudson, 2002), vi. Available online from Mandell L. Berman Institute, North American Jewish Data Bank, at http://www.jewishdatabank.org.

169. MacKenzie Ewing quoted by Paula Span, "Interfaith Marriage '83," *Glamour* 81, November 1983, 296.

170. I am particularly grateful to Brandy Simon, who first brought the issue of a triple marginality to my attention, which is a useful way to conceptualize the marginalized identity of the intermarried Jewish woman (interview by author, tape recording, Brookline, Mass., 23 January 2001). For a discussion of the American cultural norm as a non-ethnic Christian male, and women and Jews as outsiders or the "other," making the Jewish woman the other twice over, see Pogrebin, *Deborah, Golda, and Me*, xiii.

171. Fishman, *Double or Nothing*, 13.

172. Robin Elk, interview by author, tape recording, Newton, Mass., 10 January 2001.

173. Zena Jethro, interview by author, tape recording, Lexington, Mass., 8 January 2001.

174. Ibid.; Heidi Laker, interview by author, tape recording, Newton, Mass., 26 January 2001.

175. Heidi Laker, interview by author, tape recording, Newton, Mass., 26 January 2001.

176. Penina Mintz Jennings, interview by author, tape recording, Newton, Mass., 4 January 2001.

177. Rachel Lyon, interview by author, tape recording, Brookline, Mass., 18 January 2001; Robin Elk, interview by author, tape recording, Newton, Mass., 10 January 2001.

178. David W. Belin, "Confronting the Intermarriage Crisis with Realism and Effective Action," in *The Intermarriage Crisis: Jewish Communal Perspectives and Responses* (New York: American Jewish Committee, 1991), 39. An earlier version of this speech was delivered at the American Jewish Committee Annual Meeting, 8 May 1990.

179. "American Jewish Committee Deplores Chief Rabbi's Attack on Reform Judaism," The American Jewish Committee Press Release, 26 January 1999, available at http://ajc.org/InTheMedia/PressReleases.

180. McClain, *Embracing the Stranger*, 3.

181. Roberts and Roberts, *From This Day Forward*, 157-158.

182. Span, "Interfaith Marriage '83," 359.

183. Melissa Sherman, interview by author, tape recording, Brookline, Mass., 5 January 2001.

184. Zena Jethro, interview by author, tape recording, Lexington, Mass., 8 January 2001.

185. Penina Mintz Jennings, interview by author, tape recording, Newton, Mass., 4 January 2001.

186. Heidi Laker, interview by author, tape recording, Newton, Mass., 26 January 2001.

187. "Report of the Task Force on Intermarriage," Combined Jewish Philanthropies (Boston), January 1997, 6.

188. *The Connection* (spring 2004), InterfaithFamily.Com; Ellen S. Glazer, "The Religious Conundrum: Mixed Marriages," *Newton Magazine* 3, no. 2 (2004), 37-39; Ed Case to author, e-mail communication, 2 April 2004.

189. Rabbi Benjamin Samuels, "Jewish Families and Mixed Marriage: Speculating on Our Jewish Future," *Forum*, 23 March 2004, Temple Emanuel, Newton, Massachusetts. Although Rabbi Samuels of Congregation Shaarei Tefillah in Newton, Massachusetts, at a widely attended public forum on intermarriage,

characterized intermarriage as not only forbidden by Jewish law but as a "tragedy," he also uttered encouraging words: "Part of our willingness to engage an expansive complex definition of Jewish peoplehood is also to recognize that different parts of the Jewish community play different roles."

190. Jonathan D. Sarna, "Is Judaism Compatible with American Civil Religion? The Problem of Christmas and the 'National Faith,'" in *Religion and the Life of the Nation*, ed. Rowland A. Sherill (Urbana: University of Illinois Press, 1990), 153; cited in Sarna, *American Judaism*, 371.

191. Heidi Laker, interview by author, tape recording, Newton, Mass., 26 January 2001; also, among others, Brandy Simon, interview by author, tape recording, Brookline, Mass., 23 January 2001; and Robin Elk, interview by author, tape recording, Newton, Mass., 10 January 2001. Those women who were neutral or positive about having a tree were exceptions; usually they had grown up with some form of Christmas decorations in their Jewish family of origin or because their mother remarried a non-Jew. Rachel Lyon, interview by author, tape recording, Brookline, Mass., 18 January 2001; Hannah Noble, interview by author, tape recording, Brookline, Mass., 9 January 2001.

192. Jane Praeger, "When Is a Tree Not a Tree? . . . When You're Jewish and Your Husband Wants a Tree in Your Living Room," *Newsweek* 132, no. 25, 21 December 1998, 12. For an account about increasing intolerance of Christian artifacts by a woman raised as an Orthodox Jew who intermarried in the 1980s, see Tirzah Firestone, *With Roots in Heaven: One Woman's Passionate Journey into the Heart of Her Faith* (New York: Dutton, 1998), 260.

193. Karal Ann Marling, *Merry Christmas! Celebrating America's Greatest Holiday* (Cambridge, Mass.: Harvard University Press, 2000); for a history of the Christmas tree specifically, see 160, 163.

194. Paul Cowan and Rachel Cowan, *Mixed Blessings: Overcoming the Stumbling Blocks in an Interfaith Marriage* (New York: Penguin Books, 1987), 196. See also Barbara Kantrowitz and Deborah Witherspoon, "The December Dilemma: How to Reconcile Two Faiths in One Household," *Newsweek*, 28 December 1987, 56.

195. Evelyn Kaye, "Interfaith Marriages," *Ladies' Home Journal* 99, December 1982, 76-77, 130-135.

196. Bonnie Aaronson, interview by author, tape recording, Brookline, Mass. 24 January 2001.

197. Joyce Antler, *The Journey Home: Jewish Women and the American Century* (New York: Free Press, 1997), 299.

198. Zena Jethro, interview by author, tape recording, Lexington, Mass., 8 January 2001.

199. Heidi Laker, interview by author, tape recording, Newton, Mass., 26 January 2001.

200. Cohen and Eisen, *The Jew Within*, 186, 206. See also Fishman, *Double or Nothing*, 85.

201. Zena Jethro, interview by author, tape recording, Lexington, Mass., 8 January 2001.

202. Praeger, "When Is a Tree Not a Tree?" 12.

203. Penina Mintz Jennings, interview by author, tape recording, Newton, Mass., 4 January 2001.

204. Bethamie Horowitz, "Connections and Journeys: Shifting Identities among American Jews," *Contemporary Jewry* 19 (1998): 89.

205. Firestone, *With Roots in Heaven*, 339.

CONCLUSION

1. Steven M. Cohen and Arnold M. Eisen, *The Jew Within: Self, Family, and Community in America* (Bloomington: Indiana University Press, 2000), 184.

2. Ruth R. Wisse, "American Jewry through the Lens of NJPS," Session at the Thirty-fifth Annual Conference of the Association for Jewish Studies, 21 December 2003, Boston, Mass.

3. Tirzah Firestone, *With Roots in Heaven: One Woman's Passionate Journey into the Heart of Her Faith* (New York, Dutton: 1998), 262.

4. Samuel G. Freedman, "Freedom: The Promise and the Challenge," *Hadassah,* March 2004,, 11.

5. Steven Bayme, foreword to *Jewish and Something Else* by Sylvia Barack Fishman (New York: American Jewish Committee, 2001), vi.

6. Egon Mayer, "Why Not Judaism?" *Moment,* October 1991; cited in *The Inclusive,* Jewish Outreach Institute, spring 2004, 6.

7. Sarah Coleman "Not Lost: A Jewish Feminist Atheist Meditates on Intermarriage," in *Yentl's Revenge: The Next Wave of Jewish Feminism,* ed. Danya Ruttenberg (New York: Seal, 2001), 75.

8. J.D. Heyman, *People* 61, no. 3, 26 January 2004, 55.

9. For example, research in England found that 65 percent of women said they did all the Christmas shopping in their families, 32 percent reported that shopping was shared equally, and fewer than 1 percent indicated that their partners did most of the shopping ("Women Bear Brunt of Christmas Shopping," Lloyds TSB Online, 1 December 2004, available at http://www.manchesteronline.co.uk/christmas/s/138/138869_women_bear_brunt_of_christmas_shopping_.html).

10. Other recent scholarship by Jane Kaplan likewise found "very few situations in which a woman who strongly identified as Jewish was willing to let her children be raised as Christians." See Kaplan, *Interfaith Families* (Westport, Conn.: Praeger, 2004), xiv.

11. I am drawing an analogy between intermarried women's Jewish-feminist ethnicity in the late twentieth century and the "cult of true womanhood" in the nineteenth century that combined the attributes of piety and domesticity with

submissiveness and passivity. See Barbara Welter, "The Cult of True Woman-hood," *American Quarterly* 18, no. 2, pt. 1 (summer 1966): 151-174.

12. Susannah Heschel, foreword to Ruttenberg, *Yentl's Revenge*, xvi-xvii.

13. Ann Braude, "Women's History *Is* American Religious History," in *Retelling U.S. Religious History*, ed. Thomas A. Tweed (Berkeley: University of California Press, 1997), 97.

14. Egon Mayer quoted in Edward S. Shapiro, *A Time for Healing: American Jewry since World War II* (Baltimore, Md.: Johns Hopkins University Press, 1992), 237.

15. Hasdai Westbrook, "Walleye," *Newvoices: The National Jewish Student Magazine*, September/October 2003, 5.

16. Bruce A. Phillips, *Re-examining Intermarriage: Trends, Textures, Strategies* (The Susan and David Wilstein Institute of Jewish Policy Studies and The William Petschek National Jewish Family Center of the American Jewish Committee, 1997), 71.

17. Barry Kosmin, *The Demographic Imperatives of Outreach, Journal of Jewish Communal Service* 66 no. 3 (1990): 210. Cited in Phillips, *Re-examining Intermarriage*, 69.

18. Steven Bayme, "Ensuring Jewish Continuity: Policy Challenges and Implications for Jewish Communal Professionals," *Journal of Jewish Communal Service* 68, no. 4 (summer 1992): 338.

19. *The State of Jewish Outreach Today*, inaugural report of the Jewish Outreach Institute (New York: Jewish Outreach Institute, November 2002). JOI publications include Egon Mayer, ed., *Jewish Intermarriage, Conversion and Outreach* (1990); Paul Ritterband, ed., *Jewish Intermarriage in Its Social Context* (1991); David Belin, *Choosing Judaism* (1992); Egon Mayer and Luann Dragone, eds., *Jewish Connections for Interfaith Families: A National Directory of Outreach Programs* (1992); Egon Mayer, ed., *Imperatives of Jewish Outreach* (1993); David Sacks, *Welcoming the Intermarried into Your Jewish Family* (1995); Egon Mayer, *Making Jewish Outreach Work: Promoting Jewish Continuity among the Intermarried* (1996); Rela Mintz Geffen and Egon Mayer, *The Ripple Effect: Interfaith Families Speak Out* (1997); and Barbara Chaiken, *Interfaith Discussion Groups: A Manual for Bringing Interfaith Couples and Parents of Interfaith Couples into Dialogue* (1998).

20. "Report of the Task Force on Intermarriage," Combined Jewish Philanthropies (Boston), January 1997, 6; Advertisement, ". . . And Baby Makes Three," *The Boston Parents' Paper*, January 2004, 16. Saxe et al., *The 2005 Boston Community Survey*, 12. For the debate about how to interpret the findings, see, for example, Nathaniel Popper, "Boston Study Shows 60% of Interfaith Kids Raised Jewish: Outreach Is Credited for Rise in Community's Population," *Forward*, 17 November 2006, A1; Steven M. Cohen, Jack Ukeles, and Ron Miller, "Read Boston Study on

Intermarriage with Caution," *Forward*, 8 December 2006, A15; and Leonard Saxe et al., "Boston Study Did Not Bias Results," *Forward*, 15 December 2006, A12.

21. Eric Yoffie quoted by H.S. in "Are We Embracing the Intermarried or Diluting Judaism?" *Moment*, June 1997, 48, 51.

22. Sue Fishkoff, "Intermarriage," *Moment*, October 2000/Tishrei 5761, 76.

23. Ami Eden, "Conservative Body Extends Hand to the Intermarried," *InterfaithFamily.com* 70, October 2001, available online at http://interfaithfamily.com/article/issue70/eden.phtml. Reprinted with the permission of the *Forward*. Under different auspices, the Jewish Discovery Institute (JDI), formerly the Gerim Institute and the Keruv Initiative, was founded in 2002. A joint effort of the New England regions of the United Synagogue of Conservative Judaism and the Rabbinical Assembly, the JDI began offering courses and workshops for interfaith couples "to encourage learning about Judaism, to foster Jewish identity and to support those interested in conversion to Judaism." Announcement in *Newton Magazine*, February 2005; available at http://interfaithfamily.planitjewish.com; and phone conversation with Rabbi Judith Kummer, Executive Director of the Jewish Discovery Institute, 4 April 2005.

24. Steven Bayme, "To Condone or Not to Condone—Is That the Question?" *Comment & Analysis* 2, no. 4, November 1991, 2-3.

25. Steven Bayme, quoted by H.S. in "Are We Embracing the Intermarried or Diluting Judaism?" *Moment*, June 1997, 49.

26. National Jewish Outreach Program, home page "About Us," available at http://www.njop.org/html/about_us.html.

27. Sue Fishkoff, "Intermarriage," *Moment*, October 2000/Tishrei 5761, 85.

28. Egon Mayer, *Intermarriage and the Attitudes of American Jewish Leadership: The Issues and the Controversies* (New York: Jewish Outreach Institute, 1990), 2.

29. Debra Nussbaum Cohen, "New Coalition Formed to Fight Intermarriage," *The Jewish Week*, 2 March 2001; reprinted in *InterfaithFamily.com* 57; available online at http://interfaithfamily.com/article/issue57/news.phtml; Robert Wiener, "In-marriage vs. outreach: A new organization promoting Jewish-Jewish marriage sparks debate over resources and sensitivity," *New Jersey Jewish News*, n.d. Available at http://www.njjewishnews.com/njjn.com/112703/njinmarriage.html.

30. Egon Mayer quoted in Rahel Musleah, "Jewish Jeopardy," *Reform Judaism* 30, no. 1 (fall 2001): 22.

31. Debra Nussbaum Cohen, "New Coalition Formed to Fight Intermarriage," *InterfaithFamily.com* 57, reprinted with permission of *The Jewish Week*, 2 March 2001.

32. Egon Mayer, epilogue to *Making Jewish Outreach Work: Promoting Jewish Continuity among the Intermarried* (New York: Jewish Outreach Institute and the Center for Jewish Studies, Graduate School of the City University of New York, 1996), 132.

33. "Toward a New Definition of Outreach," The Egon Mayer Memorial Conference program flyer, 8-10 June 2004, Boston, Mass., Jewish Outreach Institute.

34. Phone conversation with Kari Colella, Coordinator of Marriage Ministry, Office of Family and Life, Catholic Archdiocese of Boston, 22 April 2004. Also see Amy Traverso, "Living on a Prayer," *Boston Magazine*, December 2000, 38.

35. Terry Golway, "Life in the '90s," *America* 180, no. 6, 27 February 1999, 6.

36. "Interfaith Marriage," Ecumenical and Interfaith Relations, Presbyterian Church (USA), 1998 distribution date; "Interfaith Marriage: A Resource by Presbyterian Christians," Ecumenical and Interfaith Relations, Presbyterian Church (USA), 1998 distribution date; *A Theological Understanding of the Relationship between Christians and Jews,* 199th General Assembly of the Presbyterian Church (USA), 1987, 12-13.

37. Samuel Johnson, liaison to the United Methodist Church for Boston University, School of Theology, e-mail to author, 22 June 2004. Confirmed with Info Serv of the United Methodist Church.

38. Jay Rock, coordinator for interfaith relations of the Presbyterian Church U.S.A., telephone conversation with author, 23 June 2004.

39. Laurence Kotler-Berkowitz et al. *The National Jewish Population Survey 2000-01: Strength, Challenge and Diversity in the American Jewish Population* (New York: United Jewish Communities, 2003), 2.

40. Marc J. Perry and Paul J. Mackun, *Population Change and Distribution, Census 2000 Brief, 1990 to 2000,* U.S. Department of Commerce, Economics and Statistics Administration, U.S. Census Bureau, April 2001. Available at http://www.census.gov/population/www/cen2000/briefs.html (accessed 16 June 2004).

41. Gary Langer, analysis of "Poll: Most Americans Say They're Christian," ABCNEWS.com, 18 July 2001, available at http://abcnews.go.com/sections/us/DailyNews/beliefnet_poll_010718.html, accessed 16 June 2004. ABCNEWS/Beliefnet poll was conducted 20-24 June 2001 among a random national sample of 1,022 adults. The researchers who conducted ARIS 2001 found a slightly lower total number of Christians and a higher number of Catholics; they classified 77 percent of American adults as Christian and 24.5 percent as Catholic. Barry A. Kosmin, Egon Mayer, and Ariela Keysar, *American Religious Identification Survey* (New York: Graduate Center of the City University of New York, 2001), 10, 12. Figures in 2008 differed only slightly from either the ABC News Poll or ARIS 2001: 78.4 percent Christian, 51.3 percent Protestant, and 23.9 percent Catholic. See "Summary of Key Findings," *U.S. Religious Landscape Survey,* 5.

42. Elie Wiesel responding to *Jewish Week* editor Gary Rosenblatt during a forum at Park East Synagogue, Manhattan, New York, 4 December 2002, available at http://joi.org/news/quote.php?archives=yes or http://joi.org/news/njps.shtml.

43. Cressida Heyes, "Identity Politics," *Stanford Encyclopedia of Philosophy* (2002), available at http://plato.stanford.edu/entries/identity-politics/ (accessed 20 October 2004).

44. Jack Wertheimer, Charles S. Liebman, and Steven M. Cohen, "How to Save American Jews," *Commentary* 101, no. 1, January 1996, 50.

45. I am grateful to the Stonehill College students who introduced me to the term "cashew" during one of our many lively discussions. See responses to a 28 March 2005 blog posting titled "Half-Jew for You!" Available at http://www.jewlicious.com. Robin Margolis, "Why Does the Half-Jewish Network Exist?" Available at http://www.half-jewish.net.

46. Sherry Israel, "Contemporary American Jewish Life" (comment, Thirty-second Annual Conference of the Association for Jewish Studies), 18 December 2000, Boston, Mass.

47. Jack Wertheimer, Charles S. Liebman, and Steven M. Cohen, "How to Save American Jews," *Commentary* 101, no. 1, January 1996, 48-50.

48. Statement by the International Federation of Secular Humanistic Jews at its second biennial conference, 1988, *The State of Jewish Outreach Today,* inaugural report of the Jewish Outreach Institute (New York: Jewish Outreach Institute, 2002).

49. Deborah Dash Moore, "Intermarriage and the Politics of Identity," *The Reconstructionist* 66, no. 1 (fall 2001): 49.

50. Joel Perlmann, "Who's a Jew in an Era of High Intermarriage? Surveys, Operational Definitions, and the Contemporary American Context," Working Paper No. 507, Levy Economics Institute of Bard College, July 2007, 1.

51. *The State of Jewish Outreach Today,* inaugural report of the Jewish Outreach Institute (New York: Jewish Outreach Institute, 2002).

52. Steven Bayme, comments at the Double or Nothing? Jewish Families and Mixed Marriage conference sponsored by the Hadassah-Brandeis Institute and the Cohen Center for Modern Jewish Studies, Waltham, Mass., 26 April 2004. Bayme's talk responded to the paper of Dru Greenwood, Director of the William and Lottie Daniel Department of Outreach and Synagogue Community at the Union for Reform Judaism and of the URJ-CCAR Commission on Outreach and Synagogue Community. Also see *The State of Jewish Outreach Today,* inaugural report of the Jewish Outreach Institute (New York: Jewish Outreach Institute, 2002).

53. Steven Bayme, phone conversation with author, 16 July 2004.

54. Sylvia Barack Fishman, *Double or Nothing: Jewish Family and Mixed Marriage* (Hanover, Mass.: Brandeis University Press, 2004), 152-153.

55. Douglas Rushkoff, "The Medium Is the Message: Getting over Racehood," *The Inclusive,* Jewish Outreach Institute, spring 2003, 2-3.

56. For a discussion of intermarriage from the beginning of Jewish history to the nineteenth century that rejects Jewish purity as fiction, see Ephraim Feldman, "Intermarriage Historically Considered," *Yearbook of the Central Conference of American Rabbis* 19 (9-16 November 1909): 282-283.

57. Mik Moore, "Sex, Miscegenation, and the Intermarriage Debate," *newvoices,* November 1997, 4. I am grateful to Deborah Dash Moore for bringing this editorial to my attention and to Hasdai Westbrook for sending it to me.

58. Edgar M. Bronfman quoted by Douglas Davis, "Children of Intermarriage Are Also Jews," *Jerusalem Post*, 8 October 2004, 6.

59. Wendy Cadge and Lynn Davidman, "Ascription, Choice, and the Construction of Religious Identities in the Contemporary United States," unpublished paper, Judaic Studies Faculty Seminar, Brown University, 6 November 2003, 13.

60. Bethamie Horowitz, "Connections and Journeys: Shifting Identities among American Jews," *Contemporary Jewry* 19 (1998), 76. I am grateful to Bethamie Horowitz for sharing her work with me. See also idem, "Connections and Journeys: Assessing Critical Opportunities for Enhancing Jewish Identity," *A Report to the Commission on Jewish Identity and Renewal, UJA-Federation of New York* (New York: UJA-Federation of Jewish Philanthropies of New York, September 2003 [June 2000]).

61. Bethamie Horowitz, "Vanishing Jew," comments at the Thirty-second Annual Conference of the Association for Jewish Studies, Boston, Mass., 19 December 2000. Lauren Bacall's autobiography says very little about her Jewish identity except that her grandmother disapproved of her, a "nice Jewish girl," becoming an actress (Lauren Bacall, *By Myself* [New York: Knopf, 1979], 7).

62. Calvin Goldscheider, "Are American Jews Vanishing Again?" *Contexts* 2 (winter 2003): 18.

63. Mary Antin, *The Promised Land* (Boston: Houghton Mifflin, 1912), 248-249.

64. Jeanne Ross-Neuwirth, telephone conversation with author, 21 February 1997, and baby naming celebration, 19 August 2000.

65. Bruce A. Phillips, *Re-examining Intermarriage: Trends, Textures, Strategies*, Susan and David Wilstein Institute of Jewish Policy Studies and the William Petschek National Jewish Family Center of the American Jewish Committee, 1997, 78.

66. Samuel Stein, letter to the editor, *Modern Maturity*, published by AARP, January-February 2001, 10. I am grateful to Mae R. Tupa for finding this clipping for me.

67. Pamela S. Nadell and Jonathan D. Sarna, *Women and American Judaism: Historical Perspectives* (Hanover, Mass.: Brandeis University Press, 2001), 1.

68. Alan M. Dershowitz, *The Vanishing American Jew: In Search of Jewish Identity for the Next Century* (Boston: Little, Brown, 1997; first Touchstone edition, 1998), 24.

AFTERWORD

1. For a popular analysis of Gentile women, see Christine Benvenuto, *Shiksa: The Gentile Woman in the Jewish World* (New York: St. Martin's, 2004).

2. Arnold Dashefsky, "Living Mixed Traditions: Jewish Connections and Intermarriage in the United States," paper presented at the Double or Nothing? Jewish Families and Mixed Marriage conference sponsored by the Hadassah-Brandeis Institute and the Cohen Center for Modern Jewish Studies, Waltham, Mass., 26 April 2004.

APPENDIX

1. Fred Massarik et al., *National Jewish Population Study: Intermarriage, Facts for Planning* (New York: Council of Jewish Federations and Welfare Funds, 1971), 10.

2. Barry A. Kosmin et al., *Highlights of the CJF 1990 National Jewish Population Survey* (New York: Council of Jewish Federations, 1991), 14.

3. Applying a parallel definition of "born Jews" to the NJPS 2000-2001 data that was applied to the 1990 data (Table 2), the intermarriage rate among those married in 1985-90 is 52 percent; in 1991-95, 53 percent; and in 1996–2000, 54 percent. From Laurence Kotler-Berkowitz et al., *The National Jewish Population Survey 2000-01: Strength, Challenge and Diversity in the American Jewish Population* (New York: United Jewish Communities, 2003), 16–17.

4. Kotler-Berkowitz et al., *The National Jewish Population Survey 2000-01*, 17.

5. The 2000-2001 NJPS reported that 33 percent of the children in households with one non-Jewish spouse were being raised Jewish, a slight increase from 1990. Analysis by Laurence Kotler-Berkowitz, NJPS Research Director at United Jewish Communities, via Sherry Israel, 5 January 2006. The data from Kotler-Berkowitz are based on the randomly selected children of all currently intermarried Jews that are being raised as Jewish, 38 percent of children; the 33 percent in the NJPS was based on a multiple response analysis of all children in the household. Kotler-Berkowitz et al., *The National Jewish Population Survey 2000-01*, 18.

6. Pearl Beck, *A Flame Still Burns: The Dimensions and Determinants of Jewish Identity among Young Adult Children of the Intermarried* (Jewish Outreach Institute, June 2005), 28-29.

7. Table 7, by author.

Selected Index

Abie's Irish Rose, 90

Advice about intermarriage: Black, Algernon D., "If I Marry Outside My Religion," 79; book titles for comparative analysis, 218; how to avoid, 79; *How to Stop an Intermarriage: A Practical Guide for Parents,* 126; *Ladies Home Journal,* 79; Mack, Rebecca E., on "an everlasting life destroyer," 79; Pike, James, suggests select one religious affiliation, 249n115; religious advocates warned against, 77; *Woman's Home Companion,* "My Mixed Marriage Was Happy," 81

Affiliation: proportion of adult Americans, 155; religious, 18; synagogue membership rises once Jews have children, 280n114; *U.S. Religious Landscape Survey,* 270n1, 271n2

Alba, Richard: Jewish-Jewish marriages "well below the in-marriage tendencies of eastern and central European groups" 156–157; and Nee, Victor, on definition of assimilation, 4

American Jewish Chronicle, 20

American Jewish Community (AJC): and comparison between intermarriage and the Holocaust, 188; *The Intermarriage Crisis: Jewish Community Responses and Perspectives,* 176

American Jewish Identification Survey (AJIS): nearly half adult U.S. Jews regarded themselves as secular to some degree in outlook, 168

American Jewish Yearbook (AJYB): in 1963, 13; in 1970, 14

American Religious Identity Survey (ARIS): increased religiosity of intermarried Jewish women over time reflected the national trend, 178–179; self described religious identification and reported household membership, 270n1; women more likely than men to describe their outlook as "religious," 170–171

Antin, Mary, 18–20, 22, 25–35, 58–60, 134, 199, 203; analysis of her age, 232n35, 235n96; descendants Ross, Anne, and Ross-Neuwirth, Eliana, Julia, and Jeanne, 214–215; Grabau, Amadeus W., 26; Hale, Edward W., 26; Lazarus, Josephine and Emma, 28; Roosevelt, Theodore, letter to, 60; Zangwill, Israel, letter to, 27

Antisemitism: American, decline of, and growing rate of Jewish intermarriage, 114; *Daughters of Kings,* 166; decline after World War II, archbishop of Boston Richard Cushing, and "psychological insecurity," 83; encouraged assimilation, 67;

Six-Day War, 129; sense of security about group survival, 263n116; Yom Kippur War, 142

Israel, Sherry, *Boston's Jewish Community: The 1985 Demographic Study* and *Comprehensive Report on the 1995 Demographic Study,* 271n5; demonstrates the more recent the marriage the higher the intermarriage rate, 156

Jewish Liberalism: direction and influence of, and contradiction with cultural nationalism, 114; quest for full equality, 115

Jewish men, 1, 12; disappearance from organized Jewish life, 137, 175, 279n104; Conservative Federation of Jewish Men's Clubs, 205; father's last name and mother's religious identity, 184; Kaplan, Jane, *Interfaith Families,* "not very active in Judaism," 279n106; Klein, Calvin, Schlossberg, Edwin A., and Silberstein, Charles Henry, 171; married Catholic and Protestant women, 226n43; Neuwirth, Michael, 215; Roberts, Steve, *From This Day Forward,* 180; sexual relations with Gentile women, 14; Stein, Samuel, 215

Jewish mothers, 8; coeditors of *Jewish Mothers Tell Their Stories* describe identities as fluid, 179; having children while intermarried, 177; Jewish motherhood was socially constructed to be responsible for endogamy, 94; Kaplan, Marion, *The Making of the Jewish Middle Class,* and European Jewish women as cultural transmitters, 282–283n156; Kaufman,

Debra, identified a pattern, 179; maternal death, 93–94; "maternal keeper of the domestic flame of Judaism," 184; and matrilineal descent, 10; Maushart, Susan, *The Mask of Motherhood,* becoming a mother, 177; mothers cause all the problems, 93; "Over my dead body!" response, 93; scholarly consensus on Jewishness of mothers raising children as Jewish, 185–186. *See also* Fishman, Sylvia Barack

Jewish Outreach Institute. *See* Outreach

Judaism: American Jewry's decreasing traditionalism, 65; conflation with Jewish identity, 77; diminished attendance and observance, 68; Orthodox parents' lack of instruction, 100; Reform, 29; secularization theory, 136

Labor: boundaries between women's and men's work, 244n43; dual-career family, 133; Executive Order 10980, 131; inequality in the workplace and in the home, 157; Kessler-Harris, Alice, on intermarried women continuing to be active politically, 46; rate of mothers of children less than six years of age, 157; *The Second Shift,* 158; women who worked outside the home, 133; women who worked more liberal, 134; Women's Trade Union League, 44

Ladies Home Journal, 43

Liberalism, 110

Mack, Rebecca, *You Are a Jew and a Jew You Are!,* 105, 248n105

About the Author

KEREN R. MCGINITY is the Mandell L. Berman Postdoctoral Research Fellow in Contemporary American Jewish Life at the University of Michigan's Frankel Center for Judaic Studies. Previously she was Visiting Assistant Professor in History at Brown University.